PELICAN BOOKS

A423

BODY AND MIND IN WESTERN THOUGHT

JOAN WYNN REEVES

BODY AND MIND
IN WESTERN THOUGHT

An introduction to some origins
of modern psychology

BY

JOAN WYNN REEVES

PENGUIN BOOKS

Penguin Books Ltd, Harmondsworth, Middlesex
U.S.A.: Penguin Books Inc., 3300 Clipper Mill Road, Baltimore 11, Md
AUSTRALIA: Penguin Books Pty Ltd, 762 Whitehorse Road,
Mitcham, Victoria

—

First published, 1958

—

Made and Printed in Great Britain
by Robert MacLehose and Co. Ltd
The University Press, Glasgow

CONTENTS

LIST OF PLATES 7

EDITORIAL FOREWORD 9

ACKNOWLEDGEMENTS 11

INTRODUCTION 13

PART ONE
Historical Introduction

1. THE EARLY GREEKS 25

2. CLASSICAL GREECE AND ROME 32
   i. *Hippocrates and Democritus* – ii. *Plato* – iii. *Aristotle* –
   iv. *Transitional Greece and Rome*

3. DUSK AND DAWN 51
   i. *St Augustine to St Anselm* – ii. *Abelard to Aquinas* –
   iii. *Petrarch's Problem*

4. CONTRAST AND CONFLICT 70

5. FEAR AND FACT 86

6. THE SEVENTEENTH-CENTURY SEARCH FOR
   CERTAINTY 99

7. EIGHTEENTH-CENTURY ADAPTATION 131

8. SIX POLARITIES IN SEARCH OF A PERSON 145
   i. *The Nineteenth Century* – ii. *Twentieth-Century Postscript*

9. ANTITHESES 171

PART TWO
The Thinkers Speak for Themselves

HIPPOCRATES 183

PLATO 188

Contents

ARISTOTLE 214

TITUS LUCRETIUS CARUS 229

GALEN 241

ST AUGUSTINE 245

ST THOMAS AQUINAS 250

FRANCESCO PETRARCA 254

THE DEVIL, THE WITCH, AND THE DOCTOR 263

FRANCIS BACON 273

RENÉ DESCARTES 282

BENEDICT DE SPINOZA 305

GOTTFRIED WILHELM LEIBNIZ 330

DAVID HUME 339

DAVID HARTLEY 346

ÉTIENNE BONNOT, ABBÉ DE CONDILLAC 352

JAMES BRAID 363

JOHN STUART MILL 373

EWALD HERING 376

WILHELM WUNDT 385

WILLIAM JAMES 389

INDEX 401

LIST OF PLATES

1. Hsia Kuei (*c.* 1180–1230): Talking with a friend under pines by a precipice. Ink on sella (National Palace Museum, Peking). *Reproduced by permission of Lawrence Sickman, Esq.*
2. Christ casting out the devil. Part of an illuminated initial from Psalm 1 in the Winchester Bible. *Reproduced by permission of the Dean and Chapter of Winchester*
3. Aristotle. From the Portail Royal of Chartres Cathedral. *Reproduced by permission of M. Étienne Houvet*
4 and 5. Uta and Regelindis. Sculpture from Naumburg Cathedral. *Reproduced by permission of Helga Schmidt-Glassner*
6. Bigallo: Exorcism. From the Museo dell'Opera del Duomo, Florence. *Reproduced by permission of Messrs Alinari*
7. Giotto: Death of the Virgin. From the Kaiser-Friedrich Museum, Berlin. *Reproduced by permission of Messrs Alinari*
8. Masaccio: Heads of Apostles and St Peter. From Santa Maria del Carmine, Florence. *Reproduced by permission of Messrs Alinari*
9. Benozzo Gozzoli: The Journey of the Magi. From the Palazzo Medici-Riccardi, Florence. *Reproduced by permission of Messrs Alinari*
10. Meister des Hausbuchs: The Three Living and the Three Dead Kings. *Reproduced by permission of the Staatliche Kunstsammlungen, Stuttgart*
11. Hieronymus Bosch: Punishment of the Gamblers, detail from The Garden of Delights. From the Museo del Prado, Madrid. *Reproduced by permission of Ampliaciones y Reproducciones Mas, Barcelona*
12. School of Hieronymus Bosch: The Witches. From the Musée du Louvre. *Reproduced by permission of the Caisse Nationale des Monuments Historiques, Paris*
13. Jan de Bisschop: The Walls of Delft and the 'Kolk'. *Reproduced by permission of the Fodor Museum, Amsterdam*
14. Chardin: A lady dressing her little girl. *Reproduced by permission of the National Museum, Stockholm*
15. J. Collier: Thomas Henry Huxley (1825–95). *Reproduced by permission of the National Portrait Gallery, London*
16. Käthe Kollwitz: Woman Worker. *Reproduced by permission of A. C. Cooper and Sons Ltd*
17 and 18. Mondriaan: The Grey Tree 1910–11 *and* Tree 1909–10. *Reproduced by permission of the Gemeentemuseum, The Hague (S. B. Slijper)*

EDITORIAL FOREWORD

THERE are readers of three kinds who will find in this book what they are looking for. The first are those who will be interested chiefly in its theme. They will almost certainly be in the majority, for there must be something a little odd about a person who has never had occasion to think about body and mind, who has never been puzzled by their relations, and who cannot be either attracted or provoked by any of the theories concerning these relations.

Readers of the second kind will be those who in addition are interested in history as such, and more especially in the history of ideas, and perhaps in the philosophy, the sociology, and the psychology of movements of thought. There are, it would seem, two sorts of theory about the nature of history. One view is that history is just the record of what actually happened, when what actually happened is taken to be just one thing after another without any evidence of order or pattern in the sequence of events. Opposed to this is the view that history unfolds in accordance with immanent and timeless laws, or at least that in what actually happens there are pendulum swings, uprisings and declines, or cycles of some kind. An extreme example of this sort of theory was that developed by the philosopher Hegel and turned to surprising account by Karl Marx. This is the theory of the dialectical progression. A state of affairs describable as a *Thesis* leads inevitably to an *Antithesis*, and in turn (to give the story a happy ending) is followed by a *Synthesis* which eliminates the faults and combines the merits of *Thesis* and *Antithesis*. There are sociological and psychological variants of this metaphysical theory. Perhaps some will find in these opposing views concerning history yet another *Thesis* confronted by its *Antithesis* and awaiting a *Synthesis*. But this is not among the aims of this book. An author who takes readily to Ranke, Huizinga, and Pieter Geyl is bound to find both extremes indigestable and to be chary of attempting, let alone claiming to achieve, a *synthesis*.

A third class of readers to whom this book will be of special interest consists of those who would like to believe that Psychology has a place among the 'humanities' as well as among the sciences. All psychologists agree that a very proper study of mankind is man, but there are very sharp divergencies of opinion

Editorial Foreword

concerning the way in which man should be studied. Through most of its history Psychology has been a branch of philosophy and, as this volume shows, man has been studied through this long period in the way in which philosophers study things. Today, however, Psychology claims, and has established the claim, to be a natural science; and some would say that the way of natural sciences is the only proper way in which man should be studied. They deplore all forms of philosophical speculation and are suspicious even of the philosophical analysis of psychological concepts. Sharper still is the antithesis between those who think and those who do not think that psychologists should conduct their studies with some regard to the 'insights' of the poets and other artists. This conflict is verbalized in terms of the distinction between 'understanding' and 'explanation'. The poet attempts to 'understand', the scientist is content to 'explain'.

There can be few psychologists so well qualified as the author of this book to make a just appraisal of the various opinions on these difficult and controversial issues. Joan Wynn Reeves, as this book displays, is a skilled discerner of polarities and antitheses. Coming into psychology through the door at its philosophical end, she has spent most of her working life in teaching and applying the empirical science, and she has spent much of her leisure time looking at pictures and generally enjoying the arts.

In this volume the reader is introduced to a number of great and distinguished thinkers in what is surely the way in which these thinkers would themselves wish to be introduced. After introduction and commentary the philosophers and scientists whose works are discussed are invited to speak for themselves. They accept the invitation. The reader is left to form his own opinions, to discern his own patterns in the history of ideas, and to extract his own enjoyments from the pictures which illuminate the themes of the text.

January 1958   C. A. MACE

ACKNOWLEDGEMENTS

A BOOK of this kind could be written with enjoyment only under the aegis of imaginative professors and editors, with the stimulus of colleagues and friends, and with ready access to first-class libraries. It is a pleasure to acknowledge all of these. Individual thanks are due to Professor Harding and Professor Mace for opportunity to do the work and for their positive interest in it. Informal discussion with Professor Acton has proved invaluable. Professor Onians was generous enough to read and comment on Chapter 1, which is based on his *Origins of European Thought*, detailed with its publisher on p. 31. The author hopes that all of these, together with scholars and friends in other fields on whose knowledge she has drawn, will accept her thanks and while recognizing their own influence will not object wholly to the book which reflects it. In any case, for that book, and for possible misunderstanding or mistakes in it, they are in no way responsible.

For the background of general history and the biographical details of authors, the standard works cited and, normally, their editors' notes have been used as a basis.

Grateful thanks of author and publisher are due to the owners of copyright material quoted, details of which are given at the end of each chapter or section, and to the copyright owners of the plates, whose names are given in the List of Plates on p. 7.

Writers of the stature that must be its own reward and whose age precludes them from copyright protection can be offered only affection – and apology for plunder.

London,   JOAN WYNN REEVES
January 1958

INTRODUCTION

Donde viene non so. Dove vado non m'è dato saperlo

I

'ORIENTAL ART' says Eric Newton, 'is not concerned with the nature of visual experience as is the art of the west. The work of art is not a picture of a particular thing, and therefore the laws that govern the appearance of things are of very little importance.' And later, comparing western and oriental treatment of light and shade, he adds: 'Like Constable, the Chinese landscapist is concerned with truth but truth of a different kind. Constable takes the utmost pains to be faithful to what his eye sees: the Eastern artist to what his mind knows.' One might add that both are also trying to be faithful to their way of feeling, but their emotions are integrated into different evaluations of living and with them different evaluations of time.

This may seem a far cry from the history of Western European ideas on the relations of body and mind in so far as the history is relevant to modern psychology. But the cry is not so distant, for into the little phrase 'a particular thing' Newton, wittingly or not, has packed western civilization's tendency to be absorbed with observable events that are time-linked; this rock, this leaf, this tree, this dog, this cat, this person, either at this moment or living for a period of time within our emotional and intellectual grasp. To misquote Marvell: at our backs we are apt always to hear Time's winged chariot hurrying near.

Eric Newton said something suggestive when contrasting the outlooks of East and West, as reflected in their art forms. There are, however, three other marked tendencies encouraged in Western European culture which are specially interesting from our point of view. First, the West, alive to empirical dailyness, has often tried to organize and administer it. Sometimes the results have been good, when, for instance, futile clan or tribal clashes have given place to the more humane aspects of centralization. Again, we can often praise the administration that has led to better order, food, and health for humble human lives. Sometimes ill-inspired organization has brought disaster: the twentieth-century West will not easily forget the evils of organized persecution, power-mongering, and war-mongering.

A second and opposite tendency is reflected in the older Western European variants of dream-spinning. This for the moment we will avoid calling fantasy or projection, so that neither the falsity of dreams nor a theory of their latent content is lightly assumed from the start. It is simpler to realize that, in western literature and the arts alone, expression has been given to a staggering range and depth of human need, emotion, and sentiment; from the sublime, the gay, and the playful at one extreme to devastating nightmare at the other. For us the lovely variants of the free and winged psyche that has enchanted Western European aspiration for some three thousand years, provide the most relevant example of the first extreme. By contrast, in witches, devils, and all their destructive doings we can find reflections of fear, horror, sadism, disgust, and the like strewn across European literature and living. Some of their varied forms are easily observed in certain of the sixteenth- and twentieth-century landscapes described by Sir Kenneth Clark as those of fantasy. Breughel's *Mad Margaret* and even more the *Malleus Maleficarum*, the twisted psychiatric textbook of the Inquisition at its worst, provide excellent illustration of the kind of horror which Western Europe has wanted from time to time to externalize. Both extremes, the sublime and the deeply horrible, have been important in the history of psychology.

Western Europe, however, has not only observed and identified itself with specific events, organized them when it could, and expressed itself in dreams and fantasies great and appalling. It has also abstracted from concrete experience in another direction, namely that of science, in which the laws governing the behaviour of particular things have been of very great importance. The motives, of course, and the conditions of any sustained activity are immensely complex, but reflected in the development of western science, and with it psychology, we seem to see desires for explanation or intellectual understanding, for prediction and for the power it implies, and for a security which cold logic and evidence from other people are felt in their different ways to reinforce. Following Whitehead, we may suppose that in the modern world science has to some extent played the role for which Fate was needed in Classical Greece. But in recent times, the more general recognition that scientific method leads not to certainty but to known chance has given its role a changed emphasis.

In the history of western thinking, scientific psychology has emerged naturally, but as a mongrel in conflict, with all the mongrel's curious resilience. Though rooted in biology its very attempt to be objective entails, ruthlessly, that it must come to terms with the sources and products of creative fantasy both at its greatest and its most tragic extremes. (In the mid twentieth century it is oddly necessary to add that this is not equivalent to announcing that 'everything is something else but rather less worthy'.) Rooted in philosophy as well as biology, psychology claims, with some justice, the status of an empirical study framing and answering factual questions in its own way. Arising often from the practical necessity of understanding particular people, it is yet obliged, in theory and in practice, to think in general and quantitative terms and accurately to estimate the chances of its guesses being right. Sometimes the difference between a psychologist and a layman is that the former is more appallingly aware of the risks he is taking. Rooted in the life, the literature, the arts, the culture, and the specific problems of the period to which it belongs, psychology has somehow to turn round upon itself and them as if a mirror were trying to check the veracity of its own reflections. Thus the pulls in different directions are very strong. In this respect the history of psychology, which as a science has until recently been largely a Western European product, seems clearly to reflect something which the great German historian Ranke once remarked of Europe as a whole. Ruminating on the Elizabethan reaction to Spain and her Armada he wrote: 'Whenever any principle, be it what it may, tends to the establishment of absolute dominion in Europe, there is invariably opposed to it a vigorous resistance, having its origin in the deepest springs of human nature.' Underlying this remark is a spirit very different from acceptance of fate.

Some of the most interesting of the antitheses between which psychological thinking has swung, the opposite directions in which it has been pulled, seem to be reflected in the history of Western European views about the relation of body or bodies and mind or minds. Few people would venture in a short life or a short book to attempt to deal with these thoroughly or from all points of view. Some aspects of the history of these theories, however, seem to be specially interesting psychologically and to have some bearing on understanding how psychology itself developed into an empirical study with a foot in the faculties of both Arts and Science. To show this, I have selected certain older views about the relations of body and mind, starting with those of the early Greeks, and have tried to link them both to views that are outstanding in later centuries and to some theories current in our own day. Where feasible, I have used selections so that the original writers may have a chance to speak for themselves. They are so much more interesting than their expositors. On the other hand, it seemed necessary to begin with a brief historical survey. This is no more than a sketch map drawn to the editor's projection, to be thrown away, or at most employed as a lamp-shade, when the reader embarks on the exploring that he alone can do freely and fully for himself.

II

Before we go back to the Greeks, let us take a glance at the place from which we start. In what circumstances do we naturally ask about body-mind relations? What standard theories have been proffered? What main questions and theories are current today?

In answer to the first question, we are puzzled usually by practical problems, such as how to prevent our friends worrying themselves into physical illness, how to cure a paralysis that has no apparent physical cause, or what is the relation between a vitamin deficiency or underactive thyroid gland and intellectual performance. With *how*, in fact, to deal with these situations we are not here concerned. It is enough to suggest that we should not be finally satisfied unless the answers given both prevented the worrying, diminished the paralysis, restored a lost level of intellectual capacity, and showed us *how* these effects were brought about. But in this question of *how* are hidden all the queries that have been raised about the relations of so-called mental and physical happenings. Scientific development has been described as the slow progress from one 'Oh! I see' to another. And if our curiosity is once truly aroused we don't quite rest until we have looked more closely at what we mean by 'mental' and 'physical'. Very little acquaintance with neuro-physiology, biochemistry, psychology, and psychiatry is needed to realize how intricate are the familiar practical situations which thus arouse our questioning. Plenty of other examples could be given, some of the most difficult issues being raised when we pause to reflect on the social responses of a newly-born baby, those of an old person within a few seconds of natural death, or on responsibility for our own behaviour.

What main theories of body-mind relations have been offered in the past? These may be classified roughly into three main groups. First there are theories that take seriously the apparent effects of bodily events on minds. Where the question of mental events affecting physical ones is not fully discussed, these views are illustrated by the old Hippocratic theory whereby a man's temperament depended on the proportions of blood, phlegm, and black and yellow bile in his body. This theory, via Galen's nine temperaments, penetrated to literature in a restricted version, namely that of the four humours: the sanguine, the phlegmatic, the melancholic, and the choleric. There are plenty of more subtle modern variants. Some writers in this first group would definitely maintain that the mind can retaliate, in which case those theories are known as interactionist. Such writers get into difficulties, as Descartes did, if they try to maintain simultaneously that cause and effect must be similar, body and mind are substances different by definition, the body's behaviour is determined by mechanistic laws, and that the person has a free will that makes his actions subject to praise and blame. Descartes had the peculiar merit of being so clearly and distinctly confused that the difficulties of this position became apparent. He wanted to maintain that *le libre arbitre* could at least stall the action of animal spirits, but it bears some resemblance, as Morton Prince once half implied, to '"an anima or animus sitting", as you may remember Tristram Shandy's father used to say, "like a tadpole all day long both summer and winter", dabbling its feet in the fluid of the pineal gland.' The inconsistencies in Descartes' view are obvious but hard to deal with. They will be more fully discussed later.

Writers after Descartes, aware of the difficulties of the standard interactionist position, have sometimes regarded the effect of bodily on mental happenings as a one-way process of an odd sort, mental events being but a by-product of physical. This view is designated epiphenomenalism, as exemplified in T. H. Huxley's remark:

The consciousness of brutes would appear to be related to the mechanism of their body simply as a collateral product of its working, and to be as completely without the power of modifying that working as the steam whistle, which accompanies the working of a locomotive engine, is without influence upon its machinery.

If a theorist of this sort also maintains (writing some eighty years after Huxley) that physical laws are deterministic in mass if not in miniature, it is still hard for him consistently to hold both that praise and blame should relate to personal responsibility and that there is any one person to whom they apply. In his dilemma he may decide to jettison his notions of causal necessity, his notions of substance, his notions of one- or of two-way traffic between mind and body, or his notions of the applicability or nature of praise and blame. Any such discarding requires an immense amount of very careful thought.

We now turn to the second big group of theories. Fundamentally these are so entangled either in ancient notions of substance, or in the assumption that to affect each other things must be in some way alike ('it takes a fat herdsman to drive fat swine'); that for these, combined with other, reasons their authors have to take one of three steps. If partly inspired by a horror of things physical, such theories may rest on assuming that there are only mental events. A view of this sort is to be found in Berkeley. Other authors, unalarmed by the deadliness of matter, may try to be consistently materialist, as do Lucretius,

Hobbes, and some modern defenders of 'reductionist' theories in explaining human behaviour. It is worth noting in passing that neither 'mentalists' nor materialists are denying the apparent effects of body on mind or the reverse. They tend tacitly or explicitly to assume that cause and effect must be alike but deny there are two kinds of event or substance. When, for example, we think that our minds are affecting something outside us, it is an illusion, really it is our brains and bodies that are doing all the work. A materialist may or may not hold that physical events occur according to strictly mechanical principles.

Theories of a third kind in this second big group may allow minds and bodies to be substances as different as possible but their apparent relations are explained in terms of parallel function rather than causality. Thinkers such as Leibniz and Geulincx, who followed Descartes and could see some of his difficulties, tried to evolve plans of this sort. Hence we get the analogy of mind and matter as synchronized clocks or as orchestras which cannot hear each other on and off stage but nevertheless play together. Such theories seem to require either a conductor or some other means of ensuring that changes in mind and matter satisfactorily coincide. For this purpose, as is well known, Leibniz fell back on the pre-Established Harmony in God's choice of the best of all possible worlds and was severely satirized by Voltaire.

We now turn to the third big group of theories which seems to contain a more subtle and interesting collection of views. These tend to challenge either the notion of substance or, more clearly than Leibniz, the notion of causality, or they challenge both these notions. Such theories derive in general from Aristotle when he was not thinking in terms of 'essences', from Spinoza, possibly from Hume, and, in our own day, from Russell and those whom he has influenced. Advocates of what may be called 'aspect' theories may themselves adopt one of several courses. They may, like Russell at one time, suggest that the ultimate furniture of the world is neither mental nor physical but events of a neutral kind that can be ordered in different ways. This view can be stated provocatively, as Russell once did, by saying that mind and matter, like the lion and the unicorn fighting for the crown, are simply heraldic inventions. But the provocation is apt to distract attention from the valuable core of the view, namely: it may prove useful scientifically to distinguish mental and physical happenings by the systems of relations to which they belong in preference to distinguishing kinds of events or 'things'. For instance, in some cases it may be important to relate a pain in the head to a cracked skull or a brain tumour. In others its relation to frustrated aspiration may be of greater interest in understanding and treating it. In either case the pain remains (or we hope eventually ceases) as something experienced, which it may not be very profitable to call either mental or physical except in terms of its relations as just outlined. A snag occurs when some enterprising reader then inquires what in principle is the difference implied between an aspiration and a skull. Neutral monists, and their descendants the logical positivists, have yet to show successfully that they can answer this question without begging linguistically or otherwise the very distinction they set out to avoid.

Professor Ryle's version of an aspect theory need not, as Russell's, rest on assuming neutral events. He can, I think, in principle have numberless different kinds of happenings of the same logical type in the sense that they can be indicated by simple pointing. His theory turns on suggesting we have been wrong in supposing that the terms 'mind' and 'matter' just point to two different sorts of happening. (So far he is following Russell in treating both as logical constructions.) He seems, though not always very clearly, to be trying to say that whereas significant sentences about 'matter', 'bodily', and the like must terminate eventually (although their usual reference is indirect) in nouns, pronouns, or demonstratives indicating items of some kind which could perhaps be seen, heard, tasted, smelt, touched, or felt in movement, sentences about 'mind' or 'mental' terminate not in logical subjects, but in verbs, adverbs, and, possibly, adjectives. Though, therefore, 'mind' and 'matter' both refer to logical constructions in Russell's sense, they are logical constructions of quite a different logical nature. The distinction, therefore, that Ryle needs to clarify without going round in a linguistic circle is the distinction we think we can make in ordinary living between something and the 'way' or 'style' in which it is what it is. Here he seems to be searching after a solution of a kind which Aristotle also sought. It would be premature to judge whether he has found it. A scientist, in contrast to a philosopher, would ask that in further clarifying this distinction Professor Ryle should keep in mind the practical needs of coordinating different branches of inquiry, (such as physiology and psychology), both to satisfy curiosity, to increase the chances of accurate prediction, and to solve the practical problems of human functioning and dysfunctioning about which we care as ordinary people.

What main theories are current today ? Here we must confine ourselves to outlining some English views. French, German, Italian, and American writers might answer this question very differently. Philosophically, probably Professor Ryle's attack on the problem has been the most exciting in the last few years. Among ordinary people, physiologists, and psychologists, broadly there are four main groups. First, in everyday life most of us are incuriously interactionist until we come up against something we do not understand, and then we are puzzled by the kind of problem suggested on p. 16. Secondly, there are plenty of scientists and technicians who would defend some attempt to seek the final explanation of human behaviour in terms of physical events – whether neuro-physiological, biochemical, electro-mechanical we cannot here consider in detail. Some have been discussed profitably by other writers in this series. Thirdly, there are groups of workers, often to be found among clinicians, who make use of concepts such as 'the self', 'traits', 'sentiments', that seem to serve a purpose but at any rate as yet have had no successful definitions in clearly nonpsychological terms. At most such clinicians would entertain the possibility of 'ultimate' explanation being sought elsewhere, but would regard this search as premature until better questions have been formulated at the psychological level. To some the bare possibility of final explanation in physical terms is distasteful. Fourthly, there are those with a special interest in the scientific methods appropriate to psychology who fall into two distinct groups. On the one hand some would put aside all questions about body and mind as philosophically senseless and scientifically a waste of time. They would concentrate in preference upon improving and objectifying methods of observing and describing human behaviour. The second group does not find this wholly satisfactory. They would ask us to look more closely at current theories of explanation, believing that there, if anywhere, may lie the key to better understanding both of psychological theory and psychological practice. Possibly neither of these groups need logically be committed from the start to any decision about the ingredients of the strangely interesting world around us.

Now let us turn to the Greeks and trace the story of how we have reached the confused position in which we find ourselves.

REFERENCES

Clark, Sir Kenneth. *Landscape into Art*. London: Murray, 1949, Penguin Books, 1956

Huxley, T. H. *Fortnightly Review*, November 1874, quoted by Morton Prince in *Psychologies of 1925*. Edited by Carl Murchison. The International University Series in Psychology. Worcester, Mass.: Clark University Press; London: Oxford University Press, 3rd Edn., 1928, p. 200

Newton, Eric. *European Painting and Sculpture*. Harmondsworth: Penguin Books, 3rd Edn., 1945, pp. 31 and 32

Prince, Morton. 'A Biological Theory of Consciousness', in *Psychologies of 1925*, p. 223

Ranke, Leopold Von. *The History of the Popes*. Translated by E. Foster, London: Bell, 1891, Vol. I, p. 517

Ryle, Gilbert. *The Concept of Mind*. London: Hutchinson's University Library, 1949

PART ONE

Historical Introduction

*

Whenever any principle, be it what it may,
tends to the establishment of absolute dominion
in Europe, there is invariably opposed to it a
vigorous resistance, having its origin in the
deepest springs of human nature.

LEOPOLD VON RANKE

CHAPTER I

THE EARLY GREEKS

God . . . breathed into his nostrils the breath of life;
and man became a living soul.

GENESIS

WHILE modern western European thought later incorporated
much from the East, historically we seem justified in starting
with the early Greeks. This task has been eased of late by Professor R. B. Onians. His *Origins of European Thought* shed new
light on a topic which has been the subject of controversy for
more than a century. Now, among many things in a rich store,
we find a better basis for understandin gearly Greek psychology,
particularly the concepts associated with φρένες (phrenes).

According to Onians, to understand the early Greeks, familiar
as they seem, we must not overlook the emotional expressiveness of the tradition reflected in the *Iliad* and the *Odyssey*. 'The
manliest warriors weep copiously and publicly. Because the
Achaeans are driven back, imperial Agamemnon stands un-
ashamed before the assembled host, "weeping like a fountain
of black water that from a beetling crag pours its dakr stream".'
Equally to be noted is the savagery in battle and the fact that
women are an avowed aim and approved prize of war. To quote
Onians again, 'when a city is taken, the men are slain, the children are dashed to death or enslaved, and the women violently
dragged away to serve as slaves or concubines of their married
or unmarried conquerors'. The attitude to physical injury was
in fact savagely harsh and the attitude to sex wholly naturalistic.

As Onians suggests, there is aligned with this a totality of
response not wholly dissimilar to that of certain types of primitive outlook, which is falsified by our habit of drawing a sharp
distinction between thought and feeling. Hence, and here we
come to a crucial point in understanding Homeric conceptions,
φρονεῖν (phronein) which in later Greek came to mean 'to
think', or 'have understanding', primarily in an intellectual

25

sense, carries in Homer a more comprehensive meaning, i.e., that of undifferentiated psychic activity, the action of the φρένες (phrenes) involving emotion and conation as well as thought. This concept is compatible with those ideo-motor theories in psychology which assert that an idea is not merely a state or act of awareness but carries with it a tendency to movement. As Onians points out, the popular phrase 'to see her is to love her' carries the same implication.

So far so good, but what is the meaning of φρένες as used by the early Greeks? Onians has been at pains to establish that, although by the time of the Hippocratic treatises and Plato, (that is already by the fifth century B.C.) φρένες had come to mean 'diaphragm', in Homer and the tradition he represented φρένες seems better translated as the 'lungs'. This is important because in Homeric literature θυμός (thymos), the stuff of mind or consciousness, is said to be contained in the φρένες. We are thus led to realize that in its turn thymos connoted breath. Moreover, since phrenes with the heart were organs of mind, the quality of the mind was related to their quality. Also 'thought', 'breath', and 'words' were intimately associated.

Now, still following Onians, let us look more closely at this early Greek conception of consciousness. First of all Homer's language makes clear that it is not a function but a thing. Secondly, however, it would be mistaken to identify thymos with mere outer air received and expelled. Onians presumes that the Greeks must have observed that breath is warm and moist, containing as it does a good deal of water vapour from the body, which becomes visible by condensation when it meets a bright surface or the air is cooler. 'The cognates,' he says, 'of θυμός (θυμιάω, etc.) suggest that it should mean vapour. Whence? From what liquid but blood, the hot liquid which is in fact concentrated in the heart and around it in the lungs.' And so he reaches the conclusion that θυμός is not the blood-soul as opposed to the breath-soul nor indeed mere breath but breath related to blood, not mere air but something which diminishes if the body is ill-nourished, but is increased when the body is well nourished. For Onians' fascinating evidence in favour of this interpretation I must refer readers to his book.

If we now consider what was said about early Greek expressiveness, and that thought and feeling must not be too sharply distinguished, we can appreciate that this connexion of thymos, vapour, with blood, carries with it implications about thinking, emotion, and character qualities. Emotion for the early Greeks was in fact as heart-centred as it has tended to be for most of their successors. They seem also to have noted fluctuations of emotion with variations in breathing. This is an observation familiar to most people and one to which psychology students about three thousand years later are used to giving a little extra precision with a simple piece of apparatus.

In the opinion of Onians, 'for the Homeric Greeks the $\theta\upsilon\mu\delta s$ is the spirit, the breath that is consciousness, variable, dynamic, coming and going, changing as feeling changes and, we may add, as thought changes'.... 'Upon a man's "spirit" or "breath-soul" depend the fierceness or energy ($\nu\epsilon\nu os$) and courage ($\theta\acute{a}\rho\sigma os$).' He can be of good blood, and all that this implies, or the reverse. Through his lungs he is (literally) 'inspired' by Gods and Goddesses not only with emotion but with thoughts or relatively intellectual devices. For example, Penelope had breathed into her $\phi\rho\acute{\epsilon}\nu\epsilon s$ the idea of setting up a great loom and weaving a robe. Fainting at the sight of Hector's corpse, Andromache loses consciousness (thymos). Hence consciousness may quit the body when the blood is spilt. On the other hand, the deepest emotions may be reinforced from the liver which is full of blood and bile. Homeric heroes and others, including animals, when grievously or mortally wounded lie struggling, as well they might, for breath ($\theta\upsilon\mu\delta s$) or consciousness, in the full and complicated sense so far explained.

It appears that a case can also be made for believing that consciousness, thus understood, was but the medium of all forms of sense perception then recognized, i.e., seeing, hearing, touch, taste, and smell. Various, to us odd, physiological theories about passages from the appropriate sense organs to the lungs were invoked to explain perception. To account for Homeric notions of tactile sensation, and when the writing suggests that thymos leaves dying heroes' limbs, Onians points out that for the early Greeks consciousness, while centred in the lungs, was apparently believed in some way to permeate the whole body.

We may now ask the question: what happened after death? The early Greek thymos appears normally to have perished when it left the organs on which it depended. Only in very exceptional circumstances, as, for instance, in the case of Teiresias, the blind seer, whom Odysseus was to consult in Hades, could the dead mortal retain his lungs and therefore consciousness in the sense explained. Generally, the dead were fleshless, lungless shadows without consciousness and unable to recognize or to communicate with earthly visitors unless they had, like Elpenor and Patroklos, remained unburned or had somehow managed to taste blood and acquire thymos for the occasion. To quote Onians: 'Thrice does Odysseus try to clasp the psyche of his mother but thrice she flew out of his hands "like a shadow or even as a dream" and she explained: "This is the way with mortals, when one dies, for the sinews no longer hold the flesh and the bones, but the mighty energy of burning overcomes these (as soon as the $\theta\nu\mu\sigma\varsigma$ has left the white bones) and the psyche like a dream flies away and flutters".'

In referring to the psyche, as distinct from the thymos, we have introduced the early Greeks' immortal soul in contrast to their mortal mind or spirit. Let us summarize very briefly something of what Onians has to tell us about this concept. First, he seems fairly convinced that for the early Greeks the distinction was a valid one. Secondly, psyche the immortal soul, in contrast to thymos the mortal spirit, was associated with the head. Thirdly, save for two vital respects and one less common, it played but a small part in the dailyness of living. When we say vital, however, we mean the word in its strictest sense, for psyche seems to have been considered as the immortal vitality of a man, that by which he lives. Moreover, in identifying the liquid noticed in the brain, i.e., cerebro-spinal fluid, with seminal fluid, the early Greeks reached the second vital aspect of psyche: it was not only one man's living principle but was the life that is transmitted in procreation.

The implications of such a view of the psyche are, of course, enormously complex. We can draw attention to only a very few of those traced by Onians. First, this interpretation of Greek thought is significant in relation both to later European customs, and to those in other civilizations, of sanctifying the head in some way. Laurel wreaths, haloes, diadems, anointings, crownings, and innumerable other signs of respect for the head may probably be associated with the same line of thought. Some of these are less attractive to modern readers, such as the Celtic custom of fixing up a set of human heads in one's house to obtain protection from their ghosts. Or, even more horrific, there was Kleomenes, the King of Sparta, who preserved the head of his friend Archonides in a pot of honey and professed to consult it before every undertaking. In this and in other examples there is an obvious sense in which the early Greek views, as portrayed by Onians, reveal also many of the primitive tendencies to endow the hair with magical properties.

A second implication of the early Greek view of the psyche is of more direct relevance to understanding later European attitudes to the mind-body problem. In spite of the naturalism of the early Greek attitude to sex, their view of psyche facilitated, as Onians points out, a positive attitude to chastity so that it could come to be seen as a means whereby a man conserved his vitality and his immortal soul. This is, I think, important for understanding both the complexity and the tenacity of later writers' ascetic convictions, and the intensity of those of their opponents to whom the concept of chastity appeared to be based only on fears of defilement or even on the kind of political reason making it desirable for a priesthood to be distinctively celibate. Sociologically it is interesting also that in an early Greek view it appears that the psyche was transmitted by the father and not the mother.

From the point of view of the history of psychology, there is something very interesting in the fact that the immortal soul, when it appears first in explicit evidence in Europe, is in effect vitality unencumbered and unassociated with any of the usual psychological functions which at times have been attributed to the mind. Such elegant simplicity was not to remain, and, among other causes, for the straightforward one that somebody was bound sooner or later to have a closer look at the brain. The person who did this appears to have been Alcmaeon of Croton, or at least 'he is the earliest writer whose explicit teaching on these subjects is recorded'. He lived in the sixth century B.C., was an empiricist, and is said to have practised dissection. 'He discovered "passages" leading from the eyes to the encephalos and urged that the latter received the perceptions of sight, sound, and smell, and was the seat of thought.'

One cannot help wishing at times that the earlier Greeks had started with thymos, not as a thing but as a function of head and heart, and had not tried to lodge the immortal soul anywhere. We might, thereby, have been saved the consequences that follow once the attributes, functions, and locations of the original thymos and those of the immortal and creative psyche become intermingled and confused. As Onians comments: 'The great dispute between subsequent thinkers as to whether the head or the chest is the seat of the ruling part follows this breakdown of the original duality ψυχή and θυμός and their fusion in a more complex ψυχή.' He adds in a footnote: 'e.g. Plato favoured the head, Aristotle the heart, and Epicurus the chest, while the Stoics were divided.' One may ruefully add that round related problems the Middle Ages, the Renaissance, the seventeenth, eighteenth, nineteenth, and twentieth centuries have in their own way struggled. Emphasis has shifted away from attempts to 'locate' the immortal soul, for with the rise of empirical science mental functioning in this life and its physiological accompaniments (or whatever they may eventually be deemed) have engaged, on the whole, more specialized interest. Also, we have come to think less readily in terms of an immortal soul as something capable of being in a 'place' at all. But omitting to consider the immortal soul's location as such, might not have saved any of the centuries from struggling over the closely interwoven problem of thought versus sensation or feeling. Many people, mistakenly, have approached this latter problem exclusively in terms of 'control' versus 'abandon'. In this respect, with their relative fusion of thought, feeling, and sensation, if not necessarily in their ways of living, the early Greeks did their best to serve us well.

REFERENCES

Onians, R. B. *The Origins of European Thought about the Body, the Mind, the Soul, the World, Time, and Fate.* Cambridge: University Press, 1951, Parts I and II, especially pp. 3, 4, 17, 47, 47–8, 50, 56, 61, 109 ff, 115, 117

CHAPTER 2

CLASSICAL GREECE AND ROME

> Take wings to climb the zenith,
> Or sleep in Fields of Peace;
> By day the Sun shall keep thee,
> By night the rising Star.
> > EGYPTIAN BOOK OF THE DEAD,
> > 3500 B.C. et seq.

> Happy the man, and happy he alone,
> He who can call his day his own.
> He who, secure within, can say:
> 'Tomorrow do thy worst, for I have lived today'.
> > HORACE, 65–8 B.C.

> Animula, vagula, blandula
> Hospes, comesque, corporis.
> > HADRIAN, A.D. 68–134

(i) HIPPOCRATES AND DEMOCRITUS

WHEN we turn to classical and later Greece we find that the distinctions alien to primitive thought had been made and sharpened. In some ways this was an achievement. From our twentieth-century standpoint, however, we may wish that the sharpness, and one might say the direction of abstraction, had not taken quite the form that it did, for differentiating thought from other human functioning brought with it problems of its own. These, however, we cannot discuss in detail. I therefore propose (with the continued purpose of giving a rapid historical orientation) very briefly to outline certain views of Hippocrates, Plato, and Aristotle. These are given more fully in quotations on pp. 183–228.

First let us look at Hippocrates. Living in the fifth century B.C. he was a contemporary of Pericles, Anaxagoras, Thucydides, Democritus, Phidias, Sophocles, Euripides, Aristophanes, and Socrates. He was a busy, practical physician trained at the medical school of Cos and, like Thucydides, liable to be very critical of the superstition, current in Athens, which was to spread as the civilization passed its height and began to fall into decay. Zilboorg, in his *History of Medical Psychology*, praises Hippocrates' clinical observation, regarding its acuteness as far in advance of his capacity to treat the illnesses that he recognized. Hippocrates is credited with turning the first page of the history of medical psychology when he sharply protests against the supposition that epilepsy, popularly called the Sacred Disease, was due to divine inspiration: – 'It thus appears to me to be in no way more divine or more sacred than other diseases, but has a natural cause from which it originates like other affections.'

This rings sympathetically in modern ears, but in Hippocrates' general theory, such as it was, there are distinct traces of the earlier Greek views which we have just outlined on the basis of Onians' work. In Hippocrates' writings the old psyche turns up fairly clearly as a species of vital force presiding over all organic functions, including those of the brain; but, be it noted, the concept appears to be filling out. The thymos is to be found in a pneuma or breath that is intimately connected with thought and feeling. Hippocrates, however, while apparently considering that the brain, to which pneuma eventually penetrated, might be the principal centre of reasoning, was more convinced that sensation and motor activities were associated with the brain, than he was that the brain itself thought.

Apart from this general position, Hippocrates had a good deal to say of a physiological nature, and we see a development and variation of the older role played by the liver in what he thought about the chemical basis of temperament. This he found not only in the secretion of blood but also in black and yellow bile and in phlegm. In Hippocrates, in fact, we find the first clear statement of the theory of humours which, with additions from Galen, was still underlying Elizabethan thought 2,000 years later.

From the point of view of the history of medical psychology Hippocrates is possibly most interesting for his passing clinical observations and comments. From our point of view, as the outstanding doctor of fifth-century Athens, he reveals an interesting mixture of the old and the new. Both in his doctrine of the humours, and in flashes of clinical observation shown, e.g., in his belief that disturbed emotion could in itself have physical effects, he took views about the relation of body and mind historically one stage further.

From Democritus, his contemporary, we get something quite different; that is the effective introduction into European thought of the notion of atomism and of mechanical principles of explanation. According to Democritus, everything occurs by the movement and interaction of atoms, soul atoms being simply a somewhat more subtle version of the others. Democritus was, in fact, the advocate of the billiard-ball theories of the universe which recurred in Epicurus and Lucretius and which were later to trouble European philosophers so much.

(ii) PLATO

From our point of view what are the salient facts about the Platonic notions of body, mind, and soul? There are three points of introduction necessary. First, to understand Plato's notion of individual body-mind relations one must grasp his main conception of the world soul. This Plato outlined at the beginning of the *Timaeus* which is his least typical dialogue. For the magnificence of this dialogue's imaginative sweep, its intrinsic interest, including some of its curious qualities, and for the historical fact that it was the only fragment of Plato known to the Middle Ages, it is however of special concern to us. The conceptions outlined in the more poetic dialogues and the *Republic* are referred to on pp. 188–213. Secondly, Plato, in spite of his classical Greek objectivity, his respect for the facts as he saw them, and his sometimes forgotten humour, is perhaps the greatest of those philosophers who by disposition appear to respond to a stimulating but changing period, with a search for epistemological and almost mystic certainty. For some people, Plato provides one of the most satisfying literary expressions of the individual human need to identify successfully and (here is the mystical and perhaps masochistic element) completely with something greater than himself. Thereby the individual believes he may attain both a purification and a security which, rightly or wrongly, he does not feel able to achieve in any other way. Thirdly, it would be profoundly mistaken to over-simplify Plato, suggesting either that he is intelligible and easy or that just one opinion can be drawn from what he said. The *Timaeus* alone has caused classical scholars not a little perplexity. Here, as indeed elsewhere, there are various possible interpretations and many questions that are left unanswered.

With this introduction, and the other citations on pp. 188–213, we may at this stage summarize Plato's *Timaeus* treatment of body-mind relations as follows.

God, the Creator, first made a world soul according to a mathematical formula for producing an essence from the mixing of diametrically opposite ingredients. First, there is that which is eternal, can neither develop nor change, and can only be apprehended by the purest form of thinking. Second, there is that which is continuously developing and changing, and about which we can never have more than probable opinion based on the senses. This world soul, whose dual aspect we may slightly stress in passing, was infused into the body of the world which was also created by God according to a complex mathematical recipe for mixing earth, air, fire, and water. Soul and body, when creation was complete, constituted the whole and only world, which was made in the likeness of a pattern which is eternal in the most 'absolute' sense that we can give to this term. Of the fused aspects of the world the soul was the senior in the order of creation and for Plato it takes ethical precedence. Having completed the main structure, including the stars, accomplished the ordering and revolution of the system, and lighted a fire (the sun) by which the animals, as many as nature intended, could understand the passage of time, the Creator from the remaining ingredients made the Demiurgoi (the lesser Gods), the birds, the water species, and finally the pedestrian and land creatures including man. This series of creations he did not entirely complete himself, for to the Demiurgoi, once themselves in existence, other creations were in part delegated.

In the case of man, the Creator made the immortal soul himself. For this purpose he used the remains of the elements left after creating the world soul, mixed in much the same proportions but now diluted. He divided this mixture into as many souls as there were stars and assigned a star to each soul. The souls were then taken to see the world as a whole and told of their future destiny as human beings, each man being given an equal start in so far as he would have the capacity for sensation, for love with all its pleasures and pain, for fear, anger, and the feelings akin or opposed to these. If a man conquered his lesser self in living righteously his soul would return to a blessed existence in its native star. If he lived unrighteously, failing to subdue his mortal impulses, then his soul would find reincarnation as a woman. If the person still did not desist from evil, the soul would go through a series of animal reincarnations until by the help of reason it at last overcame the mob of later accretions from earth, air, fire, and water and so dragged itself back to its initial state. It is to be noted that the individual immortal soul, with which reason is implicitly connected, takes evaluative precedence over the rest of the human being, just as for Plato the soul is the senior and superior in the world as a whole.

Having thus made and informed the human immortal souls, the Creator handed them over to the Demiurgoi, who were responsible for making the human mortal souls and their appropriate bodies, guiding these mortal animals as best they could and guarding them from all but self-inflicted evils. These instructions the Demiurgoi carried out but, one gathers, not without difficulty. The text has more than a suspicion of the mature vitality and humour which Plato's sentimentalizers sometimes forget to notice.

What remains to be said about the individual human being? The Demiurgoi, borrowing earth, air, fire, and water from the world, which later must be returned, fashioned human bodies, the head for containing the immortal soul, and the body, so suggests one passage, for carrying the head. The mortal soul, subject to terrible and irresistible affections, was given a separate habitation in another part of the body, so that it would not pollute the divine more than was absolutely necessary. In fact, the mortal soul itself had two parts; the one capable of courage, passion, and love was lodged in the chest, the other 'which desires meats, drinks, and other things of which it has need by reason of its bodily nature' was lodged between the diaphragm and the navel. Communication between this section and those above was considered in the *Timaeus* to be made via the liver acting as a reflector, with the spleen nearby as a napkin 'always ready prepared and at hand to clean the mirror'. As already noted, the *Timaeus* is recognized to be very different from many of the other Dialogues. Those who find Plato's juxtaposition of heavenly creation and internal housewifery a little odd, may pause and reflect on how much of this is due to Plato's evaluative hierarchy, which expresses one general approach to these matters, permeating as it did the whole of European culture. Jowett goes so far as to remark that 'of all the writings of Plato the *Timaeus* is the most obscure and repulsive to the modern reader, and has nevertheless had the greatest influence over the ancient and mediaeval world'.

For the rest of what Plato had to say in the *Timaeus* about the immortal and mortal souls and the body in which they dwell we may refer readers to the dialogue itself. The extracts given on pp. 188–213 have been chosen, so that the reader may compare this view with parts of the exquisite myths and the discussions of the *Phaedo*, *Phaedrus*, and the *Republic*. Meanwhile, we can understand how, blended later with a Christianity that brought from the East further intimations of immortality, the influence of Platonic theories on the interpretation of human ways was to become incalculable.

(iii) ARISTOTLE

Now let us turn to the very different Aristotle. Here we find the logician, the biologist, the lively critical sifter of other people's views, the, at times, extraordinarily penetrating, realistic commentator on men and affairs, the thinker who at other times cannot be wholly absolved from conventionality, expediency, and sententiousness. This last is usually so inextricably mixed up with shrewdness and satire that it is sometimes very difficult to disentangle the threads of gold and of dross. Similar difficulty surrounds the interpretation of Aristotle's views on the body, the mind, and the soul. (We need for the moment to use these undefined terms for expounding him.) In the past, the worst arguments raged over Aristotle's believing or not believing in a personal or any other kind of immortality. St Thomas Aquinas, who was seeking to reconcile Aristotelian and Christian views, infers immortality from Aristotle's position. The Averroists, interpreting Aristotle in a different way, argued that the soul, in so far as it was individual, was not immortal; this last attribute belonged only to reflective reason which is impersonal and identical in different beings. As heretics in this and other respects they were cruelly disposed of. As Russell suggests, in spite of St Thomas' excellent knowledge of Aristotle, it is hard not to think that as interpreters, if nothing else, the Averroists had a case. In the twentieth century, wherein, for the time being, fewer penalties attach to the consequences of interpreting Aristotle one way or another, we can entertain the simple possibility that Aristotle himself was not sure what he thought. In this respect he would be very interesting; for those who can endure uncertainty seem to be either single-minded, of rare courage, or indifferent. Here again we come back to the difficulty of the gold and the dross. Perhaps it is correct that to Aristotle the constitution and fate of an individual person were not of primary interest or importance; perhaps he was unimaginative; perhaps in his impersonality Aristotle has much to give us. For we can get too emotionally involved in individual and personal interests and thereby defeat our best aims. Aristotle's detachment may strike some people as a little bleak, but on the other hand it may be a necessary condition of the genuine contributions to psychological theory that we find in him. With these reservations we may try to outline his views.

In the eyes of the twentieth century, which reached a comparable position by the complicated route we are trying to sketch, Aristotle's greatest contribution was his interest in functioning and his tendency to move at least one step away from the earlier Greek assumption that the mind or soul was a substance in the same logical sense as the body, however differently it might be constituted. We get a hint of Aristotle's capacity for analytic criticism when he neatly summarizes his predecessors by remarking that all, or almost all, distinguish the soul by three of its attributes: movement, perception, and incorporeality. What else they hold, says Aristotle, tends to depend on their general metaphysic, e.g. their preference for earth, air, fire, or water as the ultimate 'stuff' out of which the world is made. 'In fact', he adds, 'each of the elements in turn has found a supporter except earth; but this no one has suggested except in so far as one has said that the soul is composed of or identical with all the elements'. What has Aristotle to offer instead? He distinguishes three kinds of substance: first, matter or that which is not in itself any particular thing; secondly, shape or form in virtue of which it is called some particular thing; and, thirdly, a compound of the two. Working on from this, he concludes that the soul is substance in the second sense and is the form of a natural body which potentially has life.

Before trying to understand more what he means by 'form', let us look at Aristotle's criteria for regarding something as living. These are threefold. First, and at the most primitive level, something is living if it can move in the sense of growing, decaying, feeding, and reproducing itself. Second, it is living if it has sensation, which carries with it desire, for sensation involves the experience of pleasure or pain, and also movement in a more general sense. Thirdly, something is living if it can think. Living at each of these levels presupposes those at the more primitive. What does Aristotle mean by thinking? In one sense of the word he is content to say that the whole man thinks, but we can only reconcile this with other comments by taking into account the distinction between speculative and practical thought which he makes clearer in the *Nicomachean Ethics* than in the *De Anima*. We need also to face the problems connected with Aristotle's distinction between mind (*nous*) and soul (*psyche*). Here we run into an awkward question of translation; for it seems arguable that *nous* resembles an intellectualized version of the Homeric psyche, but generalized so that one person only partakes of something which is common to man and presumably to higher beings. St Thomas held that this capacity was shared to an advanced degree by the angels. In contrast to *nous*, Aristotle's *psyche* appears to think more concretely. This would make sense of Aristotle's remark: 'Mind (*nous*) seems to have an independent existence and not to suffer any decay. Thinking, loving, and hating are not then qualities of the mind (*nous*) but rather of the individual man who possesses the mind in so far as he does. Memory and love then fail because he fails, for they were never part of the mind but of the whole entity which has perished.'

On this interpretation anything which is living (in the sense explained) has psyche in the correlative sense; plants having the first, animals the second, while the third, thinking, is the specific psychic function of man, who may or may not always be capable of thought of the highest and different nature involved in *nous*. Aristotle had clearly got the notion of increasing complexity of function as one moves up the biological scale, each level potentially possessing the functions of that below it. Personally, I do not consider that the valuable part of what Aristotle has to say here is clarified by talking (as many historians of psychology are wont) of different kinds of soul, e.g. vegetative, sensitive, rational. From this we slip so easily into thinking in terms of souls as substances 'lodged' in bodies, which Aristotle seems to have tried to escape, if not wholly successfully. Even more important, perhaps, we may lose sight of the notion of gradual differentiation of functions, which is latent but not fully developed in Aristotle.

Writing after Darwin, after Piaget, and in the light of the many current doubts about the nature of intelligence and its development, we can too easily read into Aristotle meanings which would make classical scholars and historians wince. But we must perhaps risk this rather than lose sight of Aristotle's stress on the importance of the tactile and kinaesthetic senses. Having, elsewhere, made touch fundamental among the senses, Aristotle says, in passing, that in respect of touch man 'is much more discriminating than most of the rest of creation. This is why he is of all living creatures the most capable of thought.' It is worth pausing to reflect on this in relation to modern views about the possible significance of tactile and kinaesthetic communication in early infancy. Historically, in spite of Aristotle's straightforward biological outlook, his own intellectualism and the logic and language which reinforced thinking in 'essences' contributed to a condemnation of the senses and emotions in later centuries. The contact senses, as the most fundamental, incurred a taboo which really began to lift only during the nineteenth century and is barely cleared in our own day. There are plenty of other reasons for this besides the extraordinary influence of Plato and Aristotle. Such other reasons include all the complexities of sexual mores and the fact, shrewdly observed by the old Victorian Bain in 1855, that touch and movement play a crucial role in any expression of tenderness. It will be interesting, however, if, in fifty or a hundred years' time, the importance attached to Freud for what he had to say about sex as such, gives place to his implication that the tactile and kinaesthetic senses play a more important part in successful living than has always been recognized by theorists.

Meanwhile we must not lose sight of the problems centred in Aristotle's notion of 'form'. It may help, first, to connect this with his discussion of causality, of which he distinguished four conceptions. First there is a material cause, that out of which something is made, e.g. the stone from which a statue is carved. Second, there is an efficient cause, e.g. the sculptor who does the carving. Thirdly, there may be a final cause, e.g. the purpose for which the statue is made. Finally, and much harder to understand, Aristotle distinguished a formal cause. This is not quite like the pattern, for example, in the Platonic sense of that in accordance with which the Creator was said to have made the world. Nor is it quite the shape of the statue, though it is something akin to this last. Nearer than these two negative statements I doubt if we can go with any certainty. There is, however, a sense in which Aristotle is wanting to suggest that the formal cause is the defining potentiality of something. Aristotle does not use this example, but we might say that the capacity to sleep in the winter, though he is now awake, could be seen as at least part of the 'form' of a dormouse. Any boy, expert in mouse breeding, would add details of movement, response, colour, shape, size, length of fur, whiskers, ears, etc., collectively making for individuality and without which his pet would not be a dormouse at all. Together these would constitute its 'form'.

It is in a partly comparable sense of 'form' that Aristotle thought psyche to be the form of a natural body which potentially has life. The Aristotelian psyche thus becomes the form of the body, in the sense that without it the body would no more realize its capacity for living (which it has in a way that a painted eye cannot potentially see) than an axe without a sharp edge is able to cut. The distinctive point is that an axe without an edge remains an axe, though inefficient. A body without a psyche is not the kind of body (i.e. capable of living) which Aristotle set out to consider. To quote: 'The psyche is that whereby we live and feel and think in the most fundamental sense, so that the psyche would be the notion or form, and not the matter or underlying material. As we have already said, substance is used in three senses, form, matter, and a compound of the two. Of these, matter is potentiality, and form actuality; and since what has psyche is a compound of the two, the body cannot be the actuality of a psyche, but the psyche is the actuality of some body. For this reason those are right in their view who maintain that the psyche cannot exist without a body, but the psyche is not in any sense a body. It is not a body, but it is something connected with a body, and exists in a body, and in a body of a particular kind, not at all as our predecessors supposed, who fitted it to any body, without adding any limitations as to what body or what kind of body'. Thus Aristotle begins to move from the earlier Greek and more limited conception of the psyche as a '*thing*'.

There is much in Russell's exposition of Aristotle with which one ventures to disagree. Moreover Russell seems to skate, with almost unbelievable superficiality, over the difficult empirical psychological issues which concern personal integration. Nevertheless he has a witty and logical comment on the notion of substance which may serve to underline the dangers of taking this concept for granted. Thus Russell: 'Substance when taken seriously is a concept impossible to free from difficulties. It is merely a convenient way of collecting events into bundles. What can we know about Mr Smith? When we look at him, we see a pattern of colours; when we listen to him talking, we have a series of sounds. We believe that, like us, he has thoughts and feelings. But what is Mr Smith apart from all these occurrences ? A mere imaginary hook, from which the occurrences are supposed to hang. They have in fact no need of a hook, any more than the earth needs an elephant to rest upon.' We may not think the problem is thereby solved, but without such warning it is all too easy to make the mind or soul play either the role of Russell's elephant or that of an immaterial thread uniting a string of all too material beads. We will return to this later.

The often interesting details of Aristotle's physiological psychology we must omit except for the following. First, he thought Hippocrates' views on the liver were only partly correct. Secondly, Aristotle's feeling for total functioning seems both to have rescued him from lodging a rational substance 'in' or 'on' the cortex and to have led him to underestimate the interest and importance of the brain. The function of this he reduced to that of condensing hot vapours which rise from the heart. These when cooled could be re-distributed in the form of dew and result in more temperate human activity. One somehow wishes this suggestive view were right.

Discussing Plato and Aristotle together, Zilboorg draws attention to the interesting anomaly that 'Plato the idealist, the mystic, the deductive philosopher, was a proponent of studies of organic cerebral pathology; Aristotle the pure biologist, the inductive scientist, stimulated the study of psychology proper'.

(iv) Transitional Greece and Rome

Aristotle, who, it will be remembered was Alexander's tutor, died in 322 B.C. Alexander himself had died in 323, and about this time Athens lost precedence, cultural supremacy shifting to Alexandria. The period, which was one of oppression, revolution, and social change, did not lend itself to free and detached speculation. Moreover into the relatively homogeneous Greek culture of the fifth century, very different and often pantheistic or mystical elements were filtering from the East. The two main groups of thinkers, following Epicurus (342–270 B.C.) on the one hand and Zeno, the Stoic, (336–264 B.C.) on the other, were concerned primarily with an honourable and intelligible struggle to formulate a way of living in an age of reorientation. Their followers faced similar problems as Rome successfully overcame Carthage and Syracuse in the third century Punic wars, and proceeded, in the second century, to conquer the Macedonian monarchies.

I do not propose to say much about the ways of living that Stoics and Epicureans advocated.* In any case the Stoic theories appear to have developed and changed and it is impossible either to debit or credit them with one coherent point of view. Certain aspects of the main schools do, however, concern us.

Let us deal with the Stoics first. There is much in their viewpoint which can be regarded as early Greek, influenced and overlaid by Democritus, Plato, and Aristotle. They appear to think of a world consisting of some kind of flamelike substance which is capable of acting and being acted upon and is also capable of various degrees of refinement. It behaves in a deterministic fashion in accordance with laws of nature and/or reason, there being a sense in which 'reasonable' means in conformity with nature. One already suspects unclarity, and that nature was considered 'reasonable' in some other sense as well. Man's soul was thought to partake of the most refined form of the ultimate stuff of the world, i.e. of universal reason. There is a sense, therefore, in which the Stoics were committed to a severe form of psychological materialist determinism.

On the other hand, they were very much aware that human behaviour is by no means 'reasonable' if one means by this 'always intelligently adaptive'. Their major practical problem was thus to find a way of helping human nature to escape its all too common lapses. Stoic interest in the passions therefore became paramount, and they tried to work out a theory whereby man develops, through various stages of the inadequate, to the adequate functioning of his reasoned judgement. This last was thought to be unimpeachable if left to itself, but could be disturbed by passions which are diseases of reason. The acute

* For the views of the Stoics and Epicureans I have relied on Brett, Russell, and Zilboorg. For the history of medical psychology I have used Brett, Zilboorg, Greenwood, and Smith.

reader will easily see that these views cannot all be held together, for it is hard to understand, on Stoical premises, how reason can be diseased or the passions inevitably vile. Even greater difficulty occurs when the admirable Stoic respect for courage and sense of style finds expression in a will capable of influencing events. It seems likely that the key term 'reason' was used in several different senses either by them or their expositors. This question we must leave to classical scholars and philosophers to disentangle.

From our standpoint the Stoic views, rightly or wrongly interpreted, are important for three reasons. First, because their opinions raised the awkward questions about determinism and free will which have continuously befogged discussion of mind-body relations. Secondly, they introduced a change of emphasis by their interest in human behaviour generally, and in passions or emotions particularly. Thirdly, in what they had to say about undisturbed 'reasonableness', which was achieved apparently by withdrawal and resignation to the all-pervading natural reason of the universe, one may detect an eastern element. Later on, in the period of Roman decadence, a Stoical revulsion from hedonistic laxity, combined both with eastern mysticism, neo-Platonism and ascetic Christianity, seems to have contributed to a network of views that encouraged the separation of mental and physical functioning. While initially well-intentioned, this eventually had disastrous results for those who were thought 'possessed'.

Epicurus, like the earlier Stoics, was interested in finding a philosophy of life. He is best known through Lucretius' apparently scrupulous exposition in the *De Rerum Natura*. This was written in the first half of the first century B.C. Epicurus, like the Stoics, is interesting more for his general attitude than on points of detail. We can, I think, follow most historians in dismissing the alleged encouragement of abandoned sensuality sometimes popularly attributed to his views. Epicurus himself appears to have been one of those naturally moderate, kindly people who can safely delight in happiness which is sensory (and even sensuous) because they need not fear excess, and who wish to others the same enjoyment. It is also possible to see

45

Epicurus as restrained to the point of needing to express desire for more care-free delight in the joys of this world than was open to him personally. Neither of these attitudes implies abandon. Lucretius, who gave supreme literary expression to Epicurean theory, lived in Rome through a period of severe civil war and some glorification of laxity. With this, orthodox Epicureanism contrasts rather than conforms, and so does the sensitive feeling for nature which pervades the *De Rerum Natura*. The fact of historical interest is that, with the slow decline of the Greek scientific spirit and the eventual rise of occultism and asceticism, even orthodox Epicureanism was on the losing side. Yet, until the senses were slowly reprieved, there could be few great developments in empirical science. With Renaissance interest in the world around us Lucretius was also rediscovered. In the seventeenth century Gassendi advanced an atomic theory based upon his writing.

Turning now to other interesting aspects of Epicureanism we have to note two points. First, Epicurus followed Democritus in making the world consist of atoms, some of which, the finer sort, were soul atoms. To this extent he may be dubbed 'materialistic', though 'substantival' might be a better epithet. In contrast, however, to the Stoics and to innumerable thinkers until the twentieth century, Epicurus was not caught in the assumption that every event must have a cause in the sense of something which gives it a push on predetermined lines. Though an Epicurean universe obeys general laws, it is logically possible for an Epicurean atom to behave unpredictably somewhat after the fashion of Heisenberg's electrons. Secondly, Epicurus thought of individual people as composed of innumerable atoms, in themselves eternal, but dispersing on death. On this score personal immortality was out of the question. Historically the significant point to note about this view in its setting is its aim to give freedom from fear. One gathers that third century B.C. religious beliefs on the after life and on retribution were such as to give one pause, and in the days of Lucretius Roman religious views were a mass of sinister superstition. An extract from Lucretius is given on pp. 229–40.

It is neither necessary nor possible to follow the intricate history of Stoic and Epicurean views from the time of Lucretius onwards. In regard to attitudes on body-mind relations there are three strands of history that the reader could profitably pursue but which we shall only list.

The first links the history of Roman medicine from the time of Asclepiades, about the middle of the first century B.C., to Galen (130–200 A.D.). This history is outlined by Brett, Zilboorg, and Greenwood and Smith. Asclepiades seems to have mingled a humanistic outlook on medicine and mental disorder with Epicurean principles. His successors in enlightened medicine were doctors such as Aretaeus of Cappadocia (?30–90 A.D.), Caelius Aurelianus, who practised and wrote under Trajan and Hadrian, and the medical historian Celsus, who may have been born under Augustus and writing under Tiberius. It is worth noting that this period of humanized medicine seems to coincide with that of Rome's more stable history, and it shaded into obscurantism as the empire began to disintegrate. Galen, who is the last great name in medicine before the Dark Ages, was a writer full of unmanageable inconsistencies. He was in principle a follower of Hippocrates, and is best known for crystallizing the doctrine of temperaments. This is commonly condensed to four: choleric, sanguine, phlegmatic, and bilious (or melancholic). More correctly, as shown by May Smith, it should be seen as a system of nine. Galen reached this by adding four intermediate temperaments and the one which is derived from a perfect balance. It is interesting as an early attempt to associate personality traits with the body's chemical functioning. For an account of this view and of its interesting later history the reader is referred both to May Smith and to Greenwood and Smith in the *British Journal of Medical Psychology*.

Galen's interests were wide and he was also prone to philosophize. At one moment he hazarded a summary of different views on the nature of substance as he found them colouring the thought and the medicine of his day. The passage seems to be so illuminating for our own time as well as his that he is allowed on pp. 241–4 to speak for himself.

The second strand of history would lead the reader through Stoical writers such as Cicero and Plutarch, wherein we again find clinical insight, combined in Cicero's case with clear recognition of the legal problem of the responsibility of the insane. Seneca (*c.* 4 B.C. to A.D. 65), Epictetus (*c.* A.D. 60 to A.D. 100), and Marcus Aurelius (A.D. 121–80) fit into this Stoic tradition and we can thus glimpse the stature of those who supported it. One need hardly underline the respect that is due to Stoical behaviour under stress. But in less exacting circumstances Stoicism has been known to offer ready-made rationalizations for grim kinds of egocentricity.

The third thread followed in full would link up Roman and early Christian history, revealing, as life under the Empire deteriorated, an increasing incentive to seeking happiness inwardly or in another world. Plotinus can be seen meeting this need in one way by his form of Neo-Platonism; the Catholic tradition met it in another by the fusion of Neo-Platonism and the teaching of the Gospels that we find in such a writer as St Augustine. In its early history this tradition has also been seen as offering security both from rising superstition and inexorable law, reflected among other things in dictates from unsaintly but deified emperors.

In his Stoical and authoritarian moments St Paul thought in terms of law, but could nevertheless exhort the Romans to love their neighbours as themselves. Indeed a route to freedom from fear different both from Epicurean and Stoic, and subtly different from its Socratic ancestry, entered Europe with the advent of Christianity. It inspires the famous comment:

For sin shall not have dominion over you; for ye are not under the law but under grace.

What then? Shall we sin, because we are not under the law but under grace? God forbid.

St Augustine thought of matter as extended and mind as immaterial without delving systematically into their relations. Thus his significance to us has a slightly different slant. He was important, of course, for his fusion of Platonic and Neo-Platonic thought with that of Christian theology and, therefore, for the influence of Plato on Christian philosophy up to the time of Aquinas. As Copleston has pointed out, we can see these Platonic elements in St Augustine's description of man as a rational soul using a mortal or earthly body or 'a certain substance participating in reason and fitted for ruling a body'. We must also remember St Augustine's early allegiance to Manichaeanism, according to which matter was created by an evil principle equal in status to God but in opposition to Him. Augustine's early sympathy with this, taken together with parts of the *Confessions*, suggests that he had many and complex individual motives for wanting to separate bodily from psychological functions. We must not, however, err by debiting this aspect of early theology solely to St Augustine's personal and Platonic viewpoint. Christian theology as it came from the east was already suffused with mysticism and, as we have seen, the times were propitious for other-worldly aspirations.

This caveat introduces St Augustine to our topic from a different angle. He was clearly a person of immense natural responsiveness and, in spite of the fierce rejection of sensory experience we find in *Confessions* Book x, he could also maintain unemotionally that knowledge is derived from the senses. In his treatment of memory he raises one of the most acute issues that body-mind theorists have to face. Stated in modern and practical terms this is: In what sense if any does remembering depend on a filing system and where and by what methods is this system kept and operated? This question is still one that troubles psychologists, and is directly relevant to mind-body problems. St Augustine is therefore represented on pp. 245–9 by part of the brilliant introspections on this subject that have given him permanent status in the history of psychology.

REFERENCES

SECTIONS i–iii

Aristotle. *De Anima*. Translated by W. S. Hett. Loeb Classical Library, London: Heinemann, 1935, pp. 29, 49, 121, 79
    Ethica Nichomachea. Translated by W. D. Ross. London: Oxford University Press, 1931
Bain, Alexander. *The Emotions and the Will*. London: Longmans, 3rd Edn., 1888, Chaps. III and IV
Jowett, Benjamin. *The Dialogues of Plato*, Vol. III. London: Oxford University Press, 3rd Edn., 1892, pp. 341 ff.

Plato. See Jowett, especially pp. 458–68 and 491–4

Russell, Bertrand. *History of Western Philosophy*. London: Allen and Unwin, 1946. Book I, Chaps. XIX, XX, XXII; Book II, Chap. XIII and p. 224

Zilboorg, G., and Henry, G. W. *A History of Medical Psychology*. London: Allen and Unwin, New York: Norton, 1941, Chap. III and p. 58

SECTION iv

Augustine, St. *Confessions*. Translated by E. B. Pusey. London: Dent (Everyman's Library), 1939, pp. 204 ff.

Brett, G. S. *History of Psychology*. Edited and abridged by R. S. Peters. London: Allen and Unwin, 1953, pp. 136–215

Copleston, F. C. *Aquinas*. Harmondsworth: Penguin Books, 1955, pp. 151–2

    A History of Western Philosophy. Vol. II. Medieval Philosophy: Augustine to Scotus. London: Burns, Oates and Washbourne, 1950, Chaps. III to VIII

Greenwood, Major, and Smith, May. 'Some Pioneers of Medical Psychology'. *The British Journal of Medical Psychology*. Cambridge: University Press. Vol. XIV, 1934, pp. 1–30 and 158–91

Lucretius. *De Rerum Natura*. Translated by R. Latham. Harmondsworth: Penguin Books, 1951

Paul, St. *Epistle to the Romans*. vi, 14, 15

Russell, Bertrand. *History of Western Philosophy*. London: Allen and Unwin, 1946, Bk I, Chaps. XXVII, XXVIII and XXIX

Smith, May. 'The Nervous Temperament'. *British Journal of Medical Psychology*. Cambridge: University Press. Vol. X, 1930, pp. 99 ff.

Zilboorg, G., and Henry, G. W. *A History of Medical Psychology*. London: Allen and Unwin. New York: Norton, 1941, Chap. III, specially pp. 61 ff.

CHAPTER 3

DUSK AND DAWN

The delight of the senses is rarely good, mostly bad
ST ANSELM

Laudato si, mi Signore, cum tucte le tue creature
le quale lo jorno allumeni per nui;
spetialmente messer lo frate sole,
et ellu è bellu e radiante cum molto splendore;
de te, altissimo, porta significatione
ST FRANCIS

'THREE different paths,' says Huizinga in *The Waning of the Middle Ages*, 'at all times have seemed to lead to the ideal life. Firstly, that of forsaking the world. The perfection of life here seems only to be reached beyond the domain of earthly labour and delight, by a loosening of all ties. The second path conducts to amelioration of the world itself, by consciously improving political, social, and moral institutions and conditions. Now, in the Middle Ages, Christian faith had so strongly implanted in all minds the ideal of renunciation as the base of all personal and social perfection, that there was scarcely any room left for entering upon this path of material and political progress' . . . But, he continues: 'It would be a mistake to think that the medieval mind, lacking the ideas of progress and conscious reform, had only known the religious form of the aspiration to ideal life. For there is a third path to a world more beautiful, trodden in all ages and civilizations, the easiest and also the most fallacious of all, that of the dream'.

Having suggested its dangers Huizinga goes on to indicate the positive role played in the later Middle Ages by attempts to act out some of these dreams in aristocratic reality. In this way Europe could begin to escape a dilemma, one of whose horns had been sharpened by St Augustine's somewhat Manichean asceticism. 'In the Middle Ages the choice lay, in principle,

only between God and the world, between contempt or eager
acceptance, at the peril of one's soul, of all that makes up the
beauty and the charm of earthly life. All terrestrial beauty bore
the stain of sin. Even where art and piety succeeded in hallow-
ing it by placing it in the service of religion, the artist or the
lover of art had to take care not to surrender to the charms of
colour and line. Now, all noble life was in its essential manifestations full of such beauty tainted by sin. Knightly exercises
and courteous fashions with their worship of bodily strength;
honours and dignities with their vanity and their pomp, and
especially love; – what were they but pride, envy, avarice and
lust, all condemned by religion ! To be admitted as elements of
higher culture all these things had to be ennobled and raised to
the rank of virtue.

'It was here that the path of fancy proved its civilizing value.
All aristocratic life in the later Middle Ages is a wholesale
attempt to act the vision of a dream. In cloaking itself in the
fanciful brilliance of the heroism and probity of a past age, the
life of the nobles elevated itself towards the sublime. By this
trait the Renaissance is linked to the times of feudalism.'

In short we find a sub-culture faced with the kind of conflict
seen to this day in individual personalities, who, at once too
discriminating and too loosely knit to trust their spontaneous
impulses to have style, may adopt a solution equally familiar to
modern psychology – that of externalizing at different conscious
levels some form of *via media*. Thanks partly to this, in the late
thirteenth and early fourteenth centuries responsiveness, in
sculpture and the visual arts especially, escaped both from condemnation and from symbolizing fantasy into heights of innocent naturalism it has hardly since attained again. By the High
Renaissance such naturalism was overblown. We glimpse it
again in seventeenth-century Dutch landscape and, oddly
enough, in the eighteenth century in the undeceived affection
of a Chardin. Elsewhere it was usually merged in the humanist and later scientific realism to which it had given birth,
but which inescapably was harsher and more complex.

Where meanwhile were theories of bodies and minds ? A
lightning survey would leave St Augustine, pause to take in St

Thomas Aquinas and emerge at the time of Shakespeare and Elizabeth I only to find that 'official' theorizing was a curious mixture of Plato and Aristotle modified by Augustine and Aquinas and haunted by Galen and witchcraft. But so swift a survey would only leave in utter darkness both the reasons for theoretical stagnation and the sources of immense future change. Let us, therefore, at least glance at the history within which western European culture and the future prospects of natural psychology were equally embedded.

(i) ST AUGUSTINE TO ST ANSELM*

St Augustine completed the *City of God* in 426 against the background of the disintegrating Roman Empire. It is sometimes supposed that he wished to refute the belief that conversion to Christianity had caused that disaster. Be that as it may, Constantine in 330 had already shifted the administrative centre of the Empire from then pagan Rome to Christianized Byzantium. The western empire did not formally end until 476, but in Augustine's lifetime Roman unity was already threatened by invasion from two quarters. On the one hand Germanic tribes – Ostrogoths, Visigoths, Vandals, Burgundians, and Lombards – were spreading out from the east. A more westerly threat came from the second quarter via Angles, Saxons, Jutes, Friesians, and the like. Historians seem generally agreed about the largely pagan and limited culture of these tribes. While there seems to have been some penetration of Christianity, this was of the Arian form which Christianized Rome regarded as heretical.

Ganshof sums up the contrast between the Germanic and the Roman worlds as that of 'savage tribes confronting a hyper-civilized society'. He adds, nevertheless, that 'certain deep-seated similarities in social structure were to make fusion possible, once the violent shock was over: primarily the existence on either side of a powerful aristocracy based on large landed properties'.

'Other "barbarian" nations encircled the Roman Empire

---

* For the background history of this section see Ganshof in *The European Inheritance*.

either directly or at a distance.' For our purposes it is sufficient to remember that: 'Between the last quarter of the fourth century and the end of the sixth, the migrations of many of these barbarian peoples overturned the whole structure of Europe.... The Germans were not the only peoples to take part in these invasions, but they played the chief part in them.'

The Eastern Empire meanwhile survived, though considerably harassed, as a political unit making periodic and sometimes successful attempts to regain and retain parts of Italy, but more seriously absorbed by eastern and then Moslem threats. In the fifth and sixth centuries Ravenna, open at that period to Byzantine influence, bears witness to the richness of culture the Eastern Empire could transmit. This culture moreover was not only artistic. Through Justinian, transfixed to this day in the golden mosaics of San Vitale, western culture was to retain the influence of the Roman Law coded during his rule. That would appear a mixed inheritance but for Whitehead's interesting suggestion that Greek notions of fate, Roman feelings for law, and modern respect for the laws of science have affinities. All three tend to be endowed with the objectivity and finality which western humans are apt to seek in suppliers of security. Only in the twentieth century have we begun fully to realize the man-made nature of our guardians, and that scientific 'laws' are open to change.

At the time of Justinian (527–565) the western, in contrast to the eastern, ages were dark. Slowly in the fifth and sixth centuries the Franks were beginning to gain the lead among the Germanic kingdoms. Some forms of sustained government emerged under Clovis and the other Merovingian kings and links were made between Church and State. But the cultural poverty of these kingdoms contrasted sharply with Byzantine civilization.

In the eighth century much of the Merovingian power came to be wielded by the Frankish aristocrat Charles Martel. His son Pepin later usurped the throne, making thereafter a further alliance with the Holy See, which was again under Lombard threat. It is worth realizing that since the time of Gregory the Great (590–604) the Roman Church had been driven to exercise civil and military authority under threats of invasion with which Byzantium was too busy elsewhere to assist. From our point of view the sustained influence of the Roman Church is important for two reasons. First, when Pepin's son Charlemagne succeeded his father in 768, strong papal influence was integral to the temporary re-creation of western unity and with it a fleeting cultural Renaissance. Secondly, during the Carolingian Empire of the eighth and ninth centuries we find the foundations both of episcopal organization and of the Latin education of the clergy. Both of these are relevant to understanding the extent to which Western culture, such as existed, was under the influence of a largely Latin theology. In this respect, again, there are important contrasts with Byzantium, where both the relations of Church and State and the balance of secular and ecclesiastical culture were different. Such facts we need for appreciating the kind of impact Byzantine and Arab influence had on our own thirteenth century.

The details of ninth- and tenth-century history do not concern us. Suffice it that, on the final disintegration of the Carolingian Empire in the late ninth century, there succeeded a period of semi-anarchy to which, Ganshof suggests, weak kings, rising nobility, and further aggravation by foreign invasion were all to contribute. On the other hand it is beginning to be possible to think of Francia as France and of Eastern Francia as Germany with various peripheral states. The same period showed a religious decline in which the Papacy was in danger from the rising aristocracy of Rome.

When we turn from the centre to the environs of Western Europe three facts are needed for understanding the setting for the social changes of the tenth and eleventh centuries, whose impact upon Western thinking appears to have been fairly direct. First, in the seventh century, there was the rapid rise of the Moslem religious empire. This was soon to disintegrate as a unit, but its adherents remained a permanent political danger, a stimulus to crusading, and a direct and an indirect influence on Western attitudes. For example, Aristotle's re-introduction to Western thought was due in large part to the interest aroused in him by Averroes whose influence on thirteenth- and fourteenth-

century Paris was profound. But Aristotle's temporary condemnation in the late thirteenth century appears also to have
been associated with political attitudes to his Arabian escort.
Secondly, though the details are unimportant, the tenth century
was to see the gradual stabilizing of northern countries such as
Norway, Sweden, and England, which about 950 was on the
way to recovery from Danish invasions and to an integration in
which social structure and institutions had a better chance of
stability than almost anywhere else. Thirdly, we must not quite
forget the northern trading activity through which, for example,
via Scandinavian settlers of the Baltic, both the rich mercantile
civilization of Byzantium and the Moslem countries came to
have trade links with the West.

Now in the tenth and eleventh centuries what social changes
do we have to reckon with ? The answer appears primarily to be
those associated with a gradual and fundamental increase in
population. Its causes need not here concern us. Its effects,
mainly visible in the eleventh century, are considered of first
importance. Following Ganshof's already condensed account,
let us try to summarize them still further so that their relevance
to our topic is obvious.

First is the remarkable eastern expansion of Western Europe's
boundaries: 'before 1300 the countries to the west of the Oder
had been Germanized to a large extent by the influx of these
new elements of population. An analogous phenomenon took
place in the region of the middle Danube'.

Secondly, increasing population meant increasing need for
food production. Hence from the mid eleventh century, through
the twelfth and thirteenth, we find continuous extension of the
areas under cultivation. This meant, among other things, reclaiming fallow and marsh lands, and sometimes reclaiming and
draining whole districts. Whitehead long ago and art historians
more recently have hazarded a relation between agricultural
developments, including those fostered by monastic foundations, and the thirteenth-century signs of naturalism in sculpture already mentioned.

A third and associated effect of population increase seems to
have been a hastening and intensification of the break-up of the

great domains of land. Hired labour at last began to replace services due from tenants. Sections of the population had some incentive for shifting to areas where labour was short, encouraged in some cases by overt promises of more privileged status and liberty. Ganshof suggests analogous effects among the lay aristocracy, where population shifts could and did take the form of military expeditions and settlement, such as the Norman Conquests and settlements in England and Italy in the second half of the eleventh century. Crusading, slightly later in date, may have had an element in common.

The social categories encountered prior to demographic change divide broadly into the Church, the aristocracy, and the rural population feudally employed. The Church was influential on account both of its spiritual authority and of its landed property. After the reforms initiated in the tenth century (e.g. by the monastery of Cluny) and greatly reinforced in the eleventh, the Church increased in power to the point of challenging secular influence on its appointments. Indeed in the eleventh and twelfth centuries it came to wield political power that offered a threat to the very kings and emperors who had enhanced its prestige. Socially the aristocracy tended to be a 'military caste' drawing its revenues from inherited property. On the continent in the eleventh century and in England after 1066, the aristocracy became identified with chivalry (via chevaliers or knights who fight on horseback). By the end of the eleventh century a knight had his own separate status in France, England, Germany, and Italy, and knighthood (chivalry) was coming to represent an international brotherhood of knights with common ideals. Henceforward there was a nobility becoming hereditary in the twelfth century (except in England) and as a legal class less extensive than knighthood as a social class. Ganshof suggests that in the ninth and tenth centuries the feudal relations between overlords and their rural dependents may have been a stabilizing influence in a period of declining and chaotic sovereignty. In the eleventh century, with somewhat greater security and the population changes we are considering, trade and urban developments began to come to the fore. Hence, from the eleventh century onwards, the social picture shifts to include such urban elements as traders and their staffs and artisans. The knightly families sometimes entered and sometimes withdrew from commercial activity, keeping themselves apart like the clergy. With urban, trade, and commercial developments there was slowly to rise the new social group of the bourgeoisie which, towards the end of the eleventh and early twelfth centuries, achieved in some parts a status based on freedom and associated with distinctive legal and administrative institutions.

Let us now try to epitomize from our own standpoint. We leave Augustine with his serial statement of the dangers and temptations of this world and the senses. We emerge between 1093 and 1109 to St Anselm, then Archbishop of Canterbury, who retains the old Augustinian withdrawal theme intact. Things, he maintained, and the art historians constantly quote it against him, are harmful in proportion to the number of senses they delight. Whether or not any case could be made for St Anselm, by his time the first signs of social conditions making for a change of attitude were clearly beginning to emerge.

By the close of the eleventh century, one aspect of the conflict of this world and eternity, overlaid as usual by historical complexities, is reflected in the struggles of the Emperors and the Popes. From the mid tenth to the twelfth century Germany was weakened less than the neighbouring Western European States. German Kings such as Henry and Otto I both defended their country from Slavs and Hungarians and restored something approximating to the Carolingian State. We see in fact the growth of that curious structure the Holy Roman Empire, imposing for a time its own organization on the Church. The imperial mantle symbolized diverse things, including mere ratification of worldly dominance, a stick with which to beat one's rivals or obstreperous barons and dukes, a dying feudal vision of supremacy, and a hold on this world's promise, sometimes overlaid with a vast sense of theatre.

Some of the Emperors, such as Henry III, were instrumental in Papal reforms and strengthened both the Papacy's ecclesiastical and temporal position. Some of the finest were providing a security elsewhere less to be found. But, holy or unholy, an imperial claim needed the status of Papal crowning. Hence the

Papacy, with its hold on this status and capacity to threaten eternal perdition, could wield an authority in this world which Emperors had reason to fear. It would be false to reduce this struggle either to one of essentially temporal claims or to that of vested interests in this world versus those in unworldly eternity. Suffice it for our purpose that these elements were there; the disputants, as is usual, sometimes changed sides.

(ii) ABELARD TO AQUINAS

Russell in his *History of Western Philosophy* extracts four aspects of the twelfth century for attention:

'(1) the continued conflict of empire and papacy,
(2) the rise of the Lombard cities,
(3) the crusades; and
(4) the growth of scholasticism.

All these four continued into the following century. The crusades gradually came to an inglorious end; but, as regards the other three movements, the thirteenth century marks the culmination of what, in the twelfth, is in a transitional stage.' If we realize that the social changes indicated by Ganshof were also steadily evolving, we can perhaps safely by-pass the political ramifications of the era to pick up the scent of empirical revolt in the lively thinking of Abelard (1079–1142) and John of Salisbury (1115–1180).

Psychologically, Abelard, and perhaps even more Éloise, must have lived through both of Huizinga's main alternatives in their most intolerable forms. The historical influence of this episode has not, so far as I know, ever been thoroughly traced. We can, however, detect in Abelard's thinking, specially on the subject of universals, a vein of speculation which awakened Parisian thinking to the point of storm and had its ramifications in the Schools of Chartres and St Victor. In brief, as Copleston and Taylor show, we find in Abelard a challenge to the notion evident in Plato that 'ideas' are more 'real' than anything else. Instead, without quite landing in the strictly nominalist view, whereby generality of thinking pertains exclusively to the vehicle of language, we find Abelard arguing, as a modern psychologist would, for the formation of concepts by abstraction from observation of particulars. Though this is not, at any rate in Abelard, to deny some ontological status to the general ideas so conceived, it lessens the impact of Platonic ultra-realism and suggests a distinct promotion for direct observation of individual things.

In the case of John of Salisbury this trend of thought continued. As Copleston notes, Salisbury was a student of Abelard's, became secretary to two Archbishops of Canterbury (the second was Thomas à Becket), and was later appointed Bishop of Chartres in 1176. After Paris, this was one of the two most important centres of learning and was soon to be the hub from which French Gothic architecture radiated. Though he died in 1180, it is not inappropriate that we should find its eminent Bishop asserting that 'anyone who looks for genera and species outside the things of sense is wasting his time'. 'Genera and species are not things, but are rather the forms of things which the mind, comparing the likeness of things, abstracts and unifies in the universal concepts'. Here, if anywhere, we may claim to see the theoretical foundations of a new respect for empirical knowledge being slowly filled in. It was not to gain a superstructure without enormous struggles.

Much of Chartres Cathedral was rebuilt between 1194, after damage by fire, and 1220. It was consecrated in 1260. As we enter the thirteenth century, we can see the outward turning of medieval thought becoming a little more marked. The Chartres of soaring architecture and radiant glass was the innovator and probably more influential than the Chartres of theological theory. On the other hand, the underlying psychological issues in the endless arguments of scholasticism have sometimes, I think, been overlooked. The rival claims of withdrawal to inner, and response to outer, experience are very much involved in the old epistemological problems of 'universals' and 'particulars'.

In the political setting of the thirteenth century, perhaps the dominant factors are the rise of the Papacy in the first half together with the struggles of the Emperors to hold their own. The second half shows the decline both of the Papacy and of the Empire, alike exhausted by strife; by which time French influence had crystallized politically under Louis IX (St Louis) and spread artistically in architecture and sculpture. In England we cannot lose sight of the start of Parliamentary institutions and of challenges at any rate to inefficient autocratic kingship, such as the signing of Magna Carta. Thanks partly to international trade, to the Latin conquest of Byzantium in 1204, and to the contacts established in crusading, both Byzantine (and thereby Greek) and Arabian secular culture were filtering into the strongholds of Augustinian theology and the newly-founded western universities.

While we must not underestimate medieval symbolism, reflected alike in most religious art and in the enormously complex rituals and hierarchies of medieval social and court life, there were factors undermining both 'withdrawal' and fantasy. Changes in the economic life entailing further changes in society, such as the emergence of patriciate families and the slow emancipation of serfs, provide one kind of example. Another lies in the founding of the great mendicant orders; the Dominicans in 1216 and the Franciscans in 1223. These orders seem to have acted as fertilizers of awakening cultural interest, and what could be a clearer sign of a new feeling for nature than the *Laudes Creaturarum* of St Francis. Spontaneous affection for the world around is turned, as it were, into homage to its Creator.

The art history of the second half of the thirteenth century provides more evidence both of 'withdrawal's withdrawal' and of the network of artists, masters, journeymen, and apprentices, some of whom were the carriers of naturalistic expression. On the one hand, for example, there are the exquisite flowers, leaves, and animals of Rheims, Southwell, and Bamberg which Pevsner discusses. Still more enthralling are the individual women who look across Europe from Naumburg (plates 4 and 5). These, be it noted, were carved at a time when many a woman's status was nearly as deplorable as that of the evil senses with which she was apt to be identified – in all but the ideals of courtly love and the visions of Dante.

Naturalistic sculpture, seen elsewhere in the work of Niccola and Andrea Pisano, gave impetus to the fresh awareness of touch, gesture, and movement, and the deepened emotional insight, that came into painting via Giotto. A way of realizing the significant change in progress is to steep oneself in Byzantine mosaics at Ravenna, cross to the Pisano fountain in Perugia, and emerge in the upper Church of Assisi where Giotto completed the Franciscan frescoes between 1290 and 1300. Giotto, be it noted, in the Italy to which Gothic architecture remained very largely alien, still had church walls left on which to paint. So also did his Italian successors.

Last but not least we must briefly consider thirteenth-century literature and philosophy. Huizinga has clearly shown the complexities of medieval attitudes, and it would be seriously wrong to suggest that the many signs of naturalism we have mentioned were typical of the ordinary outlook and culture of the time. They were outstanding, and signs of the future. The same is true of the romantic literature, such as Guillaume de Loris' *Romaunt de la Rose*. Its idealization of natural love provides probably the best example of a positive fantasy about whose latent content the court and university circles of Paris later came to fight battles. The licentiousness implied in naturalism if pushed to its logical extreme was soon to be detected by conservative (and often sensitive) defenders of the faith. In the midst of the Parisian cultural commotion of the fifteenth century, we can find the same Gerson (1362–1428), who as Chancellor of the University could argue that the Church had supremacy over the Pope, writing a polemical attack on the *Romaunt's* insidious influence. Gerson had an ascetic trait, but he was far from being unenlightened. Elsewhere, for example, we find him uniquely courageous in attacking superstition and witchcraft, and at his time he is almost alone in arguing that a brain lesion could be the cause of phenomena attributed by others to diabolical possession. Would that this flash of insight had carried more weight.

Of the thirteenth-century philosophy we can hardly overstress the importance. Three names come to the fore. First chronologically (his dates 1126–1198, but not his main western influence, belong to the twelfth century), we must place the

Arabian Averroes. His importance lies mainly in his stimulus to Aristotelian studies, whereby western medieval thinking was confronted, almost for the first time, with a fully developed secular philosophy. Secondly, and of prolonged influence both in his lifetime (1193–1280) and after, is the encyclopedic, rambling intelligence of St Albertus Magnus. Last, and greatest as a system maker, stands his pupil St Thomas Aquinas. As he is quoted on pp. 250 ff., a few points only of outstanding importance will be mentioned here. Although sympathetic to Augustine, Aquinas gave impetus to an enormous change in shifting the basis of Christian theology away from that form of Platonic mysticism which is latently masochistic, towards the biological intellectualism of Aristotle. This is not to detract from St Thomas's conception of the end of man as apprehension of God. But, in H. O. Taylor's happy phrase, St Thomas Aquinas emerged in faith 'trailing clouds of reason'. What is more, his views on the ascent of man were founded on a notion of biological development in which the senses and natural functions did not stand from the start condemned. They are indeed integral to human perfection, and the significance of this point can hardly be over-stressed. Temperamentally St Thomas was born to detest the Manichees and with them the spirit of negation. Finally, in giving to Aristotelian thought (whether or not his interpretation was correct) the blessing of official theology, historically Aquinas gave a cultural charter to an objective philosophy that need not intrude upon faith. The war was not won at a blow. In the 1270s and 80s, mainly after St Thomas's death in 1274, Thomist Aristotelianism savouring alike of Averroist heresies and Arabic threats came under considerable fire. This was not finally diverted until the canonization of St Thomas in 1323. In the thirteenth century however we can see in many directions signs of a widening outlook.

(iii) PETRARCH'S PROBLEM

Uta, the early eleventh-century aristocrat dreamed into stone by a thirteenth-century craftsman, gathers her cloak a little apprehensively and shivers at what she sees. As well she might.

For one thing, those Gothic architects with their passion for light had made windows everywhere and, with windows, draughts and far less wall space offering shelter and room for interesting frescoes. In fact, at the time of Uta's creation in the 1260s, artists outside Italy – whose churches we have noted retained their wall space more generally – were being driven to work in other media. Of these the most important were stained glass and manuscript illumination, which in the northern fourteenth and fifteenth centuries was to be another carrier of naturalism. Uta, however, would have shuddered at worse than draughts had she known the future of the fourteenth century:— famines and plagues that were to decimate Europe, in whose population trends there were already signs of recess; the bitter struggles of the Papacy and the crown leading in 1378 to the Great Schism, and the mood of depression expressed in the current saying that no-one had entered paradise since the Schism occurred; some sixty of the hundred years' war between England and France ending later in mutual exhaustion; the fourteenth and earlier fifteenth centuries' economic depression; signs of the backward lash of witch-hunting and persecution in which women were to be the greatest sufferers. In these respects the fourteenth century had little to give the tenth. Indeed towards its end Europe had another fit of thinking the world would end.

But what other facts and trends were at work? For understanding the future of psychology three related fourteenth-century trends are interesting. First, we have a group of sociological facts shown, for example, in changes of trading emphasis (London and Bruges stole the dominance from Italy), in the rising status of the Hanse towns, and in new economic forms which, in spite of depression, permitted for some a greater luxury in living. Together with the drop in population these facts bore both on the break-up of big estates, on the increased status of the merchants, traders, and artisans, and on the further rise of the peasant classes, now in a position to claim more independence and pay. The English peasants' revolt of 1381 and the continued growth of the guild system are particular examples of this much more general tendency. These would seem familiar but irrelevant history but for the tempting supposition that these changes reinforced the need to think in causal terms instead of withdrawal or fantasy, which could not form the basis of economic realism. A second trend, weakening the withdrawal theme and hence eventual resistance to science, concerns the internal and external state of the Church. Omitting the complex details, it is broadly true that the bitter strife with the State, fits of Avignon luxury, heavy taxation, and ultimate loss of authority by division, could only undermine the force and the favour of appeal to other-worldliness. By 1378 two, and by 1409 three, Popes could be found contending for supremacy. Clear authority came not from on high, so men were being forced into choosing for themselves. So, for example, by the second half of the fourteenth century the Papacy and methods of Papal election came well in sight of intellectual scrutiny from such diverse sources as Wycliff in Oxford, William of Ockham, Paris University, and later from those, like Hus, whom these influenced.

To understand the third trend is to grasp the more subtle overtones of the early Renaissance on which volumes of scholarship lie open to be read. Here we can do no more than recall a few familiar pointers to a complexity of outlook which we cannot discuss but in which the diverse facets of a scientific attitude also have their historical roots. Such an attitude has come to mean, among other things, respect for empirical observation provided it is checked, suspended judgement about conclusions presented on *a priori* grounds, the attempt to evaluate only upon evidence and not at a stage where preference can distort, and the attempt to withdraw receptiveness only at the point of direct attack on freedom of inquiry – on receptiveness and responsiveness themselves. The attitude began to develop in the context of liberal humanism, an essential difference lying in the emphasis on prediction and on time. The scientist can sometimes go back on his tracks or wait; this is entailed by his need to verify. The humanist, supposing he is also an administrator, must more often take courage for a decision, knowing that for a better answer he lacks only time. Both must be resilient enough to be at ease with doubt. This ease is some-

c

thing which we have hardly yet acquired. Now what was the early setting of liberal humanism? We can but briefly suggest it:

Giotto's Assisi frescoes belong to the thirteenth century, those of the Scrovegni Chapel at Padua to the fourteenth – the same Padua wherein the philosopher Marsiglio was maintaining by 1324 that the study of this life must be allowed to progress without assumptions about eternity. In the charter to philosophy given by Aquinas the word 'independence' was thereby underlined. It is fair to remark that Marsiglio encountered opposition.

Giotto had brought to frescoes a feeling for human movement and expression, which was enlivening to his century and remote from Byzantine decorative formality. But he was not truly a painter of landscape or of texture. His scenery resembles rather chunky stage props providing a background for man's relation to man and to God. Indeed, Sir Kenneth Clark suggests that Europe re-discovered nature more through the paradise garden of the *Romaunt de la Rose*, through Dante and literary settings such as that of Boccaccio's charming companions, who withdrew to 'a plot of ground like a meadow, the grass deep-spangled with a thousand different flowers'. Natural landscape entered fourteenth-century art not so much through Giotto's vision as that of the Sienese artists, the Lorenzetti and Simone Martini. But these, be it noted, contrived to work at Assisi.

At Siena 'the first surviving landscapes, in a modern sense', writes Sir Kenneth, 'are in Ambrogio Lorenzetti's frescoes of *Good and Bad Government*. They are so factual that they hardly belong to the landscape of symbol and remain unique for almost a century'. We may add that as a sign of awakening interest in how this world should be run they were not unique. Indeed they resemble the tip of an iceberg whose unseen base was gathering momentum under the still symbolic surface of the century.

This surface was gloomy as well as symbolic. Andrea Pisano died in 1348. In the same year, according to Dupont, both the Lorenzetti are said to have died of the plague, known to England as the Black Death, which ravaged Italy, Spain, France,

Germany, and Norway between 1347 and 1351. Ganshof shows that in the second half of the fourteenth and the early fifteenth centuries, other epidemics 'local, regional, or extending over several countries' augmented the effects of the mid-century's outbreak. In England alone the drop in population between 1348 and 1374 is estimated at forty per cent. Plague in Florence is sometimes considered to explain in part the temporary artistic lead taken by Siena, which was somewhat less affected. Be that as it may, this dark background forces into focus the dependence of early humanism on a very few human beings who in these times of intermittent famine as well as plague established direct or indirect contact with each other. One pauses to wonder what their travels must have been like. Chaucer, with a head full of Canterbury pilgrims, got himself to Italy on a diplomatic mission in 1373. By whose most patient journeying did Petrarch influence Bohemian thought ? What meanwhile of Simone Martini, by whose art the tactile and kinaesthetic senses were further emancipated ? 'His golden fabrics', continues Clark, 'are such as are laid up in heaven for the blessed, and the rhythmic flow of his draperies echoes the angelic song. In all this he was at one with the finest Gothic art of France, and it was no accident that, in 1339, he found his way to Avignon. It was presumably at Avignon that Simone met the man whose name has come to stand for the junction of the medieval and the modern worlds, Petrarch.'

Now Petrarch's cultural influence was enormous: it spread all over Europe. He was above all the man who could externalize the underlying but rising antinomies of his time. So if we had to choose a context for early humanism it would centre in Arezzo where Petrarch was born. To this day one may climb the narrow uneven streets overhung by the buildings of his period to the eleventh-century church of Santa Maria della Pieve. Its older architecture belongs and entices to a world where time has no hold, while Gothic overtones faintly suggest the future. Into its dusky and soaring security one enters from Italian sunshine and clatter to understand the emotional appeal of withdrawal and eternity. In the twentieth century, however, a friendly old Italian woman, like a culture's she-ancient, detaches herself from a shadow and potters off to a switch. And there in the east of the church's vast span glows none other than a Lorenzetti altarpiece. Its distant golds and scarlets are mingled as in a dawn, and the dawn is of a love of living to the full. By accident or by design, we do stand at the junction of the medieval and Renaissance worlds. I know no better way of understanding Petrarch's dilemma than in this setting and through his account of ascending Mount Ventoux. (pp. 254-62).

Simone Martini died at Avignon in 1344, but not before he had become a friend of Petrarch and made a frontispiece to Petrarch's favourite copy of Virgil. Once more from Sir Kenneth: 'It represents the poet seated in a flowery orchard while near him a shepherd and a vine-tender symbolize the *Eclogues* and the *Georgics*. For the first time since antiquity the pursuits of country life are represented in art as a source of happiness and poetry.' Petrarch, says Fisher, was 'prosecuted as a wizard at the instance of a cardinal for his undue addiction to Virgilian studies'. But among the pursuits of country life, nurtured already by Albertus Magnus, are the still early, but living roots of our later modern biology.

By the close of the century, the weakening of 'withdrawal', the first signs of causal thinking, the dawn of Renaissance humanism, and even the Wife of Bath had reached western Europe. The phase of the pastoral, which succeeded the chivalric ideal of living, had linked itself to natural observation and spontaneity. The century had coloured these both with respect for ancient learning and with a challenge to authority. Infused into this already complex outlook was a spirit of individual independence, shown in ways as diverse as the Paris arguments about Averroes, William of Ockham's empirical nominalism, and the introspective distinction of the great mystic Meister Eckhart. A body had been secretly dissected and Roger Bacon, the Oxford Franciscan, who spent ten years in prison, had been heard to say that nothing can be fully known without experiment.

All this, however, must be seen against the general background of depression induced by the causes we began to list earlier: a straggling Empire neither secure, Roman, nor Holy; a Church in 'Babylonian Captivity' from 1305 to 1370 and then divided against itself; plague, famine, economic depression; war between England and France and, increasing in the fifteenth century, war close at hand between almost any noble with enough followers to fight a king, a burgher, or a neighbour, and between any cities with rival claims to status. Nobody was safe yet living continued. Not wholly surprisingly the portraits of the people, in Chaucer for example, were beginning to take on toughness, realism, complexity, and, as Eileen Power has shown, some of his characters had foundation in fact. Regelindis might, one supposes, have found a role in the Canterbury Tales. She and her like must have been alive somewhere for Europe to withstand the impact of the era at all. The haunting aristocratic Uta of Chivalry was, however, a more elusive spirit and as we turn into the Quattrocento she can find no real place in a crowd of Masaccio faces.

REFERENCES

Anselm, St. See Pevsner p. 65

Clark, Sir Kenneth. *Landscape into Art*. London: Murray, 1949, Chap. 1, pp. 5, 6, and Penguin Books, 1956

Copleston, F. C. *A History of Philosophy:* Vol. II, Medieval Philosophy: Augustine to Scotus. London: Burns, Oates, and Washbourne, 1950

Dupont, Jacques, and Gnudi, Cesare. *Gothic Painting*. Geneva: Editions d'Art Skira, 1954

Fisher, H. A. L. *A History of Europe*. London: Arnold, 1943, p. 431

Francis, St. 'Laudes Creaturarum'. *The Golden Book of Italian Poetry*. Edited by L. de Bosis. London: Oxford University Press, 1932

Ganshof, F. L. 'The Middle Ages' in *The European Inheritance*. Edited by Barker, Clark, and Vaucher. Oxford: Clarendon Press, 1954, Vol. I pp. 313–487, especially pp. 314–15, 381 ff., 422 ff.

Huizinga, J. *The Waning of the Middle Ages*. London: Arnold, 1952, pp. 28, 29, 30, 31 and Penguin Books, 1955

Pevsner, Nikolaus. *The Leaves of Southwell*. London and New York: Penguin Books, 1945

Power, Eileen. *Medieval People*. Cambridge: University Press, 1924. Penguin Books, 1937

Russell, Bertrand. *History of Western Philosophy*. London: Allen and Unwin, 1946, p. 450

Salisbury, John of. See Copleston pp. 152–3

Taylor, H. O. *The Mediaeval Mind*. London: Macmillan, 4th Edn., 1930. Vol. II, Chap. XLI

CHAPTER 4

CONTRAST AND CONFLICT

Quant' è bella giovinezza
che si fugge tuttavia!
Chi vuol esser lieto, sia:
di doman non c'è certezza.
LORENZO DE' MEDICI

Meglio una piccola certezza che
una grande bugia.
LEONARDO DA VINCI

THE fifteenth century could be fairly called the century of sharpened contrasts. Let us look at some of them.

First there is the great contrast of birth and death thrown by the culture into strong relief. To those who have experienced a Florentine spring, the word 'Quattrocento' is apt to enter the mind at the head of an enchanted procession. Akin to Benozzo Gozzoli's in the Palazzo Medici Riccardi, it emerges from silver olive groves on the slopes of Fiesole where the snows of intermingled cherry blossom cast shadows on the brilliant green grass. Moving down through the city it pauses at San Marco, crosses to encompass San Lorenzo, and returns to Giotto's tower and Ghiberti's Paradise Doors. We must visualize them gold and gleaming in the sun much as, newly cleaned, they shone out at the end of World War II. In one's mind's eye one continues to watch the procession threading in and out to the Bargello's lovely courtyard and the Badia, to disperse eventually in an Italian crowd, no longer a procession, but arguing excitedly and cruelly in the Piazza della Signoria. 'Cruelly' because history's procession leads us to people being tortured and burned.

The word 'Renaissance' was coined meaning 're-birth', in particular the re-birth of classical learning. In Quattrocento Florence, Renaissance indeed there was; the glories of its scholarship, its craftsmanship, its colours have remained a perennial inspiration. But to the onlooker thinking of implied attitudes to body and to mind the opposing identifications of the

wider fifteenth century are so great that one is tempted to misuse some lines of Eliot:

> There was a Birth, certainly,
> We had evidence and no doubt. I had seen birth and death,
> But had thought they were different; this Birth was
> Hard and bitter agony for us, like Death, our death.

We may say prosaically enough that the Middle Ages were
dying and a new outlook gradually spreading across Europe.
But the point is that events of this kind do not happen entirely
seriatim. In part they overlap and conflict, and some people
may encounter both points of view. We may retain the image of
our Florentine spring but, if Huizinga is right,

No other epoch has laid so much stress as the expiring Middle
Ages on the thought of death. An everlasting call of *memento mori*
resounds through life. Denis the Carthusian in his *Directory of
the Life of Nobles* exhorts them: 'And when going to bed at night,
he should consider how just as he now lies down himself, soon
strange hands will lay his body in the grave'. In earlier times, too,
religion had insisted on the constant thought of death, but the
pious treatises of these ages only reached those who had already
turned away from the world. Since the thirteenth century, the
popular preaching of the Mendicant orders had made the eternal
admonition to remember death swell into a sombre chorus ring-
ing throughout the world. Towards the fifteenth century, a new
means of inculcating the awful thought into all minds was added
to the words of the preacher, namely the popular woodcut. Now
these two means of expression, sermons and woodcuts, both ad-
dressing themselves to the multitude . . . could only represent
death in a simple and striking form.

With few exceptions, the greatest being Tepl's *Der Acker-
mann aus Böhmen*, complex notions of death seem generally to
have been condensed into the dominant idea of the perishable
nature of all things, of which there were three principal versions.
To quote Huizinga again: 'The first is expressed by the question: where are now all those who once filled the world with
their splendour? The second motif dwells on the frightful spec-
tacle of human beauty gone to decay. The third is the death-
dance: death dragging along men of all conditions and ages.'

Compared with the other two, Huizinga regards the treatment of the first of these themes as 'but a graceful and elegiac sigh'. Quite different in force is that of the second, dominated by the worms, dust, and decomposition of putrefying corpses, which had awaited the realism that painting and sculpture attained about 1400 to find full visual expression. Huizinga suggests that in this fearful awareness and portrayal of physical death and decay there was less of piety than of 'spasmodic reaction against an excessive sensuality'. He may well have been right. He also detects an intense attachment to bodily parts, which is represented symbolically, as in veneration of saints and others supposed to be exempt from decay, or literally in preserving relics. It is shown too, so Huizinga thinks, in perpetuation of the custom, usual in the twelfth and thirteenth centuries, of cutting up and boiling* the bodies of eminent people dying abroad (Henry V was amongst them) so that their bones could be returned in chests to their home lands for interment.

The third theme, that of the death-dance, links, if I interpret Huizinga correctly, with the increasingly spectral and fantastic shape taken by death in European art and literature towards 1400. He attributes this macabre vision to deep underlying fear which was immediately turned by religious thought to a means of moral exhortation. For this the death-dance was an excellent focal point and a whole group of conceptions centred in this theme. The most important was the motif of the three living men who encounter three hideous dead men who tell them of their past grandeur and warn the living of their own near end. The theme was carved on the portals of the Church of the Innocents in Paris. Miniature painting and woodcuts widened its circulation. The *danse macabre* proper, which is a representation of the living of all social grades as they may expect to find themselves when dead, was painted, carved, engraved, and presented dramatically. The most famous version appears to have been that which, by 1424, covered the walls of the cloister of the Innocents. The cemetery, here, where poor and rich were interred without distinction, was preferred to every other place of burial.

* For the much older roots of this custom, including that of boiling the old to rejuvenate them, see Onians: *Origins of European Thought.*

The demands on space (and a theory that in nine days a body decomposed to the bones) made it necessary to dig up the departed and re-sell the tombstones in a very short time. Hence at the time when Masaccio had just enriched the Carmine with men of all conditions and ages but radiant with human vitality, and at the time when other Quattrocento artists were idealizing mother and child, at the Innocents in Paris:

Skulls and bones were heaped up in charnel houses along the cloisters enclosing the ground on three sides and lay there open to the eye by thousands, preaching to all the lessons of equality. ... Under the cloisters the death dance exhibited its images and its stanzas.... Such was the place which the Parisians of the fifteenth century frequented as a sort of lugubrious counterpart of the Palais Royal of 1789. Day after day, crowds of people walked under the cloisters, looking at the figures and reading the simple verses which reminded them of the approaching end. In spite of the incessant burials and exhumations going on there, it was a public lounge and a rendezvous. Shops were established before the charnel-houses and prostitutes strolled under the cloisters. A female recluse was immured on one of the sides of the church. Friars came to preach and processions were drawn up there. A procession of children only (12,500 strong, thinks the Burgher of Paris) assembled there with tapers in their hands, to carry an Innocent to Notre Dame and back to the churchyard. Even feasts were given there.

'To such an extent', quietly comments the historian, 'had the horrible become familiar'. We shall see in a moment how his comment rings true. But before adding witchcraft and heresy to our list let us recall a few fifteenth-century contrasts of a rather different kind from the procession of the Florentine Renaissance and the procession of Death.

*

The remaining contrasts, unlike the simultaneous emphasis on vitality and on death, might be better described as changes. Instead of pervading the century, which went on producing its Fra Angelico, its Botticelli, its Donatello, its Limbourgs, its Van Eycks – but later on its Bosch, the contrasts we now encounter are more obviously time linked. They might appear irrelevant

73

to our main theme but for two reasons. First, it is hard to see the force of the seventeenth and eighteenth century demands for evidence, empiricism, and rationalism, unless we glimpse the circumstances gradually stimulating passionate interest in the basis of knowledge, the nature of authority and freedom and the validity both of praise and of blame. These conditions include the witch-hunts of the fifteenth, the religious strife of the sixteenth, and the wars, persecution, and political upheavals to which the seventeenth century found itself exposed. Secondly, it wanted only the monarchies and the mechanistic physics of the seventeenth century, to transform these tempestuous topics of certain knowledge, freedom, and the basis of evaluation, into a veritable cat's cradle of inquiries, within which mind-body problems became inextricably knotted. They grew so entangled partly because of the age-long identification of matter with the sensory (and sensual), the emotional (and licentious), the enclosing (the soul's or devil's container), the inert (unresponsive) or the spatially relatable (soon to mean 'the determined'). 'Matter' also came to have an ambiguous existence as the 'outside' or 'common' and the 'unknowable' substratum. 'Mind' by contrast was apt to connote the thinking (and pure), the rational (and controlling), the incarcerated (but immortal), the vital (and spontaneous), the unextended (therefore 'free'). It remained the 'personal' and the 'private'. We shall see in the seventeenth, eighteenth, and, indeed, the nineteenth centuries the headlong collisions to which the confusions latent in these identifications gave rise. When the Romantics linked the emotions, which no one had disembodied, with the spontaneity that an overdose of sententiousness had made everyone desire, they gave a crown to the chaos from which we have by no means emerged.

With this long forward glance let us now return to the fifteenth century by way of a person of fantasy who surprises by being real, none other than Kublai Khan.

It is familiar fact that Coleridge's opium dream is rooted in *Li divisament du monde*, the account dictated in French by Marco Polo of his own, his father's, and his uncle's visits to Central Asia and China in the late thirteenth century. During this period

74

of Mongol supremacy, in particular the reign of the Khan Kublai, there had been relative peace in these parts. Thanks alike to this, to the Khan's liberal treatment of foreigners, and to the almost unbelievable journeyings of the Polo family of Venetian merchants, a basis of trade and even cultural relations had been established between East and West. Such trade relations prospered in the fourteenth century to the extent that, as Ganshof says, a Florentine merchant writing about 1340 could quote £12,000 of silk stuff as a normal load between Italy and Cathay. Ganshof indicates that such contacts between East and West were apt to fluctuate with the conflicts of various Mongol chiefs and the rivalry of Italian cities, Venice and Genoa, for example, which got involved with these. But, to quote Ganshof: 'towards the middle of the fourteenth century, direct relations with central Asia and China declined and ended. Persia passed into the hands of fanatic Moslems and it became difficult, if not impossible, for Christian travellers to pass through it. Before long the same thing happened in Central Asia, particularly when, in 1363, it fell into the hands of the Emir Timur (Tamerlaine), who laid there the foundations of a Turkish empire which was also fanatically Moslem. Finally, in 1368–70, the Mongol dynasty in China was overthrown by a national dynasty, that of the Ming . . .'. This dynasty reverted to the xenophobia which is so startlingly absent from the liberal receptiveness of Kublai, as shown, for example, in Eileen Power's attractive essay on Marco Polo.

Such a closing of Eastern communications was important in many ways. Among them we have to visualize the Europe of the early fifteenth century driven in upon itself and experiencing cultural as well as commercial isolation. The Russias in the north-east were fluctuating entities with an independent culture little affected by the west. (The Russias were soon to expand towards the east). All along the southern Mediterranean and the Middle East, Moslem influence was presenting to Western Europe not merely a passive, but an active, source of frustration and danger. The fall of Constantinople in 1453 can be seen merely as the culminating point of a process tending to leave Western Europe's only hope of outlet in the far South-West. That she took this outlet is due to many things, among them the gradual integration and rallying of Spain, broadly unified in 1469 by the marriage of Ferdinand and Isabella, and secondly the vitality of Portuguese and Spanish explorers. It is interesting also to speculate on how far the success of this exploration can also be related to provision of more effective sailing vessels and to the imagination of Don Pedro of Portugal, who in 1428 picked up a copy of Marco Polo's book in Venice and brought it back as a present to his brother Prince Henry the Navigator. Historians are apt to imply that among those who pored over Polo was the Genoese sailor Christopher Columbus.

This change therefore can be epitomized as that between an enclosed and an opened Europe. The closed had every incentive to go rooting in its own past and cling to classical Greece for safety, as the fifteenth century inclined to do. To the interests and trade routes of this ego-centred Europe the first half of the century added Madeira, the rounding of Cape Bojador, the Azores, Cape Verde, and in 1456 the Gulf of Guinea. The second half brought the mouth of the Congo, the rounding of the Cape of Good Hope, and, in 1498, Vasco da Gama reached the west coast of India. Meanwhile Columbus, having sailed down the western coast of Africa, had persuaded Ferdinand and Isabella that the route across the Atlantic would be a shorter way of reaching India (i.e. Asia) than that adopted by the Portuguese. 'In 1492', to quote Ganshof again, 'he landed in the Bahamas, in Cuba which he took for the Asiatic continent, and at Haiti, which he took for Japan.' In the same year that Columbus discovered America, Spain gave to Europe a smaller but also interesting gift, that of the scholar Vives. Born in democratic and progressive Valencia, nurtured in aristocratic and also in authoritarian scholarship, he soon, nevertheless, saw through Parisian worship of authority, and, dividing the intellectuals in twain proved a leader of educational, social, and psychological thought.

If fifteenth-century Europe began by being enclosed, European man, says Professor Clark, was even more decidedly a very 'local animal'. The common social structure of different countries, and a culture still dominated by ecclesiastical influence, underlay the 'medieval internationalism' of which we have already encountered examples. We have, however, only to note a few facts about living and the languages other than scholars' Latin to realize the influence of local pressures on ordinary people's lives.

'For many generations', writes Clark, 'the peoples had been used to fixed settlements. The main work of clearing the land, draining it, and of breaking it in for cultivation had been done for them already by former generations'. 'Almost all the land had its owners'. The exceptional wanderers moved 'in the interstices of a settled world. The outward aspects of life were much more diversified by contrasts, by local and regional peculiarities, than they are now, because travel and transport were so slow and difficult, and technology was so primitive that the physical character of each plot of ground dictated, within very narrow limits, what kind of life could be lived upon it.' Mountain and plain, light or heavy soil, wet or dry climate, the presence or absence of navigable river or sea affected as they do now such matters as the kinds of crop or the tools to be used. But living was affected too by much smaller accidents of environment. 'Everything had to be done with local materials if possible, and so in most places farming, whether individual or communal, was not specialized but provided all the requirements of a neighbourhood. . . . There were local styles of architecture, based on the available materials, timber or brick, hard stone or soft. In dress, tools, furniture, conveniences of every kind, the craftsmen of each town had their local fashions.'

And Clark continues: 'This variety went deep. It extended to the realm of thought, as may be seen from the instance of language. Each district had its dialect, and although the dialects belonged to greater languages, such as French or Provençal, Low German or High German, not many people read books or needed to talk to anyone who came from more than a day's journey away, so that standards of correctness in speech hardly existed. The man who lived at a distance of two days' journey was a foreigner.'

Now let us bring in another main change. We have seen how this local animal had been exposed to sermons and woodcuts.

By the end of the century he was to be exposed to print, a fact quite as unsettling as the increased communication of our own day. Let us look at just two examples that show both the printer's dilemma and the likely impact of printing first on a housewife's language and, second, on a scholar's way of life.

Here, from Trevelyan, is Caxton ruminating on how to translate from a French paraphrase of Virgil's *Aeneid*:

After dyuerse werkes made translated and achieued, hauing noo werke in hande, I, sittyng in my studye where as laye many dyuerse paunflettis and bookys, happened that to my hande came a lytyl booke in frenshe, whiche late was translated oute of latyn by some noble clerke of fraunce, whiche booke is named *Eneydos* made in latyn by that noble poete and grete clerke Vyrgyle.

And whan I had aduysed me in this sayd boke, I delybered and concluded to translate it in-to englysshe, And forthwyth toke a penne and ynke, and wrote a leefe or tweyne whyche I ouersawe agayn to corecte it. And whan I sawe the fayr and straunge termes therin, I doubted that it sholde not please some gentylmen whiche late blamed me, sayeng that in my translacyons I · had ouer curyous termes whiche coude not be vnderstande of comyn peple and desired me to vse olde and homely termes in my translacyons. And fayn wolde I satysfye euery man; and so to doo, toke an olde boke and redde therein and certaynly the englysshe was so rude and brood that I coude not wele understand it. . . . And certaynly our langage now vsed varyeth ferre from that whiche was vsed and spoken when I was borne. . . . And that comyn englysshe that is spoken in one shyre varyeth from another. In so moche that in my dayes happened that certayn marchauntes were in a shippe in Tamyse, for to haue sayled ouer the see into Selande, and for lacke of wynde thei taryed atte Forlond [North Foreland in Kent], and wente to lande for to refreshe them; And one of theym named Sheffelde, a mercer, cam in-to an hows and axed for mete; and specyally he axyed after eggys; and the goode wyf answerde, that she coude speke no frenshe. And the marchaunt was angry, for he also coude speke no frenshe, but wolde haue hadde 'egges' and she vunderstode hym not. And theene at laste another sayd that he wolde haue 'eyren' then the good wyf sayd that she vnderstod hym wel. Loo, what sholde a man in thyse dayes now wryte, 'egges' or 'eyren'?

Certainly it is harde to playse euery man by cause of dyuersite and chaunge of langage. And som honest and grete clerkes haue ben wyth me, and desired me to wryte the moste curyous termes that I coude fynde. And thus between playn, rude and curyous, I stande abasshed, but in my judgemente the comyn termes that be dayli vsed, ben lyghter to be vnderstonde than the olde and auncyent englysshe. And for as moche as this present Booke is not for a rude vplondyssh man to laboure therein ne rede it, but onely for a clerke and a noble gentylman that feleth and vnderstondeth in faytes of armes, in loue, and in noble chyualrye, therefor in a meane bytwene bothe I haue reduced and translated this sayd booke in to our englysshe, not ouer rude ne curyous, but in suche termes as shall be vnderstanden, by goddys grace, accordynge to my copye.

Trevelyan adds:

We thus see that Caxton had a choice to make. He had no dictionaries to cramp or to guide him. As he sat in his book-littered study considering the matter, he had not, as we have and as even Shakespeare had, an English language 'given' whose limits he might extend but whose framework he must accept. The dialects were almost as numerous as the counties of England, and moreover they were perpetually changing. The Northerner, the West countryman, even his housewife of Kent with her 'eyren', could not easily understand either the London merchant or one another. The victory of the speech of London and the Court may perhaps have been ultimately inevitable, but it was rendered certain and rapid first by Chaucer and his fifteenth-century imitators, who drove the West Midland dialect of *Piers Plowman* out of the field among the educated classes; then, by the products of Caxton's press; and last and most of all by the English Bible and Prayer Book, which in Tudor times, thanks to the printing press, reached everyone who could read and many who could only listen.

Now let us turn to Vives, writing as an international scholar in the early sixteenth century when the full implications of unlimited literature had begun to dawn on someone with the wry insight that should befit a psychologist:

As in everything connected with observation there are no limits ... so we find books have increased to such uncountable numbers. Some writers publish what they themselves have written; others limit themselves to compilations from other writers.

So much is this so, that, now, a man's life would not suffice, I do not say for the reading what has been written on many arts and sciences, but on any of them – let alone the time for understanding them. Seneca remarks that Cicero maintains that if his own life were doubled in length, time would not suffice for him to accomplish the reading of all the poems of the lyric bards. But if everything written by those old philosophers, historians, orators, poets, physicians, theologians, had reached this age, then we could put nothing but books in our houses; we should have to sit on books; we should have to walk on the top of books; our eyes would have to glance over nothing but books. Even now there is a terror fallen upon not a few people, and a hatred of study, when they find offered them in any subject of study the volumes which will need indefatigable industry to master. They instantly depress the minds of those who look at them, and the wretches moan inwardly, and ask: Who can read all these?

Finally let us glance at the political scene. The peace concluding the Hundred Years War in 1453 found France in disintegrated exhaustion and left England soon to witness the political suicide of her nobles in the profitless Wars of the Roses. In contrast as yet to some of the continental strivings, England's internal warfare was not calling in question the system of central government by king, council, and parliament. The quarrel concerned not the system but who should be allowed to work it. By the close of the century the Tudors had come to settle this. In France the central system was less well entrenched, partly because of the sharp rivalry of the Monarchy and the Burgundian Duchy. Charles VII, under whom France emerged from the war with a government and an army, died in 1461, leaving his son Louis XI (Fisher's 'eavesdropping, cheeseparing, cautious monarch') to continue rehabilitating his country. This he did. But it is worth noting how the strength of the central government was aided by such dynastic accidents as Charles the Bold, René King of Aix, and Francis Duke of Brittany's all dying without male heirs. By the first Burgundy, Picardy, and Artois, by the second Maine, Anjou, and the imperial fief of Provence, and by the third Brittany, came, by the time of Louis' death in 1483, to be part and parcel of a compact and potentially powerful, instead of an almost disrupted, country.

Italy almost throughout the century was the battle arena of rival trading states. And though by the end of the century strong groupings of territorial princes existed, their very existence laid Italy open to the Franco-Spanish depredations of the sixteenth century. The Empire itself, with which Germany had become increasingly identified, weakened as territorial principalities grew stronger. The fifteenth-century picture of Germany is of a political and social structure at the mercy of an over-wealthy Church, a selfish aristocracy, and other disintegrating factors making for private warfare and considerable unrest. This was consistent with brilliant achievements in learning, culture, and the arts. But, in the second half of the century, against the rising strength of the electors and princes not even an Emperor as outstandingly able and generous as Maximilian could give to Germany the unity and security of central control.

In sum, the fifteenth century politically was something of a melting pot. Spain was the first country to begin to attain stability under a centralized monarchy, with England under the Tudors and France under Louis XI achieving the conditions of this towards the century's end. For Italy and Germany there was a long way still to go. It is significant that in the sixteenth century Italy is so much at the mercy of stronger powers, and that conflicts between the Papacy and German protestantism play so large a part in Europe as a whole.

With this brief sketch of fifteenth-century changes let us return to the contrast with which we started, that between emphasis on vitality and on death. It would be sociologically presumptuous to indicate direct causation on the evidence cited, but one cannot help speculating on the bearing of the taste for the macabre, of the contrast of withdrawal (or death) and vitality, and of the unsettlement we have glimpsed, upon the fifteenth- and sixteenth-century witch hunts. The first could anaesthetize, the second arouse guilt, and the third encourage terrifying rumour.

Historians seem clear that there had always been witches in Europe. But as late as the eleventh and twelfth centuries they could be exorcized confidently with holy water and prayers. Some ecclesiastics, delightfully exemplified as long ago as St

Cuthbert, seem to have realized that effective exorcism involved 'the will to believe'. By the fifteenth century this will was beginning to waver. Such doubting in itself could engender a sense of sin. And what with plague and political unsettlement there was ample occasion for anxiety in a culture wherein, as Lecky implies, few people had been trained to the otherwise intolerable tensions of uncertainty.

Modern studies of rumours, their functions, and the conditions under which they spread, put insecurity, lack of reliable information, need of explanation, heightened suggestibility, need to externalize and justify underlying anxiety and guilt, high on the list of factors to be considered. In the early and middle fifteenth century all these conditions were fulfilled. To help explain the intensification of witch hunts towards the century's end we have I think to add two main complications.

First there were particular and political reasons for fusing the notions of witchcraft and of heresy. We can already see a combination of this sort in the trial of Joan of Arc in 1430. Heresy hunting on the part of the Church was almost bound to intensify as she was more obliged to fight a rearguard action against charges both of sensual worldliness and illegitimate extortion. A second complication lies in the addition of what we should call neurosis and probably psychosis, to the concept of witchcraft, which was in its day a well entrenched form of explanation. Another famous trial, that of Gilles de Rais, who was put to death in 1440 for devil worship combined with the murder of children, shows all too obviously the fusion and confusion of pathology and magic. Indeed in the late seventeenth century, as shown by Williams, in the complex case of Le Voisin, politics, pathology, and necromancy were still inextricably entwined.

If such a fusion of ideas were possible, and if indeed otherwise unexplained neurotic and psychotic behaviour was no less common than it is today, it is hardly surprising that witch hunts came to the fore. We can add therefore one final contrast to the closing fifteenth century, that of remaining faith in phantom and that of new faith in fact. Nowhere is phantom clearer than in the *Malleus Maleficarum* and the witch hunts which, as the textbook of the Inquisition, the *Malleus* supported. The facts suggesting heresy and lunacy were legion. The fantasy lies both in the confessions to which the tragic facts of torture could give rise, and in the form of explanation to which superstition and orthodoxy now joined in giving credence.

The *Malleus Maleficarum* was published about 1490 (pp. 263 ff.). Before 1669 it was printed ten times and in less than another century it went through nine more editions. It was the work of two Dominican monks, one Julius Sprenger who about 1480 became Provincial of the German Provinces and Inquisitor General for Germany, the other Heinrich Kramer. It begins with an argument on the error or heresy of doubting witchcraft. It goes on to state conscientiously and coldly the phenomena alleged to warrant diagnosis of possession and of the methods of collecting and checking observations. Thirdly it passes to the trial and treatment – torture and burning – which should be applied. Many of the phenomena would now find their place in a standard textbook of psychiatry. Others, such as the brewing of sinister potions from dismembered children's corpses, could mean pathology, but in a detailed study would have to be related to the burial customs we have noted. In broomstick-riding and devilish intercourse we can see all too clearly the current cultural slant that is often given to neurotic fantasy or psychotic hallucination. While detailed comment is inappropriate, we must face both historically, sociologically, and psychologically the fact that, in the trials of the time, accusations of witchcraft far outnumbered those of sorcery and the evidence of witchcraft was often sexual in nature. Women were the scapegoats and bore the brunt of persecution.

Sprenger and Kramer took all precautions to establish official right to proceed, obtaining support from the Emperor, the University of Cologne, and finally a Papal Bull, the text of which historically is worth consultation. It is important because it represents one of the few occasions when the Roman Church was led to acknowledge the existence of witchcraft at all.

From our special standpoint on the history of psychology, we cannot omit the appalling witch hunts, the persecution, and the thousands of cruel deaths for which in effect the *Malleus Maleficarum* supplied alike a textbook and a textual support. In the hands of the frightened, the obsessional, and the perverted the old notion of the body as a carcass that could be occupied gave rise to terrible results. The position may, as Williams suggests, have been worsened by the notion of a spirit that desires embodiment and of a pathological neutral stuff existing apart from matter and mind. From this one reaches the ideas of 'incubi' and 'succubi' that are capable of sexual relations but not themselves of giving birth to those with immortal souls.

To the sinister details of torture we mercifully need not turn. Witch trials and torture continued still it seems in their thousands through the sixteenth and into the seventeenth centuries. Some of the latest and cruellest were Scottish. Only in the eighteenth century are they found to have died down, presumably under the impact of more subtle ways of identifying and of cooler interest in fact. And who to link the fifteenth and sixteenth centuries can we find more interested in facts and the conditions of their finding than Leonardo, Copernicus, and the Machiavelli of the *Discourses*?

REFERENCES

Clark, G. N. 'The Early Modern Period' in *The European Inheritance*. Edited by Barker, Clark, and Vaucher. Oxford: Clarendon Press, 1955, Vol. II, Part IV. Chap. I, especially pp. 3, 4

Eliot, T. S. 'Journey of the Magi'. *Collected Poems 1909–1935*. London: Faber and Faber, 1941, p. 31. New York: Harcourt, Brace and Coy, Inc.

Fisher, H. A. L. *A History of Europe*. London: Arnold, 1943. Bk. II, Chaps. III, IV, V. Especially p. 459

Ganshof, F. L. 'The Middle Ages' in *The European Inheritance*. Edited by Barker, Clark, and Vaucher. Oxford: Clarendon Press, 1954, Vol. I, Part III, Chap. XII, especially pp. 420, 421, 483

Huizinga, J. *The Waning of the Middle Ages*. London: Arnold, 1952, Chap. XI, especially pp. 124–5, 126, 133, 134

Kramer, H. See Summers

Lecky, W. E. H. *History of the Rise and Influence of the Spirit of Rationalism in Europe*. London: Longmans, 1910

Machiavelli, Niccolò. *The Discourses*. Translated by L. J. Walker, London: Routledge and Kegan Paul, 1950

Onians, R. B. *The Origins of European Thought about the Body, the Mind, the Soul, the World, Time, and Fate*. Cambridge: University Press, 1951, Part II, Chaps. IX and X

Contrast and Conflict

Power, Eileen. *Medieval People*. Cambridge: University Press, 1924. Penguin Books, 1937

Sprenger, J. See Summers

Summers, Montague. *Malleus Maleficarum*. Translated with an Introduction, Bibliography, and Notes. London: The Pushkin Press, 1948

Trevelyan, G. M. *Illustrated English Social History*. London: Longmans, 1952, Vol. 1, pp. 78–9

Vives, Juan Luis. *On Education*. Translated from *De Tradendis Disciplinis* by Foster Watson. Cambridge: 1913, pp. 44–5

Williams, Charles. *Witchcraft*. London: Faber and Faber, 1941

CHAPTER 5

FEAR AND FACT

Mephistopheles:
> Why, this is hell, nor am I out of it:
> Think'st thou that I, who saw the face of God,
> And tasted the eternal joys of heaven,
> Am not tormented with ten thousand hells,
> In being depriv'd of everlasting bliss?

MARLOWE

> Firste of all he made a decree, that it should be lawfull for everie man to favoure and folow what religion he would, and that he mighte do the best he could to bring other to his opinion, so that he did it peaceablie, gentelie, quietlie, and soberlie, without hastie and contentious rebuking and invehing against other. If he could not by faire and gentle speche induce them unto his opinion yet he should use no kinde of violence....

SIR THOMAS MORE: Utopia

ONE way of focusing the sixteenth century is to imagine a Faustian study in Bonn, complete with the paraphernalia of astrology and alchemy. In the study are a doctor, well versed in the sciences, his student and a Poodle, an innocent Poodle but one endowed by the neighbours with just the supposed significance of Faust's unusual visitor. But whereas the poodle's master Agrippa did have his mad and flamboyant moments, his medical student Johannis Weyer had all the independence, gentleness, and integrity of the Dutch and Germans at their best. He was born at Grave on the Maas, Northern Brabant in 1515 or 1516, and can be claimed by both countries. For after a period as city doctor in Arnhem he was appointed in 1550 physician to Duke Wilhelm of Jülich-Cleves-Berg. This he remained till his death in 1588. It is not wholly inappropriate to take persecution, the poodle, and the doctor as the poles of sixteenth-century thought on our subject. The conflicts of the century have been rivalled only by our own.

At the century's beginning we may see liberal humanism reflected, for example, in the writings and works of More, Erasmus, the Spaniard Vives, not unjustly claimed as the father of modern psychology, and in Mantua's sturdy Pietro Pomponazzi who, as a humanist Aristotelian, incurred not a little wrath from the Pope: 'Peter of Mantua has asserted that, according to the principles of philosophy and the opinion of Aristotle, the reasoning soul is or appears to be mortal, contrary to the determination of the Lateran Council; the Pope commands that the said Peter shall retract, otherwise that he be proceeded against, 13 June 1518' (Contelori). Pomponazzi retained his professorship but the Papal wrath was a foretaste of things soon to come. Towards the end of the century Montaigne, steeped in travellers' tales of other ways of living, appears as one sitting on the edge of chaos making wide-eyed ironical comment: '*Après tout, c'est mettre ses conjectures à bien haut pris que d'en faire cuire un homme tout vif.*'

Conflict indeed there was, linked in the first place with the national rivalries of England, France, and Spain; for the last two Italy initially provided the battleground. It will be remembered from p. 81 that the fifteenth century had seen Spain unified under Ferdinand and Isabella, England unified under the Tudors, and France established under Charles VII and Louis XI, her central government reinforced by a series of dynastic accidents. Between 1477 and 1519 a further series of dynastic links, some family tragedies, and a 'vast expenditure of money and intrigue', prepared the way for Charles V to succeed to the Spanish possessions of his grandparents Ferdinand and Isabella, to the Netherlands inheritance of his grandmother Mary of Burgundy, and to the empire of his other grandfather Maximilian I. By then Charles was a nineteen-year-old, serious, Flemish, and Catholic, with his father dead and his mother insane. Broadly, the first half of the century saw the struggle of France, which was pro-Catholic but alarmed at the Spanish accession to power, to prevent Charles V from also dominating Italy. This, partly because of Papal links with Spain, France did not succeed in achieving. By the Treaty of Cambrésis in 1559, after Charles had abdicated in favour of Philip II, France withdrew, leaving Italy for the time being politically and culturally open to Spanish influence. This is relevant for understanding the interstices both of the Inquisition and of the Italian Counter-Reformation which was well on the way by the middle of the century. Meanwhile, in England the rejection of Papal authority by Henry VIII in 1534 can be seen as a partial consequence of hostility to entanglement in Spain's great empire.

Now let us look at the second source of conflict, namely religion. In Italy, at the century's start, a series of Popes, some disastrously evil, had been caught by the cultural pressure also to become great princes. Some of the nature of this pressure we can see from a letter written, about 1489, to the relatively scrupulous Innocent VIII by none other than Lorenzo de' Medici:

> Others have not so long postponed their efforts to attain the papal chair, and have concerned themselves little to maintain the retiring delicacy so long evinced by your holiness. Now is your holiness not only exonerated before God and man, but this honourable conduct may cause you to incur blame, and your reserve may be attributed to less worthy motives. Zeal and duty lay it on my conscience to remind your holiness that no man is immortal. Be the pontiff as important as he may in his own right, he cannot make his dignity and that importance hereditary; he cannot be said absolutely to possess anything but the honours and emoluments he has secured to his kindred.   (Fabroni)

Quoting this, Ranke points out that Lorenzo had a personal interest in the Pope's affairs, having married his daughter to a son of the Pope; but Lorenzo could hardly have written thus directly had not current governing class opinion made plausible this form of 'zeal and duty'.

In Germany, disgust at ecclesiastical worldly living, the complex relations of papal politics with those of the Emperor, Italian and German princes, the King of France, Henry VIII, and the like, the rising independence of German princes and the people themselves, and the passionately-resented Papal levies and costly pardons, provided a chance for reformers. In 1517 Luther, inspired by an Augustinian visionary asceticism, posted the ninety-five theses on the church door of Wittenberg which, aided by a friendly press, lit the fires of the German Reformation. Thereby he rallied not only those whose religious needs were no longer met by a sensualized Catholicism and Borgia methods of achieving power. There were others; namely those who had political and financial reasons for resenting Papal influence. Psychologically fascinating though such a study could be, we cannot begin to consider the complex economic, social, political, and other causes of Luther's rise and hold, not only on Germany, but on other northern and middle European countries.

Up till the Council of Ratisbon in 1541 it seems that it might, conceivably, have been possible to find some *modus vivendi* between a Catholicism, wherein already there were signs of internal reform, and a liberal protestantism. One can hardly read of the great Cardinal Contarini's attempt to achieve this without being moved to consider the misery it might have prevented. He failed and the breach between Catholic and Protestant views widened and deepened. In 1543 the Jesuit order, founded by the Spaniard Ignatius Loyola, was unconditionally established, in due season to become the spearhead of the Counter-Reformation.

To Germany, after long years of strife and alternating balance of power by differing religious persuasions, a lull came in 1555. By the Peace of Augsburg it was left for the then three hundred different secular states to decide for themselves which practice should prevail. The penalty for religious dissent was displacement rather than death. For some seventy years after Augsburg religious strife diminished. In the surrounding countries, however, France, the Netherlands, and to a lesser extent England, the story of persecution, rebellion, conspiracy and war continued. Calvinism became the focus of the French religious wars which centred in the struggles of the Catholics and Huguenots. By this time the French central government had been weakened again, financially and politically, by the unsuccessful struggle with Spain in Italy.

The Netherlands can best be very briefly characterized as an unwilling element in the Spanish domains, uninterested in Italian conquest, pining for peace for commercial enterprise, and strongly resenting the Catholic persecution which Philip II intensified.

Meanwhile, in Italy, internal Catholic reform was bringing to the fore some Popes who had marked ascetic traits and others who made different and varied approaches to the problem of reconciling religion, ethics, and power politics. Caraffa, who became Pope Paul IV in 1555, had had an important hand in reviving the Inquisition, the atmosphere of which is suggested in the rules he drew up as being 'the best he could devise for promoting the end in view':

First. When the faith is in question, there must be no delay; but at the slightest suspicion, vigorous measures must be resorted to with all speed.

Second. No consideration to be shown to any prince or prelate however high his station.

Third. Extreme severity is rather to be exercised against those who attempt to shield themselves under the protection of any potentate: only he who makes plenary confession shall be treated with gentleness and fatherly compassion.

Fourth. No man must debase himself by showing toleration towards heretics of any kind, above all towards Calvinists.

(Caracciolo)

When they are not reflecting struggles for power, the theological disputes of the sixteenth century, which are seen to some extent in the proceedings of the Councils of Trent, seem often to be arguments about the most effective way of relieving the tragedies of human guilt and fear. Can a sense of sin be allayed, and re-identification with goodness in the person of God be assured, by means of grace alone, or will guilt be purged to the person's (and other people's) own satisfaction only by good works to which the blessing of grace is added? Nobody in those days would have entertained the empirical chance that differences in individual personality-structure might conceivably be relevant even if for social peace there must be some shreds of approach in common. Another crucial question concerned who was, and who was not, entitled and by what methods to provide absolution and, as it were, transmit the magical quality of grace. Moreover, of those who were born to original sin, which were also the recipients of grace and by what criteria were they chosen?

I have used the word 'magical' with intention, not to make light of a theological issue, but now to bring in a different aspect of the century as a whole. This is the amount of superstition floating at all levels of a society which was experiencing the start of another increase of population and in which economic developments were enhancing differences in the social balance of power.

This brings us back to Agrippa and the poodle. Superstition at its most innocent can be noted when the stars were thought of sufficient importance for the Pope himself to consult them before negotiating with the King of France and to defer arrangements until they were thought to be propitious. It was more sinister for an Italian to 'let not a day pass without taking the horoscopes and turning the screws in the life-size figures of Coligny and Condé' (made by the Germans) and for the Spanish ambassador to report on this to Catharine de Medici with the comment that 'neither of them will live long'. More dangerous still was the widespread belief in sorcery and witchcraft. Zilboorg quotes the Burgundian Judge Boguet who lived in the reign of Henri IV of France as saying: 'I believe that the sorcerers could form an army equal to that of Xerxes, who had one million eight thousand men. Trois-Échelles, one of those best acquainted with the art of sorcerers, states that under King Charles IX [1560–74] France alone had three hundred thousand sorcerers (some read it as thirty thousand). This being the case, what are we to estimate the total number to be if we include other countries and regions of the world?'

A good deal of comparable floating superstition, left to flourish in the intervals of religious strife, which very probably encouraged general insecurity and neurosis, seems to have crystallized into excesses of relic collection and belief in miracles. Take, for instance, these examples from Ranke's *History of the Reformation in Germany*:

Elector Frederick of Saxony gathered together in the church he endowed at Wittenberg, 5005 particles, all preserved in entire standing figures, or in exquisitely wrought reliquaries, which

were shown to the devout people every year on the Monday after
Misericordia ... Miraculous images of Our Lady were discovered: one, for example, in Eischel in the diocese of Constance;
at the Iphof boundary, by the roadside, a sitting figure of the
Virgin, whose miracles gave great offence to the Monks of Birk-
lingen who possessed a similar one. ... Miracles were worked
without ceasing at the tomb of Bishop Benno in Meissen; mad-
men were restored to reason, the deformed became straight;
those infected with the plague were healed; nay, a fire at Merse-
burg was extinguished by Bishop Bose merely uttering the name
of Benno; while those who doubted his power and sanctity were
assailed by misfortunes. When Trithemius recommended this
miracle worker to the Pope for canonization, he did not forget to
remark that he had been a rigid and energetic supporter of the
church party, and had resisted the tyrant Henry IV. So intimately
were all these ideas connected.

We have noted earlier how fantasy, in which an element of
distortion and fear is all too apparent, was reflected in certain
aspects of highly-developed fifteenth- and sixteenth-century art.
This is clearly shown in the work of Hieronymus Bosch, who
links these centuries. He was much admired by the gloomy
Philip II of Spain, whom we can visualize operating from the
vast and oppressive Escorial with its roof designed like a grid-
iron to remind him of expiatory martyrdom. Though, in a sense,
Germany had provided a textbook, it was Spain who led in light-
ing Inquisitorial fires. As the sixteenth century moves on we
pass in Italy from the High Renaissance through Mannerism towards the academic and ecclesiastical dominance of art, and to
its use in the development of Catholic Baroque in the late sixteenth and in the seventeenth century. Mannerism, which was
far from being confined to Italy, also reflects both an element of
fantasy and at times the slightly distorted emotionalism that
one has in mind. In Germany, Grünewald and Altdorfer in the
first half of the sixteenth century suggest fairly clearly some of
the haunting horrors of the period in which they lived. The
most obvious example of this is the Isenheim altarpiece at Col-
mar. As Van der Meer points out, these two artists illustrate
one extreme which finds its sharpest contrast in the ultra-realism of painters such as Dürer, who sometimes reveals both ten-

dencies, but whose emotional climate is much nearer that of Erasmus, who admired him, as did also Giovanni Bellini. A similar realism is clearly revealed in the work of Holbein the Younger, who in 1526 had to flee to England, from the Basel of the Reformation, with a letter of introduction from Erasmus. The letter refers to the fact that 'the arts here are freezing'. Even by then it appears that to Protestant reformers, art, specially of a religious nature, was savouring of Popish idolatry.

It may not be unfair to suggest that in proportion to the High Renaissance worldliness of Catholicism at the century's start, and the hardening of Lutheran and Calvinist views towards the middle, persecution by all parties had probably got to reach morbid intensity to convince anyone, including the persecutors themselves. So as the century passes before our eyes we watch the parade of princes and Popes' nephews go out and back to *professio fidei*, via all the paraphernalia of occupational persecution, torture, witch burnings, heretic burnings, beheadings, massacres, internecine and major wars, Reform and Counter-Reform. In 1543 Copernicus announced that the sun does not go round the earth, while the homely ordinary people who went on living look at us from the altarpiece carved for Bordesholm by Bruggemann in 1521.

For those who seek crumbs of comfort in a period all too comparable in some ways to this same sixteenth century, it is consoling that among the elements salvaged by later centuries were, first, the quieter humanism that, for example, via Erasmus, eventually led to the Dutch secular magistrates abolishing witch burnings a hundred years ahead of any other country. Secondly, the ultra-realism and also the gentleness of Dürer returns us to Weyer who, in Zilboorg's words, proceeded

with implacable will and stubborn systemization to refute all the superstitions and practices connected with the whole problem of witchcraft. He leaves not a stone unturned. He reviews in detail all Biblical references to witches and wizards. He reviews the same problem in Greek mythology and history. He subjects to careful analysis the phenomena mentioned in the *Malleus Maleficarum*: transvection, sexual relations with the devil, sexual impotence of man, the witches' alleged ability to affect the health of man and beast, the confessions made by witches, their propensities to elaborate on their crimes, their alleged impiety. Weyer goes over in minute detail all the practices from exorcism to the endless varieties and refinements of torture, from the days of the past to his own. He leaves no doubt that but one conclusion is warranted: the witches are mentally sick people, and the monks who torment and torture the poor creatures are the ones who should be punished.

He seems to have unearthed seventy-two Princes of Darkness under Lucifer, and 7,405,926 lesser devils administering the affairs of the empire. He was a quiet doctor, religious, humble, and respected. His magnum opus the *De Praestigiis Daemonum* was published in Latin in 1563 and translated by himself into German in 1567. He concludes it with the statement:

I do not pretend to be so absolutely certain of everything which I propound in this book and I submit it in its totality to the most equitable judgement of the Catholic Church of Jesus Christ, and I stand ready to correct myself if I am convinced that in any part I have made a mistake.

Within a few years Weyer's name was listed, probably for good as well as bad reasons, on the Catholic index as an *Auctor primae classis*. In 1581 he was reprieved to *Autores secundae classis*, only reading of the *De Praestigiis* being forbidden. In 1590 all his books were banned again and remained so until the early twentieth century, which for his clinical insight and patient attempt to be factual lays claim to Weyer as the father of modern psychiatry.

What can we glean from all this about the history of the mind-body problem? Apart from the tragedies which an over-simplified notion of a soul lodged in a tenement of clay (also capable of diabolical occupation, see p. 263 ff.) could be used to rationalize, there are I think five points to note. First, the sixteenth century has something to teach us of the storms that had to be weathered before even a limited empirical approach to human functioning was remotely possible. It is of interest, when we look at some of the history, that Weyer could get a German prince to take seriously his indictment of false evidence and some of his cool com-

ments on hysteria. We cannot, I think, credit this directly to
Erasmus, but we can say that the very importance attached to
him by his contemporaries shows that he was giving some expression to a liberal humanist trend that was alive and needed
outlet and that he helped it to survive. In point of fact Erasmus,
for all his fame and scholarship, his dislike of meaningless ritual,
his passion for etymological purity, his sense of style and corresponding detestation of dirt, smells, ill-health, addled eggs, and
squalid bedrooms, did not wholly fulfil the expectations of those
around him. The reasons for this are discussed with subtlety
and insight in Huizinga's interesting biography. But as the focus
of a trend his importance is unquestionable.

The second item to be salvaged from the sixteenth century is
the work of Vives and Weyer. From our specific point of view,
Erasmus is in some ways less important than Vives, whose reflective subtlety and extraordinarily integrated personality make
him worthy of greater attention than he has received. It is to
Erasmus' credit that at the age of fifty-five he wrote to More:
'Vives is one who will overshadow the name of Erasmus'. Born
in 1492 Vives was then twenty-seven, with his major works on
education and the *De Anima* yet to be written. He was unusual
and clear-headed enough to combine sincere religious feeling
with detached empiricism, original thought with practical application, fine scholarship with a flair for simple vernacular style.
His relations with other people appear to have been unimpeachable and in the statement 'What the soul is, it is not our concern
to know; what it is like, and what are its manifestations are of
first importance' he sidesteps Aristotle and theology to psychological observation and reflection. Perhaps even more important, he made considerable contributions to the study of
emotions which historically were still tending to suffer from
invidious comparison with reason and intellect.

The sixteenth century's third contribution lies in Montaigne's stress on considering the whole person. There is too
the gift of Montaigne's objective irony, shown significantly
in his suggestion that man's exalted reason may not be wholly
successful in maintaining his superior status to other animals
and that the senses, particularly the kinaesthetic and tactile,

may play a most interesting and important part in successful communication. In the middle sixteenth century it had taken a Palestrina to smuggle sound back into the favour of an ascetic Pope at a time when too much local song and associated ribaldry had, now intelligibly, brought Church music under almost Augustinian condemnation. Early Renaissance Italy had delighted in, and as it were emancipated, the senses both in living and in art. The High Renaissance did not stop short of the sensual. Conversely the period of the Councils of Trent has been described as 'the birthday of prudery'. As far as I know, Montaigne is the first theorist of significance to review with different and detached irony the unobtrusive claim to natural value on the part of the senses. The tactile and kinaesthetic, in particular, had found few besides Aristotle and Lucretius in their defence. It is a matter of passing historical interest that Montaigne read and frequently quoted Lucretius and that he also cites Vives on a point culled from the latter's edition of St Augustine, which came, as did Montaigne himself, under Papal condemnation. Descartes in *The Passions of the Soul* was once more to cite Vives.

Fourth, in noting the liberal and the tortured we must not forget the more or less conventional literary and scientific notions of body, mind, and soul, in the last quarter of the sixteenth and the early part of the seventeenth century; for these in some form also influenced later thought. To grasp these quickly we can hardly improve on Stewart's slim volume *The Little World of Man*. This shows, as we have noted already, that at the time Shakespeare wrote, ordinary cultural views on body and mind rang the changes on Aristotle and Plato with or without interpretation by St Augustine and St Thomas. Mixed up with these ingredients were variants on the old Hippocratic and Galenical humours. Many reflected the familiar macrocosm-microcosm setting. Physiologists' opinions may be considered more conveniently with those of the seventeenth century.

Finally there remains the important fifth point to be made. As we look more closely at the last part of the sixteenth century, and list a few dates, we become aware of the impact of personalities who, drawing their stimulus from all kinds of sources, were to transform literature, philosophy, and science. While, at intervals, Montaigne was writing the *Apologie de Raymond Sebond*, Francis Bacon, born in 1561, was growing from a boy of eleven or twelve to a young man about twenty. Shakespeare was three years younger than Bacon, and so was Galileo, who was born in 1564, the year that Michelangelo died. Kepler was born in 1571, Harvey in 1578, and ten years afterwards, the year of Weyer's death, came Hobbes. Eight years later in 1596 Descartes was born. With this we must turn to the extraordinary line of literary, philosophical, and scientific developments, bearing on our topic, which belong to the turn of the sixteenth, and to the progress of the seventeenth, century.

REFERENCES

Caracciolo. *Vita di Paolo IV*. MS., c. 8. See Ranke; *History of the Popes*, Vol. I, p. 159

Contelori. *Papal Letters*. See Ranke, *History of the Popes*, Vol. I, p. 55

Erasmus. See Gombrich E. H., *The Story of Art*, p. 277. See Watson, Foster, *Juan Luis Vives*, See Huizinga, *Erasmus of Rotterdam*

Fabroni. *Vita Laurentii*. See Ranke, *History of the Popes*, Vol. I, p. 33

Fisher, H. A. L. *A History of Europe*. London: Arnold, 1943, Bk. II, Chaps. VIII and X and p. 503

Gombrich, E. H. *The Story of Art*. London: Phaidon, 1950. Dürer, p. 251 ff. Erasmus, p. 277

Hauser, A. *The Social History of Art*. Translated Stanley Godman. London: Routledge and Kegan Paul, 1951. Vol. I, p. 377

Huizinga, J. *Erasmus of Rotterdam*. London: Phaidon, 1952

Medici, Lorenzo de'. See Ranke, *History of the Popes*, Vol. I, p. 33

Meer, Van der. *Atlas de la Civilization Occidentale*. Amsterdam: Elsevier, 1952, p. 138

Montaigne, M. de. *Essais*. Edited by P. Villey. Paris: Alcan, 1923, Vol. III, p. 335

Ranke, Leopold von. *The History of the Popes*, Translated E. Foster. London: Bell, 1891, Vol. I, pp. 55, 33, 159

Ranke, Leopold von. *History of the Reformation in Germany*. Books I–VI. Translated Sarah Austin. London: Routledge, 1905, p. 120

Watson, Foster. (1) *Juan Luis Vives el gran Valenciano 1492–1540*. Oxford: University Press, 1922

(2) 'The Father of Modern Psychology'. *Psychological Review*, 1915, pp. 352 ff.

Weyer, (Wierri) Johannis. *De Praestigiis Daemonum et meantationibus ac veneficiis*. Basileae: Per Johannis Oporinum. 3rd Ed. 1566. Translation of 1579 reprinted as *Histoires, disputes et discours des illusions et impostures des diables*. Paris : Bibliothèque Diabolique, 1885

Zilboorg, G., and Henry, G. W. *A History of Medical Psychology*. London : Allen and Unwin, New York : Norton, 1941, Chap. 7, especially pp. 180–95 and 201–35

CHAPTER 6

THE SEVENTEENTH-CENTURY SEARCH
FOR CERTAINTY

> When thou hast done, thou hast not done,
>   For I have more.
> I have a sinne of feare, that when I have spunne
> My last thread, I shall perish on the shore;
> Sweare by thy selfe, that at my death thy sonne
> Shall shine as he shines now, and heretofore;
>   And, having done that, thou hast done,
>   I feare no more.
>   JOHN DONNE

OUR brief historical survey has aimed in part at recalling some of the ingredients of the culture in which the great original thinkers of the European seventeenth century were to find themselves. We may thereby see a little more clearly the extent to which their originality lay, as it usually does, in a distinctively personal mixture of assimilation and revolt.

To provide a contemporary setting, though inevitably inadequate, for people such as Bacon, Harvey, Hobbes, Descartes, Spinoza, Leibniz, and Locke, it is useful to keep in mind a few aspects of seventeenth-century history and some samples of sixteenth-century biology and psychology which bring into focus the immensity of seventeenth-century achievement.

Politically the seventeenth century was ushered in by the exorcism of Spanish domination. Henri III, the pathetic and futile son of Catharine de Medici under whose aegis the Massacre of St Bartholomew occurred in 1572, succeeded his brother Charles IX in 1574 and was assassinated in 1589. His successor Henri IV of Navarre, who entered Paris eventually in 1594, is associated with three facts of importance. First is the formulation of the Edict of Nantes whereby more than one religious communion could have political rights. Even limited Huguenot toleration was an indirect gain to those who sought to check the last bid for general Catholic dominance of which

Charles V's and Philip's monarchy had been the spearhead. Spanish influence in France was further halted by Henri IV's direct attacks on the Spanish pockets in Amiens, Calais, and Blavet in Brittany. Thirdly, under Henri IV the foundations were laid for the greatness which France attained at a later stage under Richelieu and Louis XIV.

France was by no means the only or even the most important exorcizer of alarming Spanish ghosts. In 1588 the Spanish Armada had suffered defeat by weather and the English in what Fisher calls the 'first act of a long war which outlasted Philip II and Elizabeth and was only concluded in 1604'. A little later the great fight for Dutch independence, in which the House of Orange played so important a part, subsided with the twelve-year truce of 1609 by which Holland established a freedom which she never wholly lost.

These three checks by the Dutch, the English, and the French, showed Spain's invincibility to be something that could at least be questioned. Fisher makes the following comment on Spain's internal reaction; which as a kind of displacement activity has its own psychological interest:

A long succession of reverses experienced by a religious people may either shake or confirm them in the faith. In the agony of the great Channel fight the Spanish sailors exclaimed: 'God has deserted us'. Later the nation was persuaded to believe that it was punished because it had deserted God. The losses at sea, the miscarriage in Ireland, the failure of the plan to convert England or subdue the Dutch, were ascribed by the priests to a dark taint of heresy wickedly tolerated in Spain itself. In their view the first step to the revival of the country was no plan for fiscal or naval reformation, but the propitiation of an angry and jealous God. The Moriscoes must confess or leave the country. The advice was taken. The Moriscoes were disliked on many grounds: because they were dark in skin, because they were skilled and industrious, because they were thought to be at heart heretical and to sympathize with the African corsairs who raided the Spanish coast. Accordingly no act of Philip III was so popular with the Spanish nation as his expulsion of this deserving community, numbering half a million of the most skilled agriculturalists and artificers of the country.

On a long-term view, the importance of seventeenth-century Dutch independence and of England's relative freedom to develop her own affairs could hardly be over-emphasized, though the Grand Siècle in France must have the greater limelight.

Holland, the haven of personal refuge, of printing, and of pictures, became the guardian of European liberty and an active contributor to scientific thought. The great age of Dutch interiors, portraits, and landscapes claims its own if less obvious relevance when one realizes the extent to which contemporary Italian and French artists were becoming the auxiliaries of church, state, and academy. Hauser sees the best of Dutch seventeenth-century art as the product of the bourgeoisie, shall we say at their most enlightened. John Evelyn in his diary has some shrewd comments to make on the Dutch investment value of pictures. The fact remains that much of this art escaped the sensual and sententious elements traceable in Church and Catholic court Baroque. And for many young people, to whom power-mongering is alien, a Dutch landscape embodies a desire to observe and accept which a scientific subject should like to claim in its ancestry. It is not silly to read Spinoza beside the *View of Delft*.

Seventeenth-century English literature proffers a different excitement, whose touches of private and metaphysical fantasy someone might relate to mannerist art at a less exalted (and perhaps more defensible) level than Hauser's comments on Shakespeare. More immediately relevant to psychology's history are England's experiments, to her own dissatisfaction, in king-slaying, puritan protection, restoration ribaldry and its aftermath in James II. From these she was lucky enough to emerge at the century's close, in such company as that of the Shaftsburys, Locke, and another William of Orange, offering diplomatic alternatives to 'enthusiasm', innate ideas, and undivinely arbitrary kingship.

From 1618 to 1648 the Thirty Years' War, with its intricate mixture of religious, dynastic, Spanish, Imperial, local, and personal causes, was fought, like many other sixteenth- and seventeenth-century wars, to the appalling detriment of the way of life and the unity of the territories involved, in this case mainly

German. Historians differ in assessing its consequences in comparison with other wars of the period, but the low ebb of Germany at its end is undeniable. The Congress of Westphalia by which the war was closed is regarded as the first conference in which international agreements were negotiated. It was marked among other things by the interest of the international law embodied in the resulting treaties and to which Grotius had contributed so much. Noteworthy too is the relatively small part played by ecclesiastical diplomacy. This last is of interest to us because in it, and in Richelieu's earlier cross-breeding of religious and political issues to the great advantage of France's rise to power, we can see another stage in the shift of Western European culture from the ecclesiastical to the secular. This shift is undeniably relevant to the development of science.

Henri IV of France was assassinated in 1610. Richelieu, Louis XIII's minister from 1624, died in 1642 a year before his king, who left the five-year-old Louis XIV to grow up in the atmosphere of the First and Second Fronde, a time of unrest which would make many welcome authoritarian government. Fisher asserts that Louis directly inferred the necessity of the strong personal government he later put into effect. According to Fisher: 'The autocracy of Louis XIV, reflecting the mounting ardour of French national feeling, is the dominant fact in the history of Europe from that king's assumption of power in 1661 until his death in 1715'. Such was one method of achieving certainty. From our point of view equal interest lies in Hazard's portrait of the underlying currents of thought from 1680 onwards, wherein the effects of seventeenth-century scientific philosophizing are so clearly shown and the way is also prepared for the English influence in the eighteenth century. By the turn of the century a different sense of security had loomed into view, an undefensive variety resting on reserves of resilience. It is shown most naturally in Harvey and Locke, less easily, and at its greatest, in Spinoza.

Now let us sample, from Nordenskiöld, the biology and psychology which the early seventeenth century inherited. Via Hippocrates, Aristotle, and Galen, the sixteenth-century biologists still held to the ancient idea of the 'breath' soul or 'vital spirit' as somehow associated with air and with the blood of the lungs and heart, to which 'pneuma-laden' blood was conveyed by the arteries. Blood of a less exalted kind was sometimes alleged to emanate from the liver and was associated with man's vegetable soul, as was the heart with his animal soul. To question this version of the cardio-vascular system, still more to study it empirically, was a dangerous pastime because all too easily the status of the immortal soul might loom into view. From the mid sixteenth century the empirical inquirer ran the risk of Inquisitorial scrutiny.

This risk was taken by Harvey's immediate predecessors. These include Servet, with his extraordinary mixture of heretical religious enthusiasm, astrology, and hatred of Calvinistic despotism (he was burned at the stake by the Protestants in 1553); Renaldo Columbus, Professor of Anatomy at Padua; and Cesalpino, born at Arezzo in 1519, Professor of Pharmacology at Pisa. He was appointed in his old age as body-physician to the Pope and died at Rome in 1603. Even he, who was loyally Aristotelian, fell into the Inquisition's hands from which he escaped, so Nordenskiöld suggests, by 'dialectical cleverness and perhaps also by his being in the Papal service'.

As a way of confounding body-mind relations Servet's theories could hardly be improved. Their early Greek origins are patent. He seems to have maintained that to understand the relations of the spiritual and physical life we must take into account the three vital elements of the body, namely: blood with its seat in the liver and the veins; *spiritus vitalis* in the heart and the arteries; and *spiritus animalis* which is a ray of light and situated in the brain and the nerves. The power of God's Spirit dwells in all of these.

The heart, to which the vital spirit is first communicated by God (inferred from the heart being the first point to live in the embryo), in turn communicates the vital spirit to the liver. The liver on the other hand provides material to the spirit in the form of blood. The spirit in fact ends up in the best Homeric tradition as something formed from uniting the finest components of blood with inhaled air. This union takes place in the lungs, to which blood is conveyed from the right chamber of the heart. In due season blood 'purged of soot through exhalation and mixed with inhaled air' is conveyed from the lungs back to the left chamber of the heart. Contrary to current assumption, Servet argued that blood could not go through anything as resistant as the heart wall. Moreover, the powerful structure of the pulmonary veins could not be explained simply by the function of feeding the lungs. All this, he seems to have thought, was obvious if only one took care in interpreting Galen's observations correctly.

In study of the workings of the heart Renaldo Columbus appears to have arrived independently at the notion of the arterial system originating in the heart, whose right and left ventricles were separated by an intermediate wall which again he held to be impenetrable. From the right side the blood was conveyed to the lungs, where it was mixed with air and, thus diluted, was conducted back to the left side of the heart. This fact, says Nordenskiöld, he claimed that no one had hitherto observed or described, but it was none the less true and could be verified on experimental subjects whether alive or dead.

Cesalpino, Renaldo Columbus' pupil, followed his master in maintaining that the blood passes through the lungs from the right to the left side of the heart. He was the first to call the process 'circulation', but this important step seems to have been entangled, among other things, in attempts to prove that the veins originate in the heart and not in the liver and that the nerves likewise originate in the heart and not in the brain. This latter point he inferred *inter alia* from the fact that grief and happiness are felt first in the heart, while the function of the brain is to cool the blood, like the receptacle in a distilling apparatus. In this, apart from the delightful traces of Aristotelian irony, we can detect something of the line of thought which Descartes later attempted to dislodge when he argued that from emotion being experienced at the level of the heart we cannot infer that centre to be also its point of origin.

Let us now consider a representative sample of psychologizing current in England about 1582.

In diverse bodyes the soule is sayde to be three folde, that is to saye, *Vegetabilis*, that giveth lyfe and no feeling, and that is in plants and rootes, *Sensibilis*, that giveth life and feeling, and not reason, that is in unskilfull beastes, *Racionabilis* that giveth lyfe, feeling and reason, and this is in men. The Philosopher lykneth the soule that is called *Vegetabilis*, to a Triangle. For as a Triangle hath three corners, this manner soule hath three vertues, of begetting, of nourishing, and of growing. And this soule *Vegetabilis* is like to a Triangle in Geometrie. And hee lykneth the soule *Sensibilis* to a quadrangle square, and foure cornered. For in a Quadrangle is a line drawne from one corner to another, before it maketh two Triangles; and the soule sensible maketh two triangles of vertues. For wherever the soule sensible is, there is also the soule *Vegetabilis*, but not backwarde. And hee lykeneth the soule *Racionabilis* to a Circle, because of his perfection and conteining. (Bartolomeus Anglicanus)

About a hundred years separate this exposition of Aristotle from Locke's *Essay on Human Understanding*. Meanwhile in 1621 there is a flavour of seventeenth-century challenge in Burton's dry comment on the threefold division of the soul in the *Anatomy of Melancholy*:

How these three principal faculties are distinguished and connected . . . is beyond human capacity.

Meanwhile momentous events were occurring in astronomy and physics. Copernicus' *De Revolutionibus Orbium Caelestrium*, maintaining that the earth went round the sun, had been published in the year of his death, 1543. Apart from upsetting a lot of people, Luther not excepted, the theory was not theologically condemned till the time of Galileo. It awaited further empirical confirmation for some fifty or sixty years, that is till the sixteenth century's last and momentous decade. In the fifteen-nineties we find Kepler enthralled with it partly because of the status it gave his beloved sun:

In the first place lest perchance a blind man might deny it to you, of all the bodies in the universe the most excellent is the sun, whose whole essence is nothing else than the purest light, than which there is no greater star; which singly and alone is the producer, conserver, and warmer of all things; it is a fountain of light, rich in fruitful heat, most fair, limpid, and pure to the sight, the source of vision, portrayer of all colours, though himself empty of colour, called king of the planets for his motion, heart of the world for his power, its eye for his beauty, and which alone we should judge worthy of the Most High God, should he be pleased with a material domicile and choose a place to live in with the blessed angels.

Interested by his teacher Mästlin at Tübingen, and coming to work with Tycho Brahe, Kepler devoted his mathematical genius to supporting and developing Copernicus' explanation of natural events in terms of motion and mathematics. If H. E. Burtt is correct, it is in Kepler that we begin to see most clearly the signs of a theory of explanation based on functional dependence. With it comes the renewed separation of secondary observable qualities from those that are primary by virtue of lending themselves to advanced mathematical treatment. Such a separation hinted at in the thinking of Democritus had recently been found again in writers such as Vives and Montaigne.

Motion, mathematics, and the distinction of primary and secondary qualities come into focus even more clearly in the hands of Kepler's contemporary Galileo. His views influenced his century profoundly as part of *Il Saggiatore* suggests:*

It remains for me . . . to express my thoughts concerning the proposition: motion is the cause of heat: I will show in what way it appears to me that this is true. But first I must put forward some considerations about that which we call heat, of which I strongly suspect the generally accepted notion to be pretty far from correct, in so far as it has come to be considered a true accident, affection and quality residing in the thing by which we feel ourselves warmed. For my part I say, indeed I feel obliged to maintain, that as soon as I conceive an object or corporeal substance, I immediately think of it as limited and formed in this or that shape, that in relation to other things it is large or small, that it is in this or that place, in this or that moment, that it moves or stays still, that it touches or does not touch another body, that it is one, few, or many, indeed it cannot be separated conceptually from these conditions; but that it might be white or red, bitter or

* For this section I have relied to a considerable extent on H. E. Burtt but have ventured to differ slightly from his translation of this passage.

sweet, noisy or silent, of pleasant or unpleasant smell, by these conditions I do not feel intellectually forced to think of it as inevitably accompanied. Thus if the senses had not escorted us, perhaps reason or imagination by itself would never have arrived at them. On this account I think that these tastes, smells, colours etc., in whatever part of the object they appear to us to reside, may be none other than mere names, having their location only in the responsive body; so that if the creature were taken away, all these qualities would be removed and annihilated. Nevertheless, in so far as we have given them names that are particular and different from those of the other primary and real accidents, on this account we want to believe that they exist just as truly and genuinely as those others.

I think that I can make my meaning clearer with some examples. I move one hand now over a marble statue, now over a living man. So far as concerns events originating in the hand, whether on one object or the other they are the same in respect of the primary qualities of the hand itself, that is movement and touch, for we cannot call them anything else; but the living body which suffers such operations is affected in different ways according as it comes to be touched in different parts; if it is touched on the soles of the feet, on the knees, or in the armpits, it experiences besides the common touch another sensation to which we have given a special name, calling it tickling; which experience is completely ours and nothing to do with the hand. Anyone who wished to maintain that the hand, besides movement and touch, had in itself another distinct ability, that of tickling, would be among the seriously mistaken; in so far as the tickling were an event occurring in him. A piece of paper or a feather, lightly brushed over any part of our body that you care to choose, performs as far as it is concerned the same function everywhere, that is it is moving and touching; but in us, if touched between the eyes, on the nose or under the nostrils, it arouses an almost intolerable titillation, while in other parts it hardly makes itself felt at all. Now this tickling is entirely in us and not of the feather and if the living and sensitive body is removed it is nothing more than a mere name. Now of similar and no greater reality I believe to be many qualities which we have come to attribute to natural objects, such as tastes, smells, colours, and others.

Among these Galileo proceeds to include heat.

H. E. Burtt has pointed out that the distinction Galileo emphasized between primary and secondary qualities was the first step in the extrusion of man's experience from the scientist's world of nature. Galileo himself can easily be defended; far from being a sceptic or idealist philosopher he is much nearer a modern scientific St Michael destroying an old devilish notion of substance. In fact, however, with the extrusion of some qualities (the others soon came up for philosophic scrutiny) there tended to go a devaluation of the world as experienced. This is hinted at in Galileo's remark that we want to believe that colours, sounds, and smells are 'real' just because we have given them names. It is further suggested in the argument that without the experiencing creature they are '*only* names'.

Such devaluation of sensory experience was not of course new. It was at least as old as Plato, who in the seventeenth century, if less of an authority than Aristotle, was still very much alive and speaking to those who sought for a permanent source of support. About 1597 in Galileo's lifetime we find a charming sidelight on this from an unknown Elizabethan writing of his lady:

> I heard a noise and wishĕd for a sight,
> I looked for life and did a shadow see
> Whose substance was the sum of my delight,
> Which came unseen, and so did go from me.
> Yet hath conceit persuaded my content
> There was a substance where the shadow went.
>
> . . . .
>
> Shadow, or she, or both or choose you whither
> Blest be the thing that brought the shadow hither!
> [Ault]

Turned, however, to successful scientific account, Galileo's half-implied devaluation gave rise to enormous problems, only one of which is shown in the long struggle of psychology to win itself status as a scientific subject. Not unnaturally, human beings have been cautious of accepting a subject which, if a science, is supposedly based on extruding many of the data that go to make life as it is lived. At a trivial level, the roses and honeysuckle on my desk at the moment unite in scented protest at some unwariness in Galileo's suggestion that their smell is less 'real' than their resistance to being plucked. They find contemporary support:

> What's in a name? That which we call a rose
> By any other name would smell as sweet.

Physical scientists, whose subject only progressed in explanation and prediction when the analysis and quantification advocated by Galileo got into full swing, have equally naturally hesitated to accept as a colleague the psychologist who puts a premium on human response and whose attempts at analysis and quantification still lag very far behind.

A revised understanding of the nature of abstraction, and with it of explanation, which I do not think yet available, seems necessary before we can put our fingers on the fallacy of associating success in being quantified with distinctions in 'reality'. One aspect of the problems raised in the seventeenth century may perhaps be shown by a modern example. In the best Galilean tradition, the B.B.C. relays sound waves and light waves in certain formations. As ordinary people we do not think the transmission depends, except financially, on any radio or television set being in action. With this Galileo would agree. We think there is something peculiar, however, about maintaining that the waves transmitted are 'more real' than the symphony or Coronation that we experience on tuning in. Though we are nearly far gone enough in the Platonic aspects of Galilean science almost to swallow this pronouncement. Unthinkingly, however, we should strongly resist the suggestion that in either case we are experiencing 'the real thing' as we would in the Festival Hall or in Westminster Abbey. Physics, bedevilled by Plato, and by success in handling material and efficient causation, has tended historically to put a premium on what we may dub the relatively permanent waves. Idealist philosophers, modern logicians, and some psychologists, for reasons equally open to scrutiny, have concentrated on the unchallengeableness of experience as lived. In their extreme form, Russell's for example, their last stand for certainty is on passing experience

'Now'. Though few have been psychotic enough to hold this constantly, they have sometimes at least come in sight of maintaining that the events in the Abbey and Hall have a dream status or at best are 'hypothetical constructs' useful in marshalling sensory and emotional events or experiences. These to them either constitute the 'ultimate furniture of the world' or alternatively provide the last lorn hope of unchallengeable evidence.

As yet, common sense has disregarded both extremes and stridden off to the Hall or the Abbey when it could manage to get there. It is fair to state that Galileo's successors, the Einsteins and Infelds and Russells of our day, have been the first to warn the human race of the dangers to its entire existence of mislaying human values. The interesting theoretical problem, with an overpowering practical one lurking at its heels, is that of connecting these different and legitimate frames of reference without introducing emotional issues by references to 'reality' or 'ultimate'. A further problem is that of whether the biologist's explanation of how things develop represents a fourth frame or whether it fits legitimately into one of the other three.

To return to Galileo: he was far too great an Italian and scientist to be trapped into being an *a priori* philosopher. Though he sometimes tried to be, he was never completely enmeshed in the Platonic and mathematical search for eternal security that denigrates sense and emotion because they are known to change. He had to carry out experiments if only to convince the ignorant. Thereby hangs a tale. For the apparently flirtatious evidence of the senses on delivering her data at the front door was shut out and went round to the back. There she waited demurely as the only if passing means of verifying hypotheses and shooting down the prejudices of Padua. Being one of the greatest of physicists Galileo of course accepted her with unerring insight. Here we have him writing to his friend and colleague in Germany:

O my dear Kepler, how I wish we could have one hearty laugh together! Here at Padua is the principal professor of philosophy whom I have repeatedly and urgently requested to look at the moon and planets through my glass which he pertinaceously refuses to do. Why are you not here? What shouts of laughter we should have at this glorious folly. And to hear the professor of philosophy at Pisa labouring before the Grand Duke with logical arguments, as if with magical incantations, to charm the new planets out of the sky.

Meanwhile the empirical English, as tolerant of passing ambiguity as they are reputed to be of draughts, tended without thought to leave the garden door ajar. Through it some birds, beasts, and fishes made their way, often be it said to their own great peril. With them, however, came not only more stress on the value of observation, provided it is controlled, but also the biological notion of explanation which tries to show how one thing develops into another. In the age of the master build-ups of Bernini and Baroque, there is something curiously refreshing in the simplicity of this entrance:

We have a small shrimp in these countries, which is taken in the Thames and in the sea, the whole of whose body is transparent; this creature, placed in a little water, has frequently afforded myself and particular friends an opportunity of observing the motions of the heart with the greatest distinctness, the external parts of the body presenting no obstacle to our view, but the heart being perceived as though it had been seen through a window.

I have also observed the first rudiments of the chick in the course of the fourth or fifth day of the incubation, in the guise of a little cloud, the shell having been removed and the egg immersed in clear tepid water. In the midst of the cloudlet in question there was a bloody point so small that it disappeared during the contraction and escaped the sight, but in the relaxation it appeared again, red and like the point of a pin; so that betwixt the visible and invisible, betwixt being and not being, as it were, it gave by its pulses a kind of representation of the commencement of life.

Thus Harvey, who had studied at Padua in the time of Galileo, marshalling supporting data on the circulation of the blood. The short treatise was published at Frankfurt in 1628.

With Kepler, Galileo, and Harvey, flanked by Bacon's politically-useful support for the empirical sciences, the seventeenth-century stage is set both for the inquiries of philosophers and, I hope, for seeing where these could be exciting to their contemporaries and to us. Both the cultural history of the period and the strictly scientific developments, give character to the problems raised and show why reliable knowledge was becoming so vitally important. Chronologically, the first philosopher to take into account was one of the greatest in terms of his influence, that is Descartes.

As he is quoted fairly fully on pp. 282 ff. I will add here only three main comments to those already made on pp. 17–18. Broadly, when he thinks of matter he is largely Galilean. Matter is defined as extended substance and is subject to the laws of motion. Ideally it is treated as a self-contained mechanical system. It is worth comment that in Descartes' era mechanical gadgets were coming into cultural view much as electronic brains in our own day. When Descartes thinks of a living body he takes after Harvey, though with rather more use of animal spirits than Harvey would have approved. Physiologically the body works for Descartes on mechanical principles of a plumbing variety, save that the mind operating through the pineal gland can stall or redirect the activities of animal spirits who travel by the nerves and blood vessels. When he thinks of the mind Descartes shifts to Thomist theology coloured by a slightly Platonic notion of essence. Mind is defined as unextended thinking substance. But in the *Passions of the Soul* it is not the cause of the body's heat or movement. In fact at death it leaves the carcass when the latter is (uncomfortably?) cold and slow.

The primary qualities of extension and movement belong to the world of matter, secondary qualities are experienced by the mind when exposed to material stimulus. On strict Cartesian scientific principles, one would expect the mind's activity to be limited to registering sensations and emotions and revolving in inner reflective circles in accordance with the 'simple notions' with which it is innately endowed. In fact, and here is another concession to theology, the mind or soul has the limited function of willing by which it stalls, diverts, or calls up the rival sets of animal spirits already referred to above. This function is the essence of the '*libre arbitre*'.

Descartes' profoundest contribution to European thought lay in his development of mathematics and his defence of clearness and distinctness as criteria to be satisfied before ideas could be accepted. His views on body and mind were indefensible as they stood, specially, as noted earlier, when he added interaction between two substances which he had so defined as to make interaction impossible. What we can say in Descartes' defence is that historically he was unrivalled in bringing impossible problems to the fore. To his credit he at least tried to retain a place in the world for psychological initiative.

It is also possible that, indirectly, by his attempt to separate psychological functioning so sharply from physical, Descartes enabled physical science to make progress comparatively unmolested by theological politics.

The inconsistencies in Descartes' thought were seen at the time to be so flagrant that some, such as Hobbes, suspected him of uncourageous motives. Spinoza pointed more simply to the problems left unsolved. Into Descartes' deepest feelings it is senseless to probe three hundred years later. It is of more general interest that most of the scientific philosophers of the seventeenth century still thought in an atmosphere that took religion for granted even if they felt justified in questioning scriptural authority. Most, in fact, evolved systems wherein God was needed in some form to guarantee veracity or beneficence. Descartes was no exception. Faced alike with the deceptiveness of the senses and with the chances of error in deduction, not to mention the logical possibility that the world and man's knowledge of it was made by a malignant demon with deliberate intent to deceive, Descartes is supported by thinking, by clarity, and by his trust in a kindly Creator. Some say that in the *Cogito* he stopped short too soon and 'I think therefore I am' is an illegitimate extension of 'there is doubting'. In fact as Descartes uses the *Cogito* his theory of knowledge needs God, and if one must have certainty the position is hard to argue.

'From 1637, the date of the *Discours*, the relation between matter and mind, body and soul, was a cardinal problem – *the* cardinal problem. Descartes had awarded to each substance co-ordinate, independent, absolute rights. The future business of Cartesianism was to find a *trait d'union* – an explanation for a relation in fact which had been demonstrated in theory inconceivable' (Pogson Smith).

Now let us turn from Descartes to Hobbes (1588–1679). He has been described as thinking in this dualism while being one of its most resolute opponents. An empirical realist by temperament and experience, coming to mathematics only after he was forty, Hobbes had visited Galileo in Padua and was familiar with Descartes' thought. That Francis Bacon had found Hobbes a congenial amanuensis is a tribute more to Bacon than to Hobbes, who must have been an explosively intelligent secretary. The association may possibly be relevant to Hobbes' desire to rough in a theory of human nature for social and political reasons: 'Let one man read another by his actions never so perfectly, it serves him onely with his acquaintance, which are but few. He that is to govern a whole Nation, must read in himself, not this or that particular man; but man-kind.' In this he surely glimpses a practical need to go outside one's own limited experience by whatever means available. At its best the twentieth century is more cautious of claiming to have the means, than this somewhat over-confident ancestor.

Hobbes nevertheless puts us to shame as a writer. Descartes' enormous asset in advocating clarity was the lovely lucidity of a leading French stylist – writing as an officer in a German stove in the midst of the Thirty Years' War. Hobbes' is the writing of a trenchant individualist who abominated illusion in himself and in others. He has a force and fury which Bacon cannot touch and a wicked wit which Descartes would not have dared to release. From our vantage point he can be seen as reviving the views of Democritus (also latent in Galileo) or as anticipating some Behaviourism. Emotionally he writes at times as if he were 'tone-deaf', but if one may comment on a question of taste he remains for the most part uproariously unpuerile.

Hobbes has been described by a provocative essayist as deserving a place among masters of English theology. But piety it may be said was not his main trait. His royalism, which was passionate, offended the parliamentarians, so he deemed it advisable to take refuge in France. There in turn his rationalism offended a Catholic government. He returned to England, made his peace with Cromwell, and abstained for a while from political writings, his collected works being published eventually

(1688) in Amsterdam. At the Restoration of Charles II he returned to uncertain favour on which we have evidence from Aubrey and Pepys: 'there was a report (and surely true) that in Parliament, not long after the King was settled, some bishops made a motion to have the good old gentleman burnt for a heretique.' A fellow of Corpus Christi was forced to recant his Hobbism, but Hobbes, though frightened, was not in fact burnt. The main result Pepys tells us was to send up the price of his books. I mention all this here to point a changing outlook. Hobbes is remembered by most as the man who said of life that it was 'nasty, brutish and short'. They forget that this comes from a description of life as it is in a 'state of Warre' and Hobbes thought it deplorable. Aubrey's notes reveal him as 6 feet tall or above, raven-haired, ginger-whiskered, and (to live longer) singing to keep himself healthy. At the age of 84 he wrote his own life in Latin verse having 'nothing else to do'. At 87, he produced a translation of Homer. Russell 'cannot find' that Hobbes wrote any large books after that age.

Now what were Hobbes' views on the nature of body and mind? The briefest answer is 'materialist'. Starting from Galileo's view that there are external objects in motion and in relation to others, Hobbes defined sensation in terms of the direct or indirect impact of external bodies or objects on the organs proper to each sense: 'which pressure, by the mediation of Nerves, and other strings, and membranes of the body, continued inwards to the Brain, and Heart, causeth there a resistance, or counter-pressure, or endeavour of the heart, to deliver itself: which endeavour because *Outward*, seemeth to be some matter without. And this *seeming*, or *fancy*, is that which men call *Sense*.' In other words, the attribution to external things of qualities coloured by our own experience, which Galileo debited to inveterate belief that anything named is 'real', Hobbes explained by the projection of resistance. What we call sense 'consisteth as to the Eye, in a Light or Colour figured; To the Eare in a Sound' and so on through the senses. 'All which qualities called Sensible, are not in the object that causeth them, but so many several motions of the matter, by which it presseth our organs diversely.' So far so good.

Imagination is decaying sense. Dreams are the imaginations of them that sleep and have been before 'either totally or by parcells in the Sense'. In the long run, the distinction between vision and a waking or sleeping dream boils down to coherence in practice: 'because waking I often observe the absurdity of Dreames, but never dream of the absurdities of my waking Thoughts; I am well satisfied, that being awake I know I dreame not; though when I dreame, I think myself awake'. In Hobbes' opinion, ignorance of how to distinguish dreams and other strong fancies from sensation was largely responsible for the 'Religion of the Gentiles' and the 'opinion rude people have of Fayries, Ghosts and Goblins; and of the power of Witches'. These last he considered justly punished not because they had any power but for their false belief in their power and intent to use it maliciously. But looking at the Scottish witch trials of his lifetime one cannot but hesitate.

Now Hobbes proceeded to try to work out a consistent theory of human behaviour assuming only two kinds of motion (vital as in generation, animal or voluntary as in moving our limbs), sense and its derivatives, desire and aversion, the laws of association, and the capacity on the part of man to think symbolically by means of language. Desire and aversion are explained as endeavours 'towards' or 'away'. Symbolic thinking enables man to evolve general laws of a causal and mathematical nature. With this equipment Hobbes was led to maintain that:

The Felicity of this life consisteth not in the repose of a mind satisfied. For there is no such *Finis Ultimus* (utmost ayme) nor *Summum Bonum* (Greatest Good) as is spoken of in the Books of the old Morall Philosophers. Nor can a man any more live, whose Desires are at an end, than he, whose Senses and Imaginations are at a stand. Felicity is a continuall progresse of the desire, from one object to another; the attaining of the former, being still but the way to the later. The cause whereof is, That the object of man's desire, is not to enjoy once onely, and for one instant of time; but to assure for ever, the way of his future desire. And therefore the voluntary actions, and inclinations of all men, tend, not onely to the procuring, but also to the assuring of a contented life; and differ only in the way: which ariseth partly from the

diversity of passions, in divers men; and partly from the difference of the knowledge, or opinion each one has of the causes,
which produce the effect desired.

So that in the first place, I put for a generale inclination of all
mankind, a perpetuall and restlesse desire of Power after power,
that ceaseth only in Death.

If this is Hobbes' 'materialism' it is lively and dangerous
rather than stagnant, but it is determined. One is tempted sometimes to suppose that, having accepted material objects as
moving, Hobbes simply forgot about the belief that their movements are subject to law and so assumed 'voluntary motion'
without any further ado. In fact he so defined 'fancy', and
voluntary motion in terms of it, that the consistent determinism
he advocated in argument with Bishop Bramhall can just be
maintained. He does not make the common mistake of excluding
man's determined striving from the contributory causes of
events. How to distinguish speech that is reasonable and therefore is reasoning from that which is not, presents for Hobbes, as
it does for orthodox Behaviourists, a harder problem on the
principles laid down.

When we turn from Hobbes to Spinoza, whom he and Descartes clearly influenced, we encounter one of those rare spirits
who move independently, lacking illusion, through a universe
still loved. In living and in thinking his sense of style is unrivalled. Here to his credit is Oldenburg, Secretary of the newly
founded Royal Society, trying to persuade Spinoza to publish:

I would by all means advise you not to begrudge to the learned
those works in philosophy and theology, which you have composed with the talent that distinguishes you. Publish them, I beg,
whatever be the verdict of petty theologians. Your country is
free; the course of philosophy should there be free also. Your
own prudence will, doubtless, suggest to you, that your ideas and
opinions should be put forth as quietly as possible. For the rest,
commit the issue to fortune. Come, then, good sir, cast away all
fear of exciting against you the pygmies of our time. Long enough
have we sacrificed to ignorance and pedantry. Let us spread the
sails of true knowledge, and explore the recesses of nature more
thoroughly than hereto.

Spinoza's major work, the *Ethics*, wherein he presents his views in geometrical form, is, however, as difficult as any theoretically intelligible philosophical writing can be. (I do not count those German philosophers in whom mystification is merit.) If I attempt to extract the core of Spinoza's system as it affects us, I do so with more than usual diffidence and desire to refer to what a supreme artist says for himself.

Spinoza's aim in writing was ethical, namely: so to help man understand his position in the world that he could achieve the blessedness potentially open to him and, one may add, cease to be afraid. Defined as an entity whose non-existence cannot be conceived, substance for Spinoza can be but one, that is the entire universe. Modern logicians have argued that he reached this position by tacitly assuming a subject-predicate rather than a relational logic. If they are right, Spinoza's standpoint for all its magnificence and rationality need not necessarily be accepted. There is a sense, the argument runs, in which his 'substance' is technically the logical subject of all attributes. But if a logical subject can also be the term of a relation such as 'equals', and such relations are as plausible as predicates, then not only can there be more than one substance in the technical sense but in fact there must be more than one.

Be that as it may, for Spinoza one sufficed. Conceived as having spatial characteristics, *Natura naturata*, it is the whole of infinitely extended nature. Conceived as spiritual or thinking, *Natura naturans*, it is infinitely active, spontaneous, sublime, and divine. In fact it is God. There is the clear suggestion in Spinoza that he is using matter and mind, extension and thought, as two frames of reference from which the whole universe can be considered. They are, however, logically different frames of reference and must not be confused. In considering particulars Spinoza is quite clear: 'mind and body are one and the same thing, conceived first under the attribute of thought, secondly under the attribute of extension.'

As Spinoza so defines substance that there can be only one, thought and extension being its two infinite attributes, individual minds and bodies have to be seen from one point of view as limited modulations or modes of something much greater.

Nevertheless it is perfectly legitimate and even desirable to abstract from the whole and treat the modes that are individual persons in relative isolation. Such a worm's eye view is incomplete but workable. Spinoza was not of those so paralysed by uncertainty in understanding the whole of life that they hesitated to live it. He had a sense of irony and the worm analogy is his own. Man *sub specie aeternitatis* is nevertheless but a facet of the whole. In the long run his blessedness consists in understanding and accepting this humble position in a whole scheme of happenings which is God, and which is the only subject of which freedom in the sense of complete self-determination can be predicated.

There are three main degrees of human understanding, of which the third and highest is a species of profound intellectual insight and acquiescence. Modes, themselves finite and always to some extent determined, achieve increasing spontaneity as they get nearer and nearer to achieving this insight, which, for Spinoza, carries with it a capacity to identify with the system in which they both realize and accept their role. Just as the whole system determines itself, so also it is in the nature of finite modes to persist in their own being, which is the same as achieving bodily and mentally the maximum possible active integration and insight into the universe. (On the detailed bodily aspects of this we quote Spinoza, pp. 325 ff.). Most of us fall far short of what we could achieve; to no mode is infinite achievement possible. We are ourselves to the extent that we actively participate in a necessitated freedom and acquiesce in so doing. To glimpse the grandeur he endeavours to understate let us cite these passages near the end of the *Ethics*.

In proportion as the mind is more capable of understanding things by the third kind of knowledge, it desires more to understand things by that kind.

From this third kind of knowledge arises the highest possible mental acquiescence.

Whatsoever we understand by the third kind of knowledge, we take delight in, and our delight is accompanied by the idea of God as cause.

The intellectual love of God, which arises from the third kind of knowledge, is eternal.

The intellectual love of the mind towards God is part of the infinite love wherewith God loves himself.

This love of the mind must be referred to the activities of the mind; it is itself, indeed, an activity whereby the mind regards itself accompanied by the idea of God as cause; that is an activity whereby God, in so far as he can be explained by the human mind, regards himself accompanied by the idea of himself; therefore this love of the mind is part of the infinite love wherewith God loves himself.

Hence it follows that God, in so far as he loves himself, loves man, and, consequently, that the love of God towards men, and the intellectual love of the mind towards God are identical.

From what has been said we clearly understand wherein our salvation, or blessedness, or freedom consists: namely, in the constant and eternal love towards God, or in God's love towards men. This love or blessedness is, in the Bible, called Glory, and not undeservedly. For whether this love be referred to God or to the mind, it may be rightly called acquiescence of spirit, which is not really distinguished from glory.

[from *Ethics*: v, 26 to 36]

Those encountering Spinoza for the first time may need some help in recognizing the steely resilience that pervades his system. While here obvious, it is often masked by fierce aloofness as the argument proceeds. One may make the point by contrasting Spinoza with Freud who shared certain views and also Hebrew culture: Freud's world sometimes savours of Galileo's, without its Maker, defended by a Victorian and haunted by Goethe's devil – '*Ich bin der Geist der stets verneint*'. Spinoza occasionally verges on resignation; despair was something he was near enough to know. But the positive evil of final negation hasn't a chance. His universe with all its austere impersonality, and it is very austere, is the all in all to a man who knows persecution, is dying, but in whom living is undefeated. In his artistry Spinoza is rivalled perhaps by the *Phaedo*, but not by much else. I do not think one realizes this until the geometrical writing suddenly proves the most satisfying. Even here, though more in his correspondence, we can detect his friendliness and his tolerance as well as his integrity: 'assuredly nothing forbids man to enjoy himself, save grim and gloomy superstition'.

We can hardly be surprised that Spinoza's thinking was opposed. If God is nature and nature is extended, then, said his critics, Spinoza is a peculiarly heretical pantheist. If man's behaviour is determined within a system and praise and blame are in the long run senseless, then Spinoza is seeking to undermine the whole basis of morality. It was of little avail for Spinoza to believe that frightened piety is a travesty of goodness and the behaviour of a wicked man no less harmful because it happens to be necessary. In that case, said the onlookers, on your view God must willingly cause evil. Here is a summary of a five-page letter from the Dutch merchant Blyenbergh, in hot pursuit, with part of Spinoza's answer.

If our essence is equivalent to our state at a given time, we are as perfect when sinning as when virtuous: God would wish for vice as much as virtue. Both the virtuous and the vicious execute God's will – what is the difference between them? You say some actions are more perfect than others; wherein does this perfection consist? If a mind existed so framed, that vice was in agreement with its proper nature, why should such a mind prefer good to evil? If God makes us all that we are, how can we 'go astray'? . . . If we have no free will are not our actions God's actions, and our will God's will? I could ask several more questions but do not venture.

He adds another in a postscript. 'Whether we cannot by foresight avert what would otherwise happen to us?'

Spinoza's answer turns among other things on arguing that evil and essence are incompatible and it is essence that is determined by God. Things differ in essence as well as in degree. 'A mouse no less than an angel depends on God; yet a mouse is not a kind of angel, neither is sorrow a kind of joy.' An action or a person may be perfect though unblessed, blessedness being at variance with those dispositions called bad:

Lastly, as to your third question, it assumes a contradiction, and seems to me to be as though one asked: If it agreed better with a man's nature that he should hang himself, could any reasons be given for his not hanging himself? Can such a nature possibly exist? If so, I maintain (whether I do or do not grant free will), that such an one, if he sees that he can live more conveniently on the gallows than sitting at his own table, would act most foolishly if he did not hang himself. So anyone who clearly saw that, by committing crimes, he would enjoy a really more perfect and better life and existence than he could attain by the practice of virtue, would be foolish if he did not act on his convictions. For, with such a perverse human nature as his, crime would become a virtue. As to the other question, which you add in your postscript, seeing that one might ask a hundred such in an hour, without arriving at a conclusion about any, and seeing that you yourself do not press for an answer, I will send none.

With this and the quotations on pp. 305 ff. I leave the reader to assess these arguments and to produce better ones within or outside Spinoza's system. He may ask himself in passing whether Spinoza begs a question, by so using '*conatus*' that it cannot be evil, while defining goodness as that which we desire. The question is a genuine one for anthropological Freudians ill-content with an ideal of 'local adjustment'.

Leibniz, after Spinoza, is a greater scholar and lesser man – or perhaps we mean that to us he was not so obviously blessed. Except for three points, Leibniz's thought, though eventually influential, seems to me less immediately interesting to psychology than that of Hobbes and Spinoza to whom on this account I have given more space. The three points are: first, the faint suggestion of degrees of consciousness which lurks in Spinoza's three kinds of knowledge turns, in the hands of an inventor of the calculus, into infinite shades of awareness. Leibniz, as can be seen from p. 336, thought in terms of focal and peripheral attention, rather than consciousness and unconsciousness in the current meanings, but he contributed none the less. Secondly, there is a sense in which he attempted to combine mechanical and purposive explanation by making all his units or 'monads' have some degree of vitality and responsiveness at the start. This is interesting and saved him from the Cartesian view of animals as machines. Thirdly, though the full-blown lunacy of the 'Pre-Established Harmony' should at least be a warning to those who explain bodily events by efficient, and mental events by final, causes and think no more, it is fascinating in relation to problems of modern learning theory.

Leibniz is quoted fully on pp. 330 ff. Let us here give the briefest possible statement of his system as it reflects his views on body-mind relations. There are simple substances or monads everywhere, all having some degree of vitality and of which some form the centres and unifying principles of clusters of others. The mass of an infinity of other monads surrounding a central one constitutes that monad's body. Each monad with a particular body forms a living substance. When the monad has perception accompanied by memory, i.e., perception of which a certain echo long remains, such a living being is called an animal and its monad a soul. When this soul is raised to reason it is reckoned among spirits. Each monad is a living mirror of the universe from its own vantage-point. Its perceptions are produced according to the laws of desires or final causes of good and evil. The changes of bodies and external phenomena follow the laws of efficient causes, i.e. of motion. God, the highest monad, established a harmony from the beginning between the laws of efficient and final causes. 'It is in this way that soul and body are in agreement and are physically united, while it is not possible for the one to change the laws of the other'.

Further into Leibniz I propose not to go, but to add some comments on pp. 330–1 where readers will find they can consult his more subtle statements for themselves.

By the time we reach Leibniz (1646–1716) we are stretching into the eighteenth century. Before doing this irrevocably we must pick up the threads of English empiricism in Locke (1632–1704). As one after the other of the great arguments roll on, we come nearer to sympathy with the untidy-minded, hard-working, politically-observant doctor who presented himself compared with his colleagues – Boyle, Huygens, Newton, and the like – as an under-labourer employed in removing some of the rubbish that lies in the way to knowledge.

I shall not at present meddle with the physical consideration of the mind, or trouble myself to examine wherein its essence consists, or by what motions of our spirits, or alterations of our bodies, we come to have any sensations by our organs, or any ideas in our understandings; and whether those ideas do in their formation, any or all of them, depend on matter or no. These are speculations which, however curious and entertaining, I shall decline, as lying out of my way in the design I am now upon.

In effect Locke's alternative aim was to take a working understanding for granted and give a plain and historical 'account of the ways whereby our understandings come to attain those notions of things we have'. Under this he included inquiry into the origins of these notions, the certainty, evidence, and extent of the knowledge supplied and the nature and grounds of faith and opinion.

If by this inquiry into the nature of the understanding, I can discover the powers thereof, *how far* they reach, to what things they are in any degree proportionate, and where they fail us, I suppose it may be of use to prevail with the busy mind of man to be more cautious in meddling with things exceeding its comprehension, to stop when it is at the utmost of its tether, and to sit down in quiet ignorance of those things which, upon examination, are found to be beyond the reach of our capacities. We should not then, perhaps, be so forward, out of an affectation of an universal knowledge, to raise questions, and perplex ourselves and others with disputes about things to which our understandings are not suited, and of which we cannot frame in our minds any clear or distinct perceptions; or whereof (as it has, perhaps, too often happened) we have not any notions at all. If we can find out how far the understanding can extend its view, how far it has faculties to attain certainty, and in what cases it can only judge and guess, we may learn to content ourselves with what is attainable by us in this state.

Mind, for Locke, was a *tabula rasa* open to the imprint of experience, matter ended as an unknowable substratum. More of Locke's position can be inferred from Chapter 7. Here it is important for us that Locke tried to launch a study of how a working mind works and was willing to consider criteria for assent that falls short of certainty. This returns us to some general considerations.

*

Seventeenth-century scientific thought revolted in the name of evidence that could be checked. On questions of matter and mind it represented, as we have just seen, a challenge to authority, a threat particularly to the dominance of Aristotle and of any Aristotelian theology that sought to limit inquiry. This meant both gain and loss. The gain lay in the legacy of freedom to inquire and fascination of inquiry which the seventeenth century bequeathed to its successor. On the other hand, in spite of Harvey and Leibniz, we had later to re-discover the ideas of growth and development to be found in Aristotle and Aquinas.

Much of seventeenth-century thought can also be seen as a search for certainty. Both the English empirical and nominalist tradition (with its earlier roots but becoming obvious in Francis Bacon and Hobbes) and the continental rationalist trends can be viewed as ways, though diverse, of seeking a sure foundation of knowledge when a universal theology no longer held sway and in witch hunts, superstition, religious wars and their aftermath, the worst aspects of fantasy and fanaticism were clearly revealed. In most thinkers, both English and Continental, this search was consciously inspired by desire to place better knowledge at the service of mankind. The directions in which they sought were, however, different. From the outset the English concentrated on the content of knowledge and gave prime place to its origin in the senses. With this, in fact, was linked a willingness to let general rules emerge. Continental thinkers more naturally turned inward to scrutinize the forms of thought, taking the certainty of mathematics as their paradigm. A lifetime could go in trying to explain the personal and cultural sources of this important divergence.

Whatever its origins, I want tentatively to suggest that it may have concealed a difference in outlook on uncertainty itself and a difference in outlook on the nature of explanation. To focus the difference in attitude to uncertainty, let us consider two thinkers less profoundly influential than those we have encountered so far: Sir Thomas Browne and Pascal.

There are few more individual, serenely inconsistent, uninfluential, and, to the English, intelligible people than the Norwich doctor. His *Religio Medici* is a resilient spider's web woven over chasms of doubt and mysticism alike. He can be downright, he can call in question anything. At the same time he insists, if he must have fantasies, on having ones that are decently un-believable on any rational grounds.

In our study of Anatomy there is a mass of mysterious Philosophy, and such as reduced the very Heathens to Divinity: yet, amongst all those rare discoveries and curious pieces I find in the Fabrick of Man, I do not so much content myself, as in that I find not, there is no Organ or Instrument for the rational Soul; for in the brain, which we term the seat of Reason, there is not any thing of moment more than I can discover in the crany of a beast: and this is a sensible and no inconsiderable argument of the inorganity of the Soul, at least in that sense we usually so receive it. Thus we are men, and we know not how: there is something in us that can be without us, and will be after us; though it is strange that it hath no history what it was before us, nor cannot tell how it entred in us.

Now, for these walls of flesh, wherein the Soul doth seem to be immured before the Resurrection, it is nothing but an elemental composition, and a Fabrick that must fall to ashes. *All flesh is grass*, is not onely metaphorically, but litterally, true; for all these creatures we behold are but the herbs of the field, digested into flesh in them, or more remotely carnified in our selves.

For contrast let us turn from Browne to his greater French contemporary, inwardly racked by the inescapable uncertainties which for Browne are of peripheral importance.

Voilà notre état véritable; c'est ce qui nous rend incapables de savoir certainement et d'ignorer absolument. Nous voguons sur un milieu vaste, toujours incertains et flottants, poussés d'un bout vers l'autre. Quelque terme où nous pensions nous attacher et nous affermir, il branle et nous quitte; et si nous le suivons, il échappe à nos prises, nous glisse et fuit d'une fuite éternelle. Rien ne s'arrête pour nous. C'est l'état qui nous est naturel, et toutefois le plus contraire à notre inclination; nous brûlons de désir de trouver une assiette ferme, et une dernière base constante, pour y édifier une tour qui s'élève à l'infini, mais tout notre fondement craque, et la terre s'ouvre jusqu'aux abîmes.

To point the difference between the related English and continental attitudes to explanation it is useful to borrow D'Alembert and Cassirer's distinction between '*l'esprit de système*' and '*l'esprit systématique*'. The former emphasizes the *a priori* and inner consistency; explanation consists in showing that an event is deducible from the principles laid down at the outset. Stuart Hampshire makes use of this notion of explanation in expounding Spinoza. For *l'esprit systématique* the desire to systematize may be equally strong, but principles are derived from observational data. Facts and laws are 'objective' in the sense of being there to be discovered, but the formulation of general laws remains logically open to modification. In the long run this line of thought seems to lead to successful prediction as the criterion of adequate explanation.

L'esprit de système would flourish on unwilling and passionate doubt. It seems to me reflected in Descartes and Leibniz as well as Spinoza, though with an important difference. In all three thinkers mathematical influence is marked. In Descartes and Leibniz, however, one seems also to detect authoritarian elements in keeping with aspects of the culture to which they were otherwise opposed, though both are too complex and interesting as people to be lightly dismissed with this epithet. For instance, in Leibniz's attempt to follow Contarini in finding some bridge between warring theologies, and in the tussle with Bossuet that ensued, he emerges eventually with those who fought to be free.

To Spinoza, 'authoritarian' is in no sense applicable, even though we can see elements which in lesser folk might easily have turned that way. In fact a personal ease and humility and an eastern capacity to feel at one with the world, combined with western sympathy for individual '*conatus*', placed him beyond his century's understanding. The *Ethics* could not be published till after his death. Alive he was heretic and outcast to Jew and Christian alike. Twentieth-century psychology, forgetting Bain, is only just beginning to seek in him a better guide than Descartes.

The English seventeenth century had plenty of searing doubts. When they were not directed outwards in the business of tackling constitutional problems (or just in finding how the heart *does* work), they tended to be given private and personal expression, as for instance in Donne, in whom Harding detects a fear of not responding fully to living. (One wonders if such a fear would have been open to a medieval man.)

The doubtings of English philosophers have a cool and practical flavour. They are reflected in empirical searching rather than in the building of *a priori* systems. Bacon, said Harvey, wrote of science like a Lord Chancellor, and one can see what Harvey meant. But Bacon could talk some very good sense (see pp. 273 ff.). Quotation is not necessary to show that for him the general rule must emerge from collecting observable facts. Hobbes was greatest as a trenchant stimulator. For all his use of mechanical explanation he was by no means a great mathematician and his psychology is a cock shy put forward as a basis for discussion. When frightened into the autocratic, as he certainly was, it savours of the 'exigencies of the service'. He remains at heart uneasy with things laid down from on high and invokes a Royal force 'freely elected' for want of a better answer. Of Newton's claim to mathematical distinction there is of course no question. Even his laws, however, appear linked to observation in a spirit remote from the Leibniz of the *Monadology*. Locke was not even tempted to entertain authority: 'It is not worth while to be concerned what he says or thinks, who says, or thinks only as he is directed by another'. Whitehead has noted, and even suggests that Harvey already saw, the inadequacy of Bacon's notions of induction as an account of the processes whereby scientific generalizations come to be established. For all that Bacon was far from lost in simple enumeration. *L'esprit systématique*, which Cassirer sees as colouring the thought of the eighteenth century, can count him as an ally, and it had something profoundly useful to contribute. Its roots seem to have been nurtured in this earlier English soil.

At the close of the seventeenth century France and England at any rate seem more innured to doubt, partly through the political and cultural circumstances at which we glanced earlier. We cannot do justice here to the complex contributory factors, such as horizons widened by travel, doubts about miracles, the over-playing of classicism, Bayle's scepticism and the hostility aroused by revocation of the Edict of Nantes, so brilliantly portrayed by Hazard in *La Crise de la conscience européenne*. Suffice it that between 1680 and 1715 there developed an atmosphere in which, for instance, a Locke who not only wrote on toleration, but cited uneasiness as the very stuff of living, could be read and understood. In the eighteenth century the carrier and catalyst who turned circumstance to account was, of course, Voltaire.

REFERENCES

Alembert, J. Le Rond d'. See Cassirer

Aubrey, John. *Brief Lives*. Ed. Andrew Clark. Oxford: Clarendon Press, 1898, Vol. I, pp. 321 ff.

Ault, Norman (Editor). *Elizabethan Lyrics*. London: Longmans, 1925, p. 233

Bamborough, J. B. *The Little World of Man*. London: Longmans, 1952, p. 31

Bartolomeus Anglicanus. See Bamborough, *The Little World of Man*, p. 31

Browne, Sir Thomas. *Religio Medici*. London: Dent (Everyman's Library), 1937, pp. 41–2. New York: E. P. Dutton and Co. Inc.

Burtt, H. E. *The Metaphysical Foundations of Modern Physical Science*. London: Kegan Paul, 1925, Chaps. 1–5 and pp. 48, 66–7

Burton, Robert. See Bamborough, *The Little World of Man*, p. 31

Cassirer, Ernst. *The Philosophy of the Enlightenment*. Princeton, New Jersey: Princeton University Press, 1951, Chap. I.

Evelyn, John. *Diary*, ed. William Bray. London: Dent (Everyman's Library), 2 vols., 1952

Fisher, H. A. L. *History of Europe*. London: Arnold, 1943, Bk II, Chaps. XIV, XV, XVI, XVII, XX, pp. 607, 608, 662. (Extract reproduced by permission of Messrs Eyre and Spottiswoode, Curtis Brown & Co., and the Houghton Mifflin Co., New York)

Galileo Galilei. *Il Saggiatore*, in *Prose Scelte* edited by Augusto Conti. Firenze: Barbera, 1891. Cap. XXIII, pp. 131–3, cf. Burtt, p. 75

Hampshire, Stuart. *Spinoza*. Harmondsworth: Penguin Books, 1951

Harding, D. W. 'Coherence of Theme in Donne's Poetry', *The Kenyon Review*, XIII, 2, 1951

Harvey, William. *The Circulation of the Blood*. London: Dent (Everyman's Library), 1952, p. 36

Hauser, Arnold. *The Social History of Art*. London: Routledge and Kegan Paul, 1951, Vol. I, pp. 353–422

Hazard, Paul. *The European Mind (1680–1715)*. Trans. J. L. May from *La Crise de la conscience européenne*. London: Hollis and Carter, 1953

Hobbes, Thomas. *Leviathan*, reprinted from the edition of 1651. Oxford: Clarendon Press, 1909, pp. 10, 11–12, 13, 15–16, 17, 75

Kepler, Johannes. See Burtt, H. E. *The Metaphysical Foundations of Modern Physical Science*, pp. 48 and 66–7

Locke, John. *An Essay Concerning Human Understanding*, Abridged and edited by A. S. Pringle-Pattison. Oxford: Clarendon Press, 1924, pp. 10, 11, 11–12

Nordenskiöld, E. *The History of Biology*. Trans. from the Swedish by R. B. Eyre. New York: Tudor Publishing Co., 1946, Part I, Chap. XIV

Oldenburg, H. See Spinoza Correspondence, p. 285

Pascal, Blaise. *Pensées et Opuscules*, edited by M. L. Brunschvicg. Paris: Hachette. 18th Edn. p. 354

Pepys, Samuel. See Smith, Pogson, p. xxix

Russell, Bertrand. *History of Western Philosophy*. London: Allen and Unwin, 1946, p. 570

Smith, Pogson. 'The Philosophy of Hobbes', in *Hobbes' Leviathan*. Oxford: Clarendon Press, 1909, p. xviii

Spinoza, Benedict de. *The Chief Works of Benedict de Spinoza*. Trans. R. H. M. Elwes. London: Bell, 1884, Vol. II 'Ethics' Bk. V. Props. 26 to 36 and 'Correspondence', p. 285

Whitehead, A. North. *Science and the Modern World*. New York: Macmillan, 1926, pp. 63 ff.

CHAPTER 7

EIGHTEENTH-CENTURY ADAPTATION

Know then thyself, presume not God to scan;
The proper study of Mankind is Man.
Plac'd on this isthmus of a middle state,
A Being darkly wise and rudely great:
With too much knowledge for the Sceptic side,
With too much weakness for the Stoic's pride,
He hangs between; in doubt to act, or rest;
In doubt to deem himself a God or Beast;
In doubt his Mind or Body to prefer;
Born but to die and reas'ning but to err.

POPE, *Essay on Man*

IN so far as body and mind concern this history of psychology, the most interesting people in the eighteenth century were Berkeley, Butler, Hume, and Hartley on this side of Europe; and Condillac, Cabanis, and Pinel in France. In the second half of the century Kant looms in the background at Königsberg, of indirect importance in giving additional impetus to the 'active', in contrast to 'mechanical', treatments of mental functioning which take us into the nineteenth century. In Kant, too, lies the belief not in innate ideas, but in innate ways of structuring experience.

On the whole, the social and economic history of the period is of much more direct interest than the political, provided that to orientate ourselves we recall the following: the rise of English influence, including industrial; the decline of central power in France which was still compatible with her immense role as transmitter of culture; the achievement of American Independence; the French Revolution; and, after 1763, the rise of Prussia under Frederick the Great, who started the fashion of enlightened despotism.

The social and economic background to eighteenth-century thinking is quite beyond the scope of this introduction and only the barest references can be made to it. We are entering the era in which, under the pressure of stark need, interest shifted further from eternity and towards man's life in time. It is the period wherein Huizinga's second path (cf. p. 51) to an ideal life began to tempt the enlightened, who, from the mid-century onwards, sought to give it more concrete expression. One outward reflection of this practical turn of interest was the revision of laws. These, if culture-linked and man-made as Montesquieu maintained, should be capable of improvement in a sense that 'divine' laws were not. People seeking 'happiness' sought it not too far ahead; some were more simply seeking necessities of life. With some faint promise of better alternatives, a few people challenged avoidable pain and illness, inadequate transport, and the kind of sanitation that encourages plague. Even Hume left £50 to his brother to install a 'good main drain'. In this respect Hume was in line with a century that began by trying out inoculation against smallpox and ended with Jenner discovering vaccination.

This is not to suggest that improvement in living conditions was uniform. It was not; and that in itself constituted one of the major problems. At one extreme the century was as quietly dignified as Church Row, Hampstead, as maturely intelligent as Gainsborough's *White Lady* and as full of style and vitality as the best of the Whig aristocracy. It could be as enchanting as a Watteau drawing or the Boucher *Madame de Pompadour* who ekes out immortality in the possession of the Scots. At the other extreme it out-Hogarthed Hogarth in poverty, vice, and squalor; unimaginative vice being by no means confined to those who were abominably poor.

With these echoes of problems in the background, let us turn to the eighteenth-century philosophers to go mining in a few directions, remembering also that the seventeenth had provided a steam engine for pumping out water, a microscope for examining biological specimens, a calculating machine, and a pocket clock to keep people from dawdling. Technical invention, at first slow, gathered momentum as the eighteenth century led into the nineteenth, and it maintained this speed; until once again some people seek to explain our thinking with the aid of mechanical analogies.

Of the eighteenth-century writers the first to concern us is

Berkeley. He is to be found entering Trinity College, Dublin, in 1700 to pursue his studies in an atmosphere already alive to Newton, Locke, and the Deism of Toland's *Christianity not Mysterious*. In 1713 he proceeded on logical grounds to attack Locke's 'unknowable substratum' in the *Dialogues between Hylas and Philonous*. Berkeley belongs to the seventeenth century in the speculative sweep of his effort to dispose of material substance. It has been suggested that, like many people, he projected on to it a horror of impurity and inertia. Berkeley's denial of the reality of matter is not a denial of the world around us, but a statement that it consists of perceived ideas. As Russell has commented, it is really a statement of the relativity of perception, though Berkeley claimed for it more. For him, the unquestioned persistence of what we call physical objects, which consist of ideas, is guaranteed by the 'Permanent Perceiver' who is God. The famous limericks summarizing his view remain the neatest of mnemonics:

> There was a young man who said God
> Must think it exceedingly odd
> If he finds that this tree
> Continues to be
> When there's no one about in the Quad.

> Dear Sir:
> Your astonishment's odd:
> *I* am always about in the Quad.
> And that's why the tree
> Will continue to be,
> Since observed by
> *Yours faithfully*,
> God.

Berkeley belongs to the eighteenth century in the persuasive limpidness of his style, from which the grand manner is wholly absent. In addition, he belongs most significantly to the ring of thinkers who, this side of the Channel, were intellectual matches for the more destructive proponents of Deism. More of this in a moment, when we discuss Butler.

Finally, Berkeley is a modern in his direct attack on the problem of how we see, and in the way he uses sensations of touch to throw light on perceptions of distance and size. He is modern too, though far from aware of it, in that his system of knowledge, which has the Lockian flavour of being derived from the senses, leaves Berkeley a difficulty in accounting for knowledge of the 'self'. In his later writings he appears to have met this in part by introducing 'notions' and mental 'acts' as well as ideas (in his special sense) as different sources of knowledge. We could, he thought, have a 'notion' of the self. Brett, on the basis of the *Siris*, portrays Berkeley quoting Willis and toying with a 'vital flame' that might 'constitute the animal spirit or immediate vehicle of the soul'. Here ancient and modern combine.

Hume, whom it is useful to consider after Berkeley, brought this problem of the self to the fore. Having attempted to derive all knowledge from simple impressions, Hume came to treat mind and matter virtually as bundles of elements, the unity of the mind being explained by the body, and that of the body explained by the mind. His theory of knowledge landed him in a scepticism to which the only solution was to go out to dinner, and he did. Hume possessed the clear-headed dignity that argues that a sceptic should be sceptical of his doubts and retain respect for himself and others. Some of his contemporaries were inordinately puzzled by his ability to be likeable, good, and sceptical all at once. They failed to appreciate the remarkably orderly emotions of this great intellectual who maintained that emotions provide the mainsprings of action.

Elsewhere in the *Treatise* Hume put forward the belief, to his own and his successors' perplexity, that there is no simple impression of necessary connexion which will underpin our conception of causality. Experience of constant conjunction leads us to feel connexions to be essential. Russell shows that Hume was in danger of assuming the very causality he laid open to question, but he may perhaps be rescued. Thus considered, his position consisted of two parts, one, says Russell, objective, the other subjective. Here is Russell's summary:

The objective part says: When we judge that A causes B, what has in fact happened, so far as A and B are concerned, is that they have been frequently observed to be conjoined, i.e., A has been immediately, or very quickly, followed by B; we have no right to say that A *must* be followed by B, or will be followed by B on future occasions. Nor have we any ground for supposing that, however often A is followed by B, any relation beyond sequence is involved. In fact, causation is definable in terms of sequence, and is not an independent notion.

The subjective part of the doctrine says: The frequently observed conjunction of A and B *causes* the impression of A to *cause* the idea of B. But if we are to define 'cause' as is suggested by the objective part of the doctrine, we must re-word the above. Substituting the definition of 'cause' the above becomes:

'It has been frequently observed that the frequently observed conjunction of two objects A and B has been frequently followed by occasions on which the impression of A was followed by the idea of B.'

Into the logical intricacies of this position we cannot go. It must suffice that, by challenging the notion of causality and bringing the whole problem of the unifying principle of a 'bundled' concept of mind or matter to the fore, Hume did three things. He gave a charter to future physiologists and psychologists to search for 'sequences' without worrying too much whether the 'influence' of one series on the other is virtuous or sinister. He left us the problem (still unsolved) of the criteria used in separating the two sciences. He also left us the problem – though this language belongs to 200 years later – of reconciling the modern notion of functional dependence with the investigation of the organically unified wholes with which modern physiologists and psychologists seem to be dealing. At this point it is instructive to turn to Hering writing in 1870 (pp. 376 ff.) and to Stebbing and Smith more recently. After Hume the difficulties of elementarism or of atomistic thinking in psychology should have been obvious. In fact it took about 150 years to appreciate them. He is quoted on pp. 339–45.

In discussing Hume in this manner I have been jumping far ahead and over some water that is deep. The charter I have tentatively derived from Hume (it was not explicit) could just as well be extracted from Leibniz, except that with the later writer we seem to see speculation working itself out and at a time when scientists were soon to insist on patient verification. After

Hume, though I would not venture 'because of Hume', the body-mind problem was still dealt with by philosophers, but, except for Kant, these were hardly in the front rank and were steadily veering to a method of inquiry that is factual.

Before we pass on to Hartley and Condillac, who seem to me in this tradition, let us change our viewpoint and return to Butler who is curiously neglected in the psychological history books. He is interesting for several reasons. First, there lies in him a promising clue to one of the problems Hume bequeathed, namely: were we mistaken from the beginning in searching for a simple 'self' whether or not it could be known ? Such a question could not arise until 'soul' and 'mind' had begun to be treated separately and difficulties over personal identity had entered with an associationist view of the mind. Butler, who was a bishop, naturally retained the immortal soul; but his discussion of personal identity appended to the *Analogy of Religion* takes the war into the camp of psychologizing philosophers. He deals specifically with the kind of view worked out by Locke's more ruthless followers. Here is one of his comments:

But though we are thus certain that we are the same agents, living beings, or substances, now, which we were as far back as our remembrance reaches; yet it is asked, whether we may not possibly be deceived in it ? And this question may be asked at the end of any demonstration whatever: because it is a question concerning the truth of perception by memory. And he who can doubt, whether perception by memory can in this case be depended upon, may doubt also, whether perception by deduction and reasoning, which also include memory, or indeed whether intuitive perception, can. Here then we can go no farther. For it is ridiculous to attempt to prove the truth of those perceptions, whose truth we can no otherwise prove, than by other perceptions of exactly the same kind with them, and which there is just the same ground to suspect; or to attempt to prove the truth of our faculties, which can no otherwise be proved, than by the use or means of those very suspected faculties themselves.*

Elsewhere, in the *Sermons on Human Nature*, preached at the Rolls Chapel between 1719 and their publication in 1726, Butler

* I have chosen this passage because it underlines the point taken from Trevelyan on p. 138.

develops something else whose relation to modern psychology is interesting. Assuming that the passions are implanted in man by a wholly beneficent Creator (therefore the passions are not in themselves bad), Butler, playing delicately with the notion of 'constitutional government', handed to psychology the idea of human drives being integrated into systems characterized by 'self-love' and 'benevolence'. The first serves primarily the person's own interests, the second is directed to the needs of other people. In Butler's view conscience remains a possible arbitrator in the event of the systems coming into conflict. He was concerned as a preacher to convince his hearers that in the long run conflict dissolves: for man's own interest is that of his neighbour, and he serves his neighbour by being his best self. Here Butler walks very carefully between selfishness and masochism. The ethics of this need not here concern us; more relevant is the theoretical structuring of personality which finds its echoes in modern writers such as McDougall and Freud. Such a line of thought could lead eventually to questions about body and mind being asked not in terms of correlating the behaviour of a simple, or even a series of simple, substances with others, but that of investigating the relation of complex and organically integrated occurrences. But that way of thinking again belongs to our own day.

With the mention of Butler I would like to diverge for a moment in the company of Trevelyan and Hazard to gain some insight into the rather different fates of 'reason' and 'empiricism' in eighteenth-century England and France, for they throw light on the setting of body-mind problems.

'It is a common error', writes Trevelyan, 'to regard the eighteenth century in England as irreligious. An ethical code based on Christian doctrine was a rule of life to a much larger proportion of the community than it had been in the late medieval and Tudor periods.' He then broadly separates two schools of religious thought: the Latitudinarian, influenced by Locke and standing for toleration and reasonableness in the interpretation of doctrine, and, later, the Methodist, emphasizing renewed self-discipline and zeal, allied with active philanthropy. The English Deist movement, also influenced by Locke, 'all respectable people regarded askance'. Some very respectable and able people took the trouble to oppose it skilfully. Among the skilled, Trevelyan counts Swift, Bentley, William Law, and also Butler and Berkeley whom we have just mentioned. The combination of tolerant receptiveness to science, the mature intelligence of the Deists' opponents and, one may add, the unaffected piety of the 'scientific' philosophers contributed, it would seem, to 'that peculiarly English phenomenon, the holy alliance of science and religion, which persisted (in spite of Hume) till near the close of the Century'. (Willey).

In France, Deism, imported from England, encountered a reactionary Church, an ineffectual Court, and a State by no means equipped to respond resiliently to a challenge that had some justice. Voltaire, the Deists' most brilliant disciple, moved in fear of the police and the Bastille, and the French authorities managed to burn at least some of his books. While we cannot blame everything on inadequate administrators – Voltaire was a character who often courted trouble – the fact remains that the spirit of Deism in France became more aggressive both in proportion to the need of 'enlightenment' and the resistance to it. There was even greater need for reform and no strong ring of intelligently argumentative bishops, comparable to the English 'steadiers'. It is well to remember too that 'reason', 'equality', and 'freedom' were being preached in a country at whose core there was more economic unrest, and which was to suffer cruelly in enlightening others on the need to take this seriously.

Hazard and others have pointed out the extent to which Voltaire, in transmitting Locke, virtually contrived to suggest that a spirit of doubt is equivalent to a spirit of negation; and how often Voltaire plays with Locke's passing comment on the logical possibility that matter could have been made to think. It is very instructive to read Locke and Voltaire side by side, in particular the thirteenth of the *Lettres Philosophiques* (1734) to which Hazard makes reference. Here are relevant extracts from the two authors:

LOCKE: I know it as an opinion, that the soul always thinks; ...
and that actual thinking is as inseparable from the soul, as

actual extension is from the body: which if true, to inquire after the beginning of a man's ideas is the same as to inquire after the beginning of his soul. . . .

But whether the soul be supposed to exist antecedent to, or coeval with, or some time after the first rudiments or organization, or the beginnings of life in the body, I leave to be disputed by those who have better thought of the matter. I confess myself to have one of those dull souls that doth not perceive itself always to contemplate ideas; nor can conceive it any more necessary for the soul always to think, than for the body always to move.

VOLTAIRE: *Pour moi je me vante de l'honneur d'être en ce poin aussi stupide que Locke. Personne ne me fera jamais croire que je pense toujours. . . .*

LOCKE: We have the ideas of matter and thinking, but possibly shall never be able to know whether any mere material being thinks or no; it being impossible for us, by the contemplation of our own ideas without revelation, to discover whether Omnipotency has not given to some systems of matter, fitly disposed, a power to perceive and think, or else joined and fixed to matter, so disposed, a thinking immaterial substance.

VOLTAIRE: *Locke, après avoir ruiné les idées innées, après avoir bien renoncé à la vanité de croire qu'on pense toujours, établit que toutes nos idées nous viennent par les sens, examine nos idées simples et celles qui sont composées, suit l'esprit de l'homme dans toutes ses opérations, fait voir combien les langues que les hommes parlent sont imparfaites, et quel abus nous faisons des termes à tous moments.*

Il vient enfin à considérer l'étendue ou plutôt le néant des connaissances humaines. C'est dans ce chapitre qu'il ose avancer modestement ces paroles: 'Nous ne serons jamais peut-être capable de connaître si un être purement matériel pense ou non'.

Ce discours sage parut à plus d'un théologien une déclaration scandaleuse que l'âme est matérielle et mortelle.

Voltaire half tries to exonerate Locke, but by his very discussion – he returned again and again to the theme – he contrived to suggest the very 'materialism' which Locke had not only not deduced but from which he had tried to defend himself.

Here we must leave the reader to follow for himself the French tussles between rationalism and theology which in

England came into prominence later with Darwin and Huxley.

Let us now briefly consider Hartley and Condillac. The *Observations on Man* appeared in 1749; the *Traité des Sensations* in 1754. Both authors were influenced by Locke; neither was anti-religious. Hartley numbered an array of bishops (including Butler) among his personal friends; Condillac held aloof from La Mettrie and the Encyclopedists with whom he was contemporary, and explicitly rejected the 'materialist' account of the soul. Though technically philosophers and orthodox, both authors nevertheless seem to move a little further towards tackling psychological processes without raising the worst issues of philosophy and theology.

Hartley took over Newton's theory of vibrations, and Locke on association, and combining the two 'founded' the associationist school: 'associations' and 'vibrations' running parallel. He is very much in the tradition of *l'esprit systématique* and somewhat appalled when he thinks he sees a determinist materialism looming ahead. This is compatible with extremely useful service in insisting on the value of studying cerebral and nervous functioning (cf. pp. 346–51). He was the 'general practitioner' of the eighteenth century, whose writing echoes concrete experience of people he was concerned to cure. He is paternal, prosaic, but always kindly, as we see him through his son's eyes visiting 'with affectionate sympathy, the humblest recesses of poverty and sickness, as well as the stately beds of pampered distemper and premature decrepitude'. Alas! we do not know how Hartley handled these complaints.

If Hartley like Locke started by being a doctor, but unlike Locke spent all his life in a busy practice, Condillac is the Watteau of psychological history and Piaget's most charming forerunner. Condillac was concerned not with the 'essence of the soul' but with the way in which knowledge might be built up by experience. His interest was genetic. By the fantasy of endowing a statue with one kind of sensation after another, he tries imaginatively to reconstruct the statue's increasingly living experience. In the course of this he asks some pertinent questions, among them: Would we have ever thought of matter had we been confined to the sense of smell? One must read this in the context of a statue smelling a rose (see pp. 353 ff.). His system may be seen as remotely aristocratic and a *reductio ad absurdum* of over-simplified empiricism, but it is not merely this, even though (influenced no doubt by Geulincx and Malebranche) he does expound the odd theory of cerebral events being the 'occasional causes' of mental ones. Even this is less odd when put in the context of the discussion of memory (pp. 354 ff.). Condillac explains in terms of touch and movement the way in which the statue comes to learn of its own body and physical objects. This last piece of early genetic psychologizing has too much sense, as well as too much grace, to be consigned wholly to oblivion. So it too is quoted (pp. 357 ff.).

From a somewhat different standpoint it is interesting to sample mid eighteenth-century France by way of Helvétius, writing in 1758. Influenced by Locke, Montesquieu, and Hume among others, and using an immense assembly of literary and traveller's anecdotes, he stressed the relative and local nature of manners, customs, law, and religion alike, while commenting on the motives that make men condemn *a priori* that which to them is strange. He is often shrewd and realistic, he can be blandly superficial and not a little sententious. Having criticized him one returns to read more. He attributes human action basically to desire for pleasure and aversion from pain: he gives due weight to inertia but also to weariness of inaction whose importance he thinks understressed. Environment rather than innate ability should be used, he thinks, to explain the differences in men's intellectual achievements. Here he oversimplifies but is important for his day. That, he maintains, which distinguishes the great from the lesser man is emotional force: 'it is the strong passions, which rescuing us from sloth, can alone impart to us that continued attention productive of superior intellects.' In these views Helvétius pivots curiously between a species of intellectualist hedonism reminiscent of English empiricism, and an awareness of emotional drives more appropriate to the Romantics and Freud. *De l'esprit* was condemned by the parlement of Paris, but mainly, it appears, for the supposed insult to God and man contained in the suggestion that if man had been endowed with a hoof instead of hands he would have remained without habitation, manufactures, and, indeed, anything that depends on manual exertion.

It may be inferred from the foregoing that, by the middle of the eighteenth century, treatment of mind-body problems was shifting from the realms of the broad and speculative into those where patient validated inquiry should begin to change the scene. In the second half of the century the basis of physiology was being laid by Buffon, Priestley, and Haller among others. Haller was the last defender of animal spirits, the proponent of nervous irritability, but a stringent critic of La Mettrie's *L'Homme machine*. Just as in the psychological philosophizing of the eighteenth century a hint of the mind's 'activity' is always to be found entangled even in the largest systems of mechanical association, so also in physiology 'mechanism' and 'vitalism' were fighting their way along. In the 'educational psychology' of the closing century, the tradition of Rousseau, Pestalozzi, and later of Froebel, spontaneity was destined to challenge mechanical imprinting much as lyrical poetry and natural speech came to replace a 'style' that had frozen into formality.

During the French Revolution two events occurred which were pointers into the future. Cabanis, whose interests included translating Homer's *Iliad*, Goethe's *Stella*, and Gray's *Elegy*, laid the macabre foundations of physiological psychology in a study of the after-effects of decapitation by guillotine. Not very surprisingly, though honoured in his lifetime, he soon became, in the phrase of Brett, the 'symbol of degenerate materialism'. But this was not before he had added an idea on the relation of mental to physical life. 'This,' to quote Brett, 'was the idea that consciousness belongs to a central Ego, *le moi central*, and that this central ego is an epitome of all the separate centres which the nervous system creates. The apparent signs of life which might be exhibited by the decapitated body are then explained as activities of neural ganglia which are relatively independent of the brain or central ego.'

The other event associated with the Revolution is the death of devil possession as an explanation of lunacy. History has it that during this period Pinel successfully persuaded the authorities to allow him to unchain the mental patients in the *Bicêtre*. Drama has it that one of them subsequently saved his life from the Revolutionary mob. Pinel underlines the very slowly growing belief that maltreating the body rarely improves the mind. With this, and the Italian Beccaria's earlier attack on the crueller aspects of the criminal laws, we glimpse once more the simple humanitarian interest which the second half of the century had tried so hard to make effective. It proved one of the few interests to survive the Revolution, the Napoleonic Wars, and the era of disillusion that followed them.

REFERENCES

Berkeley, George. 'Three Dialogues between Hylas and Philonous in Opposition to Sceptics and Atheists' in *Theory of Vision and Other Writings*. London: Dent (Everyman's Library), 1920, pp. 197 ff.

Brett, G. S. *History of Psychology*. Edited and abridged by R. S. Peters. London: Allen and Unwin, 1953, pp. 408 ff., 459 ff.

Butler, Joseph. Dissertation 'Of Personal Identity', and 'Sermons on Human Nature'. *Works*. Oxford: Clarendon Press, 1874, Vol. I, pp. 326–7 and Vol. II, pp. 1–38

Condillac, Étienne Bonnot, Abbé de. *Treatise on Sensations*. Trans. Geraldine Carr. London: Favil Press, 1930

Hartley, David. *Observations on Man*. London: J. Johnson, Vols. 1 and 2, 4th Edn. Vol. 3, 3rd Edn. 1801

Hazard, Paul. *European Thought in the 18th Century from Montesquieu to Lessing*, trans. J. L. May. London: Hollis and Carter, 1954, pp. 119 ff.

Helvétius, C. A. *De l'esprit*. Translated anonymously. London: Richardson, Sherwood, Neely, and Jones, 1809

Huizinga, J. *The Waning of the Middle Ages*. London: Arnold, 1952, Penguin Books, 1955

Hume, David. *Treatise on Human Nature*. Ed. L. A. Selby-Bigge. Oxford: Clarendon Press, 1928

Locke, John. *An Essay Concerning Human Understanding* abridged and ed. by A. S. Pringle-Pattison. Oxford: Clarendon Press, 1924, pp. 47–8, 268–9

Russell, Bertrand. *History of Western Philosophy*. London: Allen and Unwin, 1946. Bk III, Chap. XVII, pp. 691–2

Smith, F. V. *The Explanation of Human Behaviour*. London: Constable, 1951. Chap. III

Stebbing, L. S. *A Modern Introduction to Logic*. London: Methuen, 5th Edn. 1946. Chap. XIX and Appendix D, pp. 510–11

Trevelyan, G. M. *Illustrated English Social History*. London: Longmans, Vol. III. 1951, pp. 60, 61 *et seq.*

Voltaire. *Lettres Philosophiques*. Ed. F. A. Taylor. Oxford: Blackwell, 1943, pp. 39–45

Willey, Basil. See Trevelyan: *Illustrated English Social History*, Vol. III, p. 61

CHAPTER 8

SIX POLARITIES IN SEARCH
OF A PERSON

Things are in the saddle and ride mankind.

EMERSON

Faust complained that he had two souls in his breast.
I have a whole squabbling crowd. It goes on as in a republic.

BISMARCK

The old logic put thought in fetters, the new logic gives
it wings.

RUSSELL

In my end is my beginning

T. S. ELIOT

(i) THE NINETEENTH CENTURY

THIS chapter has to do three things: cast a glance at the nineteenth-century setting; point to particular trends that affected
our treatment of body-mind problems; indicate certain polarities brought to the fore in the nineteenth century and between
which our understanding of individual human beings in a social
and physical environment still tends to swing.

With experience of the twentieth century it is possible to
look past the nineteenth to the eighteenth with a certain nost-
algia; in spite of its problems the eighteenth had clarity and
grace and had not been forced to see 'reason' as the product of
a rare resilient endurance. Moreover it could laugh at itself;
witness Mozart's gentle satire of Mesmer's 'magnetic' cures.
Eighteenth-century evaluations, with the added touch of lyrical
loveliness that we find, say, in Schubert and Eichendorff, and
the fusion of realism and social magic that haunts the pages of
Jane Austen, were retained in part by the nineteenth. But, compared with its predecessor, the nineteenth century as it developed
became the age of 'thickness'. Indeed it 'thickened' from all
the obvious standpoints. Its furniture grew large, its textiles

heavy, and its houses huge and ornate. Its novels grew long and crowded with incident and developing characters. The best of its plays plumbed labyrinthine emotional connexions. Its orchestras were augmented by brass and the 'kitchen' and its singers had then to outdo the lot – and the effect can still be magnificent.

As it got under way, the nineteenth century grew thicker with industry, people, and peoples. The population increase obvious by about 1600 had continued with gathering impetus as improvements in medicine and some physical conditions added a lowering death- to an increasing birth-rate. One aspect of the nineteenth-century trends can be seen from the P.E.P. table below.

POPULATION OF ENGLAND AND WALES, 1801–1947

Year	Population (million)	Density (number per square mile)	Average per cent increase per annum
1801 (Census)	8·89	152	—
1811 (Census)	10·16	174	1·43
1821 (Census)	12·00	206	1·81
1831 (Census)	13·90	238	1·58
1841 (Census)	15·91	273	1·43
1851 (Census)	17·93	307	1·27
1861 (Census)	20·07	344	1·19
1871 (Census)	22·71	389	1·32
1881 (Census)	25·97	445	1·44
1891 (Census)	29·00	497	1·17
1901 (Census)	32·53	558	1·22
1911 (Census)	36·07	618	1·09
1921 (Census)	37·89	649	0·49
1931 (Census)	39·95	685	0·55
1941 mid-year estimate	41·75	716	0·45
1945 mid-year estimate	42·64	732	0·54
1946 mid-year estimate	42·85	735	0·49
1947 mid-year estimate	43·27	742	0·98

Indeed, population statistics began to be used; they underlined the numbers and the needs of the under-privileged whose existence the eighteenth century had been forced by other means to realize. The lives of ordinary people which we find in Dickensian literature, in Balzac, and in writers such as Dostoyevsky and Gorky, made their impact on literature and living, while humanitarian and political need made social legislation a necessary cement against hardship and possible revolution. As we look at the figures above, it also becomes easier to see the pressures on psychologizing philosophers to consider the wide variations in human nature.

In the second half of the century their long-sought national unity was achieved by the loosely federated or conflicting communities that had constituted Italy and Germany. France, still an intellectual leader, was so in spite of political uncertainty. Countries tended to prosper in proportion to industrialization and to the extent to which their governments could maintain an equilibrium between continuity and change – where the changes consequent on technological development were themselves gaining momentum. England developed interests outside Europe and in the last quarter of the century was the centre of an empire, but Germany and America vied with her more and more in the economic field.

Compared with our age the nineteenth century was a period of peace and prosperity, but the ground none-the-less was thick with problems, of which rising nationalism, the conflicts of science and theology, of liberal and conservative, of the 'haves' and the 'have-nots' are only some examples. With increasing science and secularization time in the future began imperceptibly to shorten, while time in the past grew longer and longer, reaching back to the pleistocene age and beyond; till now we think backwards in millions of light years and forwards to the end of a week. Our own age of uncertainty accentuated this trend and with it, for some, the impact of living. For as Freud said after World War I, 'Transience value is rarity value in time'. Meanwhile manufacture, transport, and swifter communication had begun to thicken the ordinary living of our grandfathers both directly and indirectly with things and more things. Trains moved faster than carriages, telegrams faster than letters. So, at times, the nineteenth century looms like St Pancras Station, or an overcrowded industrial Noah's Ark lurching down time's ever rolling stream – but on the far side, to us, of waves of war.

So much for an impression roughed in for the sake of contrast and of orientation. Now let us turn to particular trends that directly affected treatment of mind-body relations. Among the most important were the following: developments in physiology; the impact of Darwinian biology; two trends in medicine, one leading to better physical treatment of neuroses and psychoses, the other eventually to modern psychotherapy. No less important was a feeling for individuality, which we can detect in people as unlike each other as Charles Lamb and Maine de Biran. With it there went a stress on activity ('willing') which is found again in Maine de Biran but which we associate more readily with the German thought that is influenced by Schopenhauer. In Germany, too, we find the special fusing of interest in status and dislike of uncheckable metaphysical speculation that contributed to the founding of experimental psychology.

Last but not least, at the turn of the nineteenth and twentieth centuries thinking of 'mind' and 'body' as 'substances' was replaced in some significant quarters by thinking of 'processes', with the underlying assumption that their owners were persons who can be neither dichotomized nor explained by simply adding two, or an indefinite number of 'bits', together. To explanations, which in physiology and psychology took unconscious functioning into account and were fast becoming organic, there was added independent encouragement to think in terms of complex relations and frequencies. This encouragement came from logic, mathematical physics, and statistics. From one point of view all these can be seen to involve highly developed variants of Spinoza's views on 'aspects'. So there was reinstated the outlook of Hippocrates, which Galen had noted so neatly in the days before St Augustine, but in a setting wherein the logic and methods of modern science put a strangely different slant on the possibilities of inquiry. Early in the twentieth century, a problem of mind and body, in so far as it was scientific, could no longer be stated in terms of 'substances' that are simple and do not change. Interest shifted to the attempt, logically or experimentally, to isolate sub-systems of interrelated processes in order to see which, if any, were functionally dependent on each other.

While we can say next to nothing about the trends here listed, let us try to see a little further what they involved. This means a series of short 'flash-backs', beginning with the biological sciences and physiology in particular.

Seventeenth-century physiology, in the person of Willis (with Christopher Wren as his draughtsman), handed on to the eighteenth both a better understanding of the brain and the possibility that nerves are not tubes, through which animal spirits travel to work on mechanical lines, but fibres along which they pass. Moreover, Willis thought the animal spirits in the blood were rather more flame-like than Descartes's exposition suggests and the corporeal soul in the brain was itself a light. 'Flamelike' was an old and aristocratic quality, but here there was added a touch of insobriety reminiscent of Sir Toby Belch. For Willis unwisely hearkened to some seventeenth-century spark maintaining that 'after an extra good bout of wine he could see to read print clearly on a very dark night'. We have seen that the animal spirits survived (whether drunk or sober I do not know), until Haller, by whom the eighteenth century handed on to the nineteenth experimental studies of nervous irritability. In the 1790s Galvani (1737–98), experimenting on muscular contraction, seems to have discovered both electricity in animals and the facts relating to dissimilar metals in contact which, after much controversy, led Volta to think of the battery and Voltaic pile. The eighteenth century also supplied Spallanzani's realization that digestion is a chemical process (a theory later accepted and extended by Hunter) and Bichat's view that organically there are both voluntary and involuntary systems at work in the body.

Equally significant are the further geographical explorations of the eighteenth century. These, in Boring's pleasant phrasing, 'had so multiplied the number of known species that it was no longer possible to conceive that Noah had crowded a pair of each into the Ark' – let alone personally guarding the loveliest peacock for its intimations of immortality. In general, it seems, the eighteenth century believed in the special creation of every species, but some who linked the eighteenth and the nineteenth centuries – Goethe, Erasmus Darwin, and Lamarck – were already either toying with or expounding the possibility of transmuting species.

Wise after the event, we can see that at the beginning of the nineteenth century the stage was set both for developments in physiology, and for the tussles in biology that centred on the change from eternally-fixed to evolutionary concepts. Such tussles were bound to be tough; for not only were Biblical authority and social status on the side of specific creation, but the scientific authority of the great Cuvier was there 'invoking a neat series of scientific guesses and last judgements' to explain 'the admitted succession of plants and animals in terrestrial history'. On its side, however, evolution had some more voyages, this time of scientific discovery, among them the trips of the *Beagle* and the *Rattlesnake*, the one with Charles Darwin and the other with Huxley on board. The *Beagle* sailed off in 1831 with Charles, Erasmus Darwin's grandson, as a newly-fledged, beetle-collecting, snipe-shooting student of theology. He was armed it is true with Cuvier, but also with the new first volume of Lyell's *Principles of Geology*, which authority in the person of Henshaw had advised Charles to 'purchase, read carefully, and emphatically disbelieve'. For five years in and off America and twenty-three years at home, Darwin prowled and pottered among objects. He learnt with his eyes, from Lyell and from Malthus, not without disturbance. Eventually he was convinced that if rocks could evolve, so could animals and man. By a different route the same idea flashed on Wallace, travelling in the wilds of Malaya. The story of the *Origin of Species*, and of its impact on Victorian society and European biology from 1859 onwards, has already been told so well by Nordenskiöld and in Irvine's recent book *Apes, Angels and Victorians*, that here we must refer readers to these sources and return to nineteenth-century physiology so far as it bears on 'body and mind'.

Among the main stages of development in physiology as a subject the following seem specially relevant. Lister (1780–1869) improved and used the compound microscope by which means cells and cell structures became directly observable. He first published a paper on this in 1830. Robert Brown (1773–1858) described cell nuclei in plant tissue in 1833, and Schwann in 1839 showed such nuclei to be present in the tissue of all animals and plants. Very slowly the interest of physiologists was to shift towards the study of such nuclei. Meanwhile, between 1807 and 1822 Bell (1774–1842) and Majendie (1783–1855) (the independence of their discovery is unimportant here) had differentiated motor from sensory nerves both spatially and functionally, and Bell had added a sixth sense, the kinaesthetic or muscular, to our hitherto official equipment of five. By 1832, reflex movement which had been recognized since Galen, but only named by Astruc in 1736, was described on the basis of experimental studies by Hall who thought in terms of voluntary, involuntary, and respiratory reflexes. Johannes Müller, a successor of Haller in Berlin, by additional studies, organization of the data and, it seems, by sheer weight of expert opinion, established the study of reflexes in systematic physiology from the time of the publication of his *Handbuch* in 1835.

At the time of the last edition of Müller's *Handbuch* in 1844, the rate of transmission of nervous impulse was believed to be instantaneous or at best unmeasurable. Decision and action presumably coincided – a view which some might defend today, but for completely opposite reasons. In the mid nineteenth century Helmholtz succeeded in measuring the rate, and, with the staunch support of Du Bois-Reymond, whose life-time went to studying the electrical phenomena of the body, Helmholtz's findings were published in 1850 and 52. He found the speed to be relatively slow. There we must pause to comment: the fifty years of nervous physiology linking Cabanis and Helmholtz were yielding an increasingly complicated body but one apparently able to do many things on its own.

Now let us glance at brain physiology and the question of localization of function, which we last glimpsed in the sixteenth century entangled with devil possession (see pp. 263 ff.). Historically, the newer line of thinking runs through Pinel, Benjamin Rush, and William Tuke, all of whom made a return to Hippocrates in believing that brain dysfunction may be related to severe psychological disorders. This trend in medicine is worth study from two different viewpoints. One is that of the humanitarian approach to behaviour difficulties, already mentioned. We can see this at work in the whole history of mental and other hospital reform which links these eighteenth- and nineteenth-century originators with our latest effort sat rehabilitation. In this story, women such as Dorothea Dix and Florence Nightingale are seen coming into action. The other viewpoint takes in the impetus given to the study of brain physiology which sober and serious medicine shared with the highly inflammable popular interest aroused by the mistaken phrenology of Gall, who, it is fair to say, suffered from unscrupulous publicity. By 1861 serious brain physiology had been put on the map by such first-class scientists as Rolando, Flourens, and Broca. From them we derive the portrait of a functioning brain as a unified system in which each part has its own main task, but also something to contribute to the communal action from which it can ill be spared. By that time too, the histology of the nervous system had revealed the almost infinite number of cells of which the brain is composed. In the latter half of the nineteenth century physiological studies suggested a greater specificity of localized function than twentieth-century research would accept. We will therefore leave the story at Flourens to pick it up later with references to Sherrington, Adrian, and Lashley.

To summarize: by the second half of the nineteenth century associationist or faculty psychologists could have found a variety of 'seats for the soul', an argument for mental functioning being 'material', arguments for epiphenomenalism, for a double aspect theory, for parallelism, or for evolutionary associationism. All of these alternatives were tried. If people combined determinist physics, evolutionary biology, current physiology, and the fear of fantasy that makes a new god of technological science, they felt themselves threatened with a 'nothing but' evaluation of humanity. The fallacy in this inference was exposed by the very T. H. Huxley who did most to popularize Darwinism and has been stressed again in our own day by his grandson Julian.

Meanwhile, physiology, safely launched as an experimental science, began to look round for a colleague. The invitation to psychology issued by Hering from Vienna in 1870 is a historical document to brood upon (pp. 376 ff.). Trends of the past are focused and lightened with sureness of touch and with charm while trends of the future are muttering in the wings of Hering's stage.

Now let us hazard a glance at nineteenth-century psychologizing. In England, associationism, in the hands of James Mill, may be said to have reached its zenith and died in 1829 of the kind of internal inadequacy apparent in the extract below. James Mill was a successor of Hartley and Hume in treating sensations and ideas as fundamental ingredients of 'the mind', the mode of combining these elements being considered largely mechanical. Mill dropped hints of more subtle fusion but did not develop them. As Boring implies, the flaws in such a system soon show when the logical conclusion is pressed:

Brick is one complex idea, mortar is another complex idea; these ideas, with ideas of position and quantity, compose my idea of a wall. My idea of a plank is a complex idea, my idea of a rafter is a complex idea, my idea of a nail is a complex idea.

These, united with the same ideas of position and quantity, compose my duplex idea of a floor. In the same manner my complex ideas of glass, wood, and others, compose my duplex idea of a window; and these duplex ideas, united together, compose my idea of a house, which is made up of various duplex ideas. How many complex, or duplex ideas, are all united in the idea of furniture? How many more in the idea of merchandise? How many more in the idea called Every Thing?

By 1843, John Stuart Mill, seven years after his father's death, was arguing that scientific method should and could take account of wholes that are more than the sum of their parts and whose qualities cannot be forecast from the ways of the parts in isolation. In the younger Mill's view the only method available for studying such complex unities was that of observation and experiment, and in this he appears to have been right. In successive editions of his *System of Logic* he elaborated the view. Here is part of his early statement as quoted by Boring:

It is obvious that the complex laws of thought and feeling not only may, but must, be generated from these simple laws [of association]. And it is to be remarked, that the case is not always one of Composition of Causes: the effect of concurring causes is not always precisely the sum of the effects of those causes when separate, not even always an effect of the same kind with them. ... The laws of the phenomena of the mind are sometimes analogous to mechanical, but sometimes also to chemical laws. When many impressions or ideas are operating in the mind together, there sometimes takes place a process of a similar kind to chemical combination. When impressions have been so often experienced in conjunction, that each of them calls up readily and instantaneously the ideas of the whole group, those ideas sometimes melt and coalesce into one another, and appear not several ideas but one; in the same manner as when the seven prismatic colours are presented to the eye in rapid succession, the sensation produced is that of white. But in this last case it is correct to say that the seven colours when they rapidly follow one another *generate* white, but not that they actually *are* white; so it appears to me that the Complex Idea, formed by the blending together of several simpler ones, should when it really appears simple, (that is when the separate elements are not consciously distinguishable in it) be said to *result from*, or be *generated by*, the simple ideas, not to *consist of them* ... These are cases of mental chemistry: in which it is possible to say that the simple ideas generate, rather than that they compose, the complex ones.

J. S. Mill's notion of mental chemistry is generally significant to us because of its 'organic' emphasis. Meanwhile, on the subject of body and mind, we must pause for a moment with his account of belief in matter as the permanent possibility of sensations that are in themselves fleeting. Below is part of what he was writing in 1865 in the *Examination of Sir William Hamilton's Philosophy*. It should be related to the fuller quotation from the *Logic* given on pp. 373 ff.

I see a piece of white paper on the table. I go into another room. If the phenomenon always followed me, or if, when it did not follow me, I believed it to disappear *é rerum naturâ*, I should not believe it to be an external object. I should consider it as a phantom – a mere affection of my senses: I should not believe that there had been any Body there. But, though I have ceased to see it, I am persuaded that the paper is still there. I no longer have the sensations which it gave me; but I believe that when I again place myself in the circumstances in which I had those sensations, that is, when I go again into the room, I shall again have them; and further, that there has been no intervening moment at which this would not have been the case. Owing to this property of my mind, my conception of the world at any given instant consists, in only a small proportion, of present sensations. Of these I may at the time have none at all, and they are in any case a most insignificant portion of the whole which I apprehend. The conception I form of the world existing at any moment, comprises, along with the sensations I am feeling, a countless variety of possibilities of sensation: namely, the whole of those which past observation tells me that I could, under any supposable circumstances, experience at this moment, together with an indefinite and illimitable multitude of others which I do not know that I could, yet it is possible that I might, experience in circumstances not known to me. These various possibilities are the important thing to me in the world. My present sensations are generally of little importance, and moreover are fugitive: the possibilities, on the contrary, are permanent, which is the character that mainly distinguishes our idea of Substance or Matter from our notion of sensation.

In effect Mill tended to treat 'mind' and 'matter' as species of Kantian '*noumena*' whose existence we feel compelled to intuit but which lie outside the logical and empirical inquiry with which Mill was primarily concerned. For an understanding of this trend in nineteenth-century thought it is exceedingly interesting to put John Stuart Mill and Wundt side by side (see pp. 373 ff. and 386 ff.).

Meanwhile, Bain had brought out *The Senses and the Intellect* in 1855 and *The Emotions and the Will* in 1859. These were to be standard English texts for nearly half a century. In 1872 he published *Mind and Body*. Bain took for granted that for the understanding of people knowledge of bodily functioning must be given due weight. Hence the then current physiology, together with the principle of conservation of energy, found a natural place in his writings. But current science suggested, as we have seen, a closed causal system, while Bain, far from 'materialist' in outlook, was on the side of those who believe that human behaviour can be spontaneous. Partly to reconcile these opposing viewpoints he suggested that central nervous functioning might be 'spontaneous' in the sense of action occurring independently of stimulation – a notion of which Darwin could make neither head nor tail.* In spite of these flashes, as Boring rightly suggests, Bain never found, to his own satisfaction, a way of squaring physical determination and mental spontaneity. He veered between treating 'mind' and 'body' as substances varying in parallel, but not interacting, and treating them both more abstractly in some form of 'aspect' theory. There he must stay, but worthy of a rather more detailed study from this as well as from other points of view.

Last but not least among Victorian theoretical empiricists we must sample Herbert Spencer, who started as an associationist but worked out an evolutionary account of the emergence of mental functioning. Spencer is important, if for no other reason, for maintaining that emotional relations should be taken seriously and indeed could be directly apprehended. He tried to identify mind and motion and, though he would not have drawn Claude Bernard's conclusions, Spencer was somewhat like this great and influential French physiologist in thinking of things as alive in proportion to the adjustment between their 'internal' relations and their relations with the environment. Hence, writes Spencer:

beginning with the low life of plants and of rudimentary animals, the progress to life of higher and higher kinds essentially consists in a continual improvement of the adaptation between organic processes and processes which environ the organism.

Along with complexity of organization there goes an increase in the number, in the range, in the specificity, in the complexity, of the adjustments of inner relations to outer relations. And in tracing up the increase we [find] ourselves passing without break from the phenomena of bodily life to the phenomena of mental life.

* In our own day Coghill put something similar in principle to experimental test, and I suspect the issue is still alive and kicking under the heap of current learning controversies. We must therefore regard the use of 'spontaneous' in relation to human behaviour as a subject for further scrutiny both of a logical and experimental kind. A full scale modern attack on these issues would raise questions far outside the scope of this editor or this book. But the courageous likeable old Victorian Bain is by no means dead as a thinker.

Starting his textbook, as did most of his contemporaries, with an account of physiological functioning, Spencer attempted to work out his evolutionary species of psychophysical parallelism in rather greater detail. Since he accepted the questionable Lamarckian theory of inheritance, and propounded some curious psychology, Spencer's general evolutionary viewpoint is of more interest than his specific discussion.

From this sketch of English nineteenth-century thought we have omitted much, attempting only to indicate a main trend which may help us to understand how, in the last decades of the century, body-mind problems were once again entangled in wider issues. But as one follows these arguments it grows easier also to appreciate the scientist's wish to avoid metaphysics and to go ahead and study by experiment the empirical questions he felt he could tackle. The Mills, Spencer, and even Bain, still tended to be writing in terms of 'the mind', without much energy left for looking at individual variation, however clear they themselves were making the need for such practical empirical inquiry.

For the actual step over into the field of experimental study, English psychology, it is generally agreed, looks back to Francis Galton (1822–1911), another grandson of Erasmus Darwin. From 1850 onwards Galton can be seen like a hound quivering in pursuit of quarry as varied as: 'A Printing Electric Telegraph'; 'The Art of Travel, or Shifts and Contrivances available in Wild Countries'; 'Hereditary Genius'; 'The Nature and Nurture of Men of Science'; 'The Efficacy of Prayer'; 'the urgent need of the camel for the close companionship of his fellows'. (This last Galton had noted on some of his early explorations across North African deserts.) He initiated psychology and biology into the use of statistics. He can be found collecting anecdotes of thirty-five pairs of twins and implying a rampantly genetic account of the association of ideas and of human social behaviour:

One of the most curious anecdotes that I have received concerning this similarity of ideas was that one twin, A, who happened to be at a town in Scotland, bought a set of champagne glasses which caught his attention, as a surprise for his brother

B; while, at the same time, B, being in England, bought a similar set of precisely the same pattern as a surprise for A.

Or Galton can be found – some time before 1879 – walking in a leisurely fashion along Pall Mall a distance of 450 yards, noting that he noted some 300 different objects and recording the numerous associations they aroused. A few days later, having carefully refrained from recall, he repeated the walk and

was struck just as much as before by the variety of the ideas that presented themselves, and the number of events to which they referred, about which I had never consciously occupied myself of late years. But my admiration at the activity of the mind was seriously diminished by another observation . . . that there had been a very great deal of repetition of thought. The actors in my mental stage were indeed very numerous, but by no means so numerous as I had imagined. They now seemed to be something like the actors in theatres where large processions are represented, who march off one side of the stage, and, going round by the back, come on again at the other.

For the details of Galton's attempt to examine this finding by experiment and statistical analysis we must refer the reader to the section called 'Psychometric Experiments' in *Inquiries into Human Faculty*.* He should look at it in conjunction with the passage from Hering quoted on pp. 376 ff., and realize the age of psychological inquiry that was being ushered in. The general impression these experiments left on Galton was:

. . . like that which many of us have experienced when the basement of our house happens to be under thorough sanitary repairs, and we realize for the first time the complex system of drains and gas and water pipes, flues, bell-wires, and so forth, upon which our comfort depends, but which are usually hidden out of sight, and with whose existence, so long as they acted well, we have never troubled ourselves.

He summarized his conclusion as follows:

* These quotations come from the first edition 1883. It is worth comparing them with Galton's earlier formulation in Vol. v of *The Nineteenth Century*, 1879. At that stage he was already emphatic on the importance of 'unconscious cerebration' and of motives that need not use consciousness to gain their ends.

I have desired to show how whole strata of mental operations that have lapsed out of ordinary consciousness, admit of being dragged into light, recorded and treated statistically, and how the obscurity that attends the initial steps of our thoughts can thus be pierced and dissipated. I then showed measurably the rate at which associations sprung up, their character, the date of their first formation, their tendency to recurrence, and their relative precedence. Also I gave an instance showing how the phenomenon of a long-forgotten scene, suddenly starting into consciousness, admitted in many cases of being explained. Perhaps the strongest of the impressions left by these experiments regards the multifariousness of the work done by the mind in a state of half-unconsciousness, and the valid reason they afford for believing in the existence of still deeper strata of mental operations, sunk wholly below the level of consciousness, which may account for such mental phenomena as cannot otherwise be explained. We gain an insight by these experiments into the marvellous number and nimbleness of our mental associations, and we also learn that they are very far indeed from being infinite in their variety. We find that our working stock of ideas is narrowly limited and that the mind continually recurs to the same instruments in conducting its operations, therefore its tracks necessarily become more defined and its flexibility diminished as age advances.

Now we must turn to France, Germany, and Austria for an even briefer survey designed to highlight a somewhat greater emphasis on emotion and activity, the more direct development by Fechner and Wundt of experimental psychology from its physiological ally, and the way in which physiology, the conservation of energy principle, and studies of hypnosis and suggestion prepared the way for Freud.

Psychologically, the beginning of the French nineteenth century was a period of transition while experimental physiology was getting under way. Maine de Biran now emerges as the most interesting psychological writer. It is here that we can see very clearly a move away from the eighteenth-century desire to identify with 'reason', or in some way to find 'a man's truest self', in the using of an inviolable tool in the search for truth. The change was of course related to Rousseau, Revolution, and Romanticism. It is possible also that the frank admission by

Locke and Voltaire to moments of sleep and idleness, and Hume's straightforward belief that thinking derived energy from desire, contributed to the gradual alteration of meaning whereby 'reason' shifted from indicating a lofty abstraction, through an inviolable tool, to denoting something nearer to our modern and more limited concept of intelligence. Suffice it here that about 1812 we can see the new identification with effort instead of reason to which Biran gave expression:

Je dis aussi que l'effort voulu, immédiatement aperçu, constitue expressément l'individualité, le moi, le fait primitif du sens intime . . .

Je caractériserai dès à présent ce sens intime d'une manière plus expresse, sous le titre de sens de l'effort, dont la cause, ou force productrice, devient moi par le seul fait de la distinction qui s'établit entre le sujet de cet effort libre, et le terme qui résiste immédiatement par son inertie propre. Je dis immédiatement, pour énoncer ici d'avance une autre distinction bien essentielle, que je crois être fondé à établir entre la résistance ou l'inertie relative du corps propre qui cède ou obéit à l'effort volontaire, et la résistance absolue du corps étranger qui peut être invincible.

Maine de Biran's writing was out of line with the French materialist trends of his day and with the later positivism, and was apt to be associated with the woollier kinds of mysticism. With these one gathers it was eclipsed until interest in de Biran revived with the study of Bergson. On the other hand de Biran seems to have been read in Germany where his own interest in Leibniz was also alive. He is important to us partly for his use of introspection, partly for his stress on activity, and partly because he attempted to give a psychological 'double aspect' account of relations of mind and matter.

When we turn to German thought the main points to highlight are the following. Broadly, the Kantian tradition in philosophy worked itself out through Fichte (1762–1814), Hegel (1770–1831), and Schelling (1775–1854), who need not concern us. Indirectly relevant is Herbart (1776–1841), a contemporary of James Mill. He was an educational theorist and concerned to base his views on scientific psychology whose nature he thought must be mathematical. Herbart is relevant to body-mind problems in so far as he also returned in some respects to Leibniz.

Ideas for Herbart were active, and able and obliged to inhibit each other in accordance with the distribution of a constant amount of energy. Those that were inhibited remained existent in some obscure sense as 'tendencies'. There was a threshold of consciousness and submerged ideas moved above this *limen* to the full focus of attention, if they were consonant with a dominant system of ideas or 'apperceptive mass'. From our standpoint it seems fair to link Herbart, Schopenhauer (1788–1860), and Von Hartmann (1842–1906) together, as forerunners of later views on unconscious functioning and as collectively contributing to a more complex and dynamic conception of the mind. It is well to realize that their conceptions also bore traces of eastern pantheist absolutism.

Against this background we must place Fechner (1801–1887) who, interested in physics, physiology, and psychology, lived through all the 'vicissitudes of European science which occupied the middle of the century'. He was obsessed with the problem of relating body and mind but avoiding materialism. From this and his special combination of interest developed the well-known psycho-physical methods whereby experimenters attempt to relate strength of physical stimulus and response. With Fechner, whose *Elemente der Psychophysik* was completed in 1860, we reach the threshold of German experimental psychology from the angle of physiology. Fechner assumed a position wherein mental and physical events were distinguished as 'inner' and 'outer'. The validity of his methods raised interminable controversy.

In 1879 Wundt, coming to his subject equipped with medicine, philosophy, and physiology, established at Leipzig the first laboratory of experimental psychology.* His views on various matters changed and developed during an enormously long and productive life. A sample of his thinking on body-mind problems is given on pp. 385 ff. Though the setting is different we again detect the desire of the empirical investigator to turn

---

* Gemelli suggests that linguistic difficulties, and the unsettled state of Italy at the time, have led to Sergi's laboratory founded in Rome in 1872 being overlooked. But he acknowledges Wundt's as the most famous and historically influential.

to observation and experiment. We can see too a rather more workable version of an 'aspect' theory, provided that 'unconscious experience' is theoretically permissible.

By the 1880s, though experiment was as yet concerned largely with sensory and cognitive functioning, the complexity of psychological life was becoming more appreciated. Even in studies of perception, e.g. by Helmholtz, the complicating factor of unconscious inference was fully realized. On the other hand early experimentation tended to have an associationist and mechanist flavour. To this, the thinking of Franz Brentano and later of Gestalt psychologists in Germany and Austria, together with the integrated individual outlook of English writers such as Ward and Stout, constituted both an opposition and the source of later developments.

The story of the last nineteenth-century trend contributing to enriched understanding of human nature, and with this to the end of over-simplified body-mind problems, is that of the development of psychotherapy. This trend has been ably described in Zilboorg and Henry's *History of Medical Psychology* and sketched in Boring's useful sections on the early studies of hypnotism. To these the reader is referred. Here he needs only to realize the extent to which hypnotic suggestion had been understood by James Braid (pp. 363 ff.), the fruitful nature of therapeutic work done by Liébeault and Bernheim at Nancy from 1860 onwards, and the kind of thinking encountered in the 1880s by Freud, with Charcot in Paris and Breuer in Vienna. For a detailed understanding of this he should consult Ernest Jones' recent biography of Freud, through whom the diagnosis and possible treatment of disturbing unconscious processes and mechanisms was put on a systematic clinical basis.

This quick survey of historical trends would be woefully incomplete without reference to the fusing of European and American psychology in the closing years of the century.

German laboratories became the Mecca of would-be psychological experimenters much as Paris and Vienna were the centres of advancing psychotherapy. Among the visitors to Wundt were Cattell and Titchener, who carried experimentation from Germany to America, where by 1892 there were fifteen psychological laboratories. Among the visitors both to Germany and England (how he disliked its 'universal expression of aggregate stupidity – stupidity heavy and massive, with a sort of voluntary self-corroboration') was William James. In 1890 on finishing *The Principles of Psychology*, parts of which are still more readable than any other modern volume we have quoted, James wrote to his publisher that it testified 'to nothing but two facts: *1st*, there is no such thing as a *science* of psychology, and *2nd*, that W. J. is an incapable'. No one did more than James to make the study of people by a mongrel science come alive. By way of illustrating the complexities that future thought about body and mind would have to take into account, William James on the notion of the self is quoted on pp. 389 ff. In 1898 Morton Prince started the study of Sally Beauchamp, the most famous textbook example of 'multiple personality', a phenomenon already familiar to nineteenth-century literature and to French psychiatry, and one which underlines a whole range of complexities in relating body and mind. With the publication of his studies and of Sherrington's *Integrative Action of the Nervous System*, both in 1906, some of the hardest puzzles of twentieth-century psycho-physiology came into focus.

With this we reach the point when psychologists were clearly thinking in terms of processes and degrees of integration. Moreover they were assuming that their unit of inquiry was no longer 'the mind' but an individual person, who cannot easily be dichotomized, however much the variations in his way of functioning can profitably be compared with those of his fellows.

We may now ask: what were the six polarities between whose extremes nineteenth-century psychological thought had tended to swing? I hazard the following list:

static and mechanical	– organic and evolutionary
passively reactive	– spontaneous
atomistic	– fused or integrated
conscious	– unconscious
individual and observable only by introspection and clinical study	– distributed and capable of clinical study, experiment or statistical analysis
solidly substantive	– airily relational

Though, as I have said, we would not now dare to ask questions about body and mind as 'simple substances' associated in any of the standard ways suggested, our practical and difficult empirical studies are still apt to be affected by these same polarities.

(ii) TWENTIETH-CENTURY POSTSCRIPT

As we have just seen, the nineteenth century pretty well reached the position wherein any general issue about body-mind relations was bound to be replaced by specialized empirical studies, by-passing an apparently insoluble problem. In these later studies we find psychologists, their medical psychological colleagues, and representatives of all the allied sciences of anatomy, physiology, neurology, biochemistry, and genetics, etc., investigating more specific questions. These may be illustrated thus: localization of functions psychologically described; intelligent problem solving and its relations with heredity, cortical development, and endocrine balance; the relation of emotional experience on the one hand to behaviour problems and on the other to the thalamus and the autonomic nervous system; the relations between remembering and brain structure or disease; variation in imagery or in degrees of consciousness in relation to the type of electrical wave recorded from the cortex; variations in human problem-solving in different physical environments, e.g. at work, at high altitudes, or under stress. The list could all too easily be extended, but to give a short account of the studies and findings, apart from its impossibility, would mean writing a history and critique of current psycho-physical inquiry which would go out of date in the process of the printing of this page. The reader is therefore provided with a few initial references in this immense field, together with a warning introduction from the wise and cautious Sherrington:

But indeed, what right have we to conjoin mental experience with physiological? No scientific right; only the right of what Keats, with that superlative Shakespearian gift of his, dubbed 'busy common sense'. The right which practical life, naive and shrewd, often exercises. To many of us a mere juxtaposition of the two sets of happenings proclaims their disparity. On the one side changing electrical potentials with thermal and chemical action making a physiological entity held together by energy relations; on the other, a suite of mental experience, an activity no doubt, but in what if any relation to energy? As for me, what little I know of the how of the one, does not, speaking personally, even begin to help me toward the how of the other. The two, for all I can do, seem to remain disparate and disconnected. I recognize that, from observation which becomes more and more precise, the time and place of the two sets of events seem to be coincident. All goes to show that they do in so far correspond. Mental experience on the one hand, and brain happenings on the other, though I cannot correlate together, I nevertheless find to coincide in time and space. We admit that the physico-chemical, to which we here seek to correlate the 'mental experience', is, for us, itself at long last mental, a thought, an idea. But that does not help because, at least to me, neither of the two appears related to the other. As mental events I should suppose them aloof. Science, nobly, declines as proof anything but complete proof; but common sense, pressed for time, accepts and acts on acceptance. (Rede Lecture)

While the relevant interests of the empirical investigators developed in directions such as these, another line of thinking suggested that the original form of the problem about body and mind posed a meaningless question. This line of thought can be traced back to English philosophical arguments that moved at the turn of the nineteenth and twentieth centuries towards sensory realism and interest in logical relationships. In nineteenth-century interest in 'fusion' and 'integration' there lurked the logical possibility, not only of the kind of idealism argued by Bradley, but of the more sinister species of absolutism wherein the distinctiveness of human and other individual objects begins to get lost. According to this argument, based on a subject-predicate logic, there is in the long run only one entity of which all others are in some obscure sense qualities. When the 'Absolute' of the philosophers turns into the 'State' of misguided politics some dubious consequences are apt to follow.

The distinctive contribution of writers in the best of the English empirical tradition, such as Moore, Whitehead, and Russell, was to put their fingers on the doubtful logical assumption underlying this view. Associated with this, specially in Russell's thinking, was wider recognition of the different logical function of similar grammatical forms and of the kind of mistake that arises if this difference in function is forgotten. If we treat all descriptive phrases as if they pointed to entities, as do demonstrative pronouns then, like Meinong, we have to invent different realms of *'Being'* for housing unicorns and chimeras. Such logical mistakes look too innocent to make, but quite sensible people have slipped into treating the 'Group Mind' as a mysterious entity, instead of realizing its indirect reference in most sentences to relations, and the active results of relations, between individual people.

Ruminations of this sort led Russell himself to cast antiseptic glances at the entities designated by 'mind' and 'matter' and to suggest still another form of aspect theory, according to which these terms function as very abstract shorthand devices whose reference to the ultimate furniture of the world is decidedly indirect. Russell himself, with a desire for certainty reminiscent of the seventeenth century, and a sensory empiricism characteristic of the English eighteenth, early sought these ultimate and indubitably hard data in fleeting sensory events. It would be possible to accept his logical theory while seeking a less atomistic empirical basis, but to seek this is to try to come to grips with the sensitive Sherrington's query. In humility, I do not think we have seen how to do this and we shall not learn if we are afraid to meet psychologically with perceptual and social relations of bewildering subtlety.

It is laborious but possible to trace a direct line of descent from the early writings of Moore and Russell, through Wittgenstein and the Vienna circle, to the logical analysts of our own day such as Ryle and Ayer. It is equally possible historically to track the fusion of relativity theory and this relational logic into Bridgman's *The Logic of Modern Physics*, by which relational thinking and operational definition penetrated modern psychological thought. It was escorted by the friendly ghost of our own William of Ockham: 'Entities should not be multiplied without necessity'.

Again, one aspect of this view is on the side of freedom from absolutism, from over-identification, from metaphysical monsters, and on the side of this experience and this individual person being very distinct from that. But the danger of analysis is a defensive linguisticism which is self-defeating. It has been said, if men cannot live by bread alone neither can they live on antiseptic, and whether mind-body problems could be solved or dismissed by logic and linguistics *only* remains, as I have indicated, a very open question. Even the new logic should be a tool not a master.

REFERENCES

THE NINETEENTH CENTURY

Bain, Alexander. *Mind and Body*. London: Kegan Paul. 6th Edn. 1878. See also Boring, pp. 233–40

Bernard, Claude. *Leçons sur les phénomènes de la vie communes aux animaux et aux végétaux*. Paris: Ballière, 1878

Biran, Maine de. *Œuvres Inédites*. Paris: Dezobry, Magdeleine, 1859, pp. 206–8, and Chap. IV, pp. 246 *et seq.*

Boring, E. G. *History of Experimental Psychology*. New York and London: Century, 2nd Edn. 1950, pp. 469, 226, 230, 231

Braid, James. See Dennis, Wayne, pp. 178–93

Brett, G. S. *History of Psychology*, abridged and ed. R. S. Peters. London: Allen and Unwin, 1953, p. 334

Bridgman, P. W. *The Logic of Modern Physics*. New York: Macmillan, 1928

Coghill, G. E. See Herrick

Dennis, Wayne. *Readings in the History of Psychology*. New York: Appleton-Century-Crofts, 1948

Findlay, J. N. *Meinong's Theory of Objects*. London: Oxford University Press, 1933

Flourens, Pierre. See Dennis, Wayne, pp. 129–39

Flügel, J. C. *A Hundred Years of Psychology*. London: Duckworth, 2nd Edn. 1951, p. 413

Freud, Sigmund. 'On Transience' *Collected Papers*, Ed. James Strachey. London: Hogarth Press, 1950, Vol. V, p. 80

Galton, Francis. 'Psychometric Experiments' in *Inquiries into Human Faculty*. London: Macmillan, 1883, pp. 185 ff. cf. *The Nineteenth Century*, Vol. V, 1879

Helmholtz, Hermann von. See Dennis, Wayne pp. 197–8

Herrick, C. J. *George Ellett Coghill: naturalist and philosopher*. Chicago: University Press, 1949

Huxley, Julian. *Evolution and Ethics 1893–1943.* London: Pilot Press, 1947

Irvine, William. *Apes, Angels and Victorians.* London: Weidenfeld and Nicholson, 1955

Mathiesson, F. O. *The James Family.* New York: Knopf, 1948, p. 300

Meinong, A. See Findlay

Mill, James. See Boring, p. 226

Mill, John Stuart. See Boring, pp. 230, 231

P. E. P. *Population Policy in Great Britain.* London: Political and Economic Planning, 1948, p. 40

Prince, Morton. *The Dissociation of a Personality.* New York and London: Longmans, 1906

Russell, Bertrand. *Our Knowledge of the External World.* London: Allen and Unwin, Revised Edn. 1926

Spencer, Herbert. *The Principles of Psychology.* London: Williams and Norgate, 3rd Edn. 1881. Vol. II, p. 294

Zilboorg, G., and Henry, G. W. *A History of Medical Psychology.* New York: Norton, 1941

Wundt, Wilhelm. *Outlines of Psychology.* Trans. C. H. Judd. London: Williams and Norgate, 3rd revised Edn. 1907. See also Boring, Chap. 16, pp. 316–47

TWENTIETH-CENTURY POSTSCRIPT

Introductory Bibliography

This list is selective and includes only some works, general and specialist, which might reasonably constitute the basis of a historical attack on twentieth century studies in which body-mind relations come under fairly direct scrutiny.

Adrian, E. D. *The Physical Basis of Perception.* London: Oxford University Press, 1947

Beach, F. H. *Hormones and Behaviour.* New York: Hoeber, Medical Book Dept. Harper Brothers, 1948

Cannon, W. B. *Bodily Changes in Pain, Hunger, Fear and Rage.* New York: Appleton-Century-Crofts, 2nd Edn. 1929

Fulton, J. F. *Functional Localization in the Frontal Lobes and Cerebellum.* Oxford: Clarendon Press, 1944

Head, Sir Henry. (1) *Studies in Neurology.* London: Hodder and Stoughton, 1920. See Lashley (2)

 (2) *Aphasia.* London: Cambridge University Press, 1926

Hebb, D. O. (1) *The Organization of Behaviour.* New York: John Wiley, 1949

 (2) 'Drives and the C. N. S. (Conceptual Nervous System)'. *Psychological Review.* Vol. LXII, 1955. pp. 243–54

Hunt, J. McV. (Editor). *Personality and the Behaviour Disorders.* New York: Ronald Press, 2 Vols. 1944

Köhler, Wolfgang. *The Mentality of Apes.* Translated from the 2nd revised edition by Ella Winter. London: Routledge and Kegan Paul, 1948

Kretschmer, E. *Physique and Character*, Trans. W. J. H. Sprott. London: Kegan Paul, Trench, Trubner, 1925

Lashley, K. S. (1) *Brain Mechanisms and Intelligence*. Chicago: University Press, 1930

(2) 'The Thalamus and Emotion'. *Psychological Review*, Vol. XLV, 1938, pp. 445–69

(3) 'Experimental Analysis of Instinctive Behaviour'. *Psychological Review*, Vol. XLV, 1938, pp. 445–69

(4) 'In Search of the Engram' in *Physiological Mechanisms in Animal Behaviour*. Symposia of the Society for Experimental Biology No. IV. Cambridge: University Press, 1950, pp. 454–82

Lindsley, D. B. 'Emotion' in *Handbook of Experimental Psychology*. Ed. S. S. Stevens. New York: Wiley. London: Chapman and Hall, 1951, Chap. XIV

Martin, J. Purdon. 'Consciousness and its disturbances considered from the neurological aspect'. *The Lancet*, Jan. 1 and 8, 1949, pp. 1 and 8

Mayer-Gross, W., Slater, Eliot, and Roth, Martin. *Clinical Psychiatry*. London: Cassell, 1954

Myers, C. S. (1) *In the Realm of Mind*. Cambridge: University Press, 1937

(2) *Shell-Shock in France 1914–1918*. Cambridge: University Press, 1940

Penrose, L. S. *The Biology of Mental Defect*. London: Sedgwick and Jackson, 1949

Robinson, Mary Frances, and Freeman, Walter. *Psychosurgery and the Self*. New York and London: Grune and Stratton, 1954

Sheldon, W. H., Stevens, S. S., and Tucker, W. B. *The Varieties of Human Physique*. New York and London: Harper, 1940

Sheldon, W. H., and Stevens, S. S. *The Varieties of Temperament*. New York and London: Harper, 1942

Sherrington, C. S. (1) *The Integrative Action of the Nervous System*. New Haven: Yale University Press. London: Oxford University Press, 1906

(2) *Man on his Nature*. Penguin Books, 1955

(3) *The Brain and its Mechanisms*. (The Rede Lecture, 1933, Cambridge University Press)

Short, P. L. 'The Objective Study of Mental Imagery', *British Journal of Psychology*, Vol. XLIV, 1953, pp. 38–51

Sluckin, W. *Minds and Machines*. Penguin Books, 1954

Stafford-Clark, D. *Psychiatry To-day*. Penguin Books, 1954

Terman, L. M. *et alia*, *Genetic Studies of Genius*, Vol. I. *Mental and Physical Traits of a Thousand Gifted Children*, Vol. III. *The Promise of Youth*, Vol. IV. *The Gifted Child Grows Up*. California: Stanford University Press, 1926, 1930, 1947

Walter, W. Grey. *The Living Brain.* London: Duckworth, 1953

Wilkie, J. S. *The Science of Mind and Brain.* London: Hutchinson, 1953

Yates, Aubrey B. 'The Validity of some Psychological Tests of Brain Damage'. *Psychological Bulletin*, Vol. LI, 1954, pp. 359–79

Young, J. Z. *Doubt and Certainty in Science* (Reith Lectures 1951). Oxford: Clarendon Press, 1952

CHAPTER 9

ANTITHESES

'If there's no meaning in it,' said the King, 'that saves a world of trouble, you know, as we needn't try to find any. And yet I don't know', he went on, spreading out the verses on his knee, and looking at them with one eye; 'I seem to see some meaning in them, after all "– *said I could not swim –*," you can't swim, can you?' he added turning to the Knave.

LEWIS CARROLL

BEFORE turning to the writers themselves, let us look back on this brief historical sketch and try to identify some of the variables with which changes in views about the relation of body, mind, and soul seem to have been connected.

First there are changes in the climate of opinion. These are of more than one kind. For example, though its operation is complex, we have seen the familiar fact that however great the achievement of one epoch, in the next there is likely to be at least a contrast in emphasis. Everything in one line seems perhaps to have been said, or it has become boring, or it has turned out to be either partly true or wholly false. Or some germ of thought has led to vast new developments – take for instance Galileo on primary and secondary qualities or nineteenth-century hints about unconscious functioning. In either case the next epoch, even generation, may want to ask new questions or find some other way of expressing its own point of view. The early twentieth century turned towards experiment and relational thought. In the second half of the twentieth century it is easy to see signs of challenge to positivism, to the more pedestrian kinds of empiricism.

Another kind of shift in climate of opinion is illustrated when, partly for historical reasons, one epoch lends itself to freedom of speculation, e.g. that of classical Greece, and the succeeding era is too oppressed with the problems of living for this to be feasible. Hence the thinking, as in the case of the Stoics and Epicureans, may become more practical, personal, or time-centred. Something comparable seemed to occur in the eighteenth century. It is worth noting, in passing, that the eras in which 'time now' has specially attracted thought, have often produced solid improvements in the standard of human living. The current attitude of any period to questions of public health and to physical and social conditions is in itself interesting in relation to people's views on body and mind.

Again under our first heading, there may be a dominant trend in an epoch which appears to permeate a great many fields of interest. For instance, the seventeenth-century interest in mechanical principles is well reflected in Descartes' physiology. Current technology has given rise to the cybernetics already discussed in this series by Sluckin. A trend comparable in generality seems to have been expressed in the twentieth-century discussions of multiple personality, relativity in physics and ethics, and portraits of people and things from multiple points of view, as by Mondriaan or Picasso or in the novels of Virginia Woolf or, for that matter, in Lewinian psychology. With an extra twist from his interest in mathematics and language, we can trace the same trend in Russell's theory of descriptions, leading him as it did to the notion of mind and matter as perspectives. Spinoza's capacity to think in 'aspects' was much less coloured by his epoch; to that extent, as Russell would probably agree, Spinoza's view was more profoundly original.

Our own era has gone through an equally marked phase of attributing everything to 'social pressures', whose existence indeed it is all too reasonable to recognize. To the widowed refugee with several cold and hungry children some events are too unreal to contemplate and others so cruel as only to be explained by a devil or human malice. The fate of a William James who had talked to Caraffa of 'consciousness as the last echo of the disappearing soul on the waters of philosophy' would have been as ugly as that which many persecuted people of our own generation have actually experienced. But Whitehead, who rediscovered the phrase 'climate of opinion', and all but the extreme adherents of environmental influence, would not wish to say that social pressure is everything.

Thus we reach our second main variable, namely the individual personalities of the writers, which must be given due weight. Between thinkers of the calibre of Plato and Aristotle there are clearly enormous individual differences; Hume and Rousseau appear to have approached human living from temperamentally opposite points of view. Who could be more diverse than Hobbes and Spinoza, in spite of the fact that one influenced the other? Such differences are reflected in what they say on our subject. We may first think of such distinctions in terms of a tendency to go forward or to withdraw from external stimuli, or in terms of the predominance of sense and intellect over intellect and emotions or the converse. These Jungian distinctions are suggestive. One is perhaps more struck by the individual complexity of each person's approach, influenced as it may have been both by temperament and the accidents of development in a special situation or period. Petrarch, for example, for whom the attractions of the world around and of withdrawal are both so strong, leaves an immortally personal document in his description of the ascent of Mont Ventoux, in spite of the fact that he is expressing a major conflict of his time.

Another aspect of individual personality, which might merit more study, is suggested by Aristotle's comment that reflective thinkers tend to have depressive traits. Until, historically, the mind-body problem became a subject to which an empirical, and perhaps even experimental approach might be relevant, many thinkers who have dealt with it might be fairly called 'arm-chair'. Few were primarily men of action, in the sense of carrying a heavy load of executive responsibility. On the other hand, the greatest are so very alive to the world in which they live that Aristotle's comment has to be treated with caution. But a writer's way of managing a depressive trait and its degree of success would be likely to be related to what he had to say. Recent experiments have suggested that there may, for example, be marked differences between depressives, schizophrenics, and ordinary people in the amount and nature of their responses to tactile and kinaesthetic stimuli. Though we can hardly check this hypothesis in relation to past thinkers, it is hard not to suppose that such differences in response would be relevant to the way a person approached mind-body relations.

This brings us to a third important variable, namely, that of the attitude of the immediate culture, and of the writer, to the senses and emotions on the one hand, and to intelligence or rationality on the other. The Renaissance interest in the senses and the related development of empirical science is of obvious importance. In the eighteenth century a tendency to be enmeshed in the present moment sometimes went with it and, as suggested at the beginning, brought into focus one prominent Western trait, that of emphasis on time. In general, the emotions had to wait till the eighteenth, nineteenth, and twentieth centuries for treatment that is not tinged from the start with some form of condemnation. From the early Greeks onwards, emotions have tended to be associated in some way with physical functioning. In our own direct, empirical, scientific, and perhaps somewhat extravert period, we may attempt, and sometimes successfully, to assess variations in intelligence; though about the nature of what we are measuring, and the infallibility of the results, psychologists are usually more cautious than the man in the street. Our attitude to 'reason' is less clear nowadays, but we are about 250 years away from thinking in 'essences' and fifty years away from responding happily to, perhaps, a study group's question about 'rational thought'. Until very recently the very phrase was alien and only slowly is an interest in thinking, as something more complex than intelligent problem-solving, reawakening (Hearnshaw, Humphrey). If in considering emotional responses a modern investigator takes empirical evidence about glandular, cortical, or thalamic functioning seriously, it may seem irrelevant to be accused of 'materialism'. This accusation is nevertheless made and it is not very surprising, specially if he tends also to underestimate the social significance of emotions. Comparable is the praise for being 'practical' or 'realistic'. Both accusation and praise, however, may miss the point that he has become more interested in how things function than in the question of what they are 'made of'. In this one seems to catch the echo of an eighteenth-century French voice somewhat drily remarking: '*Il importe peu à la*

religion de quelle substance soit l'âme pourvu qu'elle soit vertueuse'.
Or perhaps it is the nineteenth-century's Claude Bernard un-
pretentiously maintaining: 'When search for the causes determining phenomena is once posited as the fundamental principle
of the experimental method, materialism, spiritualism, inert
matter, and living matter cease to exist; only phenomena are
left, whose conditions we must determine'.

This introduces a fourth and important variable with which
changes in mind-body views appear to have been connected.
That is the stage of development of the relevant empirical
sciences, of which, clearly, physics and chemistry, neuro-
physiology, and biochemistry are specially important from our
point of view. The 'matter' of the twentieth-century universe,
and indeed the carcass of the modern neuro-physiologist, or
chemist, is, imaginatively, a far more elegant, entertaining,
subtle, and surprising affair than the impenetrable, inert, unresponsive, underlying 'something' with which, understand-
ably, some earlier philosophers found it so difficult to identify
themselves. We may have to look elsewhere for the real trouble
underlying the genuine and serious modern reproach of 'materialism'. For instance, whereas in the past the 'matter' or
'body' of the philosophers and physicists may have been a
natural target on which to project the frustrations experienced
in the face of undeniable disease, stupidity, unresponsiveness,
inertia, resistance, superior power, or threat, such an easy target
may have obscured the nature of what was so profoundly and
intelligibly resented. Sometimes an accusation of being 'materialist' may be a just comment on someone who has overlooked
the significance an event has for his neighbour. Suffice it that
we cannot safely forget the state of the relevant empirical findings, including the social-psychological facts about people's
attitudes to these findings. These attitudes may change much
more slowly than the sciences, so also may choice of projective
targets. Such slowness may have great advantages.

We must now consider four other and very different factors
which seem to bear on views about mind and body.

First, it seems to be true that, as the difficulties of earlier and
simpler views have become apparent, and our knowledge of

human mental and physical functioning has increased, an important change of attitude may have taken place in the degree of simplicity or complexity of the object with which we are willing to identify. This is a difficult point to discuss briefly. It seems, however, to be true that from the eighteenth century onwards thinkers became more aware of the complexity and possibly structural nature of human personality. I am not forgetting Aristotle's levels of human functioning. There is, however, an immense gap between Aristotle and, for example, Bishop Butler's discussions of self-love and benevolence and McDougall's comparable sentiments. We may even cite James' brilliant discussion of the social, the material, and the spiritual 'me' to illustrate the possibility of identification with something much more intricate than 'body' on the one hand, or, on the other, the early Greek *thymos* or *psyche*.

Whether we shall ever evolve a view that does justice both to the complexity of modern empirical findings and to the haunting beauty of the winged psyche hypothesis I do not know. Occasionally, the glimpse of an outstanding human being, functioning to full capacity, suggests a direction in which to look for clues. As Harding has pointed out, psychologists, by the nature of their trade, are not privileged to see this very often, nor are most of us equipped to recognize or respond to the chance when it occurs. Still less can we be too venturesome in theorizing. There is, however, a sense of 'simple' in which the personalities we call 'great' appear to function, at least more often than most of us, as spontaneous wholes of extreme though unified complexity. Sometimes this elicits a comparable though lesser response from those around; much as a crowd reacts to the outstanding performance of a great artist or a great cricketer, or a country in time of danger responds to the appeal of a great statesman. Though we cannot analyse these odd facts satisfactorily (the few remarks psychologists have made about empathy, and 'group relations' are pitifully limited), we cannot afford to neglect them, nor the special circumstances in which ordinary people may show the same quality.

Questions such as this raise difficult issues about the operation of mechanisms such as projection and identification which cannot possibly be omitted in thinking about mind-body problems. We have already implied a variation, indeed a development, in the complexity of the entities with which we may feel we can identify. We have not discussed, nor is it possible here, the extent to which one person varies in his need to identify with anything, or to project, and how far he may be encouraged or discouraged in this by the immediate group, culture, or period in which he lives. It would be interesting from this point of view to compare a Hume and a Kant.

Finally, we must briefly mention two somewhat technical philosophical issues. The first is a question of logic, and history of logic. Not until the beginning of this century, and then largely through the work of G. E. Moore, Russell, and Whitehead, was logic freed from restriction to subject-predicate forms. These tend to tie our thinking to 'substances' to which qualities can be attributed. Modern logic has led us to think more naturally in terms of relations, which is relevant to the mind-body problem, partly because it loosens our prejudices. Perhaps more important, for there have been other factors helping in the direction just mentioned, modern logic would permit us to distinguish mental and physical events in terms not of qualities, such as 'solidity' or the reverse, but in terms of the kind of relation one event or group of events has with others. In one case it may be important to relate a pain to bad fish and in others to bad feelings, we do not assume on this account that feelings are inevitably fishy or that fish are fantasies.

Over the centuries, the history of science and of logic has thrown up another development whose outcome is hard to predict, but which may provide a clue to further progress. This is reflected in our changing understanding of causality and therefore of explanation. As long as people thought almost exclusively in terms of one 'thing' making another 'thing' happen, and assumed that for this to occur the two 'things' must be in some way similar, there was no escape from the confusion which, as already suggested, it was Descartes' achievement to express so clearly that its nature became apparent. On the one hand we have a material and on the other a mental 'substance', dissimilar by definition. For no very obvious reason it is assumed that cause and effect must at all costs be alike. This assumption is at least as old as Aristotle. Query: How do mind and matter affect each other? We may well ask. As outlined earlier, pp. 17 ff., one well-known escape route is to say that they don't. At best they run parallel according to an immensely complicated pre-arranged plan. Another escape is to say that there are not two substances; either all is matter, all is mind, or all is something neutral. Whether 'matter' or 'mind' are vague and general or composed of chunky or spiritual atoms need not here concern us. A third way is to make matter fundamental and mind a Rococo decoration of no functional or causal significance; here we have epiphenomenalism. A fourth solution, the usual one of common sense, is to stick to interactionism without realizing that the ancient conceptions of 'explanation', 'causality', and 'substance' must then be jettisoned. A fifth is to look more closely at 'causality', 'explanation', and 'substance'. Our first reaction to this alternative can be deep fear. On the one hand looms a bewildering mathematical abstraction and on the other a groundless dread of determinism and inertia. We are unhappy, and psychologically this is quite intelligible, if theory appears in any way to deny us those determined but free, persistent but changing, reliable but boring, stimulating but exhausting, distinctly living nuclei which we find around us and love as our friends, our relatives, and our dogs. But we need not be afraid. As Butler said long ago, theory has to allow us, not deny us, the observations from which we start. In the West, however much in a setting, these are still individual. Put more technically, if in psychology we eventually adopted notions of functional dependence, or something comparable, in preference to unanalysed notions of causality, and some of our laws came to have a statistical nature, we should have still to ensure that our theory allowed for biological development and was not fouled by depersonalizing the distinctive human beings and animals with which it is supposed to be concerned. From these it starts and to these it must return. As people as well as scientists we do so with wonder.

Into the intensely difficult technical questions of psychology and logic which we have just raised we cannot go any further.

Suffice it if at this stage we have been able to indicate some of the factors, and perhaps assumptions, which seem to have affected the development of mind-body views and with them some directions of psychological interest.

REFERENCES

Fordham, Frieda. *An Introduction to the Psychology of C. G. Jung.* Penguin Books, 1953

Harding, D. W. 'Psychological Problems in the Recognition of Excellence'. *The Advancement of Science*, No. 38. Sept. 1953

Hearnshaw, L. S. 'Exploring the Intellect'. *British Journal of Psychology*, Vol. XLII, 1951, pp. 315–21

Humphrey, George. *Thinking, an introduction to its experimental psychology.* London: Methuen, 1951

Jung, C. G. *Psychological Types.* Trans. H. G. Baynes. London: Kegan Paul, no date. Cf. Fordham, Frieda

McDougall, William. *An Introduction to Social Psychology.* London: Methuen, Thirtieth Edn. 1950, Chaps. V–VIII and Supplementary Chap. VI

Bernard, Claude. *An Introduction to the Study of Experimental Medicine.* Trans. H. C. Green. New York: Macmillan , 1927, p. 219

PART TWO

The Thinkers Speak for Themselves

*

Everything has been said before
by someone who did not
discover it.
A. N. WHITEHEAD

HIPPOCRATES

5th Century B.C.

THE following extracts are taken from *The Sacred Disease* and are designed to illustrate Hippocrates' direct, organic, and distinctly matter-of-fact approach to his problem. It is worth noting the use he makes of the older Greek conception of consciousness as something connected with inhaled air. The four humours: blood, phlegm, black bile, and yellow bile are taken for granted in the comment on how the brain is attacked. That Hippocrates thought that these four, in certain proportions, underlie human constitution is clear from another treatise *On the Nature of Man* (pp. 202–13). The notion that air being associated with consciousness may mean that wind affects both, can be found developed in an entertaining, if not quite believable, essay in explaining national characteristics geographically. It is called *Airs, Waters, Places* and is also included in the volume from which we quote (pp. 90–111).

Readers will remember that the sacred disease was epilepsy. They should realize that in its context the main force of Hippocrates' argument lies in questioning the utility of 'sacredness' as an explanatory concept when so many events may fall within its range. Since in effect all things are sacred this idea will not suffice to explain the occurrence of one rather than another. Some two thousand two hundred years later we find William James using a similar form of argument when considering the practical value of the 'soul' as a scientific hypothesis for explaining individual differences. It is to be hoped that James and Hippocrates enjoy each other's company in Elysium. One feels that they might.

From THE SACRED DISEASE

I do not believe that the 'Sacred Disease' is any more divine or sacred than any other disease, but, on the contrary, has specific characteristics and a definite cause. . . .

It is my opinion that those who first called this disease 'sacred' were the sort of people we now call witch-doctors, faith-healers, quacks, and charlatans. These are exactly the people who pretend to be very pious and to be particularly wise. By invoking a divine element they were able to screen their own failure to give suitable treatment and so called this a 'sacred' malady to conceal their ignorance of its nature. . . .

It ought to be generally known that the source of our pleasure, merriment, laughter, and amusement, as of our grief, pain, anxiety, and tears, is none other than the brain. It is specially the organ which enables us to think, see, and hear, and to distinguish the ugly and the beautiful, the bad and the good, pleasant and unpleasant. Sometimes we judge according to convention; at other times according to the perceptions of expediency. It is the brain too which is the seat of madness and delirium, of the fears and frights which assail us, often by night, but sometimes even by day; it is there where lies the cause of insomnia and sleep-walking, of thoughts that will not come, forgotten duties, and eccentricities. All such things result from an unhealthy condition of the brain; it may be warmer than it should be, or it may be cooler, or moister, or drier, or in any other abnormal state. Moistness is the cause of madness, for when the brain is abnormally moist it is necessarily agitated, and this agitation prevents sight or hearing being steady. Because of this, varying visual and acoustic sensations are produced, while the tongue can only describe things as they appear and sound. So long as the brain is still, a man is in his right mind.

The brain may be attacked both by phlegm and by bile, and the two types of disorder which result may be distinguished thus: those whose madness results from phlegm are quiet and neither shout nor make a disturbance; those whose madness results from bile shout, play tricks, and will not keep still but are always up to some mischief. Such are the causes of continued madness, but fears and frights may be caused by changes in the brain. Such a change occurs when it is warmed, and that is the effect bile has when, flowing from the rest of the body, it courses to the brain along the blood-vessels. Fright continues until the bile runs away again into the blood-vessels and into the body. Feelings of pain and nausea result from inopportune cooling and abnormal consolidation of the brain, and this is the effect of phlegm. The same condition is responsible for loss of memory.

Those of a bilious constitution are liable to shout and to cry out during the night when the brain is suddenly heated; those of phlegmatic constitution do not suffer in this way. Warming of the brain also takes place when a plethora of blood finds its way to the brain and boils. It courses along the blood-vessels I have described, in great quantity when a man is having a nightmare and is in a state of terror. He reacts in sleep in the same way that he would if he were awake; his face burns, his eyes are blood-shot as they are when scared or when the mind is intent upon the commission of a crime. All this ceases as soon as the man wakes and the blood is dispersed again into the blood vessels.

For these reasons I believe the brain to be the most potent organ in the body. So long as it is healthy, it is the interpreter which enables us to draw anything from the air. Consciousness is caused by air. The eyes, ears, tongue, hands, and feet perform actions which are planned by the brain, for there is a measure of conscious thought throughout the body proportionate to the amount of air which it receives. The brain is also the organ of comprehension, for when a man draws in a breath it reaches the brain first, and thence is dispersed into the rest of the body, having left behind in the brain its vigour and whatever pertains to consciousness and intelligence. If the air went first to the body and subsequently to the brain, the power of understanding would be left to the flesh and to the blood-vessels; it would only reach the brain hot and when it was no longer pure owing to admixture with fluid from the tissues and from the blood, and this would blunt its keenness.

I therefore assert that the brain is the interpreter of comprehension. Accident and convention have falsely ascribed that function to the diaphragm,* which does not, and could not possess it. I know of no way in which the diaphragm can think and be conscious, except that a sudden access of pleasure or of pain might make it jump and throb because it is so thin and is under greater tension than any other part of the body. Moreover, it has no cavity into which it might receive anything good

* Gk. *phrenes* cf. p. 26 for Onians on the changing meaning of this word.

or bad that comes upon it, but the weakness of its construction makes it liable to disturbance by either of these forces. It is no quicker in perception than any other part of the body, and its name and associations are quite unwarranted, just as parts of the heart are called auricles though they make no contribution to hearing. Some say, too, that we think with our hearts and it is the heart which suffers pain and feels anxiety. There is no truth in this, although it is convulsed as is the diaphragm, and even more, for the following reasons: blood-vessels from all parts of the body run to the heart, and these connexions ensure that it can feel if any pain or strain occurs in the body. Moreover, the body cannot help giving a shudder and a contraction when subjected to pain, and the same effect is produced by an excess of joy, which heart and diaphragm feel most intensely. Neither of these organs takes any part in mental operations, which are completely undertaken by the brain. As then the brain is the first organ in the body to perceive the consciousness derived from the air, if the seasons cause any violent change in the air, the brain undergoes its greatest variations. This is my reason for asserting that the diseases which attack the brain are the most acute, most serious, and most fatal, and the hardest problem in diagnosis for the unskilled practitioner.

This so-called 'sacred disease' is due to the same causes as all other diseases, to the things we see come and go, the cold and the sun too, the changing and inconstant winds. These things are divine, so that there is no need to regard this disease as more divine than any other; all are alike divine and all human. Each has its own nature and character, and there is nothing in any disease which is unintelligible or which is insusceptible to treatment. The majority of maladies may be cured by the same things as caused them. One thing nourishes one thing, another another and sometimes destroys it too. The physician must know of these things in order to be able to recognize the opportune moment to nourish and increase one thing while robbing another of its sustenance and so destroy it.

In this disease as in all others, it should be your aim to wear it down by applying the remedies most hostile to the disease and those things to which it is unaccustomed. A malady flourishes and grows in its accustomed circumstances but is blunted and declines when attacked by a hostile substance. A man with the knowledge of how to produce by means of a regimen dryness and moisture, cold and heat in the human body, could cure this disease too provided that he could distinguish the right moment for the application of the remedies. He would not need to resort to purifications and magic spells.

REFERENCE

The Medical Works of Hippocrates. Trans. John Chadwick and W. N. Mann. Oxford: Blackwell Scientific Publications, 1950, pp. 179, 179–80, 190–3

PLATO

c. 427–*c.* 347 B.C.

ABOUT the exact date and place of Plato's birth there is some uncertainty, 430, 428, and 427 all being cited. He was born either in
Athens or Aegina. The Peloponnesian War had already started
when Plato was born, and he must have grown up during the
prolonged national struggle that ended in his country's defeat.
After the conquest of Athens in 403 B.C., there was a brief period
of rule by the Thirty, of whom Critias, Plato's uncle, was the
head. This arbitrary government was soon overthrown and the
state returned to a form of democratic government. In 399, when
Plato was about 28, there took place the trial and death of his
master, Socrates. Prior to this there might have seemed some
possibility of Plato taking an active part in political affairs. After
this event he seems to have turned almost exclusively to teaching
and writing, in which he spent the rest of an increasingly illustrious life, but in times of political uncertainty.

I adhered fairly closely to the *Timaeus* in Chap 2, because,
though untypical, it was the main dialogue known to the
Middle Ages. The following extracts therefore come not from it
but from other dialogues more representative of Plato's thought.
The first, from the *Phaedo*, have been chosen to illustrate a
general view of the relation of soul and body and the doctrine of
innate ideas as involving recollection of previous 'absolute' experience. As the discussion centres on the immortality of the soul,
we get the full force of Plato's (or Socrates'?) views on withdrawal
from bodily living.

In the extract from the *Phaedrus* we find the notion of the soul
as the initiator of activity and a further slant on the doctrine of
knowledge as reminiscence. The tripartite division of the soul is
also made clear. Some of the context of myth has been retained
and we get a glimpse of Socrates reflecting on the memory of
scenes experienced before we were 'imprisoned in the body like
an oyster in his shell'.

From the *Republic* there comes the simile of the cave to show,
once again, Plato's theory of knowledge and to enable readers to
begin to relate this to seventeenth- and eighteenth-century arguments about 'innate ideas'. The extract from Book IX has indirect

relevance to mind-body problems as we see them today. For its intrinsic psychological interest, to the passage on passions and dreams is added part of Socrates' view of tyrannical character development. The point of view is somewhat different from the necessarily dramatic austerity of the *Phaedo*.

From THE PHAEDO

Socrates, who is in prison, talking with a few friends prior to drinking the hemlock, discusses why a philosopher would be inconsistent if he hesitated to die. He begins his argument as follows:

Do we believe that there is such a thing as death?

To be sure, replied Simmias.

Is it not the separation of soul and body? And to be dead is the completion of this; when the soul exists in herself, and is released from the body and the body is released from the soul, what is this but death?

Just so, he replied.

There is another question, which will probably throw light on our present inquiry if you and I can agree about it: Ought the philosopher to care about the pleasures – if they are to be called pleasures – of eating and drinking?

Certainly not, answered Simmias.

And what about the pleasures of love – should he care for them?

By no means.

And will he think much of the other ways of indulging the body; for example, the acquisition of costly raiment, or sandals, or other adornments of the body? Instead of caring about them, does he not rather despise anything more than nature needs? What do you say?

I should say that the true philosopher would despise them.

Would you not say that he is entirely concerned with the soul and not with the body? He would like, as far as he can, to get away from the body and to turn to the soul.

Quite true.

In matters of this sort philosophers, above all other men, may be observed in every sort of way to dissever the soul from the communion of the body.

Very true.

Whereas, Simmias, the rest of the world are of opinion that to him who has no sense of pleasure and no part in bodily pleasure, life is not worth having; and that he who is indifferent about them is as good as dead.

That is also true.

What again shall we say of the actual acquirement of knowledge? – is the body, if invited to share in the inquiry, a hinderer or a helper? I mean to say, have sight and hearing any truth in them? Are they not, as the poets are always telling us, inaccurate witnesses? and yet, if even they are inaccurate and indistinct, what is to be said of the other senses? – for you will allow that they are the best of them.

Certainly, he replied.

Then when does the soul attain truth? – for in attempting to consider anything in company with the body she is obviously deceived.

True.

Then must not true existence be revealed to her in thought, if at all?

Yes.

And thought is best when the mind is gathered into herself and none of these things trouble her – neither sounds nor sights nor pain nor any pleasure, – when she takes leave of the body, and has as little as possible to do with it, when she has no bodily sense or desire, but is aspiring after true being?

Certainly.

And in this the philosopher dishonours the body; his soul runs away from his body and desires to be alone and by herself?

That is true.

Well, but there is another thing, Simmias: Is there or is there not an absolute justice?

Assuredly there is.

And an absolute beauty and absolute good?

Of course.

But did you ever behold any of them with your eyes?

Certainly not.

Or did you ever reach them with any other bodily sense? — and I speak not of these alone, but of absolute greatness, and health, and strength, and of the essence or true nature of everything. Has the reality of them ever been perceived by you through the bodily organs? or rather, is not the nearest approach to the knowledge of their several natures made by him who so orders his intellectual vision as to have the most exact conception of the essence of each thing which he considers?

Certainly.

And he attains to the purest knowledge of them who goes to each with the mind alone, not introducing or intruding in the act of thought, sight, or any other sense together with reason, but with the very light of the mind in her own clearness searches into the very truth of each; he who has got rid, as far as he can, of eyes and ears and, so to speak, of the whole body, these being in his opinion distracting elements which when they infect the soul hinder her from acquiring truth and knowledge. . . .

Later, in answer to Cebes' comment that men are apt to be incredulous, fearing that the soul may perish on the day of death, Socrates is persuaded to elaborate the famous argument for the soul's immortality. He does so both to convince himself and to reassure the others. Altogether there are five stages in the argument, which can be outlined as follows:

(1) If the Pythagorean belief in transmigration is correct then the soul must have existed before birth. Socrates attempts to reinforce this by a somewhat involved inference about regeneration from the assumption that all things, including dying, have their opposites.

(2) If knowledge is simply recollection, then the soul must have existed before. Involved in this argument is the belief that we remember one thing as like another, but in assessing the degree of similarity we make use of an abstract idea of equality which is either innate or lost to us at birth but recollected afterwards. Socrates prefers the second alternative. Here is a relevant section:

If we acquired this knowledge before we were born, and were born having the use of it, then we also knew before we were born and at the instant of birth not only the equal or the greater or the less, but all other ideas; for we are not speaking only of equality, but of beauty, goodness, justice, holiness, and of all which we stamp with the name of essence in the dialectical process, both when we ask and when we answer questions. Of all this we may certainly affirm that we acquired the knowledge before birth?

We may.

But if, after having acquired, we have not forgotten what in each case we acquired, then we must always have come into life having knowledge, and shall always continue to know as long as life lasts – for knowing is the acquiring and retaining knowledge and not forgetting. Is not forgetting, Simmias, just the losing of knowledge?

Quite true, Socrates.

But if the knowledge which we acquired before birth was lost by us at birth, and if afterwards by the use of the senses we recovered what we previously knew, will not the process which we call learning be a recovering of the knowledge which is natural to us, and may not this be rightly termed recollection?

Very true.

So much is clear – that when we perceive something, either by the help of sight, or hearing, or some other sense, from that perception we are able to obtain a notion of some other thing like or unlike which is associated with it but has been forgotten. Whence, as I was saying, one of two alternatives follows: either we had this knowledge at birth, and continued to know through life; or, after birth, those who are said to learn only remember, and learning is simply recollection.

(3) Things which are compound or changing may theoretically be dispersed. There are two kinds of existence: one seen and changing, the other unseen and unchanging. The soul more nearly resembles the latter, and therefore is not open to the objection stated at the beginning. Socrates re-emphasizes his notions of the relation of body and soul in this argument, of which the following is an extract:

If the soul exists before birth, and in coming to life and being born can be born only from death and dying, must she not after death continue to exist, since she has to be born again? – Surely the proof which you desire has been already furnished. Still I suspect that you and Simmias would be glad to probe the argument further. Like children, you are haunted with a fear that when the soul leaves the body, the wind may really blow her away and scatter her; especially if a man should happen to die in a great storm and not when the sky is calm.

Cebes answered with a smile: Then, Socrates, you must argue us out of our fears – and yet, strictly speaking, they are not our fears, but there is a child within us to whom death is a sort of hobgoblin: him too we must persuade not to be afraid when he is alone in the dark.

Socrates said: Let the voice of the charmer be applied daily until you have charmed away the fear.

And where shall we find a good charmer of our fears, Socrates, when you are gone?

Hellas, he replied, is a large place, Cebes, and has many good men, and there are barbarous races not a few: seek for him among them all, far and wide, sparing neither pains nor money; for there is no better way of spending your money. And you must seek among yourselves too; for you will not find others better able to make the search.

The search, replied Cebes, shall certainly be made. And now, if you please, let us return to the point of the argument at which we digressed.

By all means, replied Socrates; what else should I please?

Very good.

Must we not, said Socrates, ask ourselves what that is which, as we imagine, is liable to be scattered, and about which we fear? and what again is that about which we have no fear? And then we may proceed further to inquire whether that which suffers dispersion is or is not of the nature of soul – our hopes and fears as to our own souls will turn upon the answers to these questions.

Very true, he said.

Now the compound or composite may be supposed to be naturally capable, as of being compounded, so also of being dissolved; but that which is uncompounded, and that only, must be, if anything is, indissoluble.

Yes; I should imagine so, said Cebes.

And the uncompounded may be assumed to be the same and unchanging, whereas the compound is always changing and never the same.

I agree, he said.

Then now let us return to the previous discussion. Is that idea of essence, which in the dialectical process we define as essence or true existence – whether essence of equality, beauty, or anything else – are these essences, I say, liable at times to some degree of change? or are they each of them always what they are, having the same simple self-existent and unchanging forms, not admitting of variation at all, or in any way, or at any time?

They must be always the same, Socrates, replied Cebes.

And what would you say of the many beautiful – whether men or horses or garments or any other things which are named by the same names and may be called equal or beautiful, – are they all unchanging and the same always, or quite the reverse? May they not rather be described as almost always changing and hardly ever the same, either with themselves or with one another?

The latter, replied Cebes; they are always in a state of change.

And these you can touch and see and perceive with the senses, but the unchanging things you can only perceive with the mind – they are invisible and are not seen?

That is very true, he said.

Well then, added Socrates, let us suppose that there are two sorts of existences – one seen, the other unseen.

Let us suppose them.

The seen is the changing, and the unseen is the unchanging?

That may be also supposed.

And, further, is not one part of us body, another part soul?

To be sure.

And to which class is the body more alike and akin?

Clearly to the seen – no one can doubt that.

And is the soul seen or not seen?

Not by man, Socrates.

And what we mean by 'seen' and 'not seen' is that which is or is not visible to the eye of man?

Yes, to the eye of man.

And is the soul seen or not seen?

Not seen.

Unseen then?

Yes.

Then the soul is more like to the unseen, and the body to the seen?

That follows necessarily, Socrates.

And were we not saying long ago that the soul when using the body as an instrument of perception, that is to say, when using the sense of sight or hearing or some other sense (for the meaning of perceiving through the body is perceiving through the senses) – were we not saying that the soul too is then dragged by the body into the region of the changeable, and wanders and is confused; the world spins round her, and she is like a drunkard, when she touches change?

Very true.

But when returning into herself she reflects, then she passes into the other world, the region of purity, and eternity, and immortality, and unchangeableness, which are her kindred, and with them she ever lives, when she is by herself and is not let or hindered; then she ceases from her erring ways, and being in communion with the unchanging is unchanging. And this state of the soul is called wisdom?

That is well and truly said, Socrates, he replied.

And to which class is the soul more nearly alike and akin, as far as may be inferred from this argument, as well as from the preceding one?

I think, Socrates, that, in the opinion of every one who follows the argument, the soul will be infinitely more like the unchangeable – even the most stupid person will not deny that.

And the body is more like the changing?

Yes.

Yet once more consider the matter in another light: When the soul and the body are united, then nature orders the soul to rule and govern, and the body to obey and serve. Now which of these two functions is akin to the divine? and which to the mortal? does not the divine appear to you to be that which naturally orders and rules, and the mortal to be that which is subject and servant?

True.

And which does the soul resemble?

The soul resembles the divine, and the body the mortal – there can be no doubt of that, Socrates.

Then reflect, Cebes: of all which has been said is not this the conclusion? – that the soul is in the very likeness of the divine, and immortal, and intellectual, and uniform, and indissoluble, and unchangeable; and that the body is in the very likeness of the human, and mortal, and unintellectual, and multiform, and dissoluble, and changeable.

(4, 5) But, objects Simmias, the soul then resembles a harmony, perishing as a melody does when the strings of a lute are broken. This drives Socrates to use arguments (2) and (3) to undermine the alleged analogy between the soul and a harmony, which he argues, for example, can only come into being after the lyre, the strings, and the sounds already exist. Unlike the soul it is not master of the elements of which it is believed to be composed. But, Cebes objects, even if the soul is more lasting than the body it does not follow that it may not cease to exist when it has outworn several bodies. This leads Socrates to consider the notions of generation and corruption from which, in effect, (and 5) he is led so to define the soul that it is as much immortal as the number 3 is odd and cannot be even. In discussing this he refers to his excitement in finding that Anaxagoras thought the mind was the 'disposer and cause of all'. Socrates is later disappointed. As the discussion seems to be still alive, here is another extract:

As I proceeded, I found my philosopher altogether forsaking mind or any other principle of order, but having recourse to air, and ether, and water, and other eccentricities. I might compare him to a person who began by maintaining generally that mind is the cause of the actions of Socrates, but who, when he endeavoured to explain the causes of my several actions in detail, went on to show that I sit here because my body is made up of bones and muscles; and the bones, as he would say, are hard and have joints which divide them, and the muscles are elastic, and they cover the bones, which have also a covering or environment of flesh and skin which contains them; and as the bones are lifted at their joints by the contraction or relaxation of the muscles, I am able to bend my limbs, and this is why I am sitting here in a curved posture – that is what he would say; and he would have a similar explanation of my talking to you, which he would attribute to sound, and air, and hearing, and he would assign ten thousand other causes of the same sort, forgetting to mention the true cause, which is, that the Athenians have thought fit to condemn me, and accordingly I have thought it better and more right to remain here and undergo my sentence; for I am inclined to think that these muscles and bones of mine would have gone off long ago to Megara or Boeotia – by the dog they would, if they had been moved only by their own idea of what was best, and if I had not chosen the better and nobler part, instead of playing truant and running away, of enduring any punishment which the state inflicts. There is surely a strange confusion of causes and conditions in all this. It may be said, indeed, that without bones and muscles and the other parts of the body I cannot execute my purposes. But to say that I do as I do because of them, and that this is the way in which mind acts, and not from the choice of the best, is a very careless and idle mode of speaking. I wonder that they cannot distinguish the cause from the condition, which the many, feeling about in the dark, are always mistaking and misnaming. And thus one man makes a vortex all round and steadies the earth by the heaven; another gives the air as a support to the earth, which is a sort of broad trough. Any power which in arranging them as they are, arranges them for the best, never enters into their minds; and instead of finding any superior strength in it, they rather expect to discover another Atlas of the world who is stronger and more everlasting and more containing than the good; – of the obligatory and containing power of the good they think nothing; and yet this is the principle which I would fain learn if any one would teach me. But as I have failed either to discover myself, or to learn of any one else, the nature of the best, I will exhibit to you, if you like, what I have found to be the second best mode of inquiring into the cause.

From THE PHAEDRUS

Simile of the Charioteer

The soul through all her being is immortal, for that which is ever in motion is immortal; but that which moves another and is moved by another, in ceasing to move ceases also to live. Only the self-moving, never-leaving self, never ceases to move, and is the fountain and beginning of motion to all that moves besides. Now the beginning is unbegotten, for that which is begotten has a beginning; but the beginning is begotten of nothing, for if it were begotten of something, then the begotten would not come from a beginning. But if unbegotten, it must also be indestructible; for if beginning were destroyed, there could be no beginning out of anything, nor anything out of a beginning; and all things must have a beginning. And therefore the self-moving is the beginning of motion; and this can neither be destroyed nor begotten, else the whole heavens and all creation would collapse and stand still, and never again have motion or birth. But if the self-moving is proved to be immortal, he who affirms that self-motion is the very idea and essence of the soul will not be put to confusion. For the body which is moved from without is soulless; but that which is moved from within has a soul, for such is the nature of the soul. But if this be true, must not the soul be the self-moving, and therefore of necessity unbegotten and immortal ? Enough of the soul's immortality.

Of the nature of the soul, though her true form be ever a theme of large and more than mortal discourse, let me speak briefly, and in a figure. And let the figure be composite – a pair of winged horses and charioteer. Now the winged horses and the charioteers of the gods are all of them noble and of noble descent, but those of other races are mixed; and the human charioteer drives his in a pair; and one of them is noble and of noble breed, and the other is ignoble and of ignoble breed; and the driving of them of necessity gives a great deal of trouble to him. I will endeavour to explain to you in what way the mortal differs from the immortal creature. The soul in her totality has the care of inanimate being everywhere, and traverses the whole heaven in divers forms appearing; – when perfect and fully winged she soars upward, and orders the whole world; whereas the imperfect soul, losing her wings and drooping in her flight at last settles on the solid ground – there, finding a home, she receives an earthly frame which appears to be self-moved, but is really moved by her power; and this composition of soul and body is called a living and mortal creature. For immortal no such union can be reasonably believed to be; although fancy, not having seen nor surely known the nature of God, may imagine an immortal creature having both a body and also a soul which are united throughout all time. Let that, however, be as God wills, and be spoken of acceptably to him. And now let us ask the reason why the soul loses her wings.

The wing is the corporeal element which is most akin to the divine, and which by nature tends to soar aloft and carry that which gravitates downwards into the upper region, which is the habitation of the gods. The divine is beauty, wisdom, goodness, and the like; and by these the wing of the soul is nourished, and grows apace; but when fed upon evil and foulness and the opposite of good, wastes and falls away. Zeus, the mighty lord, holding the reigns of a winged chariot, leads the way in heaven, ordering all and taking care of all; and there follows him the array of gods and demi-gods, marshalled in eleven bands; Hestia alone abides at home in the house of heaven; of the rest they who are reckoned among the princely twelve march in their appointed order. They see many blessed sights in the inner heaven, and there are many ways to and fro, along which the blessed gods are passing, every one doing his own work; he may follow who will and can, for jealousy has no place in the celestial choir. But when they go to banquet and festival, then they move up the steep to the top of the vault of heaven. The chariots of the gods in even poise, obeying the rein, glide rapidly; but the others labour, for the vicious steed goes heavily, weighing down the charioteer to the earth when his steed has not been thoroughly trained: – and this is the hour of agony and extremest conflict for the soul. For the immortals, when they are at the end of their course, go forth and stand upon the outside of heaven, and the revolution of the spheres carries them round, and they behold the things beyond. But of the heaven which is above the heavens, what earthly poet ever did or ever will sing worthily? It is such as I will describe; for I must dare to speak the truth, when truth is my theme. There abides the very being with which true knowledge is concerned; the colourless, formless, intangible essence, visible only to mind, the pilot of the soul. The divine intelligence, being nurtured upon mind and pure knowledge, and the intelligence of every soul which is capable of receiving the food proper to it, rejoices at beholding reality, and once more gazing upon truth, is replenished and made glad, until the revolution of the worlds brings her round again to the same place. In the revolution she beholds justice, and temperance, and knowledge absolute, not in the form of generation or of relation, which men call existence, but knowledge absolute in existence absolute; and beholding the other true existences in like manner, and feasting upon them, she passes down into the interior of the heavens and returns home; and there the charioteer putting up his horses at the stall, gives them ambrosia to eat and nectar to drink.

Such is the life of the gods; but of other souls, that which follows God best and is likest to him lifts the head of the charioteer into the outer world, and is carried round in the revolution, troubled indeed by the steeds, and with difficulty beholding true being; while another only rises and falls, and sees, and again fails to see by reason of the unruliness of the steeds. The rest of the souls are also longing after the upper world and they all follow, but not being strong enough they are carried round below the surface, plunging, treading on one another, each striving to be first; and there is confusion and perspiration and the extremity of effort; and many of them are lamed or have their wings broken through the ill-driving of the charioteers; and all of them after a fruitless toil, not having attained to the mysteries of true being, go away, and feed upon opinion. The reason why the souls exhibit this exceeding eagerness to behold the plain of truth is that pasturage is found there, which is suited to the highest part of the soul; and the wing on which the soul soars is nourished with this. And there is a law of Destiny, that the soul which attains any vision of truth in company with a god is preserved from harm until the next period, and if attaining always is always unharmed. But when she is unable to follow, and fails to behold the truth, and through some ill-hap sinks beneath the double load of forgetfulness and vice, and her wings fall from her and she drops to the ground, then the law ordains that this soul shall at her first birth pass, not into any other animal, but only into man; and the soul which has seen most of truth shall come to the birth as a philosopher, or artist, or some musical and loving nature; that which has seen truth in the second degree shall be some righteous king or warrior chief; the soul which is of the third class shall be a politician, or economist, or trader; the fourth shall be a lover of gymnastic toils, or a physician; the fifth shall lead the life of a prophet or hierophant; to the sixth the character of a poet or some other imitative artist will be assigned; to the seventh the life of an artisan or husbandman; to the eighth that of a sophist or dema- gogue; to the ninth that of a tyrant; – all these are states of pro- bation, in which he who does righteously improves, and he who does unrighteously deteriorates his lot.

Ten thousand years must elapse before the soul of each one can return to the place from whence she came, for she cannot grow her wings in less; only the soul of a philosopher, guileless and true, or the soul of a lover, who is not devoid of philosophy, may acquire wings in the third of the recurring periods of a thousand years; he is distinguished from the ordinary good man who gains wings in three thousand years: – and they who choose this life three times in succession have wings given them, and go away at the end of three thousand years. But the others re- ceive judgement when they have completed their first life, and after the judgement they go, some of them to the houses of cor- rection which are under the earth, and are punished; others to some place in heaven whither they are lightly borne by justice, and there they live in a manner worthy of the life which they led here when in the form of men. And at the end of the first thousand years the good souls and also the evil souls both come to draw lots and choose their second life, and they may take any which they please. The soul of a man may pass into the life of a beast, or from the beast return again into the man. But the soul which has never seen the truth will not pass into the human form. For a man must have intelligence of universals, and be able to proceed from the many particulars of sense to one conception of reason; – this is the recollection of those things which our soul once saw while following God – when regardless of that which we now call being she raised her head up towards the true being. And therefore the mind of the philosopher alone has wings; and this is just, for he is always, according to the measure of his abilities, clinging in recollection to those things in which God abides, and in beholding which He is what He is. And he who employs aright these memories is ever being initiated into perfect mysteries and alone becomes truly perfect. But, as he forgets earthly interests and is rapt in the divine, the vulgar deem him mad, and rebuke him; they do not see that he is inspired.

The Experience of Beauty

But of beauty, I repeat again that we saw her there shining in company with the celestial forms; and coming to earth we find her here too, shining in clearness through the clearest aperture of sense. For sight is the most piercing of our bodily senses; though not by that is wisdom seen; her loveliness would have been transporting if there had been a visible image of her, and the other ideas, if they had visible counterparts, would be equally lovely. But this is the privilege of beauty, that being the loveliest she is also the most palpable to sight. Now he who is not newly initiated or who has become corrupted, does not easily rise out of this world to the sight of true beauty in the other; he looks only at her earthly namesake, and instead of being awed at the sight of her, he is given over to pleasure, and like a brutish beast he rushes on to enjoy and beget; he consorts with wantonness, and is not afraid or ashamed of pursuing pleasure in violation of nature. But he whose initiation is recent, and who has been the spectator of many glories in the other world, is amazed when he sees any one having a godlike face or form, which is the expression of divine beauty; and at first a shudder runs through him, and again the old awe steals over him; then looking upon the face of his beloved as of a god he reverences him, and if he were not afraid of being thought a downright madman, he would sacrifice to his beloved as to the image of a god; then while he gazes on him there is a sort of re-action, and the shudder passes into an unusual heat and per-spiration; for, as he receives the effluence of beauty through the eyes, the wing moistens and he warms. And as he warms, the parts out of which the wing grew, and which had been hitherto closed and rigid, and had prevented the wing from shooting forth, are melted, and as nourishment streams upon him, the lower end of the wing begins to swell and grow from the root upwards; and the growth extends under the whole soul – for once the whole was winged. During this process the whole soul is all in a state of ebullition and effervescence, – which may be compared to the irritation and uneasiness in the gums at the time of cutting teeth, – bubbles up, and has a feeling of uneasi-ness and tickling; but when in like manner the soul is beginning to grow wings, the beauty of the beloved meets her eye and she receives the sensible warm emotion of particles which flow to-wards her, therefore called emotion ($\mathring{\iota}\mu\epsilon\rho o\varsigma$), and is refreshed and warmed by them, and then she ceases from her pain with joy. But when she is parted from her beloved and her moisture fails, then the orifices of the passage out of which the wing shoots dry up and close, and intercept the germ of the wing; which, being shut up with the emotion, throbbing as with the pulsations of an artery, pricks the aperture which is nearest, until at length the entire soul is pierced and maddened and pained, and at the recollection of beauty is again delighted. And from both of them together the soul is oppressed at the strange-ness of her condition, and is in a great strait and excitement, and in her madness can neither sleep by night nor abide in her place by day. And wherever she thinks that she will behold the beau-tiful one, thither in her desire she runs. And when she has seen him, and bathed herself in the waters of beauty, her constraint is loosened, and she is refreshed, and has no more pangs and pains; and this is the sweetest of all pleasures at the time, and is the reason why the soul of the lover will never forsake his beautiful one, whom he esteems above all; he has forgotten mother and brethren and companions, and he thinks nothing of the neglect and loss of his property; the rules and proprieties of life, on which he formerly prided himself, he now despises, and is ready to sleep like a servant, wherever he is allowed, as near as he can to his desired one, who is the object of his worship, and the physician who can alone assuage the greatness of his pain. And this state, my dear imaginary youth to whom I am talking, is by men called love.

Simile of the Charioteer amplified

As I said at the beginning of this tale, I divided each soul into three – two horses and a charioteer; and one of the horses was good and the other bad: the division may remain, but I have not yet explained in what the goodness or badness of either consists, and to that I will now proceed. The right-hand horse is upright and cleanly made; he has a lofty neck and an aquiline nose; his colour is white, and his eyes dark; he is a lover of honour and modesty and temperance, and the follower of true glory; he needs no touch of the whip, but is guided by word and admonition only. The other is a crooked lumbering animal, put together anyhow; he has a short thick neck; he is flat-faced and of a dark colour, with grey eyes and blood-red complexion; the mate of insolence and pride, shag-eared and deaf, hardly yielding to whip and spur. Now when the charioteer beholds the vision of love, and has his whole soul warmed through sense, and is full of the prickings and ticklings of desire, the obedient steed, then as always under the government of shame, refrains from leaping on the beloved; but the other, heedless of the pricks and of the blows of the whip, plunges and runs away, giving all manner of trouble to his companion and the charioteer, whom he forces to approach the beloved and to remember the joys of love. They at first indignantly oppose him and will not be urged on to do terrible and unlawful deeds; but at last, when he persists in plaguing them, they yield and agree to do as he bids them. And now they are at the spot and behold the flashing beauty of the beloved; which when the charioteer sees, his memory is carried to the true beauty, whom he beholds in company with Modesty like an image placed upon a holy pedestal. He sees her, but he is afraid and falls backwards in adoration, and by his fall is compelled to pull back the reins with such violence as to bring both the steeds on their haunches, the one willing and unresisting, the unruly one very unwilling; and when they have gone back a little, the one is overcome with shame and wonder, and his whole soul is bathed in perspiration; the other, when the pain is over which the bridle and the fall had given him, having with difficulty taken breath, is full of wrath and reproaches, which he heaps upon the charioteer and his fellow-steed, for want of courage and manhood, declaring that they have been false to their agreement and guilty of desertion. Again they refuse, and again he urges them on, and will scarce yield to their prayer that he would wait until another time. When the appointed hour comes, they make as if they had forgotten, and he reminds them, fighting and neighing and dragging them on, until at length he on the same thoughts intent, forces them to draw near again. And when they are near he stoops his head and puts up his tail, and takes the bit in his teeth and pulls shamelessly. Then the charioteer is worse off than ever; he falls back like a racer at the barrier, and with a still more violent wrench drags the bit out of the teeth of the wild steed and covers his abusive tongue and jaws with blood, and forces his legs and haunches to the ground and punishes him sorely. And when this has happened several times and the villain has ceased from his wanton way, he is tamed and humbled, and follows the will of the charioteer, and when he sees the beautiful one he is ready to die of fear. And from that time forward the soul of the lover follows the beloved in modesty and holy fear.

From THE REPUBLIC

Simile of the Cave

And now, I said, let me show in a figure how far our nature is enlightened or unenlightened: – Behold! human beings living in an underground den, which has a mouth open towards the light and reaching all along the den; here they have been from their childhood, and have their legs and necks chained so that they cannot move, and can only see before them, being prevented by the chains from turning round their heads. Above and behind them a fire is blazing at a distance, and between the fire and the prisoners there is a raised way; and you will see, if you look, a low wall built along the way, like the screen which marionette players have in front of them, over which they show the puppets.

I see.

And do you see, I said, men passing along the wall carrying all sorts of vessels, and statues and figures of animals made of wood and stone and various materials, which appear over the wall? Some of them are talking, others silent.

You have shown me a strange image, and they are strange prisoners.

Like ourselves, I replied; and they see only their own shadows, or the shadows of one another, which the fire throws on the opposite wall of the cave?

True, he said; how could they see anything but the shadows if they were never allowed to move their heads?

And of the objects which are being carried in like manner they would only see the shadows?

Yes, he said.

And if they were able to converse with one another, would they not suppose that they were naming what was actually before them?

Very true.

And suppose further that the prison had an echo which came from the other side, would they not be sure to fancy when one of the passers-by spoke that the voice which they heard came from the passing shadow?

No question, he replied.

To them, I said, the truth would be literally nothing but the shadows of the images.

That is certain.

And now look again, and see what will naturally follow if the prisoners are released and disabused of their error. At first, when any of them is liberated and compelled suddenly to stand up and turn his neck round and walk and look towards the light, he will suffer sharp pains; the glare will distress him, and he will be unable to see the realities of which in his former state he had seen the shadows; and then conceive some one saying to him, that what he saw before was an illusion, but that now, when he is approaching nearer to being and his eye is turned towards more real existence, he has a clearer vision, – what will be his reply? And you may further imagine that his instructor is pointing to the objects as they pass and requiring him to name them, – will he not be perplexed? Will he not fancy that the shadows which he formerly saw are truer than the objects which are now shown to him?

Far truer.

And if he is compelled to look straight at the light, will he not have a pain in his eyes which will make him turn away to take refuge in the objects of vision which he can see, and which he will conceive to be in reality clearer than the things which are now shown to him?

True, he said.

And suppose once more, that he is reluctantly dragged up a steep and rugged ascent, and held fast until he is forced into the presence of the sun himself, is he not likely to be pained and irritated? When he approaches the light his eyes will be dazzled, and he will not be able to see anything at all of what are now called realities.

Not all in a moment, he said.

He will require to grow accustomed to the sight of the upper world. And first he will see the shadows best, next the reflections of men and other objects in the water, and then the objects themselves; then he will gaze upon the light of the moon and the stars and the spangled heaven; and he will see the sky and the stars by night better than the sun or the light of the sun by day?

Certainly.

Last of all he will be able to see the sun, and not mere reflections of him in the water, but he will see him in his own proper place, and not in another; and he will contemplate him as he is.

Certainly.

He will then proceed to argue that this is he who gives the season and the years, and is the guardian of all that is in the visible world, and in a certain way the cause of all things which he and his fellows have been accustomed to behold?

Clearly, he said, he would first see the sun and then reason about him.

And when he remembered his old habitation, and the wisdom of the den and his fellow-prisoners, do you not suppose that he would felicitate himself on the change, and pity them?

Certainly, he would.

And if they were in the habit of conferring honours among themselves on those who were quickest to observe the passing shadows and to remark which of them went before, and which followed after, and which were together; and who were therefore best able to draw conclusions as to the future, do you think that he would care for such honours and glories, or envy the possessors of them? Would he not say with Homer,

'Better to be the poor servant of a poor master,'
and to endure anything, rather than think as they do and live after their manner?

Yes, he said, I think that he would rather suffer anything than entertain these false notions and live in this miserable manner.

Imagine once more, I said, such an one coming suddenly out of the sun to be replaced in his old situation; would he not be certain to have his eyes full of darkness?

To be sure, he said.

And if there were a contest, and he had to compete in

1. HSIA KUEI

Chinese painting reveals a rare knack of portraying individual items in relation to a four-dimensional universe but one nevertheless in which limits of space and time appear either non-existent or irrelevant. In this respect Far Eastern Art often contrasts with Western whose greatest achievements tend to involve intensification of the individual qualities of things, persons, or places. These items may have symbolic significance but in Western Art this is almost greater the more individual and time bound they become. This is seen if this twelfth-century Chinese picture, *Talking with a friend under pines by a precipice*, is compared with those that follow.

2. WINCHESTER BIBLE

This illumination from the Winchester Bible dates from the twelfth century. It shows a devil being cast out. Such literal portrayal of devil possession (or depossession) is common in art. Another and later example is given in plate 6. A famous illustration of devils being removed from a whole village occurs in the Giotto frescoes at Assisi. For fifteenth and sixteenth-century versions of the supposed activities of devils when in possession the reader should turn to Chapters 4 and 5.

3. ARISTOTLE

This figure of Aristotle represents dialectic, one of the seven liberal
arts portrayed in the carving on the twelfth-century Port Royal of
Chartres Cathedral. It serves as a reminder of two things: first the
awakening interest in Aristotle characteristic of the twelfth and
thirteenth centuries and secondly the slow shift in sculpture from the
purely formal to the naturalistic. Aristotle though not yet quite alive
is hardly Byzantine.

4. Uta

The carving of Uta and Regelindis is usually dated about 1260. The statues are among those of twelve men and women influential in founding the first Cathedral of Naumburg early in the eleventh century. To their memory the west choir of the rebuilt thirteenth-century Cathedral was dedicated. Uta and Regelindis stand beside

5 . REGELINDIS

their husbands the Margrafin Ekkehard and Hermann, two brothers who in 1028 donated their castle as residence for the first Bishop when Otto the Great was trying to establish outposts for defence and Christian missionary work in the East. The statues are masterpieces of thirteenth-century naturalism.

6. Bigallo

Plates 6 and 7 offer further illustration of exorcism on the one hand and, on the other, the often found artistic portrayal of the soul resembling a small replica of the person from whom it is removed on death.

In this Giotto version of the death of the Virgin the soul is swathed and formal. Later artists, e.g. Fra Angelico and Hungary's Master of Mateoc, treat the same general theme but the soul more closely resembles a naturalistic miniature of the dying person. This suggests an obvious problem. In the Lady Chapel of St Mark's, Venice, the sixteenth century solves the difficulty by portraying the dying Virgin realistically as a very old lady, but showing her on arrival in Heaven as a young and lovely one standing on the hand of a somewhat startled-looking Almighty.

7. GIOTTO

8. MASACCIO

These two illustrations should be considered together with plates 10 and 11 which offer a contrast. Masaccio's portrayal of vigorous and unaristocratic individualism, from one of the Carmine frescoes, and the section of Benozzo Gozzoli's decorative procession from the Palazzo Medici-Riccardi, represent in vastly different ways one fifteenth-century theme stressed in Chapter 4. The young man on the white horse is an idealized Lorenzo de' Medici.

Most readers can supplement these scanty illustrations with a host of Quattrocento visual images, including countless variations on the theme of mother and child.

9. BENOZZO GOZZOLI

This version of the three living and the three dead men (see Chap. 4) was engraved by an artist working in the Middle Rhine district at the close of the fifteenth century. Later, though probably still within Benozzo Gozzoli's lifetime, it re-states a theme as old as the early eleventh century but sharply contrasting with the Medici procession's gaiety. The related theme of the Death Dance underlies the mid-sixteenth century's brilliant and gruesome *Triumph of Death* by Breughel.

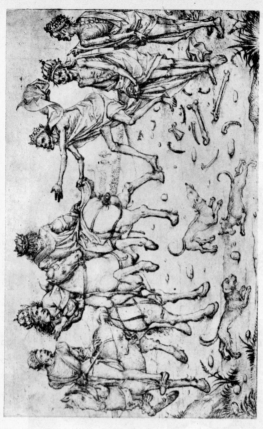

10. MEISTER DES HAUSBUCHS

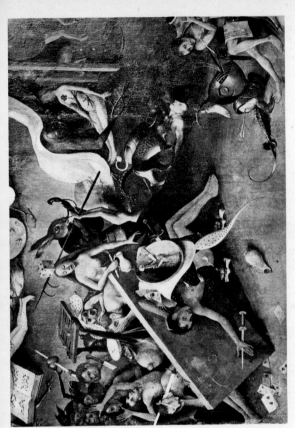

11. HIERONYMUS BOSCH

The Flemish artist Hieronymus Bosch was the greatest contemporary painter of fear and phantasy in the late fifteenth and early sixteenth century. Some of his works strike us as as morbid in the extreme, many are characterized by superb draughtsmanship and colouring. Plate 11 gives a fairly typical expression of devilish activities in hell and suggests something of the haunting and sinister quality of heresy, lunacy, and sorcery when they are linked together in one conception.

12. School of Hieronymus Bosch

This page of witches, attributed formerly to Breughel, reveals creatures of phantasy and practical nuisance value, rather than the tempestuous horrors of Breughel's more famous *Dulle Griet*, wherein the nightmare quality of Bosch still lingers. But it is interesting to note contemporary portrayal of common sixteenth-century superstitions.

This seventeenth-century sketch of Delft suggests something of the lucid realism of liberal Holland, contrasting as it does with the morbid if brilliant output of Bosch and Breughel in the previous centuries. Readers familiar with the more famous *View of Delft* by Vermeer (Spinoza's and Bisschop's great contemporary) may begin thinking in 'aspects' if, imaginatively, they stroll along the far side of Vermeer's canal.

13 . JAN DE BISSCHOP

14. CHARDIN

Chardin's genre painting of a woman arranging her little girl's hair
must stand for some eighteenth-century traits relevant to the history
of psychology and not often stressed – interest in everyday natural
things and people, in children, and in subtle personal and social
relationships. It is arguable that Chardin was the century's greatest
and most individual social observer though, as he portrayed humble
life, he was not the most typical. The reader may ask himself: has
Chardin painted 'minds', 'bodies', or 'people'?

15. T. H. HUXLEY

The nineteenth century provided so many portraits and people that for illustration here a Galtonian attempt at composite portraiture appeared at one stage the best answer. In fact a composite portrait eliminates the distinctive and individual qualities that Galton himself stressed. Instead, and not uncharacteristically, T. H. Huxley shouldered his way in lecturing on evolution and advocating technical education.

16. A WOMAN WORKER

The Woman Worker by Käthe Kollwitz was included in the exhibition of art considered by Hitler to be 'degenerate'. She might in fact be misemployed, unemployed, a refugee, an expellee, or one of millions of other tragic individuals of the twentieth century.

17 and 18. MONDRIAAN

These two versions of a tree by the Dutch artist Mondriaan date from about 1910, a period when the possibility of thinking in new 'relations', 'polarities', or 'aspects' was getting a grip on several spheres of interest, including mathematical physics and music. Dutch experts on Mondriaan sometimes look past him to Spinoza because in their different ways and centuries both made abstraction expressive.

measuring the shadows with the prisoners who had never moved out of the den, while his sight was still weak, and before his eyes had become steady (and the time which would be needed to acquire this new habit of sight might be very considerable), would he not be ridiculous? Men would say of him that up he went and down he came without his eyes; and that it was better not even to think of ascending; and if any one tried to loose another and lead him up to the light, let them only catch the offender, and they would put him to death.

No question, he said.

This entire allegory, I said, you may now append, dear Glaucon, to the previous argument; the prison-house is the world of sight, the light of the fire is the sun, and you will not misapprehend me if you interpret the journey upwards to be the ascent of the soul into the intellectual world according to my poor belief, which, at your desire, I have expressed – whether rightly or wrongly God knows. But, whether true or false, my opinion is that in the world of knowledge the idea of good appears last of all, and is seen only with an effort; and, when seen, is also inferred to be the universal author of all things beautiful and right, parent of light and of the lord of light in this visible world, and the immediate source of reason and truth in the intellectual; and that this is the power upon which he who would act rationally either in public or private life must have his eye fixed.

I agree, he said, as far as I am able to understand you.

Moreover, I said, you must not wonder that those who attain to this beatific vision are unwilling to descend to human affairs; for their souls are ever hastening into the upper world where they desire to dwell; which desire of theirs is very natural, if our allegory may be trusted.

Yes, very natural.

And is there anything surprising in one who passes from divine contemplations to the evil state of man, misbehaving himself in a ridiculous manner; if, while his eyes are blinking and before he has become accustomed to the surrounding darkness, he is compelled to fight in courts of law, or in other places, about the images or the shadows of images of justice, and is endeavouring to meet the conceptions of those who have never yet seen absolute justice ?

Anything but surprising, he replied.

Any one who has common sense will remember that the bewilderments of the eyes are of two kinds, and arise from two causes, either from coming out of the light or from going into the light, which is true of the mind's eye, quite as much as of the bodily eye; and he who remembers this when he sees any one whose vision is perplexed and weak, will not be too ready to laugh; he will first ask whether that soul of man has come out of the brighter life, and is unable to see because unaccustomed to the dark, or having turned from darkness to the day is dazzled by excess of light. And he will count the one happy in his condition and state of being, and he will pity the other; or, if he have a mind to laugh at the soul which comes from below into the light, there will be more reason in this than in the laugh which greets him who returns from above out of the light into the den.

That, he said, is a very just distinction.

But then, if I am right, certain professors of education must be wrong when they say that they can put a knowledge into the soul which was not there before, like sight into blind eyes.

They undoubtedly say this, he replied.

Whereas, our argument shows that the power and capacity of learning exists in the soul already; and that just as the eye was unable to turn from darkness to light without the whole body, so too the instrument of knowledge can only by the movement of the whole soul be turned from the world of becoming into that of being, and learn by degrees to endure the sight of being, and of the brightest and best of being, or in other words, of the good.

Very true.

And must there not be some art which will effect conversion in the easiest and quickest manner; not implanting the faculty of sight, for that exists already, but has been turned in the wrong direction, and is looking away from the truth ?

Yes, he said, such an art may be presumed.

And whereas the other so-called virtues of the soul seem to

be akin to bodily qualities, for even when they are not originally innate they can be implanted later by habit and exercise, the virtue of wisdom more than anything else contains a divine element which always remains, and by this conversion is rendered useful and profitable; or, on the other hand, hurtful and useless.

From the discussion of the tyrannical character

In Book IX of the *Republic* as an explanatory digression in discussing the tyrannical man Socrates remarks:

I do not think that we have adequately determined the nature and number of the appetites, and until this is accomplished the inquiry will always be confused.

Asked to supply the omission he starts with the following comments, which I think have considerable historical interest in relation to some of our modern theories, though I do not want to make the mistake of implying that 'everything has been said before':

Certain of the unnecessary pleasures and appetites I conceive to be unlawful; every one appears to have them but in some persons they are controlled by the laws and by reason, and the better desires prevail over them – either they are wholly banished or they become few and weak; while in the case of others they are stronger, and there are more of them.

Which appetites do you mean? DREAMS

I mean those which are awake when the reasoning and human and ruling power is asleep; then the wild beast within us, gorged with meat or drink, starts up and having shaken off sleep, goes forth to satisfy his desires; and there is no conceivable folly or crime – not excepting incest or any other unnatural union, or parricide, or the eating of forbidden food – which at such a time, when he has parted company with all shame and sense, a man may not be ready to commit.

Most true, he said.

But when a man's pulse is healthy and temperate, and when before going to sleep he has awakened his rational powers, and fed them on noble thoughts and inquiries, collecting himself in meditation; after having first indulged his appetites neither too much nor too little but just enough to lay them to sleep, and prevent them and their enjoyments and pains from interfering with the higher principle – which he leaves in the solitude of pure abstraction, free to contemplate and aspire to the know-ledge of the unknown, whether in past, present, or future: when again he has allayed the passionate element, if he has a quarrel against anyone – I say, when, after pacifying the two irrational principles, he rouses up the third, which is reason, before he takes his rest, then, as you know, he attains truth most nearly, and is least likely to be the sport of fantastic and lawless visions.

I quite agree.

In saying this I have been running into a digression; but the point which I desire to note is that in all of us, even in good men, there is a lawless wild-beast nature, which peers out in sleep. Pray, consider whether I am right, and you agree with me.

Yes, I agree.

And now remember the character which we attributed to the democratic man. He was supposed from his youth upwards to have been trained under a miserly parent, who encouraged the saving appetites in him, but discountenanced the unnecessary, which aim only at amusement and ornament?

True.

And then he got into the company of a more refined, licen-tious sort of people, and taking to all their wanton ways rushed into the opposite extreme from an abhorrence of his father's meanness. At last, being a better man than his corruptors, he was drawn in both directions until he halted midway and led a life, not of vulgar and slavish passion, but of what he deemed moderate indulgence in various pleasures. After this manner the democrat was generated out of the oligarch?

Yes, he said; that was our view of him, and is so still.

And now, I said, years will have passed away, and you must conceive this man, such as he is, to have a son, who is brought up in his father's principles.

I can imagine him.

Then you must further imagine the same thing to happen to

the son which has already happened to the father: – he is drawn into a perfectly lawless life, which by his seducers is termed perfect liberty; and his father and friends take part with his moderate desires, and the opposite party assist the opposite ones. As soon as these dire magicians and tyrant-makers find that they are losing their hold on him, they contrive to implant in him a master passion, to be lord over his idle and spendthrift lusts – a sort of monstrous winged drone – that is the only image which will adequately describe him.

Yes, he said, that is the only adequate image of him.

And when his other lusts, amid clouds of incense and perfumes and garlands and wines, and all the pleasures of a dissolute life, now let loose, come buzzing around him, nourishing to the utmost the sting of desire which they implant in his drone-like nature, then at last this lord of the soul, having Madness for the captain of his guard, breaks out into a frenzy; and if he finds in himself any good opinions or appetites in process of formation, and there is in him any sense of shame remaining, to these better principles he puts an end, and casts them forth until he has purged away temperance and brought in madness to the full.

Yes, he said, that is the way in which the tyrannical man is generated.

REFERENCES

Plato. *The Dialogues of Plato*. Trans. by Benjamin Jowett. London: Oxford University Press. 5 vols. 3rd Edn. 1931
    Phaedo, Vol. II, pp. 157 ff. Especially pp. 203–5, 216–17, 219–23, 244–5
    Phaedrus, Vol. I, pp. 391 ff. Especially pp. 451–6, 457–8, 460–1
    Republic, Vol. III, Bk. VII, pp. 214–19, Bk. IX, 280–2

ARISTOTLE

? 384–322 B.C.

Aristotle was born at Stagyra in Thrace; his father was physician
to the king of Macedonia. Becoming a student of Plato's when he
was about eighteen, Aristotle remained at the Academy until his
middle thirties when Plato died. From 343 B.C., Aristotle was for
three years tutor to Alexander the Great, until the time when the
latter was declared of age at 16. Between 335 and 323 B.C. Aristotle lived in Athens, writing and running his school. To this he
gave a scientific (especially biological) turn of interest very different from the predominantly mathematical emphasis which
characterized the later Academy. Alexander died in 323. When
the Athenians rebelled and indicted those known to have had
connexions with him, Aristotle fled from Athens and died the
following year.

It is useful to know that some of the difficulty in understanding Aristotle derives from modern editions having to be based on
a mixture possibly of lecturer's notes and excerpts from fully
written works. A. E. Taylor's *Aristotle* in the Nelson Discussion
Series is an excellent introduction for those who want to know
something more of this problem, and of Aristotle's life and times,
but cannot embark on classical scholarship.

In his early years Aristotle held a view of the soul something
like Plato's. The following extracts from the *De Anima* and the
Nichomachean Ethics, which are later, do not do justice to the
complexity and often apparently contradictory nature of what
Aristotle had to say. They have been chosen by way of introduction. There is some justification for Voltaire's comment:

'*Aristote, qu'on a expliqué de mille façons parce qu'il était ininteli-
gible, croyait, si l'on s'en rapporte à quelques-uns de ses disciples,
que l'entendement de tous les hommes était une seule et même
substance.*'

On the other hand Aristotle was often an excellent biologist
and his approach to psychological questions is of undoubted
relevance to the way we consider them now. We cannot entirely
blame Aristotle for the fact that his logic, and the somewhat un-
profitable emphasis on 'essence' associated with it, proved so
much more interesting to the Scholastics. Modern thought has

had to revolt from one facet of Aristotle's outlook in order to return more appreciatively to others.

In dealing with the passages that follow, the reader will be helped if he realizes that '*psyche*' has been translated as 'soul', but Aristotle is discussing what we would call 'mind'. '*Nous*' has been translated as 'mind'. It appears to share one characteristic, i.e. immortality, with what we should call 'soul' but seems to be impersonal. Aristotle, however, must be allowed to make clear his own usage of these key terms.

From DE ANIMA

Book I

[402a] Holding as we do that, while knowledge of any kind is a thing to be honoured and prized, one kind of it may, either by reason of its greater exactness or of a higher dignity and greater wonderfulness in its objects, be more honourable and precious than another, on both accounts we should naturally be led to place in the front rank the study of the soul. The knowledge of the soul admittedly contributes greatly to the advance of truth in general, and, above all, to our understanding of Nature, for the soul is in some sense the principle of animal life. Our aim is to grasp and understand, first its essential nature, and secondly its properties; of these some are thought to be affections proper to the soul itself, while others are considered to attach to the animal owing to the presence within it of soul. . . .

First, no doubt, it is necessary to determine in which of the *summa genera* soul lies, what it *is*; is it 'a this-somewhat', a substance, or is it a *quale* or a *quantum*, or some other of the remaining kinds of predicates which we have distinguished? Further, does soul belong to the class of potential existents, or is it not rather an actuality? . . .

[402b] We must consider also whether soul is divisible or is without parts, and whether it is everywhere homogeneous or not; and if not homogeneous, whether its various forms are different specifically or generically: up to the present time those who have discussed and investigated soul seem to have confined them-

selves to the human soul. We must be careful not to ignore the question whether soul can be defined in a single unambiguous formula, as is the case with animal, or whether we must not give a separate formula for each sort of it, as we do for horse, dog, man, god. . . .

[403a] A further problem presented by the affections of soul is this: are they all affections of the complex of body and soul, or is there any one among them peculiar to the soul by itself? To determine this is indispensable but difficult. If we consider the majority of them, there seems to be no case in which the soul can act or be acted upon without involving the body; e.g. anger, courage, appetite, and sensation generally. Thinking seems the most probable exception; but if this too proves to be a form of imagination or to be impossible without imagination, it too requires a body as a condition of its existence. If there is any way of acting or being acted upon proper to soul, soul will be capable of separate existence. If there is none, its separate existence is impossible. In the latter case, it will be like what is straight, which has many properties arising from the straightness in it, e.g. that of touching a bronze sphere at a point, though straightness divorced from the other constituents of the straight thing cannot touch it in this way; it cannot be so divorced at all, since it is always found in a body. It therefore seems that all the affections of soul involve a body – passion, gentleness, fear, pity, courage, joy, loving, and hating; in all these there is a concurrent affection of the body. In support of this we may point to the fact that, while sometimes on the occasion of violent and striking occurrences there is no excitement or fear felt, on others faint and feeble stimulations produce these emotions, viz. when the body is already in a state of tension resembling its condition when we are angry. Here is a still clearer case: in the absence of any external cause of terror we find ourselves experiencing the feelings of a man in terror. From all this it is obvious that the affections of soul are en-mattered formulable essences.

Consequently their definitions ought to correspond, e.g. anger should be defined as a certain mode of movement of such and such a body (or part or faculty of a body) by this or that cause and for this or that end. That is precisely why the study of the soul must fall within the science of Nature, at least so far as in its affections it manifests this double character. Hence a physicist would define an affection of soul differently from a dialectician; the latter would define e.g. anger as the appetite for returning pain for pain, or something like that, while the former would define it as a boiling of the blood or warm substance surrounding the heart.

[403b] The latter assigns the material conditions, the former the form or formulable essence; for what he states is the formulable essence of the fact, though for its actual existence there must be embodiment of it in a material such as is described by the other. Thus the essence of a house is assigned in such a formula as 'a shelter against destruction by wind, rain, and heat'; the physicist would describe it as 'stones, bricks, and timbers'; but there is a third possible description which would say that it was that form in that material with that purpose or end. Which, then, among these is entitled to be regarded as the genuine physicist? The one who confines himself to the material, or the one who restricts himself to the formulable essence alone? Is it not rather the one who combines both in a single formula? If this is so, how are we to characterize the other two? Must we not say that there is no type of thinker who concerns himself with those qualities or attributes of the material which are in fact inseparable from the material, and without attempting even in thought to separate them? The physicist is he who concerns himself with all the properties active and passive of bodies or materials thus or thus defined; attributes not considered as being of this character he leaves to others, in certain cases it may be to a specialist, e.g. a carpenter or a physician, in others (a) where they are inseparable in fact, but are separable from any particular kind of body by an effort of abstraction, to the mathematician, (b) where they are separate both in fact and in thought from body altogether, to the First Philosopher or Metaphysician. But we must return from this digression and repeat that the affections of soul are inseparable from the material substratum of animal life, to which we have

seen that such affections, e.g. passion and fear, attach, and have not the same mode of being as a line or a plane.

[408b] . . . We speak of the soul as being pained or pleased, being bold or fearful, being angry, perceiving, thinking. All these are regarded as modes of movement, and hence it might be inferred that the soul is moved. This, however, does not necessarily follow. We may admit to the full that being pained or pleased, or thinking, are movements (each of them a 'being moved'), and that the movement is originated by the soul. For example we may regard anger or fear as such and such movements of the heart, and thinking as such and such another movement of that organ, or of some other; these modifications may arise either from changes of place in certain parts or from qualitative alterations (the special nature of the parts and the special modes of their changes being for our present purpose irrelevant). Yet to say that it is *the soul* which is angry is as inexact as it would be to say that it is the soul that weaves webs or builds houses. It is doubtless better to avoid saying that the soul pities or learns or thinks and rather to say that it is the man who does this with his soul. What we mean is not that the movement is in the soul, but that sometimes it terminates in the soul and sometimes starts from it, sensation e.g. coming from without inwards, and reminiscence starting from the soul and terminating with the movements, actual or residual, in the sense organs.

The case of mind is different; it seems to be an independent substance implanted within the soul and to be incapable of being destroyed. If it could be destroyed at all, it would be under the blunting influence of old age. What really happens in respect of mind in old age is, however, exactly parallel to what happens in the case of the sense organs; if the old man could recover the proper kind of eye, he would see just as well as the young man. The incapacity of old age is due to an affection not of the soul but of its vehicle, as occurs in drunkenness or disease. Thus it is that in old age the activity of mind or intellectual apprehension declines only through the decay of some other inward part; mind itself is impassible. Thinking, loving, and hating are affections not of mind, but of that which has mind, so far as it has it. That is why, when this vehicle decays, memory and love cease; they were activities not of mind, but of the composite which has perished; mind is, no doubt, something more divine and impassible.

Much of the rest of Book I concerns the views of Aristotle's predecessors.

Book II

In this book Aristotle, having reviewed his predecessors' opinions in Book I, decides to make a fresh start. Parts of this follow:

[412a] We are in the habit of recognizing, as one determinate kind of what is, substance, and that in several senses, (a) in the sense of matter or that which in itself is not 'a this', and (b) in the sense of form or essence, which is that precisely in virtue of which a thing is called 'a this', and thirdly (c) in the sense of that which is compounded of both (a) and (b). Now matter is potentiality, form actuality; of the latter there are two grades related to one another as e.g. knowledge to the exercise of knowledge.

Among substances are by general consent reckoned bodies and especially natural bodies; for they are the principles of all other bodies. Of natural bodies some have life in them, others not; by life we mean self-nutrition and growth (with its correlative decay). It follows that every natural body which has life in it is a substance in the sense of a composite.

But since it is also a *body* of such and such a kind, viz. having life, the *body* cannot be soul; the body is the subject or matter, not what is attributed to it. Hence the soul must be a substance in the sense of the form of a natural body having life potentially within it. But substance is actuality, and thus soul is the actuality of a body as above characterized. Now the word actuality has two senses corresponding respectively to the possession of knowledge, and the actual exercise of knowledge. It is obvious that the soul is actuality in the first sense, viz. that of knowledge as possessed, for both sleeping and waking presuppose the existence of soul, and of these waking corresponds to actual knowing, sleeping to knowledge possessed but not employed, and, in the history of the individual, knowledge comes before its employment or exercise.

That is why the soul is the first grade of actuality of a natural body having life potentially in it. The body so described is a body which is organized.

[412b] The parts of plants in spite of their extreme simplicity are 'organs'; e.g. the leaf serves to shelter the pericarp, the pericarp to shelter the fruit, while the roots of plants are analogous to the mouths of animals, both serving for the absorption of food. If then, we have to give a general formula applicable to all kinds of soul, we must describe it as the first grade of actuality of a natural organized body. That is why we can wholly dismiss as unnecessary the question whether the soul and the body are one; it is as meaningless as to ask whether the wax and the shape given to it by the stamp are one, or generally the matter of a thing and that of which it is the matter. Unity has many senses (as many as 'is' has), but the most proper and fundamental sense of both is the relation of an actuality to that of which it is the actuality.

We have now given an answer to the question, What is soul? – an answer which applies to it in its full extent. It is substance in the sense which corresponds to the definitive formula of a thing's essence. That means that it is 'the essential whatness' of a body of the character just assigned. Suppose that what is literally an 'organ', like an axe, were a *natural* body, its 'essential whatness' would have been its essence, and so its soul; if this disappeared from it, it would have ceased to be an axe, except in name. As it is, it is just an axe; it wants the character which is required to make its whatness or formulable essence a soul; for that, it would have had to be a *natural* body of a particular kind, viz. one having *in itself* the power of setting itself in movement and arresting itself. . . .

[413a] We resume our inquiry from a fresh starting-point by calling attention to the fact that what has soul in it differs from what has not, in that the former displays life. Now this word has more than one sense, and provided any one alone of these is

found in a thing we say that thing is living. Living, that is, may mean thinking, or perception, or local movement and rest, or movement in the sense of nutrition, decay, and growth. Hence we think of plants also as living, for they are observed to possess in themselves an originative power through which they increase or decrease in all spatial directions; they grow up *and* down, and everything that grows increases its bulk alike in both directions or indeed in all, and continues to live so long as it can absorb nutriment.

This power of self-nutrition can be isolated from the other powers mentioned, but not they from it – in mortal beings at least. The fact is obvious in plants; for it is the only psychic power they possess.

[413b] This is the originative power, the possession of which leads us to speak of things as *living* at all, but it is the possession of sensation that leads us for the first time to speak of living things as animals; for even those beings which possess no power of local movement but do possess the power of sensation we call animals and not merely living things.

The primary form of sense is touch, which belongs to all animals. Just as the power of self-nutrition can be isolated from touch and sensation generally, so touch can be isolated from all other forms of sense. (By the power of self-nutrition we mean that departmental power of the soul which is common to plants and animals: all animals whatsoever are observed to have the sense of touch.) What the explanation of these two facts is, we must discuss later. At present we must confine ourselves to saying that soul is the source of these phenomena and is characterized by them, viz. by the powers of self-nutrition, sensation, thinking, and motivity.

Is each of these a soul or a part of a soul ? And if a part, a part in what sense ? A part merely distinguishable by definition or a part distinct in local situation as well ? In the case of certain of these powers, the answers to these questions are easy, in the case of others we are puzzled what to say. Just as in the case of plants which when divided are observed to continue to live though removed to a distance from one another (thus showing that in *their* case the soul of each individual plant before division was actually one, potentially many), so we notice a similar result in other varieties of soul, i.e. in insects which have been cut in two; each of the segments possesses both sensation and local movement; and if sensation, necessarily also imagination and appetition; for, where there is sensation there is also pleasure and pain, and, where these, necessarily also desire.

We have no evidence as yet about mind or the power to think; it seems to be a widely different kind of soul, differing as what is eternal, from what is perishable; it alone is capable of existence in isolation from all other psychic powers. All the other parts of soul, it is evident from what we have said, are, in spite of certain statements to the contrary, incapable of separate existence though, of course, distinguishable by definition. . . .

[414a] . . . the word substance has three meanings – form, matter, and the complex of both – and of these three what is called matter is potentiality, what is called form, actuality. Since then the complex here is the living thing, the body cannot be the actuality of the soul; it is the soul which is the actuality of a certain kind of body. Hence the rightness of the view that the soul cannot be without a body, while it cannot *be* a body; it is not a body but something relative to a body. That is why it is *in* a body, and a body of a definite kind. It was a mistake, therefore, to do as former thinkers did, merely to fit it into a body without adding a definite specification of the kind or character of that body. Reflection confirms the observed fact; the actuality of any given thing can only be realized in what is already potentially that thing, i.e. in a matter of its own appropriate to it. From all this it follows that soul is an actuality or formulable essence of something that possesses a potentiality of being besouled.

Of the psychic powers above enumerated some kinds of living things, as we have said, possess all, some less than all, others one only. Those we have mentioned are the nutritive, the appetitive, the sensory, the locomotive, and the power of thinking. Plants have none but the first, the nutritive, while another order of living things has this *plus* the sensory.

[414b] If any order of living things has the sensory, it must also

have the appetitive; for appetite is the genus of which desire, passion, and wish are the species; now all animals have one sense at least, viz. touch, and whatever has a sense has the capacity for pleasure and pain and therefore has pleasant and painful objects present to it, and wherever these are present, there is desire, for desire is just appetition of what is pleasant. . . .

. . . Certain kinds of animals possess in addition the power of locomotion, and still another order of animate beings, i.e. man and possibly another order like man or superior to him, the power of thinking, i.e. mind.

Aristotle proceeds thereafter to discuss the ways of being 'besouled' which he has distinguished. This discussion, which among other things raises the question of the nature of the senses and imagination, leads him well into Book III. The following passages seem specially important from our point of view.

Book III

[427a] There are two distinctive peculiarities by reference to which we characterize the soul – (1) local movement and (2) thinking, discriminating, and perceiving. Thinking, both speculative and practical, is regarded as akin to a form of perceiving; for in the one as well as the other the soul discriminates and is cognizant of something which *is*. Indeed the ancients go so far as to identify thinking and perceiving; e.g. Empedocles says 'For 'tis in respect of what is present that man's wit is increased', and again 'Whence it befalls them from time to time to think diverse thoughts', and Homer's phrase 'For suchlike is man's mind' means the same. They all look upon thinking as a bodily process like perceiving, and hold that like is *known* as well as *perceived* by like, as I explained at the beginning of our discussion. Yet they ought at the same time to have accounted for error also; [427b] for it is more intimately connected with animal existence and the soul continues longer in the state of error than in that of truth. They cannot escape the dilemma: either (1) whatever seems is true (and there are some who accept this) or (2) error is contact by the unlike; for that is the opposite of the knowing of like by like.

[427b] That perceiving and practical thinking are not identical is therefore obvious; for the former is universal in the animal world, the latter is found in only a small division of it. Further, speculative thinking is also distinct from perceiving. . . .

Thinking is different from perceiving and is held to be in part imagination, in part judgement: we must therefore first mark off the sphere of imagination and then speak of judgement. [428a] . . . If then imagination presents no other features than those enumerated and is what we have described, then imagination must be a movement resulting from an actual exercise of a power of sense.

[429a] And because imaginations remain in the organs of sense and resemble sensations, animals in their actions are largely guided by them, some (i.e. the brutes) because of the non-existence in them of mind, others (i.e. men) because of the temporary eclipse in them of mind by feeling or disease or sleep.

Turning now to the part of the soul with which the soul knows and thinks (whether this is separable from the others in definition only, or spatially as well) we have to inquire (1) what differentiates this part, and (2) how thinking can take place.

If thinking is like perceiving, it must be either a process in which the soul is acted upon by what is capable of being thought, or a process different from but analogous to that. The thinking part of the soul must therefore be, while impassible, capable of receiving the form of an object; that is, must be potentially identical in character with its object, without being the object. Mind must be related to what is thinkable, as sense is to what is sensible.

Therefore, since everything is a possible object of thought, mind, in order, as Anaxagoras says, to dominate, that is, to know, must be pure from all admixture; for the co-presence of what is alien to its nature is a hindrance and a block: it follows that it too, like the sensitive part, can have no nature of its own, other than that of having a certain capacity. Thus, that in the soul which is called mind (by mind I mean that whereby the soul thinks and judges) is, before it thinks, not actually any real thing. For this reason it cannot reasonably be regarded as blended with the body: if so, it would acquire some quality, e.g. warmth or cold, or even have an organ like the sensitive faculty: as it is, it has none. It was a good idea to call the soul 'the place of forms', though (1) this description holds only of the intellective soul, and (2) even this is the forms only potentially, not actually.

Observation of the sense-organs and their employment reveals a distinction between the impassibility of the sensitive and that of the intellective faculty. After strong stimulation of a sense we are less able to exercise it than before, as e.g. in the case of a loud sound we cannot hear easily immediately after [429b], or in the case of a bright colour or a powerful odour we cannot see or smell, but in the case of mind thought about an object that is highly intelligible renders it more and not less, able afterwards to think about objects that are less intelligible: the reason is that while the faculty of sensation is dependent upon the body, mind is separable from it.

[430a] ... in fact mind as we have described it is what it is by virtue of becoming all things, while there is another which is what it is by virtue of making all things: this is a sort of positive state like light; for in a sense light makes potential colours into actual colours.

Mind in this sense of it is separable, impassible, unmixed, since in its essential nature it is activity. . . .

From ETHICA NICHOMACHEA

Book I

[1102a–13] Since happiness is an activity of soul in accordance with perfect virtue, we must consider the nature of virtue; for perhaps we shall thus see better the nature of happiness. . . . But clearly the virtue we must study is human virtue; for the good we were seeking was human good and the happiness, human happiness. By human virtue we mean not that of the body but that of the soul; and happiness also we call an activity of soul. But if this is so, clearly the student of politics must know somehow the facts about soul, as the man who is to heal the eyes or the body as a whole must know about the eyes or the body. . . . The student of politics, then, must study the soul, and must study it with these objects in view, and do so just to the extent which is sufficient for the questions we are discussing; for further precision is perhaps something more laborious than our purposes require.

Some things are said about it, adequately enough, even in the discussions outside our school, and we must use these; e.g. that one element in the soul is irrational and one has a rational principle. Whether these are separated as the parts of the body or of anything divisible are, or are distinct by definition but by nature inseparable, like convex and concave in the circumference of a circle, does not affect the present question.

Of the irrational element one division seems to be widely distributed, and vegetative in its nature, I mean that which causes nutrition and growth; for it is this kind of power of the soul that one must assign to all nurslings and to embryos [1102b], and this same power to full-grown creatures; this is more reasonable than to assign some different power to them. Now the excellence of this seems to be common to all species and not specifically human. . . .

There seems to be also another irrational element in the soul – one which in a sense, however, shares in a rational principle. For we praise the rational principle of the continent man and of the incontinent, and the part of their soul that has such a principle, since it urges them aright and towards the best objects; but there is found in them also another element naturally opposed to the rational principle, which fights against and resists that principle. For exactly as paralysed limbs when we intend to move them to the right turn on the contrary to the left, so is it with the soul; the impulses of incontinent people move in contrary directions. But while in the body we see that which moves astray, in the soul we do not. No doubt, however, we must none-the-less suppose that in the soul too there is something contrary to the rational principle, resisting and opposing it. In what sense it is distinct from the other elements does not concern us. Now even this seems to have a share in a rational principle, as we said; at any rate in the continent man it obeys the rational principle – and presumably in the temperate and brave man it is still more obedient; for in him it speaks, on all matters, with the same voice as the rational principle.

Therefore the irrational element also appears to be two-fold. For the vegetative element in no way shares in a rational principle, but the appetitive and in general the desiring element in a sense shares in it, in so far as it listens to and obeys it; this is the sense in which we speak of 'taking account' of one's father or one's friends, not that in which we speak of 'accounting' for a mathematical property. That the irrational element is in some sense persuaded by a rational principle is indicated also by the giving of advice and by all reproof and exhortation.

[1103a] And if this element also must be said to have a rational principle, that which has a rational principle (as well as that which has not) will be two-fold, one subdivision having it in the strict sense and in itself, and the other having a tendency to obey as one does one's father.

Book VI

[1139a] We said before that there are two parts of the soul – that which grasps a rule or rational principle, and the irrational; let us now draw a similar distinction within the part which grasps a rational principle. And let it be assumed that there are two parts which grasp a rational principle – one by which we contemplate the kind of things whose originative causes are invariable, and one by which we contemplate variable things. . . .

. . . Now there are three things in the soul which control action and truth – sensation, reason, desire.

Of these, sensation originates no action; this is plain from the fact that the lower animals have sensation but no share in action.

What affirmation and negation are in thinking, pursuit and avoidance are in desire; so that since moral virtue is a state of character concerned with choice, and choice is deliberate desire, therefore both the reasoning must be true and the desire right, if the choice is to be good, and the latter must pursue just what the former asserts. Now this kind of intellect and of truth is practical; of the intellect which is contemplative, not practical nor productive, the good and the bad state are truth and falsity respectively (for this is the work of everything intellectual); while of the part which is practical and intellectual the good state is truth in agreement with right desire.

REFERENCES

Aristotle. *De Anima*. Trans. J. A. Smith in *The Works of Aristotle*, ed. W. D. Ross. Oxford: Clarendon Press, 1931. Vol. III

Ethica Nichomachea. Trans. W. D. Ross. London: Oxford University Press, 1931. For refs. see margin

Taylor, A. E. *Aristotle*. London: Nelson 1943

TITUS LUCRETIUS CARUS

c. 98–55 B.C.

VERY little is known of Lucretius' life apart from his probable
dates and the fact that Cicero may have been the person to see to
the publication of the *De Rerum Natura*. Lucretius has been
compared to Milton in his poetic handling of philosophical
material. He is regarded as one of the greatest of the Roman
poets, partly on account of his sympathy and persuasiveness.
The following extracts are chosen for their special relevance to
us. The lyrical quality is not stressed.

From DE RERUM NATURA
MATTER

All nature as it is in itself consists of two things – bodies and
the vacant space in which the bodies are situated and through
which they move in different directions. The existence of bodies
is vouched for by the agreement of the senses. If a belief resting
directly on this foundation is not valid, there will be no standard to which we can refer any doubt on obscure questions for
rational confirmation. If there were no place and space, which
we call vacuity, these bodies could not be situated anywhere or
move in any direction whatever. This I have just demonstrated.
It remains to show that *nothing exists that is distinct both from
body and from vacuity* and could be ranked with the others as a
third substance. For whatever *is* must also be something. If it
offers resistance to touch, however light and slight, it will increase the mass of body by such amount, great or small, as it
may amount to, and will rank with it. If, on the other hand, it is
intangible, so that it offers no resistance whatever to anything
passing through it, then it will be that empty space which we
call vacuity. Besides, whatever it may be in itself, either it will
act in some way, or react to other things acting upon it, or else
it will be such that things can be and happen in it. But without
body nothing can act or react; and nothing can afford a place
except emptiness and vacancy. Therefore, besides matter and

vacuity, we cannot include in the number of things any third substance that can either affect our senses at any time or be grasped by the reasoning of our minds.

*

Material objects are of two kinds, atoms and compounds of atoms. The atoms themselves cannot be swamped by any force, for they are preserved indefinitely by their absolute solidity.

*

In this connexion there is another fact that I want you to grasp. *When the atoms are travelling straight down through empty space by their own weight, at quite indeterminate times and places they swerve ever so little from their course,* just so much that you would call it a change of direction. If it were not for this swerve, everything would fall downwards like rain-drops through the abyss of space. No collision would take place and no impact of atom on atom would be created. Thus nature would never have created anything.

If anyone supposes that heavier atoms on a straight course through empty space could outstrip lighter ones and fall on them from above, thus causing impacts that might give rise to generative motions, he is going far astray from the path of truth. The reason why objects falling through water or thin air vary in speed according to their weight is simply that the matter composing water or air cannot obstruct all objects equally, but is forced to give way more speedily to heavier ones. But empty space can offer no resistance to any object in any quarter at any time, so as not to yield free passage as its own nature demands. Therefore, through undisturbed vacuum all bodies must travel at equal speed though impelled by unequal weights. The heavier will never be able to fall on the lighter from above or generate of themselves impacts leading to that variety of motions out of which nature can produce things. We are thus forced back to the conclusion that the atoms swerve a little – but only a very little, or we shall be caught imagining slantwise movements, and the facts will prove us wrong. For we see plainly and palpably that weights, when they come tumbling down, have no power of their own to move aslant, so far as meets the eye. But who can possibly perceive that they do not diverge in the very least from a vertical course?

Again, if all movement is always interconnected, the new arising from the old in a determinate order – if the atoms never swerve so as to originate some new movement that will snap the bonds of fate, the everlasting sequence of cause and effect – what is the source of the free will possessed by living things throughout the earth? What, I repeat, is the source of that will-power snatched from the fates, whereby we follow the path along which we are severally led by pleasure, swerving from our course at no set time or place but at the bidding of our own hearts? There is no doubt that on these occasions the will of the individual originates the movements that trickle through his limbs. Observe, when the starting barriers are flung back, how the race-horses in the eagerness of their strength cannot break away as suddenly as their hearts desire. For the whole supply of matter must first be mobilized throughout every member of the body: only then, when it is mustered in a continuous array, can it respond to the prompting of the heart. So you may see that the beginning of movement is generated by the heart; starting from the voluntary action of the mind, it is then transmitted throughout the body and the limbs. Quite different is our experience when we are shoved along by a blow inflicted with compulsive force by someone else. In that case it is obvious that all the matter of our body is set going and pushed along involuntarily, till a check is imposed through the limbs by the will. Do you see the difference? Although many men are driven by an external force and often constrained involuntarily to advance or to rush headlong, yet there is within the human breast something that can fight against this force and resist it. At its command the supply of matter is forced to take a new course through our limbs and joints or is checked in its course and brought once more to a halt. So also in the atoms you must recognize the same possibility: besides weight and impact there must be a third cause of movement, the source of this inborn power of ours, since we see that nothing can come out of nothing. For the weight of an atom prevents its movements from being completely determined by the impact of other atoms.

But the fact that the mind itself has no internal necessity to determine its every act and compel it to suffer in helpless passivity – this is due to the slight swerve of the atoms at no determinate time or place.

Mind

The next step ... is ... to elucidate ... the nature of mind and of life. In so doing I shall drive out neck and crop that fear of Hell which blasts the life of man from its very foundations.

Often from fear of death mortals are gripped by such a hate of living and looking on the light that with anguished hearts they do themselves to death. They forget that this very fear is the fountainhead of their troubles; this it is that harasses conscience, snaps the bonds of friendship, and hurls down virtue from the heights. Many a time before now men have betrayed their country and their beloved parents in an effort to escape the halls of Hell.

As children in blank darkness tremble and start at everything, so we in broad daylight are oppressed at times by fears as baseless as those horrors which children imagine coming upon them in the dark. This dread and darkness of the mind cannot be dispelled by the sunbeams, the shining shafts of day, but only by an understanding of the outward form and inner workings of nature.

First, I maintain that *the mind*, which we often call the intellect, the seat of the guidance and control of life, *is part of a man*, no less than hand or foot or eyes are parts of a whole living creature. There are some who argue that the sentience of the mind is not lodged in any particular part, but is a vital condition of the body, what the Greeks call a *harmony*, which makes us live as sentient beings without having any locally determined mind. Just as good health may be said to belong to the healthy body without being any specific part of it, so they do not station the sentience of the mind in any specific part. In this they seem to me very wide of the mark. Often enough the visible body is obviously ill, while in some other unseen part we are enjoying ourselves. No less often the reverse happens: one who is sick at heart enjoys bodily well-being. This is no different from the experience of an invalid whose foot is hurting while his head is in no pain.

Or consider what happens when we have surrendered our limbs to soothing slumber and our body, replete and relaxed, lies insensible. At that very time there is something else in us that is awake to all sorts of stimuli – something that gives free admittance to all the motions of joy and to heart-burnings void of substance.

Next, you must understand that *there is also a vital spirit in our limbs* and the body does not derive its sentience from harmony. In the first place, life often lingers in our limbs after a large part of the body has been cut off. On the other hand, when a few particles of heat have dispersed and some air has been let out through the mouth, life forsakes the veins forthwith and abandons the bones. Hence you may infer that all the elements do not hold equal portions of vitality or sustain it equally, but it is chiefly thanks to the atoms of wind and heat that life lingers in the limbs. There is therefore in the body itself a vital breath and heat which forsakes our limbs at death.

Now that we have discovered the nature of the mind and of the vital spirit as a part of the man, drop this name harmony which was passed down to the musicians from the heights of Helicon – or else perhaps they fetched it themselves from some other source and applied it to the matter of their art, which had then no name of its own. Whatever it be, let them keep it. And give your attention now to the rest of my discourse.

Next, I maintain that *mind and spirit are interconnected* and compose between them a single substance. But what I may call the head and dominant force in the whole body is that guiding principle which we term mind or intellect. This is firmly lodged in the mid-region of the breast. Here is the place where fear and alarm pulsate. Here is felt the caressing touch of joy. Here, then, is the seat of intellect and mind. The rest of the vital spirit, diffused throughout the body, obeys the mind and moves under its direction and impulse. The mind by itself experiences thought and joy of its own at a time when nothing moves either the body or the spirit.

When our head or eye suffers from an attack of pain, our whole body does not share in its aching. Just so the mind sometimes suffers by itself or jumps for joy when the rest of the spirit, diffused through every limb and member, is not stirred by any new impulse. But, when the mind is upset by some more overwhelming fear, we see all the spirit in every limb upset in sympathy. Sweat and pallor break out all over the body. Speech grows inarticulate; the voice fails; the eyes swim; the ears buzz; the limbs totter. Often we see men actually drop down because of the terror that has gripped their minds. Hence you may readily infer a connexion between the mind and the spirit which, when shaken by the impact of the mind, immediately jostles and propels the body.

The same reasoning proves that *mind and spirit are both composed of matter*. We see them propelling the limbs, rousing the body from sleep, changing the expression of the face, and guiding and steering the whole man – activities that all clearly involve touch, as touch in turn involves matter. How then can we deny their material nature? You see the mind sharing in the body's experiences and sympathizing with it. When the nerve-racking impact of a spear gashes bones and sinews, even if it does not penetrate to the seat of life, there ensues faintness and a tempting inclination earthwards and on the ground a turmoil in the mind and an intermittent faltering impulse to stand up again. The substance of the mind must therefore be material, since it is affected by the impact of material weapons.

My next task will be to demonstrate to you what sort of matter it is of which this mind is composed and how it was formed. First, I affirm that *it is of very fine texture and composed of exceptionally minute particles*. If you will mark my words, you will be able to infer this from the following facts. It is evident that nothing happens as quickly as the mind represents and sketches the happening to itself. Therefore the mind sets itself in motion more swiftly than any of those things whose substance is visible to our eyes. But what is so mobile must consist of exceptionally minute and spherical atoms, so that it can be set going by a slight push. The reason why water is set going and flowing by such a slight push is of course the smallness of its atoms and their readiness to roll. The stickier consistency of honey – its relatively sluggish flow and dilatory progress – is due to the closer coherence of the component matter, consisting, as it obviously does, of particles not so smooth or so fine or so round. A high pile of poppy seed can be disturbed by a light puff of breeze, so that it trickles down from the top, whereas a heap of stones or corn ears remains immovable. In proportion as objects are smaller and smoother, so much the more do they enjoy mobility; the greater their weight and roughness, the more firmly are they anchored. Since, therefore, the substance of the mind has been found to be extraordinarily mobile, it must consist of particles exceptionally small and smooth and round. This discovery, my dear fellow, will prove a timely aid to you in many problems.

Here is a further indication how flimsy is the texture of the vital spirit and in how small a space it could be contained if it could be massed together. At the instant when a man is mastered by the care-free calm of death and forsaken by mind and spirit, you cannot tell either by sight or by weight that any part of the whole has been filched away from his body. Death leaves everything there, except vital sentience and warmth. Therefore the vital spirit as a whole must consist of very tiny atoms, linked together throughout veins, flesh and sinews – atoms so small that, when all the spirit has escaped from the whole body, the outermost contour of the limbs appears intact and there is no loss of weight. The same thing happens when the bouquet has evaporated from the juice of Bacchus, or the sweet perfume of an ointment has escaped into the air, or some substance has lost its savour. The substance itself is not visibly diminished by the loss, and its weight is not lessened, obviously because savour and scent are caused by many minute atoms distributed throughout the mass. On every ground, therefore, it may be inferred that mind and spirit are composed of exceptionally diminutive atoms, since their departure is not accompanied by any loss of weight.

It must not be supposed that the stuff of mind or spirit is a single element. The body at death is abandoned by a sort of rarefied wind mixed with warmth, while the warmth carries

with it also air. Indeed, heat never occurs without an inter-
mixture of air: because it is naturally sparse, it must have many
atoms of air moving in its interstices.

The composition of mind is thus found to be *at least three-fold*.
But all these three components together are not enough to
create sentience, since the mind does not admit that any of
these can create the sensory motions that originate the meditations revolved in the mind. *We must* accordingly *add to these a
fourth component*, which is quite nameless. Than this there is
nothing more mobile or more tenuous – nothing whose component atoms are smaller or smoother. This it is that first sets
the sensory motions coursing through the limbs. Owing to the
minuteness of its atoms, it is first to be stirred. Then the motions
are caught up by warmth and the unseen energy of the wind,
then by air. Then everything is roused to movement: the blood
is quickened; the impulse spreads throughout the flesh; last of
all, bones and marrow are thrilled with pleasure or the opposite
excitement. To this extremity pain cannot lightly penetrate, or
the pangs of anguish win through. If they do, then everything is
so confounded that no room is left for life, and the components
of the vital spirit escape through all the pores of the body. But
usually a stop is put to these movements as near as may be at
the surface of the body. Thanks to this stoppage we contrive to
cling to life.

At this point I should like to demonstrate *how these components are intermixed* and from what mode of combination they
derive their powers. Reluctantly I am thwarted in my purpose
by the poverty of our native tongue. But, so far as I can touch
upon the surface of this topic, I will tackle it.

The atoms rush in and out amongst one another on atomic
trajectories, so that no one of them can be segregated nor its distinctive power isolated by intervening space. They co-exist like
the many properties of a single body. In the flesh of any living
thing there are regularly scent and colour and taste; and yet
from all these there is formed only one corporeal bulk. Just so,
warmth and air and the unseen energy of wind create in combination a single substance, together with that mobile force
which imparts to them from itself the initial impetus from

which the sensory motion takes its rise throughout the flesh. This basic substance lurks at our very core. There is nothing in our bodies more fundamental than this, the most vital element of their whole vital spirit. Just as in our limbs and body as a whole, mind and spirit with their interconnected powers are latent, because their component atoms are small and sparse, so this nameless element composed of minute atoms is latent in the vital spirit and is in turn its vital element and controls the whole body.

In the same way, wind and air and warmth commingled through the limbs must interact, one being relatively latent, another prominent. In appearance a single stuff is formed by them all: warmth and wind and air do not display their powers separately so as to blot out sentience and dissolve it by their disunion. First, there is at the mind's disposal that element of heat which it brings into play when it boils with rage and passion blazes more fiercely from the eyes. There is likewise no lack of that chill wind, associated with fear, which sets the limbs atremble and impels them to flight. There is lastly that calm and steady air which prevails in a tranquil breast and unruffled mien.

In those creatures whose passionate hearts and choleric dispositions easily boil up in anger, there is a surplus of the hot element. An outstanding example is the truculent temper of lions, who often roar till they burst their chests with bellowing and cannot keep the torrents of their rage pent within. But the cold hearts of deer are of a windier blend: they are quicker to set chill breezes blowing through the flesh, provoking a shuddering movement in the limbs. Cattle, again, have in their vital composition, a bigger portion of calm air. They are never too hotly fired by a touch of that smoky torch of anger which clouds the mind with its black and blinding shadow. They are never transfixed and benumbed by the icy shaft of fear. Their nature is a mean between the timidity of the deer and the lion's ferocity.

So it is with men. Though education may apply a similar polish to various individuals, it still leaves fundamental traces of their several temperaments. It must not be supposed that innate vices can be completely eradicated: one man will still incline more readily to outbursts of rage; another will give way a little sooner to fear; a third will accept some contingencies too impassively. And in a host of other ways men must differ one from another in temperament and so also in the resultant behaviour. To unfold here the secret causes of these differences is beyond my power. I cannot even find names for the multiplicity of atomic shapes that give rise to this variety of types. But I am clear that there is one relevant fact I can affirm: the lingering traces of inborn temperament that cannot be eliminated by philosophy are so slight that there is nothing to prevent men from leading a life worthy of the gods.

This *vital spirit*, then, *is present in the whole body*. It is the body's guardian and preserver. For the two are interlocked by common roots and cannot be torn apart without manifest disaster. As easily could the scent be torn out of lumps of incense without destroying their nature as mind and spirit could be abstracted from the whole body without total dissolution. So from their earliest origin the two are charged with a communal life by the intertangled atoms that compose them. It is clear that neither body nor mind by itself without the other's aid possesses the power of sensation: it is by the interacting motions of the two combined that the flame of sentience is kindled in our flesh.

*

From all this it follows that *death is nothing to us* and no concern of ours, since our tenure of the mind is mortal. In days of old, we felt no disquiet when the hosts of Carthage poured in to battle on every side – when the whole earth, dizzied by the convulsive shock of war, reeled sickeningly under the high ethereal vault, and between realm and realm the empire of mankind by land and sea trembled in the balance. So, when we shall be no more – when the union of body and spirit that engenders us has been disrupted – to us, who shall then be nothing, nothing by any hazard will happen any more at all. Nothing will have power to stir our senses, not though earth be fused with sea and sea with sky.

*

As for all those torments that are said to take place in the depths of Hell, they are actually present here and now, in our own lives.

There is no wretched Tantalus, as the myth relates, transfixed with groundless terror at the huge boulder poised above him in the air. But in this life there really are mortals oppressed by unfounded fear of the gods and trembling at the impending doom that may fall upon any of them at the whim of chance.

There is no Tityos lying in Hell for ever probed by birds of prey. Assuredly they cannot find food by groping under those giant ribs to glut them throughout eternity. No matter to what length that titanic frame may lie outstretched, so that he covers not a paltry nine acres with his spread-eagled limbs but the whole extent of earth, he will not be able to suffer an eternity of pain nor furnish food from his body for evermore. But Tityos is here in our midst – that poor devil prostrated by love, torn indeed by birds of prey, devoured by gnawing jealousy, or rent by the fangs of some other passion.

Sisyphus too is alive for all to see, bent on winning the insignia of office, its rods and ruthless axes, by the people's vote and embittered by perpetual defeat. To strive for this profitless and never-granted prize, and in striving toil and moil incessantly, this truly is to push a boulder laboriously up a steep hill, only to see it, once the top is reached, rolling and bounding down again to the flat levels of the plain.

By the same token, to be for ever feeding a malcontent mind, filling it with good things but never satisfying it – that fate we suffer when the circling seasons enrich us with their products and their ever-changing charms but we are never filled with the fruits of life – this surely exemplifies the story of those maidens in the flower of life for ever pouring water into a leaking vessel which can never by any sleight be filled.

As for Cerberus and the Furies and the pitchy darkness and the jaws of Hell belching abominable fumes, these are not and cannot be anywhere at all. But life is darkened by the fear of retribution for our misdeeds, a fear enormous in proportion to their enormity, and by the penalties imposed for crime – imprisonment and ghastly precipitation from Tarpeia's Crag, the lash, the block, the rack, the boiling pitch, the firebrand, and the branding iron. Even though these horrors are not physically present, yet the conscience-ridden mind in terrified anticipation torments itself with its own goads and whips. It does not see what term there can be to its suffering nor where its punishment can have an end. It is afraid that death may merely to intensify pain. So at length the life of misguided mortals becomes a Hell on earth.

REFERENCE

Lucretius. *De Rerum Natura*. Trans. as *The Nature of the Universe* by R. E. Latham. Harmondsworth: Penguin Books, 1951, pp. 39–40, 41, 66–8, 98–106, 121, 126–7

GALEN

A.D. *c*. 130–200

CLAUDIUS GALENUS was the son of a well-to-do architect and was born at Pergamum in Asia Minor. His father, who was highly educated, saw to it that his son received a broad and eclectic training in both philosophy and medicine, which Galen studied in several important centres of the time, emerging as a staunch disciple of Hippocrates. As a professional doctor he lived and worked in Rome for about five years, where he was highly critical of the atomistic medical tradition there current, but numbered Marcus Aurelius among his patients. Galen's contemptuously critical comments, and possibly also the ambiguous status of a Greek doctor in the Rome of the period, made it necessary for him to leave the city in A.D. 168. He returned to Pergamum where he settled down to practise and write, having refused the Emperor's request that he should return and accompany him on an expedition against the Germanic tribes who were threatening the empire in the north.

The following extract is not from the famous *De Temperamentis*, of which a modern English translation is not yet available, but from the treatise *On the Natural Faculties*. The reader will find a very helpful account of Galen on the temperaments and of this theory's historical influence in Dr May Smith's *The Nervous Temperament*.

Galen's eclectic training is sometimes reflected in his rambling and discursive writing. His vivid summary of the points at issue between those who defended an atomic, and those in favour of a more biological and organic, approach to human functioning does him rather more than justice. But it seems worth resuscitating in the light of the past hundred years of psychology, in which biological concepts have again been overhauling associationist atomism, while many have sought a means of achieving the best of both worlds. The reader should beware of Galen's flirtations with astrology. I suspect that 'principle' might be a better word than 'faculty' for the very general assimilative and expulsive processes that Galen discusses at the close of the passage quoted.

From On the Natural Faculties

Since feeling and voluntary motion are peculiar to animals, whilst growth and nutrition are common to plants as well, we may look on the former as effects of the soul and the latter as effects of the nature. And if there be anyone who allows a share in soul to plants as well, and separates the two kinds of soul, naming the kind in question vegetative, and the other sensory, this person is not saying anything else, although his language is somewhat unusual. We, however, for our part, are convinced that the chief merit of language is clearness, and we know that nothing detracts so much from this as do unfamiliar terms; accordingly we employ those terms which the bulk of people are accustomed to use, and we say that animals are governed at once by their souls and by their nature, and plants by their nature alone, and that growth and nutrition are the effects of nature, not of soul.

*

Now, speaking generally, there have arisen the following two sects in medicine and philosophy among those who have made any definite pronouncement regarding Nature. I speak, of course, of such of them as know what they are talking about, and who realize the logical sequence of their hypotheses, and stand by them; as for those who cannot understand even this, but who simply talk any nonsense that comes to their tongues, and who do not remain definitely attached either to one sect or the other – such people are not even worth mentioning.

What, then, are these sects, and what are the logical consequences of their hypotheses? The one class supposes that all substance which is subject to genesis and destruction is at once *continuous* and susceptible of *alteration*. The other school assumes substance to be unchangeable, unalterable, and subdivided into fine particles, which are separated from one another by empty spaces.

All people, therefore, who can appreciate the logical sequence of an hypothesis hold that, according to the second teaching, there does not exist any substance or faculty peculiar either to Nature or to Soul, but that these result from the way in which the primary corpuscles, which are unaffected by change, come together. According to the first-mentioned teaching, on the other hand, Nature is not posterior to the corpuscles, but is a long way prior to them and older than they; and therefore in their view it is Nature which puts together the bodies both of plants and animals; and this she does by virtue of certain faculties which she possesses – these being, on the one hand, attractive and assimilative of what is appropriate, and, on the other, expulsive of what is foreign. Further, she skilfully moulds everything during the stage of genesis; and she also provides for the creatures after birth, employing here other faculties again, namely, one of affection and forethought for offspring, and one of sociability and friendship for kindred. According to the other school, none of these things exist in the natures [of living things], nor is there in the soul any original innate idea, whether of agreement or difference, of separation or synthesis, of justice or injustice, of the beautiful or ugly; all such things, they say, arise in us *from sensation and through sensation*, and animals are steered by certain images and memories.

Some of these people have even expressly declared that the soul possesses no reasoning faculty, but that we are led like cattle by the impression of our senses, and are unable to refuse or dissent from anything. In their view, obviously, courage, wisdom, temperance, and self-control are all mere nonsense, we do not love either each other or our offspring, nor do the gods care anything for us. This school also despises dreams, birds, omens, and the whole of astrology, subjects with which we have dealt at greater length in another work, in which we discuss the views of Asclepiades the physician. Those who wish to do so may familiarize themselves with these arguments, and they may also consider at this point which of the two roads lying before us is the better one to take. Hippocrates took the first-mentioned. According to this teaching, substance is one and is subject to *alteration*; there is a consensus in the movements of air and fluid throughout the whole body; Nature acts throughout in an artistic and equitable manner, having certain faculties, by virtue of which each part of the body draws to itself the juice which is proper to it, and, having done so, attaches it to every portion of itself, and completely assimilates it; while such part of the juice as has not been mastered, and is not capable of undergoing complete alteration and being assimilated to the part which is being nourished, is got rid of by yet another (an expulsive) faculty.

REFERENCES

Galen. *On the Natural Faculties*. Trans. A. J. Brock. The Loeb Classical Library. London: Heinemann, 1928, pp. 3, 43–9. Cambridge Mass.: The Harvard University Press

Smith, May. 'The Nervous Temperament', *British Journal of Medical Psychology*. Cambridge: University Press, Vol. x, 1930, pp. 99–174

ST AUGUSTINE

354-430

St Augustine was born in Africa of a pagan father and a Christian mother. He was widely educated, intensely responsive, and in his early manhood led a passionate and irregular life. After a period of Manichean belief he was converted to Christianity in A.D. 386. About ten years afterwards he was appointed Bishop of Hippo, near Carthage.

He was a voluminous theological writer, his later period being marked by strong asceticism and a sense of sin which is apt to strike the modern reader as somewhat distorted. The following passages from the *Confessions* are not chosen to illustrate this, though a few pages later there comes St Augustine's famous serial condemnation of sensory experience. Instead he is shown, as the great introspectionist that he is, in the grip of psychological curiosity about a topic, i.e. remembering, which is crucial for any satisfactory treatment of body-mind relations.

From The Confessions

I will pass then beyond this power of my nature also, rising by degrees unto Him, who made me. And I come to the fields and spacious palaces of my memory, where are the treasures of innumerable images, brought into it from things of all sorts perceived by the senses. There is stored up, whatsoever besides we think, either by enlarging or diminishing, or any other way varying those things which the sense hath come to; and whatever else hath been committed and laid up, which forgetfulness hath not yet swallowed up and buried. When I enter there, I require what I will, to be brought forth, and something instantly comes; others must be longer sought after, which are fetched, as it were, out of some inner receptacle; others rush out in troops, and while one thing is desired and required, they start forth, as who should say, 'Is it perchance I?' These I drive away with the hand of my heart, from the face of my remembrance; until what I wished for be unveiled, and appear in sight, out of its secret place. Other things come up readily, in unbroken order, as they are called for; those in front making way for the following; and as they make way, they are hidden from sight, ready to come when I will. All which takes place, when I repeat a thing by heart.

There are all things preserved distinctly and under general heads, each having entered by its own avenue: as light, and all colours and forms of bodies, by the eyes; by the ears all sorts of sounds; all smells by the avenue of the nostrils; all tastes by the mouth; and by the sensation of the whole body, what is hard or soft; hot or cold; smooth or rugged; heavy or light; either outwardly or inwardly to the body. All these doth that great harbour of the memory receive in her numberless secret and inexpressible windings, to be forthcoming, and brought out at need; each entering in by his own gate, and there laid up. Nor yet do the things themselves enter in; only the images of the things perceived, are there in readiness, for thought to recall. Which images, how they are formed, who can tell, though it doth plainly appear by which sense each hath been brought in and stored up. For even while I dwell in darkness and silence, in my memory I can produce colours, if I will, and discern betwixt black and white, and what others I will: nor yet do sounds break in, and disturb the image drawn in by my eyes, which I am reviewing, though they also are there, lying dormant, and laid up, as it were, apart. For these too I call for, and forthwith they appear. And though my tongue be still, and my throat mute, so can I sing as much as I will; nor do those images of colours, which notwithstanding be there, intrude themselves and interrupt, when another store is called for, which flowed in by the ears. So the other things, piled in and up by the other senses, I recall at my pleasure. Yea, I discern the breath of lilies from violets, though smelling nothing; and I prefer honey to sweet wine, smooth before rugged, at the time neither tasting, nor handling, but remembering only.

These things do I within, in that vast court of my memory. For there are present with me, heaven, earth, sea, and whatever I could think on therein, besides what I have forgotten. There also meet I with myself, and recall myself, and when, where, and what I have done, and under what feelings. There be all which I remember, either on my own experience, or others' credit. Out of the same store do I myself with the past continually combine fresh and fresh likenesses of things, which I have experienced, or, from what I have experienced, have believed: and thence again infer future actions, events and hopes, and all these again I reflect on, as present. 'I will do this or that,' say I to myself, in that great receptacle of my mind, stored with the images of things so many and so great, 'and this or that will follow.' 'O that this or that might be!' 'God avert this or that!' So speak I to myself: and when I speak, the images of all I speak of are present, out of the same treasury of memory; nor would I speak of any thereof, were the images wanting.

Great is this force of memory, excessive great, O my God; a large and boundless chamber! who ever sounded the bottom thereof? yet is this a power of mine, and belongs unto my nature; nor do I myself comprehend all that I am. Therefore is the mind too strait to contain itself. And where should that be, which it containeth not of itself? Is it without it, and not within? how then doth it not comprehend itself? A wonderful admiration surprises me, amazement seizes me upon this. And men go abroad to admire the heights of mountains, the mighty billows of the sea, the broad tides of rivers, the compass of the ocean, and the circuits of the stars, and pass themselves by; nor wonder, that when I spake of all these things, I did not see them with mine eyes, yet could not have spoken of them, unless I then actually saw the mountains, billows, rivers, stars, which I had seen, and that ocean which I believe to be, inwardly in my memory, and that, with the same vast spaces between, as if I saw them abroad. Yet did not I by seeing draw them into myself, when with mine eyes I beheld them; nor are they themselves with me, but their images only. And I know by what sense of the body, each was impressed upon me.

Yet not these alone does the unmeasurable capacity of my memory retain. Here also is all, learnt of the liberal sciences and as yet unforgotten; removed as it were to some inner place, which is yet no place.

*

The same memory contains also the affections of my mind, not in the same manner that my mind itself contains them, when it feels them, but far otherwise, according to a power of its own. For without rejoicing I remember myself to have joyed; and without sorrow do I recollect my past sorrow. And that I once feared, I review without fear; and without desire call to mind a past desire. Sometimes, on the contrary, with joy do I remember my fore-past sorrow, and with sorrow, joy. Which is not wonderful, as to the body; for mind is one thing, body another. If I therefore with joy remember some past pain of body, it is not so wonderful. But now seeing this very memory itself is mind, (for when we give a thing in charge, to be kept in memory, we say, 'See that you keep it in mind;' and when we forget, we say, 'It did not come to my mind,' and, 'It slipped out of my mind,' calling the memory itself the mind;) this being so, how is it that when with joy I remember my past sorrow, the mind hath joy, the memory hath sorrow; the mind upon the joyfulness which is in it, is joyful, yet the memory upon the sadness which is in it, is not sad? Does the memory perchance not belong to the mind? Who will say so? The memory then is, as it were, the belly of the mind, and joy and sadness, like sweet and bitter food; which, when committed to the memory, are, as it were, passed into the belly, where they may be stowed, but cannot taste. Ridiculous it is to imagine these to be alike; and yet are they not utterly unlike.

*

But what when the memory itself loses anything, as falls out when we forget and seek that we may recollect? Where in the end do we search, but in the memory itself? and there, if one thing be perchance offered instead of another, we reject it, until what we seek meets us; and when it doth, we say, 'This is it;' which we should not unless we recognized it, nor recognize it unless we remembered it. Certainly then we had forgotten it. Or, had not the whole escaped us, but by the part whereof we had hold, was the lost part sought for; in that the memory felt that it did not carry on together all which it was wont, and maimed, as it were, by the curtailment of its ancient habit, demanded the restoration of what it missed? For instance, if we see or think of some one known to us, and having forgotten his name, try to recover it; whatever else occurs, connects itself not therewith; because it was not wont to be thought upon together with him, and therefore is rejected, until that present itself, whereon the knowledge reposes equably as its wonted object. And whence does that present itself, but out of the memory itself? for even when we recognize it, on being reminded by another, it is thence it comes. For we do not believe it as something new, but, upon recollection, allow what was named to be right. But were it utterly blotted out of the mind, we should not remember it, even when reminded. For we have not as yet utterly forgotten that which we remember ourselves to have forgotten. What then we have utterly forgotten, though lost, we cannot even seek after.

REFERENCES

Augustine, St. *Confessions*. Trans. E. B. Pusey. London: Dent, (Everyman's Library). 1939, p. 210 §12–213 §16, p. 216 §21, p. 221 §28

ST THOMAS AQUINAS

1224(5)–1274

St Thomas's views on body and mind are very largely Aristotelian with at least one important difference. While he seeks with Aristotle to treat the 'mind', 'soul', or living principle as the 'form' of the body, he argues simultaneously that, in so far as the soul can be aware of different material objects or of immaterial things, it must be in a sense immaterial itself. On these grounds, among others, St Thomas maintains that the soul intellectualizing is immortal in a sense in which Aristotle's *psyche* was not and it is individual in a sense in which Aristotle's *nous* does not appear to have been. It is exceedingly difficult to assess how far St Thomas could maintain all these views at once. For a sympathetic discussion of this the reader is referred to Copleston.

Consistently with his individual, and in some ways biological, notion of human functioning at increasingly subtle levels, St Thomas treats immortality as a pale affair unless the body is resurrected. At one point he assumes that the soul's desires are not within it for nothing. Hence neither the wish for eternal life nor that for perpetual exercise of inquiry would be found in man unless there were a chance of satisfaction. One may question the validity of this argument while delighting in the vitality of the thirteenth-century man who uses it in the way that St Thomas does.

For the details of St Thomas's views on more specifically psychological problems and for an initial understanding of his very difficult system as a whole, the reader should start by consulting the references given below. Meanwhile they may find helpful the schematic representation on p. 251 of St Thomas's views of psychological functioning. It is taken from Gilby.

It should be realized that St Thomas assumes the natural desires of the spiritual soul to be inevitably good and, though an intellectualist in outlook, he could also maintain that 'Love takes up where knowledge leaves off'. The extracts quoted below do little justice to a vast and complex system, but they may serve to underline some of the points made above and elsewhere in Chapter 3.

```
┌ Of cognition
│       in the body-soul compound
│                   ┌ external senses (the five senses traditionally enumer-
│                   │    ated, sight, hearing, taste, smell, touch)
│                   │ internal senses (imagination, memory, sense of what
│                   └    is beneficial and harmful, communal sense)
│       in the spiritual soul
│               the mind, intellect or reason (to which may be attached
│                   the intellectus agens)
│ of appetition
│       ┌ in the body-soul compound
│       │       the sensuality or sensitive appetite
│       │           ┌ concupiscible
│       │           └ irascible
│       └ in the spiritual soul
│               the will, with its functions of volition and choice.
```

(Note: the natural appetite is not limited to any one faculty but covers them all and the substance.)

From SUMMA THEOLOGICA

[Ia lxxv I] Let us agree on the meaning of the term. Soul is the first principle of life within living things about us: living things we term animate, things lacking life inanimate.

Now life is chiefly manifested in the two functions of motion and knowledge. According to some of the ancients its principle is bodily: this, however, was because they had not developed far enough to appreciate what lies beyond the range of the imagination; bodies alone were real, they held, and anything else unreal.

That they were at fault in their opinion may be shown in many ways, and we will take but one, confidently and in general terms. Obviously not every principle of vital operation is soul, otherwise the eye would be soul, since it is the principle of sight; and the same applies to other vital organs. The term should be reserved to the first principle of life, for though there may be bodily vital principles, the heart for instance, a body cannot be the first principle of life.

For evidently to be the principle of life, or even to be alive, does not belong to body precisely as such, otherwise every body would be a principle of life or alive. Life is in a body because it is a special kind of body; that body is in fact of such a kind comes from a factor which may be called its actuality. The soul, therefore, is not a body, but the actuality of a body, by analogy with heat where the principle of warmth, which is not itself a body, is a kind of actuality of body.

[Ia lxxvi I] We should assert that the mind, the principle of intellectual activity, is the form of the human body. The body's first animating principle is the soul. And since life is manifested by various activities in the various grades of living things, that which is the first principle of these vital activities is the soul. For by soul primarily we take nourishment, feel, walk about, and also understand. Call it mind or intellective soul, this principle is the form of body. If anyone wishes to deny this, let him explain how otherwise he can attribute the activity of understanding to the individual man. Everybody experiences in himself that it is veritably himself who understands.

[2a–2ae. xxv. 5] Our body's substance is not from an evil principle, as the Manichees imagine, but from God. And therefore by the friendship of charity, by which we love God, should we cherish the body.

[Ia lxxvi 5] The intellective soul ranks lowest in the scale of intellectual substances in that it lacks the natural inborn knowledge of truth with which pure spirits are endowed, but must piece together the fragments of truth perceived through the senses. Nature does not fail in necessaries, and therefore the intellective soul has to possess the power of sensing as well as of understanding. Now the activity of the senses is not performed without physical organs. Therefore, the soul must be united to that kind of body which can be the instrument adapted to sense. All the senses are based on touch. Among all the animals man has the best-developed sense of touch, and among men those have the finer minds who have the more delicate sense of touch. A rare mind goes with bodily refinement.

[Ia xc 4 ad 3] The soul continues to be when separated from the body by the failure of body we call death. But the soul should not suffer this dislocation at its origin.

From OTHER WRITINGS

The proposition, *souls are individuated by the matters of bodies, and they keep their individuality when disembodied, as wax the impression of a seal,* can be understood aright though it is also open to misconception. If taken in the sense that bodies are the total cause of the individuation of soul, then the proposition is false; but if the sense is that they are the partial causes, then it is true. The body is not the total cause of the being of soul, though the very being of soul is in relationship to body. Similarly, the body is not the total cause of the individuality of this soul, though it is this soul's nature to be joinable to this body, which relationship remains in the soul after the body's death.

*

To be united to body is not to the detriment of soul, but for its enrichment. There is the substantial benefit of completing human nature, and the accidental benefit of achieving knowledge that can only be acquired through the senses.

REFERENCES

Aquinas, St Thomas. *Philosophical Texts.* Selected and translated with notes and an introduction by Thomas Gilby. London: Oxford University Press, 1951, Chap. IX. § 519, 534, 541, 551, 564, 539, 543 and p. 214

Copleston, F. C. *Aquinas.* Harmondsworth: Penguin Books, 1955

Taylor, H. O. *The Mediaeval Mind.* London: Macmillan, 1930, Vol. II

FRANCESCO PETRARCA

1304–1374

THE following letter from Petrarch describes the first ascent of a
mountain, known to have been undertaken for its own sake, in
the fourteenth century. The letter is included in this volume
because it illustrates better than anything else the type of conflict
between interest in this world and withdrawal from it to which
Petrarch was exposed. As he was probably the most influential
writer of his day, the document is one of unusual importance in
understanding the thought of the period and with this the background of body-mind problems.

THE ASCENT OF MOUNT VENTOUX

*To Dionigi da Borgo San Sepolcro, of the Order of Saint
Augustine, Professor of Theology, about his own troubles*

Today I ascended the highest mountain in this region, which,
not without cause, they call the Windy Peak. Nothing but the
desire to see its conspicuous height was the reason for this undertaking. For many years I have been intending to make this
expedition. You know that since my early childhood, as fate
tossed around human affairs, I have been tossed around in these
parts, and this mountain, visible far and wide from everywhere,
is always in your view. So I was at last seized by the impulse to
accomplish what I had always wanted to do. It happened while
I was reading Roman history again in Livy that I hit upon the
passage where Philip, the King of Macedon – the Philip who
waged war against the Roman people – 'ascends Mount Haemus
in Thessaly, since he believed the rumour that you can see two
seas from its top: the Adriatic and the Black Sea.' Whether he
was right or wrong I cannot make out because the mountain is
far from our region, and the disagreement among authors renders the matter uncertain. I do not intend to consult all of them:
the cosmographer Pomponius Mela does not hesitate to report

254

the fact as true, Livy supposes the rumour to be false. I would not leave it long in doubt if that mountain were as easy to explore as the one here. At any rate, I had better let it go, in order to come back to the mountain I mentioned at first. It seemed to me that a young man who holds no public office might be excused for doing what an old king is not blamed for.

I now began to think over whom to choose as a companion. It will sound strange to you that hardly a single one of all my friends seemed to me suitable in every respect, so rare a thing is absolute congeniality in every attitude and habit even among dear friends. One was too sluggish, the other too vivacious; one too slow, the other too quick; this one too gloomy of temper, that one too gay. One was duller, the other brighter than I should have liked. This man's taciturnity, that man's flippancy; the heavy weight and obesity of the next, the thinness and weakliness of still another were reasons to deter me. The cool lack of curiosity of one, like another's too eager interest, dissuaded me from choosing either. All such qualities, however difficult they are to bear, can be borne at home: loving friendship is able to endure everything; it refuses no burden. But on a journey they become intolerable. Thus my delicate mind, craving honest entertainment, looked about carefully, weighing every detail, with no offence to friendship. Tacitly it rejected whatever it could foresee would become troublesome on the projected excursion. What do you think I did? At last I applied for help at home and revealed my plan to my only brother, who is younger than I and whom you know well enough. He could hear of nothing he would have liked better and was happy to fill the place of friend as well as brother.

We left home on the appointed day and arrived at Malaucène at night. This is a place at the northern foot of the mountain. We spent a day there and began our ascent this morning, each of us accompanied by a single servant. From the start we encountered a good deal of trouble, for the mountain is a steep and almost inaccessible pile of rocky material. However, what the Poet says is appropriate: 'Ruthless striving overcomes everything.'

The day was long, the air was mild; this and vigorous minds, strong and supple bodies, and all the other conditions assisted us on our way. The only obstacle was the nature of the spot. We found an aged shepherd in the folds of the mountain who tried with many words to dissuade us from the ascent. He said he had been up to the highest summit in just such youthful fervour fifty years ago and had brought home nothing but regret and pains, and his body as well as his clothes torn by rocks and thorny underbrush. Never before and never since had the people there heard of any man who dared a similar feat. While he was shouting these words at us, our desire increased just because of his warnings; for young people's minds do not give credence to advisers. When the old man saw that he was exerting himself in vain, he went with us a little way forward through the rocks and pointed with his finger to a steep path. He gave us much good advice and repeated it again and again at our backs when we were already at quite a distance. We left with him whatever of our clothes and other belongings might encumber us, intent only on the ascent, and began to climb with merry alacrity. However, as almost always happens, the daring attempt was soon followed by quick fatigue.

Not far from our start we stopped at a rock. From there we went on again, proceeding at a slower pace, to be sure. I in particular made my way up with considerably more modest steps. My brother endeavoured to reach the summit by the very ridge of the mountain on a short cut; I, being so much more of a weakling, was bending down toward the valley. When he called me back and showed me the better way, I answered that I hoped to find an easier access on the other side and was not afraid of a longer route on which I might proceed more smoothly. With such an excuse I tried to palliate my laziness, and, when the others had already reached the higher zones, I was still wandering through the valleys, where no more comfortable access was revealed, while the way became longer and longer and the vain fatigue grew heavier and heavier. At last I felt utterly disgusted, began to regret my perplexing error and decided to attempt the heights with a wholehearted effort. Weary and exhausted, I reached my brother, who had been waiting for me and was refreshed by a good long rest. For a while we went on together at the same pace. However, hardly had we left that rock behind us when I forgot the detour I had made just a short while before and was once more drawing down the lower regions. Again I wandered through the valleys, looking for the longer and easier path and stumbling only into longer difficulties. Thus I indeed put off the disagreeable strain of climbing. But nature is not overcome by man's devices; a corporeal thing cannot reach the heights by descending. What shall I say? My brother laughed at me; I was indignant; this happened to me three times and more within a few hours. So often was I frustrated in my hopes that at last I sat down in a valley. There I leaped in my winged thoughts from things corporeal to what is incorporeal and addressed myself in words like these:

'What you have so often experienced today while climbing this mountain happens to you, you must know, and to many others who are making their way toward the blessed life. This is not easily understood by us men, because the motions of the body lie open, while those of the mind are invisible and hidden. The life we call blessed is located on a high peak. "A narrow way," they say, leads up to it. Many hilltops intervene, and we must proceed "from virtue to virtue" with exalted steps. On the highest summit is set the end of all, the goal toward which our pilgrimage is directed. Everyman wants to arrive there. However, as Naso says: "Wanting is not enough; long and you attain it." You certainly do not merely want; you have a longing, unless you are deceiving yourself in this respect as in so many others. What is it, then, that keeps you back? Evidently nothing but the smoother way that leads through the meanest earthly pleasures and looks easier at first sight. However, having strayed far in error, you must either ascend to the summit of the blessed life under the heavy burden of hard striving, ill deferred, or lie prostrate in your slothfulness in the valleys of your sins. If "darkness and the shadow of death" find you there – I shudder while I pronounce these ominous words – you must pass the eternal night in incessant torments.'

You cannot imagine how much comfort this thought brought my mind and body for what lay still ahead of me. Would that I might achieve with my mind the journey for which I am longing day and night as I achieved with the feet of my body my journey today after overcoming all obstacles. And I wonder whether it ought not to be much easier to accomplish what can be done by means of the agile and immortal mind without any local motion 'in the twinkling of the trembling eye' than what is to be performed in the succession of time by the service of the frail body that is doomed to die and under the heavy load of the limbs.

There is a summit, higher than all the others. The people in the woods up there call it 'Sonny', I do not know why. However, I suspect they use the word in a sense opposite to its meaning, as is done sometimes in other cases too. For it really looks like the father of all the surrounding mountains. On its top is a small level stretch. There at last we rested from our fatigue.

And now, my dear father, since you have heard what sorrows arose in my breast during my climb, listen also to what remains to be told. Devote, I beseech you, one of your hours to reading what I did during one of my days. At first I stood there almost benumbed, overwhelmed by a gale such as I had never felt before and by the unusually open and wide view. I looked around me: clouds were gathering below my feet, and Athos and Olympus grew less incredible, since I saw on a mountain of lesser fame what I had heard and read about them. From there I turned my eyes in the direction of Italy, for which my mind is so fervently yearning. The Alps were frozen stiff and covered with snow – those mountains through which that ferocious enemy of the Roman name once passed, blasting his way through the rocks with vinegar if we may believe tradition. They looked as if they were quite near me, though they are far, far away. I was longing, I must confess, for Italian air, which appeared rather to my mind than my eyes. An incredibly strong desire seized me to see my friend and my native land again. At the same time I rebuked the weakness of a mind not yet grown to manhood, manifest in both these desires, although in both cases an excuse would not lack support from famous champions.

Then another thought took possession of my mind, leading it from the contemplation of space to that of time, and I said to myself: 'This day marks the completion of the tenth year since you gave up the studies of your boyhood and left Bologna. O immortal God, O immutable Wisdom! How many and how great were the changes you have had to undergo in your moral habits since then.' I will not speak of what is still left undone, for I am not yet in port that I might think in security of the storms I have had to endure. The time will perhaps come when I can review all this in the order in which it happened, using as a prologue that passage of your favourite Augustine: 'Let me remember my past mean acts and the carnal corruption of my soul, not that I love them, but that I may love Thee, my God.'

Many dubious and troublesome things are still in store for me. What I used to love, I love no longer. But I lie: I love it still, but less passionately. Again have I lied: I love it, but more timidly, more sadly. Now at last I have told the truth; for thus it is: I love, but what I should love not to love, what I should wish to hate. Nevertheless I love it, but against my will, under compulsion and in sorrow and mourning. To my own misfortune I experience in myself now the meaning of that most famous line: 'Hate I shall, if I can; if I can't, I shall love though not willing.' The third year has not yet elapsed since that perverted and malicious will, which had totally seized me and reigned in the court of my heart without an opponent, began to encounter a rebel offering resistance. A stubborn and still undecided battle has been long raging on the field of my thoughts for the supremacy of one of the two men within me.

Thus I revolved in my thoughts the history of the last decade. Then I dismissed my sorrow at the past and asked myself: 'Suppose you succeed in protracting this rapidly fleeing life for another decade, and come as much nearer to virtue, in proportion to the span of time, as you have been freed from your former obstinacy during these last two years as a result of the struggle of the new and the old wills – would you then not be able – perhaps not with certainty but with reasonable hope at least – to meet death in your fortieth year with equal mind and cease to care for that remnant of life which descends into old age?'

These and like considerations rose in my breast again and again, dear father. I was glad of the progress I had made, but I wept over my imperfection and was grieved by the fickleness of all that men do. In this manner I seemed to have somehow forgotten the place I had come to and why, until I was warned to throw off such sorrows, for which another place would be more appropriate. I had better look around and see what I had intended to see in coming here. The time to leave was approaching, they said. The sun was already setting, and the shadow of the mountain was growing longer and longer. Like a man aroused from sleep, I turned back and looked toward the west. The boundary wall between France and Spain, the ridge of the Pyrenees, is not visible from there, though there is no obstacle of which I knew, and nothing but the weakness of the mortal eye is the cause. However, one could see most distinctly the mountains of the province of Lyons to the right and, to the left the sea near Marseilles as well as the waves that break against Aigues Mortes, although it takes several days to travel to this city. The Rhone River was directly under our eyes.

I admired every detail, now relishing earthly enjoyment, now lifting up my mind to higher spheres after the example of my body, and I thought it fit to look into the volume of Augustine's *Confessions* which I owe to your loving kindness and preserve carefully, keeping it always in my hands, in remembrance of the author as well as the donor. It is a little book of smallest size but full of infinite sweetness. I opened it with the intention of reading whatever might occur to me first: nothing indeed, but pious and devout sentences could come to hand. I happened to hit upon the tenth book of the work. My brother stood beside me, intently expecting to hear something from Augustine in my mouth. I ask God to be my witness and my brother who was with me: Where I fixed my eyes first, it was written: 'And men go abroad to admire the heights of mountains, the mighty billows of the sea, the broad tides of rivers, the compass of the ocean, and the circuits of the stars – and pass themselves by.' I was stunned, I confess. I bade my brother, who wanted to hear more, not to molest me, and closed the book, angry with myself that I still admired earthly things. Long since I ought to have learned, even from pagan philosophers, that 'nothing is admirable besides the mind; compared to its greatness nothing is great.'

I was completely satisfied with what I had seen of the mountain and turned my inner eye toward myself. From this hour nobody heard me say a word until we arrived at the bottom. These words occupied me sufficiently. I could not imagine that this had happened to me by chance: I was convinced that whatever I had read there was said to me and to nobody else. I remembered that Augustine once suspected the same regarding himself, when, while he was reading the Apostolic Epistles, the first passage that occurred to him was, as he himself relates: 'Not in banqueting and drunkenness, not in chambering and wantonness, not in strife and envying; but put ye on the Lord Jesus Christ, and make no provision for the flesh to fulfil your lusts.' The same had happened before to Anthony: he heard the Gospel where it is written: 'If thou wilt be perfect, go and sell that thou hast, and give to the poor, and come and follow me, and thou shalt have treasure in heaven.' As his biographer Athanasius says, he applied the Lord's command to himself, just as if the Scripture had been recited for his sake. And as Anthony, having heard this, sought nothing else, and as Augustine, having read the other passage, proceeded no further, the end of all my reading was the few words I have already set down. Silently I thought over how greatly mortal men lack council who, neglecting the noblest part of themselves in empty parading, look without for what can be found within. I admired the nobility of the mind, had it not voluntarily degenerated and strayed from the primordial state of its origin, converting into disgrace what God had given to be its honour.

How often, do you think, did I turn back and look up to the summit of the mountain today while I was walking down? It seemed to me hardly higher than a cubit compared to the height of human contemplation, were the latter not plunged into the filth of earthly sordidness. This too occurred to me at every step: 'If you do not regret undergoing so much sweat and hard labour to lift the body a bit nearer to heaven, ought any cross or jail or torture frighten the mind that is trying to come nearer to God and set its feet upon the swollen summit of insolence and upon the fate of mortal men?' And this too: 'How few will ever succeed in not diverging from this path because of fear of hardship or desire for smooth comfort? Too fortunate would be any man who accomplished such a feat – were there ever such anywhere. This would be him of whom I should judge the Poet was thinking when he wrote:

> Happy the man who succeeded in baring the causes of things
> And who trod underfoot all fear, inexorable Fate and Greedy
> Acheron's uproar. . . .

How intensely ought we to exert our strength to get under foot not a higher spot of earth but the passions which are puffed up by earthly instincts.'

Such emotions were rousing a storm in my breast as, without perceiving the roughness of the path, I returned late at night to the little rustic inn from which I had set out before dawn. The moon was shining all night long and offered her friendly service to the wanderers. While the servants were busy preparing our meal, I withdrew quite alone into a remote part of the house to write this letter to you in all haste and on the spur of the moment. I was afraid the intention to write might evaporate, since the rapid change of scene was likely to cause a change of mood if I deferred it.

And thus, most loving father, gather from this letter how eager I am to leave nothing whatever in my heart hidden from your eyes. Not only do I lay my whole life open to you with the utmost care but every single thought of mine. Pray for these thoughts, I beseech you, that they may at last find stability. So long have they been idling about and, finding no firm stand, been uselessly driven through so many matters. May they now turn at last to the One, the Good, the True, the stably Abiding.

Farewell.

On the twenty-sixth day of April, at Malaucène.

REFERENCE

Petrarca, Francesco. Trans. by Hans Nachod in *The Renaissance Philosophy of Man*. Edited by Ernst Cassirer, P. O. Kristeller, and J. H. Randall. Chicago: University Press, 1950, pp. 36–46. The Pusey translation of St Augustine has been substituted in one passage. (Reprinted by permission of the University of Chicago Press)

THE DEVIL, THE WITCH,
AND THE DOCTOR

THE first of the following extracts comes from a relatively mild
chapter of the *Malleus Maleficarum*. The distinction made by St
Thomas between 'glamours' and 'imaginary visions', which corresponds broadly to ours between illusions and hallucinations,
has already been explained by the authors. The chapter from
which I quote is concerned to show how devils 'can enter the
heads and other parts of the body of men, and move the inner
mental images from place to place'. It is therefore an attempt to
explain hallucination by devil possession. It illustrates quite well
the odd mixture of psychiatry, theology, and fiendish hypothesis
that characterizes the book, as well as something of the more
general spiritual interference that it takes for granted. Psychological readers will note some odd comments on localization of
function.

The second extract comes from Scot's *Discoverie of Witchcraft*
which was published in 1584 and is cited by Dover Wilson to
illustrate the kind of superstition which Shakespeare may have
encountered. Scot's *Discoverie* set out to prove 'That the Com-
pacts and Contracts of Witches with *Devils* and *Infernal Spirits*
or *Familiars*, are but Erroneous Novelties and Imaginary Conceptions'. Published four years before Weyer's death, it also was
on the side of an enlightenment which unfortunately King
James I did not share. He ordered Scot's book to be burned and
wrote his *Demonologie* to refute it.

Finally, we must say a little more about Weyer, from whom
the remaining extracts are taken. According to Zilboorg he took
up the study of medicine as a young man and spent about two
years, probably 1532–4, with Agrippa in Bonn. After this he
went to France, pursuing his studies in Orleans and Paris, where
he received his medical degree in 1537. Little seems to be known
of his next moves until 1545 when he was appointed city physician
of Arnhem. This he remained for five years, at the end of which
period he became personal physician to Duke Wilhelm of Jülich
Cleves-Berg. In the intervals of this work, which he continued
almost up to the time of his death, he produced various studies
in medicine and early psychiatry based on very wide clinical ex-

perience. Among other things he wrote a treatise on the 'disease of wrath'. The *De Praestigiis Daemonum* is however his *magnum opus*. Though of its time in quoting authorities galore, it is none-the-less strewn with concrete examples of current beliefs and cases which Weyer was clearly trying to understand and explain empirically.

When nineteenth-century France began to get interested in psychotherapy, Weyer was resuscitated, and a sixteenth-century French translation of the *De Praestigiis* was re-issued with a lively introduction. It suggests that Weyer had a robust sense of fun as well as of sober kindness, startling his medical colleagues by arranging his final list of Princes of Darkness in the form of a Medical Directory, giving specialities, places, and times of con-sultation.

His French editor gives more weight than Zilboorg to the idea that Weyer himself probably believed in devils. But however we interpret Weyer on this point, it is quite clear that he was fighting hard for naturalistic and psychological explanations of the sup-posed powers of devils and witches and of people's belief in these.

The first passage, on p. 269, translated direct from the French edition, is a typical piece of expostulation on Weyer's part. It has several points of interest. Among them it suggests complex motives for the sixteenth and seventeenth centuries wanting the body (and matter) to be solid and impenetrable. The remaining extracts are from Zilboorg's translated quotations in *A History of Medical Psychology* to which the reader should refer. A beauti-ful little copy of the third Latin edition of *De Praestigiis Dae-monum*, printed in Basel in 1566, is in the possession of the Lon-don Library.

Duke Wilhelm eventually had a stroke and the symptoms associated with it led to Weyer being suspected of sorcery after all. He appears nevertheless to have died a peaceful death and been buried with honour in Teklenbourg, Westphalia.

From MALLEUS MALEFICARUM

How Devils may enter the Human Body and the Head without doing any Hurt, when they cause such Metamorphosis by Means of Prestidigitation.

Concerning the method of causing these illusory transmutations it may further be asked: whether the devils are then inside the bodies and heads of those who are deceived, and whether the latter are to be considered as possessed by devils; how it can happen without injury to the inner perceptions and faculties that a mental image is transferred from one inner faculty to another; and whether or not such work ought to be considered miraculous.

First we must again refer to a distinction between such illusory glamours; for sometimes the outer perceptions only are affected, and sometimes the inner perceptions are deluded and so affect the outer perceptions.

In the former case the glamour can be caused without the devils' entering into the outer perceptions, and merely by an exterior illusion; as when the devil wishes to hide some body by the interposition of some other body, or in some other way; or when he himself assumes a body and imposes himself on the vision.

But in the latter case it is necessary that he must first occupy the head and the faculties. And this is proved by authority and reason.

And it is not a valid objection to say that two created spirits cannot be in one and the same place, and that the soul pervades the whole of the body. For on this question there is the authority of St John Damascene, when he says: Where the Angel is, there he operates. And St Thomas, in the *Second Book of Sentences*, dist. 7, art. 5, says: All Angels, good and bad, by their natural power, which is superior to all bodily power, are able to transmute our bodies.

And this is clearly true, not only by reason of the superior nobility of their nature, but because the whole mechanism of

the world and all corporeal creatures are administered by
Angels; as St Gregory says in the 4th Dialogue: In this visible
world nothing can be disposed except by an invisible creature.
Therefore all corporeal matters are governed by the Angels,
who are also called, not only by the Holy Doctors but also by
all the Philosophers, the Powers which move the stars. It is clear
also from the fact that all human bodies are moved by their
souls, just as all other matter is moved by the stars and the
Powers which move them. Any who wish may refer to St
Thomas in the First Part, Qu. 90, art. I.

From this it is concluded that, since devils operate there
where they are, therefore when they confuse the fancy and the
inner perceptions they are existing in them.

Again, although to enter the soul is possible only to God Who
created it, yet devils can, with God's permission, enter our
bodies; and they can then make impressions on the inner
faculties corresponding to the bodily organs. And by those impressions the organs are affected in proportion as the inner perceptions are affected in the way which has been shown: that the
devil can draw out some image retained in a faculty corresponding to one of the senses; as he draws from the memory which is
in the back part of the head, an image of a horse, and locally
moves that phantasm to the middle part of the head, where are
the cells of imaginative power; and finally to the sense of
reason, which is in the front of the head. And he causes such a
sudden change and confusion, that such objects are necessarily
thought to be actual things seen with the eyes. This can be
clearly exemplified by the natural defect in frantic men and
other maniacs.

But if it is asked how he can do this without causing pain in
the head, the answer is easy. For in the first place he does not
cause any actual physical change in the organs, but only moves
the mental images. And secondly, he does not effect these
changes by injecting any active quality which would necessarily
cause pain, since the devil is himself without any corporeal
quality, and can therefore operate without the use of any such
quality. Thirdly, as has been said, he effects these transmutations only by a local movement from one organ to another, and

not by other movements through which painful transformations are sometimes caused.

And as for the objection that two spirits cannot separately exist in the same place, and that, since the soul exists in the head, how can a devil be there also? It is to be said that the soul is thought to reside in the centre of the heart, in which it communicates with all the members by an outpouring of life. An example can be taken from a spider, which feels in the middle of its web when any part of the web is touched.

However, St Augustine says in his book *On the Spirit and the Soul*,* that it is all in all, and all in every part of the body. Granting that the soul is in the head, still the devil can work there; for his work is different from the work of the soul. The work of the soul is in the body, to inform it and fill it with life; so that it exists not merely locally, but in the whole matter. But the devil works in such a part and such a place of the body, effecting his changes in respect of the mental images. Therefore, since there is no confusion between their respective operations, they can both exist together in the same part of the body.

REFERENCE

Sprenger, Julius, and Kramer, Heinrich. *Malleus Maleficarum*. Trans. Montague Summers. London: The Imago Publishing Co. Ltd., 1948, pp. 124–5

From THE DISCOVERIE OF WITCHCRAFT

Then he (the Devil) teacheth them to make ointments of the bowels and members of children, whereby they ride in the air, and accomplish all their desires. So as, if there be any children unbaptized, or not guarded with the sign of the cross or orisons; then the witches may and do catch them from their mothers' sides in the night, or out of their cradles, or otherwise kill them with their ceremonies; and after burial steal them out of their

---

* 'On the Spirit'. The treatise *De Natura et Origine Animae* was written towards the end of the year 419.

graves, and seethe them in a cauldron, until their flesh be made potable. Of the thickest whereof they make ointments, whereby they ride in the air; but the thinner potion they put into flagons, whereof whosoever drinketh, observing certain ceremonies, immediately becometh a master or rather a mistress in that practice and faculty. . . .

It shall not be amiss here in this place to repeat an ointment greatly to this purpose . . . The receipt is as followeth. R. the fat of young children, and seethe it with water in a brazen vessel, reserving the thickest of that which remaineth boiled in the bottom, which they lay up and keep until occasion serveth to use it. They put hereunto *eleoselinum, aconitum, frondes populeas*, and soot. Another receipt to the same purpose. R. *sium, acarum vulgare, pentaphyllon*, the blood of a flitter-mouse, *solanum somniferum, et oleum.* They stamp all these together, and then they rub all parts of their bodies exceedingly, till they look red, and be very hot, so as the pores may be opened, and their flesh soluble and loose. They join herewithal either fat, or oil instead thereof, that the force of the ointment may the rather pierce inwardly, and so be more effectual. By this means in a moonlight night they seem to be carried in the air, to feasting, singing, dancing, kissing, culling, and other acts of venery, with such youths as they love and desire most: for the force of their imagination is so vehement, that almost all that part of the brain, wherein the memory consisteth, is full of such conceits. And whereas they are naturally prone to believe any thing; so do they receive such impressions and steadfast imaginations into their minds, as even their spirits are altered thereby; not thinking upon any thing else, either by day or by night. And this helpeth them forward in their imaginations, that their usual food is none other commonly but beets, roots, nuts, beans, peas, etc.

REFERENCE

Scot, Reginald. *The Discoverie of Witchcraft*. Quoted by John Dover Wilson, *Life in Shakespeare's England*. Harmondsworth: Penguin Books, 1949, pp. 60-1

From Weyer's DE PRAESTIGIIS DAEMONUM

*Absurd means by which solid objects are supposed to be inserted
into the human body*

There is a certain doctor who, under the name of Jacques,
Seigneur de Lichtemberg, has written a book in German in
which he gives a quite senseless and unfounded explanation of
how these solid substances are inserted into bodies by devils at
the instigation of witches. I am very astonished that the respectable and learned Jacques Milich should have given support to
this in his book *The Devil-Sorcerer*. These two assert that the
devil opens and enlarges the pores or apertures of the human
body and passes through them straw, pig's livers, knives, pieces
of leather, parings, thread, fishbones, thorns, and other similar
sharp objects, after which he closes the apertures again. Through
them he can, however, when he pleases, withdraw these same
objects.

The doctor then proffers the following analogies. Just as it
happens, he says, that when a stone has been dropped into water
and the hand withdraws, one cannot tell how it went in, and
just as lightning naturally passes through the interstices of a
sheath without damaging it and melts the iron within, so with
those diabolical illusions which cause stigmata, scars, and even
more serious wounds. Those are his very words.

But anyone with even a little knowledge of natural things will
readily perceive that these reasons are of little account and inadequate. For I maintain that it is an impossibility that pores
or apertures, which from their first creation were made by
nature small and constricted, could, without harm, be enlarged
by the devil so that he could pass through them pieces of straw,
leather or knives, after which at his will and pleasure they could
be closed again, and that later on they could eject this substance
which has lain within for so many days or months. All the more
so, since the pores of the body have from the beginning been so
firmly constricted by their first creator that it is utterly impossible for a denser substance to pass, other than a very thin fluid

such as sweat or vapour; just as we observe in solid, thick stone, and notably in earthenware and wood, whose pores or apertures allow the passage of certain fluids, but of no other hard or solid matter, without being materially opened or broken. These things can easily be accepted in fantasy, but they cannot be so easily effected in reality.

The analogy of the stone dropped into water by the hand is utterly absurd: for it is ridiculous to compare the human body, which is solid and dense, with water, which is liquid, tenuous, and flowing, and which by nature facilitates the passage of ships and any other object. Moreover, there is no similarity or comparison between a tongue of fire of subtle substance which passes through the interstices of the sheath, and a hard and solid object which he says and maintains can enter through the pores of the human body without harm.

But for the fact that anyone can perceive without difficulty how flimsy are these proofs, I could spend longer refuting them. There are a number of such proofs scattered here and there in the course of his book.

From Weyer's Dedication of his DE PRAESTIGIIS DAEMONUM

Of all the misfortunes which the various fanatical and corrupt opinions, through Satan's help, have brought in our time to Christendom, not the smallest is that which, under the name of witchcraft, is sown as a vicious seed. The people may be divided against themselves through their many disputes about the Scriptures and church customs, while the old snake stirs the fire; still no such great misfortune results from that as from the thereby inspired opinion that childish old hags whom one calls witches or sorcerers can do any harm to men and animals. Daily experience teaches us what cursed apostasy, what friendship with the wicked one, what hatred and strife among fellow creatures, what dissension in city and in country, what numerous murders of innocent people through the devil's wretched aid, such belief in the power of witches brings forth. No one can more correctly judge about these things than we physicians whose ears and hearts are being constantly tortured by this superstition.

*

I notice more from day to day that the bog of Camarina blows its plague-laden breath stronger than ever.

*

Therefore I, with my limited means, have undertaken to challenge the grievous thing which disgraces our Christian faith. It is not arrogance which impels me. I know that I know nothing and that my work allows me little leisure. I know too that many others could do this work better than I. I would like to incite them to outdo me. I shall gladly listen to reason.

My object is chiefly of a theological nature: to set forth the artfulness of Satan according to Biblical authority and to demonstrate how one can overcome it. Next, my object is philosophical, in that I fight with natural reason against the deceptions which proceed from Satan and the mad imagination of the so-called witches. My object is also medical, in that I show that those illnesses the origin of which is attributed to witches come from natural causes. And finally, my object is legal, in that I speak of the punishment, in another than the accustomed way, of sorcerers and witches.

But in order that I shall not meet with the reproach that I have overstepped the boundaries of my intellectual power and the limits of my profession with too great a faith in my own intelligence, I have submitted my seemingly paradoxical manuscript to men of your Highness' family as well as to theologians, lawyers, and excellent physicians, that it may be read in a critical sense. The manuscript shall remain protected through their authority if it is founded on reason; it shall fall if it is judged to be in error; it shall become better if it needs supplement or revision. For there is nothing in the world which can be made immediately and at once completely perfect.

One might rejoin here that the *Malleus Maleficarum* has already fulfilled this mission. But one has only to read in that book the silly and often godless absurdities of the theologians Heinrich Kramer and Jacob (Johann) Sprenger and to compare these quietly with the content of my manuscript. Then it will be clearly seen that I expound and advocate a totally different, even an opposite, point of view.

To you, Prince, I dedicate the fruit of my thought. For thirteen years your physician, I have heard expressed in your Court the most varied opinions concerning witches; but none so agrees with my own as does yours, that witches can harm no one through the most malicious will or the ugliest exorcism, that rather their imagination – inflamed by the demons in a way not understandable to us – and the torture of melancholy makes them only fancy that they have caused all sorts of evil. For when the entire manner of action is laid on the scales, and the implements therefor examined with care and scrutiny, the nonsense and falsity of the matter is soon clear to all eyes and more lucid than the day. You do not, like others, impose heavy penalties on perplexed, poor old women. You demand evidence, and only if they have actually given poison bringing about the death of men or animals do you allow the law to take its course.

REFERENCES

Weyer, Johannis. *Histoires disputes et discours des illusions et impostures des diables etc.* par Jean Wier. Paris: Delahaye et Lecrosnier, Bibliothèque Diabolique, 1885. Vol. 1, Bk. IV. Chap. xv, pp. 554–6

Zilboorg, G., and Henry, G. W. *A History of Medical Psychology*. London: Allen and Unwin, 1941, pp. 213–15

FRANCIS BACON
1560–1626

FRANCIS BACON was born on January 22, 1560. His father, Sir Nicholas Bacon, was Queen Elizabeth's counsellor and Lord Keeper of the Privy Seal. His mother is described by Rawley, Bacon's 'first and last chaplain', as 'a choice lady, eminent for piety, virtue and learning; being exquisitely skilled for a woman in the Greek and Latin tongues'. Born of highly intelligent parents, into a home where affairs of State and wide education were taken for granted, Bacon in effect had greatness thrust upon him. He became Chancellor to James I but fell from power in 1621. He continued to write in retirement.

Bacon is in some ways a puzzling person and a puzzling writer to assess. His claim to a place in the history of psychology and of body-mind problems is, however, serious for three main reasons. First, he was genuinely critical of current pseudo-science and devoted himself tirelessly to maintaining the need to place what was then called natural philosophy on a sound observational and experimental basis. Secondly, he had some shrewd things to say about the habits, vested interests, prejudices, etc. that prevent us from observing and reasoning afresh. Thirdly, he occasionally raised awkward questions in a very direct fashion and was remarkably at home in keeping straightforward empirical inquiry away from directions that were emotionally toned.

It is easy to detect in Bacon a tendency to pontificate. It is possible that as a Chancellor people took him more seriously than his writings always warranted. The fact that a Chancellor could say the things that he did say at that time was, however, significant and Bacon's influence proved considerable and useful. We still have not achieved some of the sensible things he suggested.

From A DISCUSSION OF SCIENTIFIC METHOD

Hence it follows that the order of demonstration is likewise inverted. For hitherto the proceeding has been to fly at once from the sense and particulars up to the most general propositions, as certain fixed poles for the argument to turn upon, and from these to derive the rest by middle terms: a short way, no doubt, but precipitate; and one which will never lead to nature, though it offers an easy and ready way to disputation. Now my plan is to proceed regularly and gradually from one axiom to another, so that the most general are not reached till the last; but then when you do come to them you find them to be not empty notions, but well defined, and such as nature would really recognize as her first principles, and such as lie at the heart and marrow of things.

But the greatest change I introduce is in the form itself of induction and judgement made thereby. For the induction of which the logicians speak, which proceeds by simple enumeration, is a puerile thing; concludes at hazard; is always liable to be upset by a contradictory instance; takes into account only what is known and ordinary; and leads to no result.

Now what the sciences stand in need of is a form of induction which shall analyse experience and take it to pieces, and by a due process of exclusion and rejection lead to an inevitable conclusion. And if that ordinary mode of judgement practised by the logicians was so laborious, and found exercise for such great wits, how much more labour must we be prepared to bestow upon this other, which is extracted not merely out of the depths of the mind, but out of the very bowels of nature.

Nor is this all. For I also sink the foundations of the sciences deeper and firmer; and I begin the inquiry nearer the source than men have done heretofore; submitting to examination those things which the common logic takes on trust. For, first, the logicians borrow the principles of each science from the science itself; secondly, they hold in reverence the first notions of the mind; and lastly, they receive as conclusive the immediate informations of the sense, when well disposed. Now upon the first point, I hold that true logic ought to enter the several provinces of science armed with a higher authority than belongs to the principles of those sciences themselves, and ought to call those putative principles to account until they are fully established. Then with regard to the first notions of the intellect; there is not one of the impressions taken by the intellect when left to go its own way, but I hold it for suspected, and no way established, until it has submitted to a new trial and a fresh judgement has been thereupon pronounced. And lastly, the information of the sense itself I sift and examine in many ways. For certain it is that the senses deceive; but then at the same time they supply the means of discovering their own errors; only the errors are here, the means of discovery are to seek.

The sense fails in two ways. Sometimes it gives no information, sometimes it gives false information. For first, there are very many things which escape the sense, even when best disposed and no way obstructed; by reason either of the subtlety of the whole body, or the minuteness of the parts, or distance of place, or slowness or else swiftness of motion, or familiarity of object, or other causes. And again when the sense does apprehend a thing its apprehension is not much to be relied upon. For the testimony and information of the sense has reference always to man, not to the universe; and it is a great error to assert that the sense is the measure of things.

To meet these difficulties, I have sought on all sides diligently and faithfully to provide helps for the sense – substitutes to supply its failures, rectifications to correct its errors; and this I endeavour to accomplish not so much by instruments as by experiments. For the subtlety of experiments is far greater than that of the sense itself, even when assisted by exquisite instruments; such experiments, I mean, as are skilfully and artificially devised for the express purpose of determining the point in question. To the immediate and proper perception of the sense therefore I do not give much weight; but I contrive that the office of the sense shall be only to judge of the experiment, and that the experiment itself shall judge of the thing. And thus I conceive that I perform the office of a true priest of the sense (from which all knowledge in nature must be sought, unless men mean to go mad) and a not unskilful interpreter of its oracles; and that while others only profess to uphold and cultivate the sense, I do so in fact. Such then are the provisions I make for finding the genuine light of nature and kindling and bringing it to bear. And they would be sufficient of themselves, if the human intellect were even, and like a fair sheet of paper with no writing upon it. But since the minds of men are strangely possessed and beset, so that there is no true and even surface left to reflect the genuine rays of things, it is necessary to seek a remedy for this also.

Now the idols, or phantoms, by which the mind is occupied are either adventitious or innate. The adventitious come into the mind from without; namely, either from the doctrines and sects of philosophers, or from perverse rules of demonstration. But the innate are inherent in the very nature of the intellect, which is far more prone to error than the sense is. For let men please themselves as they will in admiring and almost adoring the human mind, this is certain: that as an uneven mirror distorts the rays of objects according to its own figure and section, so the mind, when it receives impressions of objects through the sense, cannot be trusted to report them truly, but in forming its notions mixes up its own nature with the nature of things.

And as the first two kinds of idols are hard to eradicate, so idols of this last kind cannot be eradicated at all. All that can be done is to point them out so that this insidious action of the mind may be marked and reproved (else as fast as old errors are destroyed new ones will spring up out of the ill complexion of the mind itself, and so we shall have but a change of errors, and not a clearance); and to lay it down once for all as a fixed and established maxim, that the intellect is not qualified to judge except by means of induction, and induction in its legitimate form.

From A Discussion of the Study of Man

Let us now come to that knowledge whereunto the ancient oracle directs us, which is the knowledge of ourselves; which deserves the more accurate handling in proportion as it touches us more nearly. This knowledge is for man the end and term of knowledges; but of nature herself it is but a portion. And generally let this be a rule; that all divisions of knowledges be accepted and used rather for lines to mark or distinguish, than sections to divide and separate them; in order that solution of continuity in sciences may always be avoided.

... With this reservation therefore let us proceed to the doctrine concerning Man. It has two parts. For it considers man either segregate, or congregate and in society. The one I call the Philosophy of Humanity, and the other Civil Philosophy. Philosophy of Humanity consists of parts similar to those of which man consists; that is, of knowledges which respect the body, and of knowledges which respect the mind. But before we pursue the particular distributions let us constitute one general science concerning the Nature and State of Man; a subject which certainly deserves to be emancipated and made a knowledge of itself. It is composed of those things which are common as well to the body as the soul; and may be divided into two parts; the one regarding the nature of man undivided, and the other regarding the bond and connexion between the mind and body; the first whereof I will term the doctrine concerning the Person of Man, the second the doctrine concerning the League. But it is plain that these things, being common and mixed, could not all have been assigned to that first division, of sciences which regard the body and sciences which regard the mind.

The doctrine concerning the Person of Man takes into consideration two subjects principally; the Miseries of the human race, and the Prerogatives or Excellencies of the same. And for the miseries of humanity, the lamentation of them has been elegantly and copiously set forth by many, both in philosophical and theological writings. And it is an argument at once sweet and wholesome.

But that other subject of the Prerogatives of Man seems to me to deserve a place among the *desiderata*. Pindar in praising Hiero says most elegantly (as is his wont) that he 'culled the tops of all virtues'. And certainly I think it would contribute much to magnanimity and the honour of humanity, if a collection were made of what the schoolmen call the *ultimities*, and Pindar the *tops or summits*, of human nature, especially from true history; showing what is the ultimate and highest point which human nature has of itself attained in the several gifts of body and mind....

With regard to the doctrine concerning the League or Common Bond between the soul and body, it is distributed into two parts. For as in all leagues and amities there is both mutual intelligence and mutual offices, so the description of this league of soul and body consists in like manner of two parts; namely, how these two (that is the Soul and the Body) disclose the one the other, and how they work the one upon the other; by knowledge or indication, and by impression. The former of these (that is, the description of what knowledge of the mind may be obtained from the habit of the body, or of the body from the accidents of the mind) has begotten two arts; both of prediction; whereof the one is honoured with the inquiry of Aristotle, and the other of Hippocrates. And although they have of later times been polluted with superstitious and fantastical arts, yet being purged and restored to their true state, they have both a solid ground in nature and a profitable use in life. The first is Physiognomy, which discovers the dispositions of the mind by the lineaments of the body; the second is the Interpretation of Natural Dreams, which discovers the state and disposition of the body by the agitations of the mind. In the former of these I note a deficience. For Aristotle has very ingeniously and diligently handled the structure of the body when at rest, but the structure of the body when in motion (that is, the gestures of the body) he has omitted; which never-the-less are equally within the observations of art, and of greater use and advantage. For the lineaments of the body disclose the dispositions and inclinations of the mind in general; but the motions and gestures of the countenance and parts do not only so, but disclose likewise the seasons of access, and the present humour and state of the mind and will. For as your Majesty says most aptly and elegantly, 'As the tongue speaketh to the ear so the gesture speaketh to the eye'. And well is this known to a number of cunning and astute persons; whose eyes dwell upon the faces and gestures of men, and make their own advantage of it, as being most part of their ability and wisdom. Neither indeed can it be denied, but that it is a wonderful index of simulation in another, and an excellent direction as to the choice of proper times and seasons to address persons; which is no small part of civil wisdom. Nor let any one imagine that a sagacity of this kind may be of use with respect to particular persons, but cannot fall under a general rule; for we all laugh and weep and frown and blush nearly in the same fashion; and so it is (for the most part) in the more subtle motions. But if any one be reminded here of chiromancy, let him know that it is a vain imposture, not worthy to be so much as mentioned in discourses of this nature. With regard to the Interpretation of Natural Dreams, it is a thing that has been laboriously handled by many writers, but it is full of follies. At present I will only observe that it is not grounded upon the most solid foundation of which it admits; which is, that when the same sensation is produced in the sleeper by an internal cause which is usually the effect of some external act, that external act passes into the dream. A like oppression is produced in the stomach by the vapour of indigestion and by an external weight superimposed; and therefore persons who suffer from the nightmare dream of a weight lying on them, with a great array of circumstances. A like pendulous condition of the bowels is produced by the agitation of the waves at sea, and by wind collected round the diaphragm; therefore hypochondriacal persons often dream that they are sailing and tossing on the sea. There are likewise innumberable instances of this kind.

The latter branch of the doctrine of the League (which I have termed Impression) has not yet been collected into an art, but only comes in sometimes dispersedly in the course of other treatises. It has the same relation or antistrophe that the former has. For the consideration is twofold; either how and how far the humours and temperament of the body alter and work upon the mind; or again, how and how far the passions or apprehensions of the mind alter and work upon the body. For the physicians prescribe drugs to heal mental diseases, as in the treatment of frenzy and melancholy; and pretend also to exhibit medicines to exhilarate the mind, to fortify the heart and thereby confirm the courage, to clarify the wits, to corroborate the memory, and the like. But the diets, and the choice of meats and drinks, the ablutions and other observances of the body, in the sect of the Pythagoreans, in the heresy of the Manicheans, and in the law of Mahomet, exceed all measure. So likewise the ordinances in the ceremonial law interdicting the eating of the blood and fat, and distinguishing between beasts clean and unclean for meat, are many and strict. Nay, the Christian faith itself (although clear and serene from all clouds of ceremony), yet retains the use of fastings, abstinences, and other macerations and humiliations of the body, as things not merely ritual, but also profitable. The root and life of all which prescripts (besides the ceremony and the exercise of obedience) consist in that of which we are speaking, namely the sympathy of the mind with the state and disposition of the body. But if any man of weak judgement conceive that these impressions of the body on the mind either question the immortality of the soul, or derogate from its sovereignty over the body, a slight answer may serve for so slight a doubt. Let him take the case of an infant in the mother's womb, which is affected by that which affects the mother, and yet is in due time delivered and separated from her body; or of monarchs who, though powerful, are sometimes controlled by their servants, and yet without abatement of their majesty royal.

As for the reciprocal part (which is the operation of the mind and its passions upon the body), it also has found a place in medicine. For there is no physician of any skill who does not attend to the accidents of the mind, as a thing most material towards recoveries, and of the greatest force to further or hinder other remedies. But another question pertinent to this subject has been but sparingly inquired into, and nowise in proportion to its depth and worth; namely how far (setting the affections aside) the very imagination of the mind, or a thought strongly fixed and exalted into a kind of faith, is able to alter the body of the imaginant. For although it has a manifest power to hurt, yet it follows not that it has the same degree of power to help; no more indeed than a man can conclude, that because there are pestilent airs, able suddenly to kill a man in health, therefore there should be sovereign airs, able suddenly to cure a man in sickness. Such an inquiry would surely be of noble use; though it needs (as Socrates says) a *Delian diver*; for it lies deep. Again, among those doctrines concerning the League, or the concordances between the mind and body, there is none more necessary than the inquiry concerning the proper seats and domiciles which the several faculties of the mind occupy in the body and its organs. Which kind of knowledge has not been without its followers; but what has been done in it is in most parts either disputed or slightly inquired; so that more diligence and acuteness is requisite. For the opinion of Plato, who placed the understanding in the brain, as in a castle; animosity (which he unfitly enough called anger, seeing it is more related to swelling and pride) in the heart; and concupiscence and sensuality in the liver; deserves neither to be altogether despised nor to be eagerly received. Neither again is that arrangement of the intellectual faculties (imagination, reason, and memory) according to the respective ventricles of the brain, destitute of error. Thus then have I explained the doctrine concerning the nature of man undivided, and likewise the league between the mind and body.

REFERENCE

Bacon, Francis. *Philosophical Works*. Ed. J. M. Robertson. London: Routledge, 1905, pp. 249–51, 478, 478–9, 480–2

RENÉ DESCARTES

1596–1650

MANY of Descartes' works are of great psychological interest, and the reader who wants to get a serious grasp of his views would need to study him deeply, making a start with the *Discours de la Méthode* published in 1637 and the *Meditationes de Prima Philosophia* published in 1641. Both of these are short, and there are excellent modern translations into English, of which the most convenient and up to date are those by Professor Norman Kemp Smith in *Descartes' Philosophical Writings*. In the *Discours* and *Meditations*, considered psychologically, Descartes can be seen struggling to decide with which conception of himself he is willing to identify. Descartes' reasoning, when he is thinking of the main distinctions between mind and matter, and when he concludes that mind is simple and unextended, while matter is spatially divisible, is elegant and close. One can hardly extract quotations without distortion. The following selections therefore come from Descartes' later and somewhat less familiar work *Les Passions de l'Âme* published in 1649. Here we see Descartes trying to deal with the practical problem of how mind and matter, as he understood them, may be integrated in the complex person which, in his more relaxed and unphilosophical moments, Descartes assumed himself to be.

Descartes was prompted to write the treatise by the Princess Elizabeth of Bohemia. Those who, like her, find something difficult to understand about Descartes' clearly non-material and substantive soul being able to affect his distinctly material body, would do well to go on and read the delightful correspondence between Her Highness and Descartes on this interesting topic. There they will find the harassed Descartes labouring to clarify his own thoughts as well as those of the intelligent and puzzled Princess. There are moments when he seems to be fumbling after a non-tactile conception of causality and after almost Kantian notions of the innate framework of mental functioning. He is clearly aware of enormous difficulties, and one surmises that he never quite satisfied either his favourite pupil or himself. Both may have been a little glad to accept his courteous but clear suggestion that perhaps it is unwise to try and spend too much time on the philosophical heights. Part of this tempting discussion is also available in Professor Kemp Smith's edition to which the interested reader is referred. Reference to the complete correspondence is also given. The Princess was a Protestant and daughter of the Winter Queen, Charles the First's beautiful sister, who lived as an honoured refugee in Holland after the Bohemian revolt and the death of the Elector Palatine, Princess Elizabeth's father.

Part of *L'Âme Raisonnable* is also quoted. It is taken from Fulton and is a translation from *De Nomine figuris et latinitate donatus a Florentino Schuyl* published in 1662 with Descartes' own diagrams. These include one of the perception of light by stimuli transmitted to the pineal gland. The quotation shows clearly the extent to which Descartes was influenced by current 'mechanical' models of explanation.

So far as the body was concerned its functions proceeded from 'the mere arrangement of its organs' . . . 'so that so far as these are concerned, it is unnecessary to conceive in it any soul – whether vegetative or sensitive – or any other principle of motion, or of life, than its blood and its spirits agitated by the heat of the fire which burns continually in its heart, and which is in no wise essentially different in nature from all the fires which are met with in inanimate bodies'.

From THE PASSIONS OF THE SOUL

ARTICLE I

*What in respect of a subject is passion, is in some
other regard always action.*

. . . I feel myself obliged to write as if I were treating of a matter to which no one before me had ever paid due attention. On proceeding to do so, I observe that whatever occurs in the way of novelty or change, is by the philosophers ordinarily termed a passion in respect of the subject to which it happens and an action in respect of what causes it to happen. Though agent and patient are often very different, the action and the passion are thus always one and the same thing. We are allowing it these two names because of the two diverse subjects to which we can refer it.

ARTICLE 2

*That to understand the passions of the soul we have to
distinguish its functions from those of the body.*

I note that we are not aware of any subject which acts upon our
soul more immediately than does the body with which it is conjoined, and that consequently we ought to recognize that what
in the soul is a passion is in the body usually an action. There is
therefore no better way of gaining an understanding of the
passions than to examine the difference there is between mind
and body, with a view to knowing to which of the two we should
attribute each one of the functions that are in us.

ARTICLE 3

What rule we should follow in so doing.

We shall not find much difficulty in doing this, if we take note
that whatever we experience as being in us, and which, we find,
can also exist in completely inanimate bodies, has to be attributed to our body, and on the other hand that all which is in us,
and which we cannot anywise view as appertaining to a body,
has to be attributed to the soul.

ARTICLE 4

*That the heat and movement of the limbs proceed
from the body, the thoughts from the soul.*

Thus, because we cannot view the body as in any fashion thinking, we are right in believing that all the various kinds of
thoughts which are in us appertain to the soul; and because we
do not doubt that there are inanimate bodies which can move
in as many or more diverse ways than can our limbs, and which
have as much heat or more (as experience shows us in the case
of flame, which has in itself more heat and movement than any
of our members), we ought to recognize that all the heat and
movements which are in us, in so far as they do not anywise
depend on thought, appertain exclusively to the body.

ARTICLE 5

That it is an error to believe that the soul gives the body its movement and heat.

Proceeding on these lines, we shall avoid a very serious error into which many have fallen, and which indeed I esteem to be the primary cause of our failure hitherto to explain the passions and other matters pertaining to the soul. The error is that, from observing how all dead bodies are devoid of heat, and consequently of movement, it has been thought that it is the absence of the soul which has caused these movements and this heat to cease; and thereby, without reason we have come to believe that our natural heat and all the movements of our body depend on the soul. What, on the contrary, we ought to hold is that the reason why the soul absents itself on death is that this heat ceases and that the organs which operate in moving the limbs disintegrate.

ARTICLE 6

The difference there is between a living and a dead body.

That we may avoid this error, let us recognize that death never comes through failure of the soul, but solely because some one of the principal parts of the body disintegrates. Let us hold that the body of a living man differs from that of a dead man just as any machine that moves of itself (e.g. a watch or other automaton when it is wound up and thereby has in itself the corporeal principle of those movements for which it is designed, together with all else that is required for its action) differs from itself when it is broken and the principle of its movement ceases to act.

ARTICLE 7

Brief explanation of the parts of the body and of some of their functions.

To make this more intelligible I will explain here in a few words the whole fashion in which the machinery of our body is constructed. . . .

[Here follows Descartes' account of bodily functioning, in the course of which he refers to Harvey.]

ARTICLE 17

Concerning the functions of the soul.

After having thus considered all the functions which appertain to the body alone, we easily recognize that there remains in us nothing which we should attribute to our soul save only our thoughts. These are of two principal kinds, the actions of the soul and its passions. All our volitions I name actions, because we experience them as proceeding directly from our soul and as seeming to depend on it alone: while, on the other hand, we can give the general title, passions, to all those modes of awareness which often arise in us without our soul making them to be what they are, and which in all cases it receives from the things which they [stand for and] represent.

ARTICLE 18

Concerning the will.

Our volitions, in turn, are also of two kinds. Some actions of the soul terminate in the soul itself, as when we will to love God, or in general apply our thought to some non-material object. Our other actions terminate in our body, as when from our merely willing to walk, it follows that our legs are moved and that we walk.

ARTICLE 19

Concerning cognizing [i.e. awareness].

Our cognizings are likewise of two kinds. Some have the soul as their cause, others the body. Those which have the soul as their cause are the cognizings of our volitions and of all the imagings and other things which depend on these volitions. For it is certain that we cannot will anything without cognizing by the same means that we will it; and although in respect of our soul it is an action to will something, we can say that to be aware that it wills is likewise a passion. Yet because such cognizing and such volition are really one and the same thing, it is always named from what is the more noble, and accordingly it is not customary to call it a passion but always to view it as an action.

ARTICLE 20

Concerning the imagings and other thoughts FANTASY *which are formed by the soul.*

When our soul applies itself to image something which does not exist, as in representing to itself an enchanted palace or a chimera, and also when it applies itself to think of something which is purely intelligible and not imageable, e.g. to think of its own nature, the awareness it has of these things depends chiefly [for its initiation] on the act of will which causes us to think of them. This is why we are wont to view them as actions rather than as passions.

ARTICLE 21

Concerning the imagings which have the body alone as their cause.

As to the cognizings which are caused by the body, they for the most part depend on the nerves. But there are also some which do not, and which though entitled, like those above referred to, imagings, yet differ from them in that our will plays no part in forming them. Accordingly they cannot be numbered among the actions of the soul; they come about owing to the manner in which the spirits (variously agitated and coming upon traces of diverse impressions which have preceded them in the brain) take their course fortuitously by certain pores rather than by others. Such are the illusions of our dreams and the daydreams we often have when awake – our thinking wandering carelessly without directing itself to any of them. Some of these imagings are passions of the soul, taking the term passion in its most proper and exact meaning, and they may all be so named if we take it in a more general sense. Since, however, they do not have so notable and so determinate a cause as the cognizings the mind receives by intervention of the nerves, and appear to be only their shadows and pictures, we must, to distinguish them properly, first of all consider the [two-fold] difference exhibited by these others.

ARTICLE 22

How the cognizings differ from one another.

The cognizings which I have not yet considered all come to the soul by intervention of the nerves; and between them there are these differences: that some of them we relate to outside objects which strike our senses, others to our body or to some of its parts, and others to our soul.

ARTICLE 23

Concerning the cognizings we relate to objects external to us.

The cognizings we relate to things external to us, viz. to the objects of our senses, are caused (at least when we are not mistaken in our opinion) by those objects which, in exciting certain movements in the organs of the external senses, also excite, by way of the nerves, movements in the brain, which then cause the soul to sense them. Thus when we see the light of a torch, and hear the sound of a bell, this light and this sound are two different actions which, simply by exciting two different movements in certain of our nerves, and thereby in the brain, give the soul two different sensations, which we so relate to the subjects we are supposing to be their causes, that we think we see the torch itself and hear the bell, and not that we are merely sensing the movements which proceed from them.

ARTICLE 24

Concerning the cognizings we refer to our body.

The cognizings we refer to our body, or to certain of its parts, are those we have of hunger, thirst, and of our other natural appetites – to which may be added pain, heat, and other affections which we sense as in our limbs, not as in external objects. Thus we can sense at one and the same time, and by way of the same nerves, the cold of our hand and the heat of the flame which it approaches; or contrariwise the heat of the hand and the cold of the air to which it is exposed, without their being any difference between the actions that cause us to feel the heat or the cold of our hand and the actions which cause us to feel what is external to us, excepting only that inasmuch as one of these actions follows upon the other, we judge the first to be already in us, and what supervenes upon it as not yet so, but as in the object which causes it.

ARTICLE 25

Concerning the cognizings we refer to our soul.

The cognizings which we refer exclusively to the soul are those whose effects we feel as in the soul itself, and in respect of which we do not usually know any proximate cause to which we can relate them. Such are the feelings of joy, anger, and the like, excited in us sometimes by the objects that move our nerves and sometimes by other causes. All our cognizings, both those we refer to objects external to us and those we refer to the various affections of our body, are indeed passions in respect of our soul, when we use the term passion in its most general meaning. We are, however, wont to restrict the term to signify only those which are related to the soul itself; and it is these alone that I have here undertaken to explain under the title, passions of the soul.

ARTICLE 26

That the imagings which depend solely on the fortuitous movement of the spirits may be passions just as truly as the cognizings which depend on the nerves.

We have still to note that whatever the soul is aware of by intervention of the nerves can also be represented by the fortuitous course of the [animal] spirits, without there being any other difference save only that the impressions which come into the brain by way of the nerves are usually more lively and more definite than those excited there by the spirits. This is what led me to say in Article 21 that the latter are, as it were, the shadows or the pictures of the former. We must also note that it sometimes happens that the picture is so similar to the thing it represents that while we can be deceived regarding the cognizings which refer to objects outside us, or at least regarding those which refer to certain parts of our body, we cannot be thus deceived regarding the passions. So close, so interior, to our soul are the passions, that it is impossible it should sense them unless they veritably are what it senses them as being. Often when asleep, and sometimes even when awake, we image certain things so vividly that we think we see them before us or sense them in our body, although they have yet no such existence there. But whether asleep or day-dreaming, we cannot be sad, or be stirred by any other passion, save in so far as the soul does have the passion veritably in itself.

ARTICLE 27

The definition of passions of the soul.

Having thus considered how the passions of the soul differ from all its other thoughts, we may, it seems to me, define them, in general terms, as being those cognizings, or feelings, or emotions of the soul, which we thus view as specially pertaining to it, and which are caused, upheld, and fortified by some movement of the [animal] spirits.

ARTICLE 28

Explanation of the first part of this definition.

We can entitle them cognizings when we use this word in a general manner to signify all the thoughts which are not actions, i.e. not volitions, of the soul, but not when using it to signify only evident cognitions. For experience shows us that those who are the most excited by their passions are not those who know them best, and that their passions are to be counted as belonging to that group of cognizings which the close alliance of mind and body renders confused and obscure. We may also entitle them feelings, as being received into the soul in the same fashion as the objects of the external senses, and otherwise not known by it. But it is better to name them emotions of the soul, not only because this name can be given to all the changes which take place in it, i.e. to all the various thoughts which the soul can know, but especially because, of all the various kinds of thoughts it can have, there are no others which agitate and unsettle it so powerfully as do these passions.

ARTICLE 29

Explanation of the other part of the definition.

I add that they quite specially refer to the soul, in order to distinguish them from the other feelings which are not so referred – some, such as odours, sounds, colours, referred to external objects, others, such as hunger, thirst, pain, referring to our body. I also add that they are caused, upheld, and fortified by some movement of the [animal] spirits, in order to distinguish them from those of our volitions which can also be entitled emotions of the soul, but which besides being referred to the soul are also caused by it; and also in order to explain their nearest, most proximate cause which again distinguishes them from the other feelings.

ARTICLE 30

That the soul is united to all parts of the body conjointly.

But for the more perfect understanding of all these things, we must know that the soul is really joined to the whole body, and that we cannot, properly speaking, say that it is in any one of its parts to the exclusion of the others – the body being unitary, i.e. in some fashion indivisible, in virtue of the disposition of its organs which are so related each to the others, that when any one of them is removed, the whole body is rendered defective. Again, the soul is of such a nature that it has no relation to extension, nor to the dimensions or other properties of the matter composing the body, but only to the whole assemblage of its organs, as appears from our inability to think of the half or the third of a soul, or of its occupying a space. It does not become smaller on the removal of a part of the body. When, however, the assemblage of the bodily organs disintegrates, it itself, in its entirety, withdraws from the body.

ARTICLE 31 *PINEAL*

That there is a small gland in the brain in which the soul exercises its function more specifically than in its other parts.

We have also to bear in mind that although the soul is joined to the whole body, there is yet in the body a certain part in which it exercises its functions more specifically than in all the others. It is a matter of common belief that this part is the brain, or possibly the heart – the brain because of its relation to the senses, the heart because it is there we feel the passions. But on carefully examining the matter I seem to find evidence that the part of the body in which the soul exercises its functions immediately is in no wise the heart, nor the brain as a whole, but solely the innermost part of the brain, viz. a certain very small gland, situated in a midway position, and suspended over the passage by which the animal spirits of the anterior cavities communicate with those of the posterior cavities, in such fashion that its slightest movements can greatly alter the course of those spirits; and reciprocally that any change, however slight, taking place in the course of the spirits can greatly change the movements of this gland.

ARTICLE 32

How we know this to be the chief seat of the soul.

The reason which persuades me that the soul cannot have anywhere in the body any other location for the immediate exercise of its functions is that I observe all the other parts of the brain to be double, just as we have two eyes, two hands, two ears, and indeed, all the organs of our external senses double; and that since of any one thing at any one time we have only one single and simple thought, there must be some place where the two images which come from the two eyes, and where the two impressions which come from one single object by way of the double organs of the other senses, can unite before reaching the soul, and so prevent their representing to it two objects in place of one. We can easily think of these images or other impressions as being united in this gland by mediation of the spirits which fill the cavities of the brain. There is no other place in the brain save only this gland, where they can be thus united.

ARTICLE 33

That the seat of the passions is not in the heart.

As to the opinion of those who think that the soul receives its passions in the heart, it is not of any weight. Its sole foundation is the feeling we have of the changes brought about in the heart by the passions, and it is easy to show that this alteration is felt in the heart solely owing to the intervention of a small nerve which descends to it from the brain, just as pain is felt in the foot owing to the intervention of the nerves of the foot, and just as the stars are apprehended as in the heavens owing to the intervention of their light and of the optic nerves. Thus it is no more necessary that our soul should exercise its functions immediately in the heart, in order that its passions be felt there, than it is necessary for the soul to be in the heavens in order that the stars be seen there.

ARTICLE 34

How the soul and the body act on one another.

Let us then allow that the soul has its chief seat in the small gland which is in mid-brain, and that from there it radiates through all the rest of the body owing to the intervention of the [animal] spirits, the nerves and even the blood, which, participating in the impressions of the spirits, can carry them by way of the arteries to all its members . . .

ARTICLE 35

An example of the manner in which impressions from objects unite in the gland which is in mid-brain.

If we see some animal approach us, the light reflected from its body depicts two images of it, one in each of our eyes. The two images, by way of the optic nerves, form two others in the interior surface of the brain which faces its cavities. From these, by way of the spirits which fill these cavities, the images then radiate towards the small gland which the spirits encircle, and do so in such fashion that the movement which constitutes each point of one of the images tends towards the same point of the gland as does the movement constituting that point in the other image which represents the same part of the animal; and in this way the two brain-images form but one image on the gland, which, acting immediately on the soul, causes it to see the shape of the animal.

ARTICLE 36

An example of the manner in which the passions are excited in the soul.

Moreover, if this shape is very startling and terrifying, i.e. if it is closely related to things which have previously been hurtful to the body, it excites in the soul the passion of anxious apprehension, and thereupon either of courage, or it may be of fear or terror, according to the varying temperament of the body or the strength of the soul, and according as it has been by defence or by flight that we have hitherto secured ourselves against the harmful things to which the impression stands related. Such past actions so predispose the brain, in certain men, that the spirits reflected from the image thus formed on the gland then proceed to take their course, partly in the nerves which serve in turning the back and in moving the legs for flight, partly in those which enlarge or contract the heart, partly in those which so enlarge or contract the orifices of the heart, or which so agitate the other parts whence the blood is sent to the heart, that this blood, being there, [through the heat of the heart] rarefied in some unusual manner, conveys to the brain [animal] spirits suited to the maintenance and fortifying of the passion of fear, suited, that is to say, to the holding open, or to the re-opening, of those pores of the brain which conduct them to those same nerves. And since the pores, by which they pass, mainly operate through the small nerves which serve to contract or enlarge the orifices of the heart, this causes the soul to feel the pain chiefly in the heart.

ARTICLE 37

How it seems that all passions are caused by some movement of the [animal] spirits.

This is also true of all the other passions; they are one and all chiefly caused by the spirits which are contained in the cavities of the brain, in so far as these operate by way of the nerves which serve to enlarge or contract the orifices of the heart ... From this it can be clearly understood why in my definition I have declared each of them to be caused by some one particular movement of the spirits.

ARTICLE 38

An example of the movements of the body which accompany the passions but which [unlike them] do not in any wise depend on the soul.

For the rest, just as the course which these spirits take towards the nerves of the heart suffices to give that [precise] movement to the gland through which fear is placed in the soul, so, too, this same course by which at the same instant certain spirits proceed towards the nerves which serve to move the legs for flight suffices to cause yet another movement in the gland, thereby enabling the soul to sense and apprehend this flight – the flight being thus excited in the body exclusively by the disposition of the [bodily] organs, and without any co-operation on the part of the soul.

ARTICLE 39

How one and the same cause may excite different passions in different men.

The impressions which the presence of a terrifying object makes on the gland causes fear in certain men, and yet in other men can excite courage and confidence. The reason of this is that all brains are not constituted in the same manner, and that one and the same movement of the gland which in some excites fear, in others causes the spirits to enter partly into those brain-pores which serve to move the hands for self-defence and partly into those which agitate the blood and drive it towards the heart in the manner required to provide the spirits proper for the continuing of the defence and for the persistence in the will to do so.

ARTICLE 40

The chief effect of the passions.

For it is all-important to note that the principal effect of all the passions in men is to incite and dispose the soul to will those things for which they [the passions] are preparing the body. Thus the feeling of fear incites in it the will to flee, that of courage the will to resist attack; and similarly with the others.

ARTICLE 41

The power of the soul in respect of the body.

But the will is in its nature so free that it can never be constrained; and of the two kinds of thoughts which I have distinguished in the soul (on the one hand its actions, i.e. its volitions, and on the other its passions, taking the word in its most general sense as covering cognizings of every sort), the former are absolutely in its power and cannot be changed by the body save indirectly, whereas the latter are absolutely dependent on the actions which produce them, and (except when it is itself their cause) cannot be changed by the soul save indirectly. Now the action of the soul consists entirely in this, that simply by willing it makes the small gland to which it is closely united move in the way requisite for producing the effect aimed at in the volition.

ARTICLE 42

How we find in the memory the things we wish to remember.

Thus when the soul wills to recall something, this volition, by causing the gland to bend successively now to one side and now to another, impels the spirits towards this and that region of the brain, until they come upon the part where the traces left by the object we will to recall are found. These traces consist in the manner in which the spirits, owing to the paths they have taken on the presence of that object, have so modified the pores of the brain that these have thereby acquired a greater facility than the others of being opened in that same fashion when the spirits again come towards them. The spirits on meeting these pores therefore enter into them more easily than into the others, and thereby excite that special movement in the gland which represents that same object to the soul, and so enable it to know what it has willed to remember.

ARTICLE 43

How the soul can image, be attentive, and move the body.

When we wish to image something we have never seen, this volition has the power of causing the gland to move in the manner required in driving the spirits towards the brain-pores on the opening of which the thing can be represented. Thus, too, when we wish to hold our attention fixed for some little time on some one object, this volition keeps the gland bent in this direction. And lastly, when we will to walk or to move the body in any manner, this volition causes the gland to impel the spirits towards the muscles which bring about this effect.

ARTICLE 44

That each volition is naturally connected with some movement of the gland, but that by practice or by habituation it may be connected with others.

Yet it is not always the will to excite in us some movement or some other effect which itself enables us to excite it; for that depends on how nature or habit has, in this or that case, connected each movement of the gland with some one particular thought. Thus, for instance, if we wish to adjust our eyes for the apprehension of a far-distant object, this volition causes the pupil to enlarge; and if we wish to look at a very near object, this volition causes it to contract. Should we, however, think only of enlarging the pupil, we may indeed so will, but we do not thereby enlarge it. For it is not with the volition to enlarge or contract the pupil that nature has connected the movement of the gland which serves to impel the spirits towards the optic nerve in the manner requisite for this enlarging or contracting of the pupil, but instead with that of looking at objects distant or near. When in speaking we think only of what we wish to say, this makes us move the tongue and lips much more promptly and much more effectively than if we thought of all the various actions they must go through in pronouncing the words that express this meaning. The habits we have acquired in learning to speak have connected the action of the soul, which by way of the gland can move the tongue and lips, with the meaning of the words that follow upon these movements rather than with the movements themselves.

ARTICLE 45

What the power of the soul is in respect of the passions.

This also holds in respect of the passions. They cannot be directly excited or suppressed by the action of our will, but only indirectly through representation of the things which are customarily conjoined with the passions we wish to have, and contrary to those we wish to suppress. Thus, in order to excite courage and to suppress fear, the will to do so is not sufficient; we have to bring to mind the reasons, the signs, which suggest to us that the danger is not great, that there is more security in defence than in flight, that we shall have the glory and joy of having conquered, whereas we can expect nothing but regret and shame from having fled, etc.

ARTICLE 46

What prevents the soul from having complete control over the passions.

There is one special reason why the soul is unable to change or suppress its passions in an effortless manner, and this reason is what has led me, in defining them, to say that they are not merely caused, but also upheld and fortified by some particular movement of the [animal] spirits. They are almost all accompanied by some commotion taking place in the heart, and consequently also in all the blood and [animal] spirits, so that until this commotion has subsided, the passions remain present to our thought in the same manner as sensible objects are present to us in thought during the time they act on our sense-organs. Just as the soul, in making itself closely attentive to some other thing, can prevent itself from hearing a slight noise or feeling a slight pain, but cannot in the same way escape hearing thunder or feeling fire burning the hand, it is similarly easy to overcome the lesser passions, but not those that are more violent and powerful; we have to await the abating of the commotion in the blood and spirits. The most the will can do while this commotion is in its full strength, is to refuse consent to its effects, and to restrain several of the movements to which it disposes the body. For instance if anger causes the hand to be upraised for striking, the will can usually arrest it [from further action]; if fear incites the legs to flight, the will can restrain them, and so in all other like cases.

ARTICLE 47

In what consists the contests we are wont to suppose as taking place between the lower and the higher parts of the soul.

All the contests we are wont to conceive as taking place between the inferior part of the soul which we call the sensuous and the superior which is rational, or, as we say, between the natural appetites and the will, consist solely in the repugnance there is between the two movements in the pineal gland – the movement excited by the spirits and the contrary movement excited by the will. For there is in us but one soul, a soul that has no diversity of parts, i.e. it is at once sensuous and rational, and all its appetites are volitions. The error committed in representing it as displaying diverse personalities that ordinarily are at variance with one another, arises from our failure to distinguish its functions from those of the body, to which alone we must attribute whatever in us is observed to be repugnant to our reason. There is, therefore, no contest save that which takes place in the small gland which is in the centre of the brain, when it is impelled to one side by the soul, and to another by the animal spirits which, as above said, are entirely corporeal; often the two impacts are contrary to one another; and the stronger holds the other in check. We can, indeed, in respect of movements excited in the gland by the spirits, distinguish two sorts of movement. Some of them represent to the soul the objects which are moving the senses, or, it may be, the impressions by which it is faced in the brain; and these have no influence on the will. The others do have an influence on the will, viz. those which cause the passions and the bodily movements which accompany the passions. Though the former often prevent the soul from acting, or are themselves hindered by its actions, they are yet not directly contrary to those actions; and we notice no conflict. This we observe as taking place only in respect of the latter sort of movements, i.e. between them and the volitions which are repugnant to them, e.g. between the force by which the spirits impel the gland in causing the soul to desire something, and the force through which the soul, by way of the will, impels the gland in a contrary direction, to shun this something. What gives prominence to this conflict is that, as already noted, the will, not having the power to excite the passions directly, is constrained to address itself to the task of considering in succession a number of different things. One of these, it may be, has the power to change for a moment the course taken by the spirits; but the thing next considered may have no such power, and the spirits revert to their previous condition, owing to the unchanged, but still continuing and contrary disposition in the nerves, heart, and blood. This is how it comes about that the soul feels itself, almost at one and the same time, impelled to desire and not to desire one and the same thing; and this is what has occasioned us to picture the soul as having in it two conflicting powers. There is nothing, however, to prevent our recognizing the frequent occurrence of conflict [provided we do so rightly], namely, when the cause exciting a certain passion in the soul also excites, quite independently of the soul, certain movements in the body, and when the soul immediately on apprehending the movements arrests or strives to arrest them, as happens in the case of fear. What is then exciting the fear [in the soul] is also causing the spirits to enter the muscles which serve to predispose the limbs for flight, and the resolve to be brave then counters this predisposition.

ARTICLE 48

How we come to know the strength or weakness of souls,
and what the evil is in those who are weakest.

It is by the outcome of these conflicts that each individual can come to know the force or weakness of his soul. Those whose nature is such that the will can easily conquer the passions and arrest the bodily movements which accompany them have without doubt the strongest souls. But there are those who cannot gain knowledge of their strength, owing to their never equipping the will with its proper weapons, but only with those which certain passions provide in the resisting of other [contrary] passions. What I call its proper arms are the firm and determinate judgements bearing on the good and the evil, in accordance with which it has resolved to regulate the actions of its life. The weakest of all souls are those whose will does not determine itself to follow its assured judgements, but continually allows itself to be carried away by present passions which, as being contrary to one another, draw the will now in one direction and now in another. Being thus made to battle against itself, the soul is reduced to a condition than which none can be more deplorable. Thus while fear represents death as an extreme evil, and as one that can be avoided only by flight, ambition on the other hand represents the infamy of this flight as an evil worse than death. The two passions agitate the will in opposite ways; yielding now to the one and now to the other, it is in continual opposition to itself, and the soul is thus rendered enslaved and unhappy.

In articles 49 and 50 of Part I of the *Passions* Descartes maintains that 'most men have determinate judgements in accordance with which they regulate a part of their actions' and he seems to hold that no soul is so feeble as not to be able 'if rightly directed' to acquire the capacity to do this.

From L'âme Raisonnable

The animal spirits resemble a very subtle fluid, or rather a very pure and lively flame, and are continually generated in the heart, and ascend to the brain as to a sort of reservoir. Hence they pass into the nerves and are distributed to the muscles, causing contraction or relaxation, according to their quantity.

In proportion as the animal spirits enter the cavities of the brain, they pass thence into the pores of its substance, and from these pores into the nerves; where according as they enter, or even only tend to enter, more or less, into this or that nerve, they have the power of changing the shape of the muscles into which the nerves are inserted, and by this means making all the limbs move. Thus, as you may have seen in the grottoes and fountains in our gardens, the force with which the water issues from its reservoir is sufficient to put into motion various machines, and even to make them play several instruments, or pronounce words, according to the varied disposition of the tubes which conduct the water. Indeed, the nerves of the machine may very well be compared with the tubes of these waterworks; its muscles and tendons with the other various engines and springs which seem to move these machines; its animal spirits to the water which impels them, of which the heart is the source or fountain; while the cavities of the brain are the central reservoir. Moreover, breathing and other like acts which are as natural and usual to the body or machine, and which depend on the flow of the spirits, are like the movements of a clock, or of a mill, which may be kept going by the ordinary flow of water. External objects which, by their mere presence, act upon the organs of sense; and which, by this means, determine the machine to move in many different ways, according as the parts of the brain of the machine are arranged, may be compared to the strangers who, entering into one of the grottoes of these waterworks, unconsciously themselves cause the movements which they witness. For they cannot enter without treading upon certain planks which are so disposed that, if they approach a bathing Diana, they cause her to hide among the reeds; and if they attempt to follow her, they see approaching towards them a Neptune, who threatens them with his trident; or if they pass in another direction they cause some sea-monster to dart out who vomits water into their faces; or like contrivances, according to the fancy of the engineers who made them. And lastly, when the rational soul – *l'âme raisonnable* – is lodged in this machine, it will have its principal seat in the brain, and will take the place of the engineer or 'fountaineer', who ought to be in that part of the works or reservoir with which all the various tubes are connected, when he wishes to quicken or to slacken, or in any way to alter their movements.

REFERENCES

Descartes, René. 'Les Passions de l'Âme' in *Descartes' Philosophical Writings*. Selected and trans. Norman Kemp Smith. London: Macmillan, 1952. *Correspondance*, ed. Adam and Milhaud. Paris: Presses Universitaires de France, Vol. v, 1951, Vol. vi, 1956

Fulton, J. F. *Selected Readings in the History of Physiology*. Springfield and Baltimore: Charles C. Thomas, 1930, pp. 236–40

BENEDICT DE SPINOZA
1632–1677

SPINOZA was of Jewish origin and was born in Amsterdam of parents who belonged to a group of Spanish and Portuguese Jews who fled to the United Provinces from the Inquisition. His father was a well-to-do merchant, distinguished in the Amsterdam Jewish community. Spinoza's mother died when he was five years old, his father when he was twenty-two. Spinoza received an orthodox Jewish education, including a thorough grounding in Hebrew literature and philosophy. Brett points the relevance of this to the relative ease with which Spinoza could forego the notion of the mind or soul as an immortal substance lodged in the body. It is also relevant to understanding the touch of Oriental 'oneness' with the world at large which colours his outlook. While this distinguishes Spinoza from a Western thinker, his strong feeling for individual vitality makes him un-Eastern.

Spinoza is an almost exact contemporary of Vermeer; it is possible that he knew Rembrandt, who made several studies of Spinoza's teacher, Rabbi Manasseh ben Israel.

Spinoza's interests were not confined to Jewish culture. He was influenced by Hobbes and he became acquainted with current physical science and with Descartes' philosophy, probably through Francis Van den Enden from whom he learnt Latin. Through this development of interest he became alienated from Jewish orthodoxy and was publicly excommunicated by the court of the Rabbis in 1656. The development of his views eventually made him equally open to suspicion from orthodox Christians.

From the age of twenty-four he earned his living in the trade of lens-polisher, the rest of his time being devoted to writing, and to carrying on a considerable correspondence with a large circle of friends and critics. The former included not only Oldenburg but others such as De Witt, the leader of the liberal and anti-clerical party of the time, and Ludwig Meyer, an active supporter of enlightenment and tolerance. This association is related to Spinoza's political writings. De Witt's tragic murder, and other political setbacks, threw a shadow over Spinoza's years of maturity.

For ten years or so before his death in 1677 Spinoza was suffering from tuberculosis, which cannot have been improved by his lens grinding and polishing. But one is tempted to wonder whether Leeuwenhoek's contemporary use of the microscope and Spinoza's grinding of convex, i.e. magnifying lenses, led him to think in terms of 'aspects'. He seems to have been active and working at one or other of his writings up to the day he died. It is important to think of him as still in his early forties. The *Ethics* was published posthumously in 1677.

The following extracts are chosen to support and amplify what has been said on pp. 117 ff.

From THE ETHICS

PART III

Postulates

(1) The human body can be affected in many ways, whereby its power of activity is increased or diminished, and also in other ways which do not render its power of activity either greater or less.

N.B. This postulate or axiom rests on Postulate i and Lemmas v and vii, which see after II. xiii.

(2) The human body can undergo many changes, and, nevertheless, retain the impressions or traces of objects (cf. II, Post. v), and, consequently, the same images of things (see note II. xvii).

Proposition I. Our mind is in certain cases active, and in certain cases passive. In so far as it has adequate ideas it is necessarily active, and in so far as it has inadequate ideas, it is necessarily passive.

Proof. In every human mind there are some adequate ideas, and some ideas that are fragmentary and confused (II. xl note). Those ideas which are adequate in the mind are adequate also in God, inasmuch as he constitutes the essence of the mind (II. xl Coroll.), and those which are inadequate in the mind are likewise (by the same Coroll.) adequate in God, not inasmuch as he contains in himself the essence of the given mind alone, but as he, at the same time, contains the minds of other things. Again, from any given idea some effect must necessarily follow (I. xxxvi); of this effect God is the adequate cause (III. Def. i), not inasmuch as he is infinite, but inasmuch as he is conceived as affected by the given idea (II. ix). But of that effect whereof God is the cause, inasmuch as he is affected by an idea which is adequate in a given mind, of that effect, I repeat, the mind in question is the adequate cause (II. xi Coroll.). Therefore our mind, in so far as it has adequate ideas (III. Def. ii), is in certain cases necessarily active; this was our first point. Again, whatsoever necessarily follows from the idea which is adequate in God, not by virtue of his possessing in himself the mind of one man only, but by virtue of his containing, together with the mind of that one man, the minds of other things also, of such an effect (II. xi Coroll.) the mind of the given man is not an adequate, but only a partial cause; thus (III. Def. ii) the mind, inasmuch as it has inadequate ideas, is in certain cases necessarily passive; this was our second point. Therefore our mind, &c. Q.E.D.

Corollary. Hence it follows that the mind is more or less liable to be acted upon, in proportion as it possesses inadequate ideas, and, contrariwise, is more or less active in proportion as it possesses adequate ideas.

Proposition II. Body cannot determine mind to think, neither can mind determine body to motion or rest or any state different from these, if such there be.

Proof. All modes of thinking have for their cause God, by virtue of his being a thinking thing, and not by virtue of his being displayed under any other attribute (II. vi). That, therefore, which determines the mind to thought is a mode of thought, and not a mode of extension; that is (II. Def. i), it is not body. This was our first point. Again, the motion and rest of a body must arise from another body, which has also been determined to a state of motion or rest by a third body, and absolutely everything which takes place in a body must spring from God, in so far as he is regarded as affected by some mode of extension, and not by some mode of thought (II. vi); that is, it cannot spring from the mind, which is a mode of thought.

This was our second point. Therefore body cannot determine mind, &c. Q.E.D.

Note. This is made more clear by what was said in the note to II. vii, namely, that mind and body are one and the same thing, conceived first under the attribute of thought, secondly, under the attribute of extension. Thus it follows that the order or concatenation of things is identical, whether nature be conceived under the one attribute or the other; consequently the order of states of activity and passivity in our body is simultaneous in nature with the order of states of activity and passivity in the mind. The same conclusion is evident from the manner in which we proved II. xii.

Nevertheless, though such is the case, and though there be no further room for doubt, I can scarcely believe, until the fact is proved by experience, that men can be induced to consider the question calmly and fairly, so firmly are they convinced that it is merely at the bidding of the mind, that the body is set in motion or at rest, or performs a variety of actions depending solely on the mind's will or the exercise of thought. However, no one has hitherto laid down the limits to the powers of the body, that is, no one has as yet been taught by experience what the body can accomplish solely by the laws of nature, in so far as she is regarded as extension. No one hitherto has gained such an accurate knowledge of the bodily mechanism, that he can explain all its functions; nor need I call attention to the fact that many actions are observed in the lower animals, which far transcend human sagacity, and that somnambulists do many things in their sleep, which they would not venture to do when awake. These instances are enough to show that the body can by the sole laws of its nature do many things which the mind wonders at.

Again, no one knows how or by what means the mind moves the body, nor how many various degrees of motion it can impart to the body, nor how quickly it can move it. Thus, when men say that this or that physical action has its origin in the mind, which latter has dominion over the body, they are using words without meaning, or are confessing in specious phraseology that they are ignorant of the cause of the said action, and do not wonder at it.

But, they will say, whether we know or do not know the means whereby the mind acts on the body, we have, at any rate, experience of the fact that unless the human mind is in a fit state to think, the body remains inert. Moreover, we have experience, that the mind alone can determine whether we speak or are silent, and a variety of similar states which, accordingly, we say depend on the mind's decree. But, as to the first point, I ask such objectors, whether experience does not also teach, that if the body be inactive the mind is simultaneously unfitted for thinking? For when the body is at rest in sleep, the mind simultaneously is in a state of torpor also, and has no power of thinking, such as it possesses when the body is awake. Again, I think everyone's experience will confirm the statement, that the mind is not at all times equally fit for thinking on a given subject, but according as the body is more or less fitted for being stimulated by the image of this or that object, so also is the mind more or less fitted for contemplating the said object.

But, it will be urged, it is impossible that solely from the laws of nature considered as extended substance, we should be able to deduce the causes of buildings, pictures, and things of that kind, which are produced only by human art; nor would the human body, unless it were determined and led by the mind, be capable of building a single temple. However, I have just pointed out that the objectors cannot fix the limits of the body's power, or say what can be concluded from a consideration of its sole nature, whereas they have experience of many things being accomplished solely by the laws of nature, which they would never have believed possible except under the direction of mind; such are the actions performed by somnambulists while asleep, and wondered at by their performers when awake. I would further call attention to the mechanism of the human body, which far surpasses in complexity all that has been put together by human art, not to repeat what I have already shown, namely, that from nature, under whatever attribute she be considered, infinite results follow. As for the second objection, I submit that the world would be much happier, if men were as fully able to keep silence as they are to speak. Experience abundantly shows that men can govern anything more easily than their tongues, and restrain anything more easily than their appetites; whence it comes about that many believe, that we are only free in respect to objects which we moderately desire, because our desire for such can easily be controlled by the thought of something else frequently remembered, but that we are by no means free in respect to what we seek with violent emotion, for our desire cannot then be allayed with the remembrance of anything else. However, unless such persons had proved by experience that we do many things which we afterwards repent of, and again that we often, when assailed by contrary emotions, see the better and follow the worse, there would be nothing to prevent their believing that we are free in all things. Thus an infant believes that of its own free will it desires milk, an angry child believes that it freely desires vengeance, a timid child believes that it freely desires to run away; further, a drunken man believes that he utters from the free decision of his mind words which, when he is sober, he would willingly have withheld: thus, too, a delirious man, a garrulous woman, a child, and others of like complexion, believe that they speak from the free decision of their mind, when they are in reality unable to restrain their impulse to talk. Experience teaches us no less clearly than reason, that men believe themselves to be free, simply because they are conscious of their actions, and unconscious of the causes whereby those actions are determined; and, further, it is plain that the dictates of the mind are but another name for the appetites, and therefore vary according to the varying state of the body. Everyone shapes his actions according to his emotion, those who are assailed by conflicting emotions know not what they wish; those who are not attacked by any emotions are readily swayed this way or that. All these considerations clearly show that a mental decision and a bodily appetite or determined state, are simultaneous, or rather are one and the same thing, which we call decision, when it is regarded under and explained through the attribute of thought, and a conditioned state, when it is regarded under the attribute of extension, and deduced from the laws of motion and rest. This will appear yet more plainly in the sequel. For the present I wish to call attention to another point, namely, that we cannot act by the decision of the mind, unless we have a remembrance of having done so. For instance, we cannot say a word without remembering that we have done so. Again, it is not within the free power of the mind to remember or forget a thing at will. Therefore the freedom of the mind must in any case be limited to the power of uttering or not uttering something which it remembers. But when we dream that we speak, we believe that we speak from a free decision of the mind, yet we do not speak, or, if we do, it is by a spontaneous motion of the body. Again, we dream that we are concealing something, and we seem to act from the same decision of the mind as that, whereby we keep silence when awake concerning something we know. Lastly, we dream that from the free decision of our mind we do something, which we should not dare to do when awake.

Now I should like to know whether there be in the mind two sorts of decisions, one sort illusive, and the other sort free? If our folly does not carry us so far as this, we must necessarily admit, that the decision of the mind, which is believed to be free, is not distinguishable from the imagination or memory, and is nothing more than the affirmation, which an idea, by virtue of being an idea, necessarily involves (II. xlix). Wherefore these decisions of the mind arise in the mind by the same necessity, as the ideas of things actually existing. Therefore those who believe that they speak or keep silence or act in any way from the free decision of their mind, do but dream with their eyes open.

Proposition VI. Everything, in so far as it is in itself, endeavours to persist in its own being.

Proof. Individual things are modes whereby the attributes of God are expressed in a given determinate manner (I. xxv Coroll.); that is (I. xxxiv), they are things which express in a given determinate manner the power of God, whereby God is and acts; now no thing contains in itself anything whereby it can be destroyed, or which can take away its existence (III. iv); but contrariwise it is opposed to all that could take away its existence (III. v). Therefore, in so far as it can, and in so far as it is in itself, it endeavours to persist in its own being. Q.E.D.

Proposition VII. The endeavour, wherewith everything endeavours to persist in its own being, is nothing else but the actual essence of the thing in question.

Proof. From the given essence of any thing certain consequences necessarily follow (I. xxxvi), nor have things any power save such as necessarily follows from their nature as determined (I. xxix); wherefore the power of any given thing, or the endeavour whereby, either alone or with other things, it acts, or endeavours to act, that is (III. vi), the power or endeavour, wherewith it endeavours to persist in its own being, is nothing else but the given or actual essence of the thing in question. Q.E.D.

Proposition IX. The mind, both in so far as it has clear and distinct ideas, and also in so far as it has confused ideas, endeavours to persist in its being for an indefinite period, and of this endeavour it is conscious.

Proof. The essence of the mind is constituted by adequate and inadequate ideas (III. iii), therefore (III. vii), both in so far as it possesses the former, and in so far as it possesses the latter, it endeavours to persist in its own being, and that for an indefinite time (III. viii). Now as the mind (II. xxiii) is necessarily conscious of itself through the ideas of the modifications of the body, the mind is therefore (III. vii) conscious of its own endeavour.

Proposition X. An idea, which excludes the existence of our body, cannot be postulated in our mind, but is contrary thereto.

Proof. Whatsoever can destroy our body, cannot be postulated therein (III. v). Therefore neither can the idea of such a thing occur in God, in so far as he has the idea of our body (II. ix Coroll.); that is (II. xi, xiii), the idea of that thing cannot be postulated as in our mind, but contrariwise, since (II. xi, xiii) the first element, that constitutes the essence of the mind, is the idea of the human body as actually existing, it follows that the first and chief endeavour of our mind is the endeavour to affirm the existence of our body: thus, an idea, which negatives the existence of our body, is contrary to our mind, etc. Q.E.D.

Proposition XI. Whatsoever increases or diminishes, helps or hinders the power of activity in our body, the idea thereof increases or diminishes, helps or hinders the power of thought in our mind.

Proof. This proposition is evident from II. vii or from II. xiv.

. *Note*. Thus we see, that the mind can undergo many changes, and can pass sometimes to a state of greater perfection, sometimes to a state of lesser perfection. These passive states of transition explain to us the emotions of pleasure and pain. By *pleasure* therefore in the following propositions I shall signify *a passive state wherein the mind passes to a greater perfection*. By *pain* I shall signify *a passive state wherein the mind passes to a lesser perfection*. Further, the emotion of pleasure in reference to the body and mind together I shall call *stimulation* (*titillatio*) or *merriment* (*hilaritas*), the emotion of pain in the same relation I shall call *suffering* or *melancholy*. But we must bear in mind, that stimulation and suffering are attributed to man, when one part of his nature is more affected than the rest, merriment and melancholy, when all parts are alike affected. What I mean by desire I have explained in the note to Prop. ix of this part; [cf. p. 314] beyond these three I recognize no other primary emotion; I will show as I proceed, that all other emotions arise from these three. But, before I go further, I should like here to explain at greater length Prop. x of this part, in order that we may clearly understand how one idea is contrary to another. In the note to II. xvii we showed that the idea, which constitutes the essence of mind, involves the existence of body, so long as the body itself exists. Again, it follows from what we pointed out in the Coroll. to II. viii, that the present existence of our mind depends solely on the fact that the mind involves the actual existence of the body. Lastly, we showed (II. xvii, xviii and note) that the power of the mind, whereby it imagines and remembers things, also depends on the fact, that it involves the actual existence of the body. Whence it follows, that the present existence of the mind and its power of imagining are removed, as soon as the mind ceases to affirm the present existence of the body. Now the cause, why the mind ceases to affirm this existence of the body, cannot be the mind itself (III. iv), nor again the fact that the body ceases to exist. For (by II. vi) the cause, why the mind affirms the existence of the body, is not that the body began to exist; but (II. xvii) this result follows from another idea, which excludes the present existence of our body and, consequently, of our mind, and which is therefore contrary to the idea constituting the essence of our mind.

Proposition XII. The mind, as far as it can, endeavours to conceive those things, which increase or help the power of activity in the body.

Proposition XIII. When the mind conceives things which diminish or hinder the body's power of activity, it endeavours, as far as possible, to remember things which exclude the existence of the first-named things.

Proof. So long as the mind conceives anything of the kind alluded to, the power of the mind and body is diminished or constrained (cf. III. xii Proof); nevertheless it will continue to conceive it, until the mind conceives something else, which excludes the present existence thereof (II. xvii); that is (as I have just shown), the power of the mind and of the body is diminished, or constrained, until the mind conceives something else, which excludes the existence of the former thing conceived: therefore the mind (III. ix), as far as it can, will endeavour to conceive or remember the latter. Q.E.D.

Corollary. Hence it follows, that the mind shrinks from conceiving those things, which diminish or constrain the power of itself and of the body.

Definitions of the Emotions

(1) *Desire* is the actual essence of man, in so far as it is conceived, as determined to a particular activity by some given modification of itself.

Explanation. We have said above, in the note to Prop. ix of this part, that desire is appetite, with consciousness thereof; further, that appetite is the essence of man, in so far as it is determined to act in a way tending to promote its own persistence. But, in the same note, I also remarked that, strictly speaking, I recognize no distinction between appetite and desire. For whether a man be conscious of his appetite or not, it remains one and the same appetite. Thus, in order to avoid the appearance of tautology, I have refrained from explaining desire by appetite; but I have taken care to define it in such a manner, as to comprehend, under one head, all those endeavours of human nature, which we distinguish by the terms appetite, will, desire, or impulse. I might, indeed, have said, that desire is the essence of man, in so far as it is conceived as determined to a particular activity; but from such a definition (cf. II. xxiii) it would not follow that the mind can be conscious of its desire or appetite. Therefore, in order to imply the cause of such consciousness, it was necessary to add, *in so far as it is determined by some given modification*, etc. For, by a modification of man's essence, we understand every disposition of the said essence, whether such disposition be innate, or whether it be conceived solely under the attribute of thought, or solely under the attribute of extension, or whether, lastly, it be referred simultaneously to both these attributes. By the term desire, then, I here mean all man's endeavours, impulses, appetites, and volitions, which vary according to each man's disposition, and are, therefore, not seldom opposed one to another, according as a man is drawn in different directions, and knows not where to turn.

(2) *Pleasure* is the transition of a man from a less to a greater perfection.

(3) *Pain* is the transition of a man from a greater to a less perfection.

. . . .

I, therefore, recognize only three primitive or primary emotions (as I said in the note to III. xi), namely, pleasure, pain, and desire.

PART IV

Proposition VII. An emotion can only be controlled or destroyed by another emotion contrary thereto, and with more power for controlling emotion.

Proposition XVIII. Desire arising from pleasure is, other conditions being equal, stronger than desire arising from pain.

Proof. Desire is the essence of a man (Def. of the Emotions, i), that is, the endeavour whereby a man endeavours to persist in his own being. Wherefore desire arising from pleasure is, by the fact of pleasure being felt, increased or helped; on the contrary, desire arising from pain is, by the fact of pain being felt, diminished or hindered; hence the force of desire arising from pleasure must be defined by human power together with the power of an external cause, whereas desire arising from pain must be defined by human power only. Thus the former is the stronger of the two. Q.E.D.

Note. In these few remarks I have explained the causes of human infirmity and inconstancy, and shown why men do not abide by the precepts of reason. It now remains for me to show what course is marked out for us by reason, which of the emotions are in harmony with the rules of human reason, and which of them are contrary thereto. But, before I begin to prove my propositions in detailed geometrical fashion, it is advisable to sketch them briefly in advance, so that everyone may more readily grasp my meaning.

As reason makes no demands contrary to nature, it demands that every man should love himself, should seek that which is useful to him – I mean, that which is really useful to him, should desire everything which really brings man to greater perfection, and should, each for himself, endeavour as far as he can to preserve his own being. This is as necessarily true, as that a whole is greater than its part. (Cf. III. iv.)

Again, as virtue is nothing else but action in accordance with the laws of one's own nature (IV. Def. viii), and as no one endeavours to preserve his own being, except in accordance with the laws of his own nature, it follows, *first*, that the foundation of virtue is the endeavour to preserve one's own being, and that happiness consists in man's power of preserving his own being; *secondly*, that virtue is to be desired for its own sake, and that there is nothing more excellent or more useful to us, for the sake of which we should desire it; *thirdly* and lastly, that suicides are weak-minded, and are overcome by external causes repug-

nant to their nature. Further, it follows from Postulate iv, Part
II, that we can never arrive at doing without all external things
for the preservation of our being or living, so as to have no relations with things which are outside ourselves. Again, if we consider our mind, we see that our intellect would be more imperfect, if mind were alone, and could understand nothing besides itself. There are, then, many things outside ourselves,
which are useful to us, and are, therefore, to be desired. Of
such none can be discerned more excellent, than those which
are in entire agreement with our nature. For if, for example,
two individuals of entirely the same nature are united, they
form a combination twice as powerful as either of them singly.

Therefore, to man there is nothing more useful than man –
nothing, I repeat, more excellent for preserving their being can
be wished for by men, than that all should so in all points agree,
that the minds and bodies of all should form, as it were, one
single mind and one single body, and that all should, with one
consent, as far as they are able, endeavour to preserve their
being, and all with one consent seek what is useful to them all.
Hence, men who are governed by reason – that is, who seek
what is useful to them in accordance with reason, – desire for
themselves nothing, which they do not also desire for the rest of
mankind, and, consequently, are just, faithful, and honourable
in their conduct.

Such are the dictates of reason, which I purposed thus briefly
to indicate, before beginning to prove them in greater detail. I
have taken this course, in order, if possible, to gain the attention
of those who believe that the principle that every man is bound
to seek what is useful for himself is the foundation of impiety,
rather than of piety and virtue.

PART V

At length I pass to the remaining portion of my Ethics, which
is concerned with the way leading to freedom. I shall therefore
treat therein of the power of the reason, showing how far the
reason can control the emotions, and what is the nature of
Mental Freedom or Blessedness; we shall then be able to see

how much more powerful the wise man is than the ignorant. It is no part of my design to point out the method and means whereby the understanding may be perfected, nor to show the skill whereby the body may be so tended, as to be capable of the due performance of its functions. The latter question lies in the province of Medicine, the former in the province of Logic. Here, therefore, I repeat I shall treat only of the power of the mind, or of reason; and I shall mainly show the extent and nature of its dominion over the emotions, for their control and moderation. That we do not possess absolute dominion over them, I have already shown. Yet the Stoics have thought that the emotions depended absolutely on our will, and that we could absolutely govern them. But these philosophers were compelled, by the protest of experience, not from their own principles, to confess that no slight practice and zeal is needed to control and moderate them: and this someone endeavoured to illustrate by the example (if I remember rightly) of two dogs, the one a house-dog and the other a hunting-dog. For by long training it could be brought about, that the house-dog should become accustomed to hunt, and the hunting-dog to cease from running after hares. To this opinion Descartes not a little inclines. For he maintained, that the soul or mind is specially united to a particular part of the brain, namely to that part called the pineal gland, by the aid of which the mind is enabled to feel all the movements which are set going in the body, and also external objects, and which the mind by a simple act of volition can put in motion in various ways. He asserted, that this gland is so suspended in the midst of the brain, that it could be moved by the slightest motion of the animal spirits, further, that this gland is suspended in the midst of the brain in as many different manners, as the animal spirits can impinge thereon; and, again, that as many different marks are impressed on the said gland, as there are different external objects which impel the animal spirits towards it; whence it follows, that if the will of the soul suspends the gland in a position, wherein it has already been suspended once before by the animal spirits driven in one way or another, the gland in its turn reacts on the said spirits, driving and determining them to the condition wherein they were, when repulsed before by a similar position of the gland. He further asserted, that every act of mental volition is united in nature to a certain given motion of the gland. For instance, whenever anyone desires to look at a remote object, the act of volition causes the pupil of the eye to dilate, whereas, if the person in question had only thought of the dilation of the pupil, the mere wish to dilate it would not have brought about the result, inasmuch as the motion of the gland, which serves to impel the animal spirits towards the optic nerve in a way which would dilate or contract the pupil, is not associated in nature with the wish to dilate or contract the pupil, but with the wish to look at remote or very near objects. Lastly, he maintained that, although every motion of the aforesaid gland seems to have been united by nature to one particular thought out of the whole number of our thoughts from the very beginning of our life, yet it can nevertheless become through habituation associated with other thoughts; this he endeavours to prove in the *Passions de l'âme*, I. 50. He thence concludes, that there is no soul so weak, that it cannot, under proper direction, acquire absolute power over its passions. For passions as defined by him are 'perceptions, or feelings, or disturbances of the soul, which are referred to the soul as species, and which (mark the expression) are produced, preserved, and strengthened through some movement of the spirits' (*Passions de l'âme*, I. 27). But, seeing that we can join any motion of the gland, or consequently of the spirits, to any volition, the determination of the will depends entirely on our own powers; if, therefore, we determine our will with sure and firm decisions in the direction to which we wish our actions to tend, and associate the motions of the passions which we wish to acquire with the said decisions, we shall acquire an absolute dominion over our passions. Such is the doctrine of this illustrious philosopher (in so far as I gather it from his own words); it is one which, had it been less ingenious, I could hardly believe to have proceeded from so great a man. Indeed, I am lost in wonder, that a philosopher, who had stoutly asserted, that he would draw no conclusions which do not follow from self-evident premisses, and would affirm nothing which he did not clearly and distinctly perceive, and who had so often taken to task the scholastics for wishing to explain obscurities through occult qualities, could maintain a hypothesis, beside which occult qualities are commonplace. What does he understand, I ask, by the union of the mind and the body? What clear and distinct conception has he got of thought in most intimate union with a certain particle of extended matter? Truly I should like him to explain this union through its proximate cause. But he had so distinct a conception of mind being distinct from body, that he could not assign any particular cause of the union between the two, or of the mind itself, but was obliged to have recourse to the cause of the whole universe, that is to God. Further, I should much like to know, what degree of motion the mind can impart to this pineal gland, and with what force can it hold it suspended? For I am in ignorance, whether this gland can be agitated more slowly or more quickly by the mind than by the animal spirits, and whether the motions of the passions, which we have closely united with firm decisions, cannot be again disjoined therefrom by physical causes; in which case it would follow that, although the mind firmly intended to face a given danger, and had united to this decision the motions of boldness, yet at the sight of the danger the gland might become suspended in a way, which would preclude the mind thinking of anything except running away. In truth, as there is no common standard of volition and motion, so is there no comparison possible between the powers of the mind and the power or strength of the body; consequently the strength of one cannot in any wise be determined by the strength of the other. We may also add, that there is no gland discoverable in the midst of the brain, so placed that it can thus easily be set in motion in so many ways, and also that all the nerves are not prolonged so far as the cavities of the brain. Lastly, I omit all the assertions which he makes concerning the will and its freedom, inasmuch as I have abundantly proved that his premises are false. Therefore, since the power of the mind, as I have shown above, is defined by the understanding only, we shall determine solely by the knowledge of the mind the remedies against the emotions, which I believe all have had experience of, but do not accurately observe or distinctly see, and from the same basis we shall deduce all those conclusions, which have regard to the mind's blessedness.

Proposition III. An emotion, which is a passion, ceases to be a passion, as soon as we form a clear and distinct idea thereof.

Proof. An emotion, which is a passion, is a confused idea (by the general Def. of the Emotions). If, therefore, we form a clear and distinct idea of a given emotion, that idea will only be distinguished from the emotion, in so far as it is referred to the mind only, by reason (II. xxi and note); therefore (III. iii), the emotion will cease to be a passion. Q.E.D.

Corollary. An emotion therefore becomes more under our control, and the mind is less passive in respect to it, in proportion as it is more known to us.

Proposition IV. There is no modification of the body, whereof we cannot form some clear and distinct conception.

Proof. Properties which are common to all things can only be conceived adequately (II. xxxviii); therefore (II. xii and Lemma ii after II. xiii) there is no modification of the body, whereof we cannot form some clear and distinct conception. Q.E.D.

Corollary. Hence it follows that there is no emotion, whereof we cannot form some clear and distinct conception. For an emotion is the idea of a modification of the body (by the general Def. of the Emotions), and must therefore (by the preceding Prop.) involve some clear and distinct conception.

Note. Seeing that there is nothing which is not followed by an effect (I. xxxvi), and that we clearly and distinctly understand whatever follows from an idea, which in us is adequate (II. xl), it follows that everyone has the power of clearly and distinctly understanding himself and his emotions, if not absolutely, at any rate in part, and consequently of bringing it about, that he should become less subject to them. To attain this result, therefore, we must chiefly direct our efforts to acquiring, as far as possible, a clear and distinct knowledge of every emotion, in order that the mind may thus, through emotion, be determined to think of those things which it clearly and distinctly perceives, and wherein it fully acquiesces: and thus that the emotion itself may be separated from the thought of an external cause, and may be associated with true thoughts whence it will come to pass, not only that love, hatred, etc. will be destroyed (v. ii), but also that the appetites or desires, which are wont to arise from such emotion, will become incapable of being excessive (iv. lxi). For it must be especially remarked that the appetite through which a man is said to be active, and that through which he is said to be passive is one and the same. For instance, we have shown that human nature is so constituted, that everyone desires his fellow-men to live after his own fashion (iii. xxxi note); in a man, who is not guided by reason, this appetite is a passion which is called ambition, and does not greatly differ from pride; whereas in a man, who lives by the dictates of reason, it is an activity or virtue which is called piety (iv. xxxvii note i and second proof). In like manner all appetites or desires are only passions, in so far as they spring from inadequate ideas; the same results are accredited to virtue, when they are aroused or generated by adequate ideas. For all desires, whereby we are determined to any given action, may arise as much from adequate as from inadequate ideas (iv. lix). Than this remedy for the emotions (to return to the point from which I started), which consists in a true knowledge thereof, nothing more excellent, being within our power, can be devised. For the mind has no other power save that of thinking and of forming adequate ideas, as we have shown above (iii. iii).

. . . .

I have now gone through all the remedies against the emotions, or all that the mind, considered in itself alone, can do against them. Whence it appears that the mind's power over the emotions consists:

(1) In the actual knowledge of the emotions (v. iv note).

(2) In the fact that it separates the emotions from the thought of an external cause, which we conceive confusedly (v. ii and iv note).

(3) In the fact, that, in respect to time, the emotions referred to things, which we distinctly understand, surpass those referred to what we conceive in a confused and fragmentary manner (v. vii).

(4) In the number of causes whereby those modifications are fostered, which have regard to the common properties of things or to God (v. ix, xi).

(5) Lastly, in the order wherein the mind can arrange and associate, one with another, its own emotions (v. x note and xii, xiii, xiv).

But, in order that this power of the mind over the emotions may be better understood, it should be specially observed that the emotions are called by us strong, when we compare the emotion of one man with the emotion of another, and see that one man is more troubled than another by the same emotion; or when we are comparing the various emotions of the same man one with another, and find that he is more affected or stirred by one emotion than by another. For the strength of every emotion is defined by a comparison of our own power with the power of an external cause. Now the power of the mind is defined by knowledge only, and its infirmity or passion is defined by the privation of knowledge only: it therefore follows, that that mind is most passive, whose greatest part is made up of inadequate ideas, so that it may be characterized more readily by its passive states than by its activities: on the other hand, that mind is most active, whose greatest part is made up of adequate ideas, so that, although it may contain as many inadequate ideas as the former mind, it may yet be more easily characterized by ideas attributable to human virtue, than by ideas which tell of human infirmity. Again, it must be observed, that spiritual unhealthiness and misfortunes can generally be traced to excessive love for something which is subject to many variations, and which we can never become masters of. For no one is solicitous or anxious about anything, unless he loves it; neither do wrongs, suspicions, enmities, etc. arise, except in regard to things whereof no one can be really master.

We may thus readily conceive the power which clear and distinct knowledge, and especially that third kind of knowledge (II. xlvii note), founded on the actual knowledge of God, possesses over the emotions: if it does not absolutely destroy them, in so far as they are passions (v. iii and iv, note); at any rate, it causes them to occupy a very small part of the mind (v. xiv).

Further, it begets a love towards a thing immutable and eterna
(v. xv), whereof we may really enter into possession (II. xlv)
neither can it be defiled with those faults which are inherent ir
ordinary love; but it may grow from strength to strength, anc
may engross the greater part of the mind, and deeply penetrate it

Proposition XXI. The mind can only imagine anything, o
remember what is past, while the body endures.

Proof. The mind does not express the actual existence of it
body, nor does it imagine the modifications of the body a
actual, except while the body endures (II. viii Coroll.); and
consequently (II. xxvi), it does not imagine any body as actually
existing, except while its own body endures. Thus it canno
imagine anything (for definition of Imagination, see II. xvi
note), or remember things past, except while the body endure
(see definition of Memory, II. xviii note). Q.E.D.

Proposition XXIII. The human mind cannot be absolutely
destroyed with the body, but there remains of it something
which is eternal.

Proof. There is necessarily in God a concept or idea, which
expresses the essence of the human body (Prop. xxii), which
therefore, is necessarily something appertaining to the essence
of the human mind (II. xiii). But we have not assigned to the
human mind any duration, definable by time, except in so far as
it expresses the actual existence of the body, which is explained
through duration, and may be defined by time – that is (II. vii
Coroll.), we do not assign to it duration, except while the body
endures. Yet, as there is something, notwithstanding, which is
conceived by a certain eternal necessity through the very essence
of God (Prop. xxii); this something, which appertains to the
essence of the mind, will necessarily be eternal. Q.E.D.

Note. This idea, which expresses the essence of the body
under the form of eternity, is, as we have said, a certain mode of
thinking, which belongs to the essence of the mind, and is
necessarily eternal. Yet it is not possible that we should remember that we existed before our body, for our body can bear no
trace of such existence, neither can eternity be defined in terms
of time, or have any relation to time. But, notwithstanding, we

feel and know that we are eternal. For the mind feels those things that it conceives by understanding, no less than those things that it remembers. For the eyes of the mind, whereby it sees and observes things, are none other than proofs. Thus, although we do not remember that we existed before the body, yet we feel that our mind, in so far as it involves the essence of the body, under the form of eternity, is eternal, and that thus its existence cannot be defined in terms of time, or explained through duration. Thus our mind can only be said to endure, and its existence can only be defined by a fixed time, in so far as it involves the actual existence of the body. Thus far only has it the power of determining the existence of things by time, and conceiving them under the category of duration.

Proposition XXXIX. He, who possesses a body capable of the greatest number of activities, possesses a mind whereof the greatest part is eternal.

Proof. He, who possesses a body capable of the greatest number of activities, is least agitated by those emotions which are evil (IV. xxxviii) – that is (IV. xxx), by those emotions which are contrary to our nature; therefore (V. x), he possesses the power of arranging and associating the modifications of the body according to the intellectual order, and, consequently, of bringing it about, that all the modifications of the body should be referred to the idea of God; whence, it will come to pass that (V. xv) he will be affected with love towards God, who (V. xvi) must occupy or constitute the chief part of the mind; therefore (V. xxxiii), such a man will possess a mind whereof the chief part is eternal. Q.E.D.

Note. Since human bodies are capable of the greatest number of activities, there is no doubt but that they may be of such a nature, that they may be referred to minds possessing a great knowledge of themselves and of God, and whereof the greatest or chief part is eternal, and, therefore, that they should scarcely fear death. But, in order that this may be understood more clearly, we must here call to mind, that we live in a state of perpetual variation, and, according as we are changed for the better or the worse, we are called happy or unhappy.

For he, who, from being an infant or a child, becomes a corpse, is called unhappy; whereas it is set down to happiness. if we have been able to live through the whole period of life with a sound mind in a sound body. And, in reality, he, who, as in the case of an infant or a child, has a body capable of very few activities, and depending for the most part on external causes, has a mind which, considered in itself alone, is scarcely conscious of itself, or of God, or of things; whereas, he, who has a body capable of very many activities, has a mind which, considered in itself alone, is highly conscious of itself, of God, and of things.

Having attempted to give the mind as he understands it some form of eternity, Spinoza closes the *Ethics* with the following propositions:

Proposition XLI. Even if we did not know that our mind is eternal, we should still consider as of primary importance piety and religion, and generally all things which, in Part IV, we showed to be attributable to courage and high-mindedness.

Proof. The first and only foundation of virtue, or the rule of right living is (IV. xxii, Coroll. and xxiv) seeking one's own true interest. Now, in order to determine what reason prescribes as useful, we took no account of the mind's eternity, which has only become known to us in this Fifth Part. Although we were ignorant at that time that the mind is eternal, we nevertheless stated that the qualities attributable to courage and high-mindedness are of primary importance. Therefore, even if we were still ignorant of this doctrine, we should yet put the aforesaid precepts of reason in the first place. Q.E.D.

Note. The general belief of the multitude seems to be different. Most people seem to believe that they are free, in so far as they may obey their lusts, and that they cede their rights, in so far as they are bound to live according to the commandments of the divine law. They therefore believe that piety, religion, and, generally, all things attributable to firmness of mind, are burdens, which, after death, they hope to lay aside, and to receive the reward for their bondage, that is, for their piety and religion; it is not only by this hope, but also, and chiefly, by the fear of being horribly punished after death, that they are induced to live according to the divine commandments, so far as their feeble and infirm spirit will carry them.

If men had not this hope and this fear, but believed that the mind perishes with the body, and that no hope of prolonged life remains for the wretches who are broken down with the burden of piety, they would return to their own inclinations, controlling everything in accordance with their lusts, and desiring to obey fortune rather than themselves. Such a course appears to me not less absurd than if a man, because he does not believe that he can by wholesome food sustain his body for ever, should wish to cram himself with poisons and deadly fare; or if, because he sees that the mind is not eternal or immortal, he should prefer to be out of his mind altogether, and to live without the use of reason; these ideas are so absurd as to be scarcely worth refuting.

Proposition XLII. Blessedness is not the reward of virtue, but virtue itself; neither do we rejoice therein, because we control our lusts, but, contrariwise, because we rejoice therein, we are able to control our lusts.

*

Space forbids more than one more extract. It is from a letter to Oldenburg, wherein Spinoza is trying to explain the vantage point of an element in his system.

Let us imagine, with your permission, a little worm, living in the blood, able to distinguish by sight the particles of blood, lymph, etc., and to reflect on the manner in which each particle, on meeting with another particle, either is repulsed, or communicates a portion of its own motion. This little worm would live in the blood, in the same way as we live in a part of the universe, and would consider each particle of blood, not as a part, but as a whole. He would be unable to determine, how all the parts are modified by the general nature of blood, and are compelled by it to adapt themselves, so as to stand in a fixed relation to one another. For, if we imagine that there are no causes external to the blood, which could communicate fresh movements to it, nor any space beyond the blood, nor any bodies whereto the particles of blood could communicate their motion, it is certain that the blood would always remain in the same state, and its particles would undergo no modifications, save those which may be conceived as arising from the relations of motion existing between the lymph, the chyle, etc. The blood would then always have to be considered as a whole, not as a part. But, as there exist, as a matter of fact, very many causes which modify, in a given manner, the nature of the blood, and are, in turn, modified thereby, it follows that other motions and other relations arise in the blood, springing not from the mutual relations of its parts only, but from the mutual relations between the blood as a whole and external causes. Thus the blood comes to be regarded as a part, not as a whole. So much for the whole and the part.

All natural bodies can and ought to be considered in the same way as we have here considered the blood, for all bodies are surrounded by others, and are mutually determined to exist and operate in a fixed and definite proportion, while the relations between motion and rest in the sum total of them, that is, in the whole universe, remain unchanged. Hence it follows that each body, in so far as it exists as modified in a particular manner, must be considered as a part of the whole universe, as agreeing with the whole, and associated with the remaining parts. As the nature of the universe is not limited, like the nature of blood, but is absolutely infinite, its parts are by this nature of infinite power infinitely modified, and compelled to undergo infinite variations. . . .

You see, therefore, how and why I think that the human body is a part of nature. As regards the human mind, I believe that it also is a part of nature; for I maintain that there exists in nature an infinite power of thinking, which, in so far as it is infinite, contains subjectively the whole of nature, and its thoughts proceed in the same manner as nature – that is, in the sphere of ideas. Further, I take the human mind to be identical with this said power, not in so far as it is infinite, and perceives the whole of nature, but in so far as it is finite, and perceives only the human body; in this manner, I maintain that the human mind is a part of an infinite understanding.

If we could quote further we should draw from Spinoza having intellectual sport with an unknown friend who wants to believe in ghosts and spirits provided they are pleasant and not feminine. For a further sidelight on ghosts in relation to body and mind and on Spinoza's mixture of irony and deadly seriousness, readers should turn to Letters LV onwards in Elwes' edition cited below. This has been used throughout.

REFERENCE

Spinoza, Benedict de. *The Chief Works of Benedict de Spinoza*. Trans. R. H. M. Elwes. London: Bell, 1884. Vol. II, pp. 130–5, 136–40, 173, 194, 201–2, 244–7, 248–9, 257, 259, 267, 269, 291–2

GOTTFRIED WILHELM LEIBNIZ

1646–1716

LEIBNIZ, whose father was a professor of moral philosophy, wa
born at Leipzig where, at the age of fifteen, he went to the Univer
sity to study Law, obtaining his Doctorate, however, from Alt
dorf. During his studies he became acquainted with Bacon's *D
Augmentis Scientiarum* and with the writings of people such a
Kepler, Galileo, and Descartes. On the other hand he was als
grounded in scholastic thought and mathematics, in which he i
in the front rank. He spent short periods at Jena and Nürnberg
where he became a member of a secret society of Rosicrucian
who were trying to find the philosophers' stone. Leibniz's metho
of gaining admission to the society was ' to collect from books on
alchemy all the most obscure phrases he could find and to make
of them an unintelligible letter, which he produced as evidence
of his fitness for membership'.* The society was so impressed
that it immediately appointed him secretary. Indirectly, this ad
venture in the mysterious brought Leibniz into touch with the
Elector and Archbishop of Mainz, one of the men most active in
dealing with the problems of Germany after the Thirty Years
War and at the time of Louis XIV's rise to power. Leibniz
entered the service of the Elector, and the association no doubt
explains Leibniz's intermittent essays in diplomacy. Of these the
effort, about 1686, to reconcile Catholics and Protestants is an example. His theory of substance derived initially, if Latta is right,
from Leibniz being unable to reconcile Descartes' view of matter
as pure extension with either the Catholic or the Lutheran doctrines of Transubstantiation. Leibniz therefore set out to discover a theory which would satisfy both Churches and afford
some basis of reconciliation.

In connexion with another abortive scheme, that of diverting
Louis XIV's interest to Egypt rather than Germany, Leibniz
went to Paris. There he lived for some years, paying a brief visit
to England in 1673. This was cut short by the death of the Elector
of Mainz. After several attempts at obtaining diplomatic appointments, Leibniz became, from 1676 onwards, librarian to the
Duke of Brunswick at Hanover. During these years abroad and
later, Leibniz built up an enormous network of associations with

* Quoted from Latta on the basis of Fontenelle.

men of learning. He himself was much the most learned man of his time but apparently isolated as a person. It is worth realizing that he often wrote in French and for various reasons many of his works were not published until years – even 150 or more – after his death.

The Principles of Nature and of Grace, parts of which are given below, was written it is thought in 1714, two years before Leibniz died. It has been chosen in preference to the *Monadology*, which belongs to the same period, because its expression, though perhaps less concise and philosophically elegant, seems to convey more naturally Leibniz's relevance to psychological history. It was published in 1718.

From THE PRINCIPLES OF NATURE AND OF GRACE

(1) *Substance* is a being capable of action. It is simple or compound. *Simple substance* is that which has no parts. *Compound substance* is the combination of simple substances or *Monads*. *Monas* is a Greek word, which means unity, or that which is one. Compounds or bodies are pluralities [*multitudes*]; and simple substances, lives, souls, spirits, are unities. And everywhere there must be simple substances, for without simple substances there would not be compounds; and consequently all nature is full of life.

(2) The Monads, having no parts, can neither be made [*formées*] nor unmade. They can neither come into being nor come to an end by natural means, and consequently they last as long as the universe, which will be changed, but which will not be destroyed. They can have no shape [*figure*]; otherwise they would have parts. Consequently any one Monad in itself and at a particular moment can be distinguished from any other only by internal qualities and activities [*actions*], which cannot be other than its *perceptions* (that is to say, the representations of the compound, or of that which is outside, in the simple) and *appetitions* (that is to say, its tendencies to pass from one perception to another), which are the principles of change. For the simplicity of substance is by no means inconsistent with the

multiplicity of the modifications which are to be found together in that same simple substance, and these modifications must consist in variety of relations to the things which are outside. It is as in the case of a *centre* or point, in which, although it is perfectly simple, there is an infinite number of angles formed by the lines which meet in it.

(3) All nature is a *plenum*. There are simple substances everywhere, which are actually separated from one another by activities of their own, and which continually change their relations; and each specially important [*distinguée*] simple substance or Monad, which forms the centre of a compound substance (e.g. of an animal) and the principle of its oneness, is surrounded by a *mass* composed of an infinity of other Monads, which constitute the particular body of this central Monad, and according to the affections of its body the Monad represents, as in a kind of *centre*, the things which are outside of it. This *body* is *organic*, though it forms a kind of automaton or natural machine, which is a machine not only as a whole, but also in the smallest parts of it that can come into observation. Since the world is a *plenum* all things are connected together and each body acts upon every other, more or less, according to their distance, and each, through reaction, is affected by every other. Hence it follows that each Monad is a living mirror, or a mirror endowed with inner activity, representative of the universe, according to its point of view, and as subject to rule as is the universe itself. And the perceptions in the Monad are produced one from another according to the laws of desires [*appétits*] or of the *final causes of good and evil*, which consist in observable perceptions, regular or irregular, as, on the other hand, the changes of bodies and external phenomena are produced one from another according to the laws of *efficient causes*, that is to say, of motions. Thus there is a perfect *harmony* between the perceptions of the Monad and the motions of bodies, a harmony pre-established from the beginning between the system of efficient causes and that of final causes. And it is in this way that soul and body are in agreement and are physically united, while it is not possible for the one to change the laws of the other.

(4) Each Monad, with a particular body, forms a living sub-

stance. Thus not only is there everywhere life, accompanied with members or organs, but there is also an infinity of degrees in the Monads, one dominating more or less over another. But when the Monad has organs so arranged that they give prominence and sharpness [*du relief et du distingué*] to the impressions they receive, and consequently to the perceptions which represent these (as, for instance, when, by means of the form of the eye's humours, the rays of light are concentrated and act with more force), this may lead to *feeling* [*sentiment*], that is to say, to a perception accompanied by *memory*, in other words, a perception of which a certain echo long remains, so as to make itself heard on occasion. Such a living being is called an *animal*, as its Monad is called a *soul*. And when this soul is raised to *reason*, it is something more sublime and is reckoned among spirits [*esprits*], as will presently be explained. It is true that animals are sometimes in the condition of mere [*simple*] living beings and their souls in the condition of mere Monads, namely when their perceptions are not sufficiently sharp [*distingué*] to be remembered, as happens in a deep dreamless sleep or in a swoon. But perceptions which have become completely confused are sure to be developed again in animals, for reasons which I shall presently mention. Thus it is well to make distinction between *perception*, which is the inner state of the Monad representing outer things, and *apperception*, which is *consciousness* or the reflective knowledge of this inner state, and which is not given to all souls nor to the same soul at all times. It is for lack of this distinction that the Cartesians have made the mistake of ignoring perceptions of which we are not conscious, as ordinary people ignore imperceptible [*insensible*] bodies. It is this also that has led these same Cartesians to believe that only minds [*esprits*] are Monads, that the lower animals have no soul, and that still less are there other *principles of life*. And as they came into too great conflict with the common opinion of men in denying feeling [*sentiment*] to the lower animals, so on the other hand they conformed too much to the prejudices of the crowd in confounding a *prolonged unconsciousness*, which comes from a great confusion of perceptions, with *absolute death*, in which all perception would cease. This has confirmed the ill-founded opinion that some souls are destroyed, and the bad ideas of some who call themselves free-thinkers [*esprits forts*] and who have disputed the immortality of our soul.

(5) There is a connexion among the perceptions of animals which has some likeness to reason; but it is based only on the memory of *facts* or effects, and not at all on the knowledge of *causes*. Thus a dog avoids the stick with which it has been beaten, because memory represents to it the pain which this stick has caused it. And men, in so far as they are empirics, that is to say in three-fourths of their actions, do not act otherwise than the lower animals. For instance, we expect that there will be daylight to-morrow because our experience has always been so: it is only the astronomer who rationally foresees it, and even his prediction will ultimately fail when the cause of daylight, which is not eternal, ceases. But *genuine reasoning* depends upon necessary or eternal truths, such as those of logic, of number, of geometry, which produce an indubitable connexion of ideas and infallible inferences. The animals in which these inferences do not appear are called the *lower animals* [*bêtes*]; but those which know these necessary truths are properly those which are called *rational animals*, and their souls are called *minds* [*esprits*]. These souls have the power to perform acts of reflexion and to observe that which is called ego, substance, soul, mind [*esprit*], in a word, immaterial things and truths. And this it is which makes science or demonstrative knowledge possible to us.

(6) Modern research has taught us, and reason confirms it, that the living beings whose organs are known to us, that is to say, plants and animals, do not come from putrefaction or chaos, as the ancients thought, but from *pre-formed* seeds, and consequently from the transformation of pre-existing living beings. In the seed of large animals there are animalcules which by means of conception obtain a new outward form, which they make their own and which enables them to grow and become larger so as to pass to a greater theatre and to propagate the large animal. It is true that the souls of human spermatic animals are not rational, and that they become so only when conception gives to these animals human nature. And as in general animals are not entirely born in conception or *genera-*

ion, no more do they entirely perish in what we call *death*; for it is reasonable that what does not come into being by natural means should not any more come to an end in the course of nature. Thus, throwing off their mask or their tattered covering, they merely return to a more minute theatre, where they may nevertheless be as sensitive [*sensible*] and as well ordered as in the larger theatre. And what has just been said about the large animals applies also to the generation and death of spermatic animals themselves, that is to say, they are growths of other smaller spermatic animals, in comparison with which they in turn may be counted large, for everything in nature proceeds *ad infinitum*. Thus not only souls but also animals are ingenerable and imperishable; they are only developed, enveloped, clothed, unclothed, transformed. Souls never put off the whole of their body, and do not pass from one body into another body which is entirely new to them. Accordingly there is no *metempsychosis*, but there is *metamorphosis*. Animals change, take on and put off, parts only. In nutrition this takes place gradually and by little imperceptible [*insensible*] portions, but continually; and on the other hand, in conception or in death, when much is gained or lost all at once, it takes place suddenly and in a way that can be noticed [*notablement*], but rarely.

(11) The supreme wisdom of God led Him to choose specially the *laws of motion* which are most fitting and which are most in conformity with abstract or metaphysical reasons. There is conserved the same quantity of total and absolute force, or of activity [*action*], also the same quantity of relative force or of reaction, and finally the same quantity of force of direction. Further, action is always equal to reaction, and the whole effect is always equivalent to its full cause. And it is remarkable [*surprenant*] that by the sole consideration of *efficient causes* or of matter it was impossible to explain these laws of motion which have been discovered in our time and of which a part has been discovered by myself. For I have found that we must have recourse to *final causes*, and that these laws are dependent not upon the *principle of necessity*, like the truths of logic, arithmetic, and geometry, but upon the *principle of fitness* [*convenance*], that is

to say, upon the choice of wisdom. And this is one of the mos:
effective and remarkable proofs of the existence of God fc
those who can go deeply into these things.

(12) Again, it follows from the perfection of the Suprem
Author not only that the order of the whole universe is the mos
perfect that can be, but also that each living mirror representin
the universe according to its point of view, that is to say, eac
Monad, each substantial centre, must have its perceptions an
its desires [*appétits*] as thoroughly well-ordered as is compatibl
with all the rest. Whence it also follows that *souls*, that is to say
the most dominant Monads, or rather animals themselves can
not fail to awake again from the condition of stupor into whicl
death or some other accident may put them.

(13) For all is regulated in things, once for all, with as mucl
order and mutual connexion as possible, since supreme wisdor
and goodness can act only with perfect harmony. The present i
big with the future, the future might be read in the past, th
distant is expressed in the near. We might get to know th
beauty of the universe in each soul, if we could unfold all that i
enfolded in it and that is perceptibly developed only throug]
time. But as each distinct perception of the soul includes an in
finite number of confused perceptions, which involve the whol
universe, the soul itself knows the things of which it has percep
tion, only in so far as it has distinct and heightened [*or* unveiled
perceptions of them; and it has perfection in proportion to it:
distinct perceptions. Each soul knows the infinite, knows all
but confusedly; as when I walk on the sea-shore and hear th
great noise the sea makes, I hear the particular sounds whicl
come from the particular waves and which make up the tota
sound, but I do not discriminate them from one another. Ou
confused perceptions are the result of the impressions whicl
the whole universe makes upon us. It is the same with eacl
Monad. God alone has a distinct knowledge of all, for He is th
source of all. It has been very well said that as a centre He is
everywhere, but His circumference is nowhere, for everything
is immediately present to Him without any distance from this
centre.

(14) As regards the rational soul or *mind* [*l'esprit*], there is ir

it something more than in the Monads or even in mere [*simple*] souls. It is not only a mirror of the universe of created beings but also an image of the Deity. The mind [*l'esprit*] has not merely a perception of the works of God, but it is even capable of producing something which resembles them, although in miniature. For, to say nothing of the wonders of dreams, in which we invent without trouble (but also without willing it) things which, in our waking hours, we should have to think long in order to hit upon, our soul is architectonic also in its voluntary activities and, discovering the scientific principles in accordance with which God has ordered things (*pondere, mensura, numero,* &c.), it imitates, in its own province and in the little world in which it is allowed to act, what God does in the great world.

From SECOND EXPLANATION . . .

You do not understand, you say, how I could prove that which I advanced concerning the communication or harmony of two substances so different as the soul and the body. It is true that I believe that I have found the means of doing so, and this is how I propose to satisfy you. Imagine two clocks or watches which agree perfectly. Now, this may take place in *three ways*. The *first* consists in a mutual influence; the *second* is to have a skilful workman attached to them who regulates them and keeps them always in accord; the *third* is to construct these two clocks with so much art and accuracy as to assure their future harmony. Put now the soul and the body in place of these two clocks; their accordance may be brought about by one of these three ways. The way of influence is that of common philosophy, but as we cannot conceive of material particles which may pass from one of these substances into the other, this view must be abandoned. The way of continual assistance of the creator is that of the system of occasional causes; but I hold that this is to make a *Deus ex Machina* intervene in a natural and ordinary matter, in which, according to reason, he ought not to cooperate except in the way in which he does in all other natural things. Thus there remains only my hypothesis; that is, the way of harmony. From the beginning God has made each of these two substances of such a nature that merely by following its own peculiar laws, received with its being, it nevertheless accords with the other, just as if there were a mutual influence or as if God always put his hand thereto in addition to his general cooperation.

REFERENCES

Leibniz, Gottfried Wilhelm. *The Monadology and Other Philosophical Writings*. Trans. Robert Latta. Oxford: Clarendon Press, 1898, pp. 406–14, 417–21

Rand, Benjamin. *The Classical Psychologists*. Selections illustrating psychology from Anaxagoras to Wundt. London: Constable, 1912. 'Second Explanation of the System of the Communication between Substances', 1696, pp. 218–19

DAVID HUME

1711–1776

DAVID HUME was born in Edinburgh, and it is fair to regard him as the greatest of the Scottish philosophers. The *Treatise on Human Nature* was written in France, the first two volumes appearing in 1739 and the third in 1740, when Hume was still under thirty years of age. Hume spent most of his life as a writer in philosophy, history, politics, and political economy. He had brief periods of official duties, including acting as secretary to the British Embassy in Paris and as under-secretary in the Foreign Office. His *History of England*, though widely criticized, has been described as the first comprehensive history to introduce the social and literary aspects of a nation's life as second in importance only to its political fortunes. This is another sidelight on the growth of eighteenth-century social interests.

The extracts below are chosen for their bearing on the problem of how the core of a personality can or cannot be dealt with in strict accordance with an atomistic sensory empiricism, and to show the sceptical flavour of Hume's own scepticism. Having seen the problem as stated by Hume, the reader should compare it with James' treatment, part of which is quoted on pp. 389 ff. Between Hume and James lies the whole of the nineteenth-century shift towards the more structured conceptions of personality which are found afterwards in the writings of psychologists such as McDougall, Freud, and Lewin. One is left with the interesting historical question of how Bishop Butler's eighteenth-century contribution tended to get lost.

From ON PERSONAL IDENTITY

There are some philosophers, who imagine we are every moment intimately conscious of what we call our SELF; that we feel its existence and its continuance in existence; and are certain, beyond the evidence of a demonstration, both of its perfect identity and simplicity. The strongest sensation, the most violent passion, say they, instead of distracting us from this view, only fix it the more intensely, and make us consider their influence on *self* either by their pain or pleasure. To attempt a farther proof of this were to weaken its evidence; since no proof can be deriv'd from any fact, of which we are so intimately conscious; nor is there any thing, of which we can be certain, if we doubt of this.

Unluckily all these positive assertions are contrary to that very experience, which is pleaded for them, nor have we any idea of *self*, after the manner it is here explain'd. For from what impression cou'd this idea be deriv'd? This question 'tis impossible to answer without a manifest contradiction and absurdity; and yet 'tis a question, which must necessarily be answer'd, if we wou'd have the idea of self pass for clear and intelligible. It must be some one impression, that gives rise to every real idea. But self or person is not any one impression, but that to which our several impressions and ideas are suppos'd to have a reference. If any impression gives rise to the idea of self, that impression must continue invariably the same, thro' the whole course of our lives; since self is suppos'd to exist after that manner. But there is no impression constant and invariable. Pain and pleasure, grief and joy, passions and sensations succeed each other, and never all exist at the same time. It cannot, therefore, be from any of these impressions or from any other, that the idea of self is deriv'd; and consequently there is no such idea.

But farther, what must become of all our particular perceptions upon this hypothesis? All these are different, and distinguishable, and separable from each other, and may be separately consider'd, and may exist separately, and have no need of anything to support their existence. After what manner, therefore, do they belong to self; and how are they connected with it? For my part, when I enter most intimately into what I call *myself*, I always stumble on some particular perception or other, of heat or cold, light or shade, love or hatred, pain or pleasure. I never can catch *myself* at any time without a perception, and never can observe any thing but the perception. When my perceptions are removed for any time as by sound sleep; so long am I insensible of *myself*, and may truly be said not to exist.

And were all my perceptions remov'd by death, and cou'd I neither think, nor feel, nor see, nor love, nor hate after the dissolution of my body, I shou'd be entirely annihilated, nor do I conceive what is farther requisite to make me a perfect nonentity. If any one upon serious and unprejudic'd reflexion, thinks he has a different notion of *himself*, I must confess I can reason no longer with him. All I can allow him is, that he may be in the right as well as I, and that we are essentially different in this particular. He may, perhaps, perceive something simple and continu'd, which he calls *himself*; tho' I am certain there is no such principle in me.

But setting aside some metaphysicians of this kind, I may venture to affirm of the rest of mankind, that they are nothing but a bundle or collection of different perceptions, which succeed each other with an inconceivable rapidity, and are in a perpetual flux and movement. Our eyes cannot turn in their sockets without varying our perceptions. Our thought is still more variable than our sight; and all our other senses and faculties contribute to this change; nor is there any single power of the soul, which remains unalterably the same, perhaps for one moment. The mind is a kind of theatre, where several perceptions successively make their appearance; pass, re-pass, glide away, and mingle in an infinite variety of postures and situations. There is properly no *simplicity* in it at one time, nor *identity* in different; whatever natural propension we may have to imagine that simplicity and identity. The comparison of the theatre must not mislead us. They are the successive perceptions only, that constitute the mind; nor have we the most distant notion of the place, where these scenes are represented, or of the materials, of which it is composed.

What then gives us so great a propension to ascribe an identity to these successive perceptions, and to suppose ourselves possest of an invariable and uninterrupted existence thro' the whole course of our lives? In order to answer this question, we must distinguish betwixt personal identity, as it regards our thought or imagination, and as it regards our passions or the concern we take in ourselves. The first is our present subject; and to explain it perfectly we must take the matter pretty deep, and account for that identity, which we attribute to plants and animals; there being a great analogy betwixt it, and the identity of a self or person.

We have a distinct idea of an object, that remains invariable and uninterrupted thro' a suppos'd variation of time; and this idea we call that of *identity* or *sameness*. We have also a distinct idea of several different objects existing in succession, and connected together by a close relation; and this to an accurate view affords as perfect a notion of *diversity*, as if there was no manner of relation among the objects. But tho' these two ideas of identity, and a succession of related objects be in themselves perfectly distinct, and even contrary, yet 'tis certain, that in our common way of thinking they are generally confounded with each other. That action of the imagination, by which we consider the uninterrupted and invariable object, and that by which we reflect on the succession of related objects, are almost the same to the feeling, nor is there much more effort of thought requir'd in the latter case than in the former. The relation facilitates the transition of the mind from one object to another, and renders its passage as smooth as if it contemplated one continu'd object. This resemblance is the cause of the confusion and mistake, and makes us substitute the notion of identity, instead of that of related objects. However at one instant we may consider the related succession as variable or interrupted, we are sure the next to ascribe to it a perfect identity, and regard it as invariable and uninterrupted. Our propensity to this mistake is so great from the resemblance above-mention'd, that we fall into it before we are aware; and tho' we incessantly correct ourselves by reflexion, and return to a more accurate method of thinking, yet we cannot long sustain our philosophy, or take off this bias from the imagination. Our last resource is to yield to it, and boldly assert that these different related objects are in effect the same, however interrupted and variable. In order to justify to ourselves this absurdity, we often feign some new and unintelligible principle, that connects the objects together, and prevents their interruption or variation. Thus we feign the continu'd existence of the perceptions of our senses, to remove the interruption; and run into the notion of a *soul*, and *self*, and *substance*, to disguise the variation. But we may farther observe, that where we do not give rise to such a fiction, our propension to confound identity with relation is so great, that we are apt to imagine something unknown and mysterious, connecting the parts, beside their relation; and this I take to be the case with regard to the identity we ascribe to plants and vegetables. And even when this does not take place, we still feel a propensity to confound these ideas, tho' we are not able fully to satisfy ourselves in that particular, nor find any thing invariable and uninterrupted to justify our notion of identity.

From ON SCEPTICISM

... I have already shewn, that the understanding, when it acts alone, and according to its most general principles, entirely subverts itself, and leaves not the lowest degree of evidence in any proposition, either in philosophy or common life. We save ourselves from this total scepticism only by means of that singular and seemingly trivial property of the fancy, by which we enter with difficulty into remote views of things, and are not able to accompany them with so sensible an impression, as we do those, which are more easy and natural. Shall we, then, establish it for a general maxim, that no refin'd or elaborate reasoning is ever to be received? Consider well the consequences of such a principle. By this means you cut off entirely all science and philosophy: You proceed upon one singular quality of the imagination, and by a parity of reason must embrace all of them: And you expressly contradict yourself; since this maxim must be built on the preceding reasoning, which will be allow'd to be sufficiently refin'd and metaphysical. What party, then, shall we choose among these difficulties? If we embrace this principle, and condemn all refin'd reasoning, we run into the most manifest absurdities. If we reject it in favour of these reasonings, we subvert entirely the human understanding. We have, therefore, no choice left but betwixt a false reason and none at all. For my part, I know not what ought to be done in the present case. I can only observe what is commonly done; which is, that this difficulty is seldom or never thought of; and even where it has once been present to the mind, is quickly forgot, and leaves but a small impression behind it. Very refin'd reflections have little or no influence upon us; and yet we do not, and cannot establish it for a rule, that they ought not to have any influence; which implies a manifest contradiction.

But what have I here said, that reflexions very refin'd and metaphysical have little or no influence upon us? This opinion I can scarce forbear retracting, and condemning from my present feeling and experience. The *intense* view of these manifold contradictions and imperfections in human reason has so wrought upon me, and heated my brain, that I am ready to reject all belief and reasoning, and can look upon no opinion even as more probable or likely than another. Where am I, or what? From what causes do I derive my existence, and to what condition shall I return? Whose favour shall I court, and whose anger must I dread? What beings surround me? and on whom have I any influence, or who have any influence on me? I am confounded with all these questions, and begin to fancy myself in the most deplorable condition imaginable, environ'd with the deepest darkness, and utterly depriv'd of the use of every member and faculty.

Most fortunately it happens, that since reason is incapable of dispelling these clouds, nature herself suffices to that purpose, and cures me of this philosophical melancholy and delirium, either by relaxing this bent of mind, or by some avocation, and lively impression of my senses, which obliterate all these chimeras. I dine, I play a game of backgammon, I converse, and am merry with my friends; and when after three or four hours' amusement, I wou'd return to these speculations, they appear so cold, and strain'd, and ridiculous, that I cannot find in my heart to enter into them any farther.

Here then I find myself absolutely and necessarily determin'd to live, and talk, and act like other people in the common affairs of life. But notwithstanding that my natural propensity, and the course of my animal spirits and passions reduce me to this indolent belief in the general maxims of the world, I still feel such remains of my former disposition, that I am ready to hrow all my books and papers into the fire, and resolve never more to renounce the pleasures of life for the sake of reasoning and philosophy. For those are my sentiments in that splenetic humour, which governs me at present. I may, nay I must, yield to the current of nature, in submitting to my senses and understanding; and in this blind submission I shew most perfectly my sceptical disposition and principles. But does it follow, that I must strive against the current of nature, which leads me to indolence and pleasure; that I must seclude myself, in some measure, from the commerce and society of men, which is so agreeable; and that I must torture my brain with subtilities and sophistries, at the very time that I cannot satisfy myself concerning the reasonableness of so painful an application, nor have any tolerable prospect of arriving by its means at truth and certainty. Under what obligation do I lie of making such an abuse of time? And to what end can it serve either for the service of mankind, or for my own private interest? No: If I must be a fool, as all those who reason or believe any thing certainly are, my follies shall at least be natural and agreeable. Where I strive against my inclination, I shall have a good reason for my resistance; and will no more be led a wandering into such dreary solitudes, and rough passages, as I have hitherto met with. . . .

A true sceptic will be diffident of his philosophical doubts, as well as of his philosophical convictions.

REFERENCE

Hume, David. *Treatise on Human Nature*. Ed. L. A. Selby Bigge. Oxford: Clarendon Press, 1928, Bk. 1, pp. 251–5, 267–70, 273

DAVID HARTLEY

1705–1757

DAVID HARTLEY was a Yorkshireman who practised as a physician in Newark, Bury St Edmunds, London, and then Bath. His *Observations on Man* is regarded as the first systematic attempt to interpret mental phenomena by the laws of association. As explained on p. 140, he combined this with a theory of physiological vibrations. His way of dealing with mind-body problems is fairly clearly seen in the following extracts.

From OBSERVATIONS ON MAN

Man consists of two parts, body and mind.

The first is subjected to our senses and inquiries, in the same manner as the other parts of the external material world.

The last is that substance, agent, principle, etc. to which we refer the sensations, ideas, pleasures, pains, and voluntary motions.

Sensations are those internal feelings of the mind, which arise from the impressions made by external objects upon the several parts of our bodies.

All our other internal feelings may be called *ideas*. Some of these appear to spring up in the mind of themselves, some are suggested by words, others arise in other ways. Many writers comprehend *sensations* under *ideas*; but I every where use these words in the senses here ascribed to them.

The ideas which resemble sensations, are called *ideas of sensation*: all the rest may therefore be called *intellectual ideas*.

It will appear in the course of these observations, that the *ideas of sensation* are the elements of which all the rest are compounded. Hence *ideas of sensation* may be termed *simple*, *intellectual* ones *complex*.

The *pleasures* and *pains* are comprehended under the sensations and ideas, as these are explained above. For all our pleasures and pains are internal feelings, and conversely, all our internal feelings seem to be attended with some degree either of *pleasure* or *pain*. However, I shall, for the most part, give the names of *pleasure* and *pain* only to such degrees as are considerable; referring all low evanescent ones to the head of *mere sensations* and *ideas*.

The pleasures and pains may be ranged under seven general classes; viz.

1. Sensation;
2. Imagination;
3. Ambition;
4. Self-Interest;
5. Sympathy;
6. Theopathy; and,
7. The Moral Sense; according as they arise from,
1. The impressions made on the external senses;
2. Natural or artificial beauty or deformity;
3. The opinions of others concerning us;
4. Our possession or want of the means of happiness, and security from, or subjection to, the hazards of misery;
5. The pleasures and pains of our fellow-creatures;
6. The affections excited in us by the contemplation of the Deity; or,
7. Moral beauty and deformity.

The human mind may also be considered as endued with the faculties of *memory*, *imagination*, or *fancy*, *understanding*, *affection*, and *will*.

*

My chief design in the following chapter is briefly to explain, establish, and apply the doctrines of *vibrations* and *association*. The first of these doctrines is taken from the hints concerning the performance of sensation and motion, which Sir Isaac Newton has given at the end of his *Principia*, and in the Questions annexed to his *Optics*; the last, from what Mr Locke, and other ingenious persons since his time, have delivered concerning the influence of *association* over our opinions and affections, and its use in explaining those things in an accurate and precise way, which are commonly referred to the power of habit and custom, is a general and indeterminate one.

The doctrine of *vibrations* may appear at first sight to have no connexion with that of *association*; however, if these doctrines be found in fact to contain the laws of the bodily and mental powers respectively, they must be related to each other, since the body and mind are. One may expect, that *vibrations* should infer *association* as their effect, and *association* point to *vibrations* as its cause. I will endeavour, in the present chapter, to trace out this mutual relation.

The proper method of philosophizing seems to be, to discover and establish the general laws of action, affecting the subject under consideration, from certain select, well-defined, and well-attested phenomena, and then to explain and predict the other phenomena by these laws. This is the method of analysis and synthesis recommended and followed by Sir Isaac Newton. I shall not be able to execute, with any accuracy, what the reader might expect of this kind, in respect of the doctrines of *vibrations* and *association*, and their general laws, on account of the great intricacy, extensiveness, and novelty of the subject. However, I will attempt a sketch in the best manner I can, for the service of future inquirers.

*

Proposition I. The white medullary Substance of the Brain, spinal Marrow, and the Nerves proceeding from them, is the immediate Instrument of Sensation and Motion.

Under the word *brain*, in these observations, I comprehend all that lies within the cavity of the skull, *i.e.* the *cerebrum*, or *brain* properly so-called, the *cerebellum*, and the *medulla oblongata*.

This proposition seems to be sufficiently proved in the writings of physicians and anatomists; from the structure and functions of the several organs of the human body; from experiments on living animals; from the symptoms of diseases, and from dissections of morbid bodies. Sensibility, and the power of motion, seem to be conveyed to all the parts, in their natural state, from the brain and spinal marrow, along the nerves. These arise from the medullary, not the cortical part, every where, and are themselves of a white medullary substance. When the nerves of any part are cut, tied, or compressed in any considerable degree, the functions of that part are either entirely destroyed, or much impaired. When the spinal marrow is compressed by a dislocation of the vertebrae of the back, all the parts, whose nerves arise below the place of dislocation, become paralytic. When any considerable injury is done to the medullary substance of the brain, sensation, voluntary motion, memory, and intellect, are either entirely lost, or much impaired; and if the injury be very great, this extends immediately to the vital motions also, *viz.* to those of the heart, and organs of respiration, so as to occasion death. But this does not hold equally in respect of the cortical substance of the brain; perhaps not at all, unless as far as injuries done to it extend themselves to the medullary substance. In dissections after apoplexies, palsies, epilepsies, and other distempers affecting the sensations and motions, it is usual to find some great disorder in the brain, from preternatural tumours, from blood, matter, or serum, lying upon the brain, or in its ventricles, etc. This may suffice as general evidence for the present. The particular reasons for some of these phenomena, with more definite evidences, will offer themselves in the course of these observations.

Proposition II. The white medullary Substance of the Brain is also the immediate Instrument, by which Ideas are presented to the Mind: or, in other words, whatever Changes are made in this Substance, corresponding Changes are made in our Ideas; and vice versa.

The evidence for this proposition is also to be taken from the writings of physicians and anatomists; but especially from those parts of these writings which treat of the faculties of memory, attention, imagination, etc. and of mental disorders. It is sufficiently manifest from hence, that the perfection of our mental faculties depends upon the perfection of this substance; that all injuries done to it affect the trains of ideas proportionably; and that these cannot be restored to their natural course till such injuries be repaired. Poisons, spirituous liquors, opiates, fevers, blows upon the head, etc. all plainly affect the mind, by first disordering the medullary substance. And evacuations, rest, medicines, time, etc. as plainly restore the mind to its former state, by reversing the foregoing steps. . . .

Proposition III. The Sensations remain in the Mind for a short time after the sensible Objects are removed.

This is very evident in the sensations impressed on the eye. Thus, to use Sir Isaac Newton's words, 'If a burning coal be nimbly moved round in a circle, with gyrations continually repeated, the whole circle will appear like fire; the reason of which is, that the sensation of the coal, in the several places of that circle, remains impressed on the *sensorium* until the coal return again to the same place. And so in a quick consecution of the colours,' (*viz.* red, yellow, green, blue, and purple, mentioned in the experiment, whence this passage is taken,) 'the impression of every colour remains on the *sensorium* until a revolution of all the colours be completed, and that first colour return again. The impressions therefore of all the successive colours are at once in the *sensorium* – and beget a sensation of white.' *Opt.* b. 1. p. 2 Experiment 10.

————

It may also be objected to the whole foregoing theory, as well as to the doctrine of vibrations in particular, that it is unfavourable to the immateriality of the soul; and by consequence, to its immortality. But to this I answer, that I am reduced to the necessity of making a *postulatum* at the entrance of my inquiries; which precludes all possibility of proving the materiality of the soul from this theory afterwards. Thus I suppose, or postulate, in my first proposition, that sensations arise in the soul from motions excited in the medullary substance of the brain. I do indeed bring some arguments from physiology and pathology, to shew this to be a reasonable *postulatum*, when understood in a general sense; for it is all one to the purpose of the foregoing theory, whether the motions in the medullary substance be the physical cause of the sensations, according to the system of the schools; or the occasional cause, according to *Malebranche*; or only an adjunct, according to Leibniz. However, this is not supposing matter to be endued with sensation, or any way explaining what the soul is; but only taking its existence, and connexion with the bodily organs in the most simple case, for granted, in order to make further inquiries. Agreeably to which I immediately proceed to determine the species of the motion, and by determining it, to cast light on some important and obscure points relating to the connexion between the body and the soul in complex cases.

It does indeed follow from this theory, that matter, if it could be endued with the most simple kinds of sensation, might also arrive at all that intelligence of which the human mind is possessed: whence this theory must be allowed to overturn all the arguments which are usually brought for the immateriality of the soul from the subtlety of the internal senses, and of the rational faculty. But I no ways presume to determine whether matter can be endued with sensation or no. This is a point foreign to the purpose of my inquiries. It is sufficient for me, that there is a certain connexion, of one kind or other, between the sensations of the soul, and the motions excited in the medullary substance of the brain; which is what all physicians and philosophers allow.

REFERENCES

Hartley, David. *Observations on Man*. London: 1801, Vol. I, pp. i–iii, 3–6, 7–9, 9, 511–12
    For biographical notes by his son see Vol. III

ÉTIENNE BONNOT,
ABBÉ DE CONDILLAC
1715–1780

CONDILLAC lived a quiet and somewhat independent life de
voted to philosophical writing. Apart from this his main task wa
the education of one of Louis XV's grandsons. Condillac appear
to have been a conscientious author and educationist, hard-work
ing, and in an age of brilliance – he was contemporary with Vol
taire, Rousseau, Diderot, Helvétius, and d'Holbach – he never
theless achieved a high reputation and was an influence on later
writers.

Condillac himself was considerably influenced by Locke and
took one further step towards sensory empiricism by trying to
explain the acquisition of knowledge on the basis of sensations
omitting Locke's ideas on reflection. Condillac was anxious to
avoid the type of materialism usually attributed to La Mettrie
and to do this invoked a species of occasionalism, retaining a distinction between mental and physical events.

It is perhaps worth passing comment that La Mettrie's
L'Homme machine was not (as we would now expect) a treatise
on cybernetics but a lively and intentionally provocative discourse
much of which concerns the physical facts, such as lack of sleep
and hunger, that it is wise to take into account in explaining human behaviour. While La Mettrie clearly succeeded all too well
in provoking some of his contemporaries, his personal gaiety and
common sense delighted Frederick the Great, who wrote a
eulogy on him and included some dry remarks on the prejudices
of the pious. I doubt if it would be fair to include Condillac in
this group, for it is easy to see that for other reasons the two
writers are poles apart. La Mettrie appears to us the more stimulating, robust and practical; Condillac is by far the more subtle
and charming. It would seem too that his *Treatise on Systems*
would warrant further study. Meanwhile something of his
approach can be seen in the following extract.

Étienne Bonnot, Abbé de Condillac

From THE TREATISE ON SENSATIONS

I

The First Cognitions of a Man Limited to the Sense of Smell.

(1) *The Statue Limited to the Sense of Smell can only Know Odours*

Our statue being limited to the sense of smell its cognitions cannot extend beyond smells. It can no more have ideas of extension, shape or of anything outside itself, or outside its sensations, than it can have ideas of colour, sound or taste.

(2) *Only Relatively to Itself are Odours Smelled*

If we give the statue a rose to smell, to us it is a statue smelling a rose, to itself it is smell of rose.

The statue therefore will be rose smell, pink smell, jasmine smell, violet smell, according to the flower which stimulates its sense organ. In a word, in regard to itself smells are its modifications or modes. It cannot suppose itself to be anything else, since it is only susceptible to sensations.

(3) *It Has no Idea of Matter*

Let the philosophers, to whom it appears so evident that all is material, put themselves for a moment in its place, and then imagine how they could suspect the existence of anything which resembles what we call *matter*.

(4) *It Could Not be More Limited in its Cognitions*

This is enough to prove that we have only to increase or diminish the number of senses, in order to make us pass quite different judgements from those which now seem natural to us; and our statue limited to the sense of smell, can give us the idea of a class of beings with extremely limited cognitions.

Two Kinds of Pleasures and Pains

Pleasures and pains are of two kinds. The one kind belong more particularly to the body; they are sensible. The other kind are in the memory and in all the faculties of the soul; they are intellectual or spiritual. But it is a difference which the statue is incapable of noticing.

This ignorance will guard it from an error which we have difficulty in avoiding: for these feelings do not differ as much as we imagine. Of a truth, they are all intellectual or spiritual, because, rightly understood, it is only the soul which feels. There is, indeed, a sense in which we can say they are all sensible or corporeal, because the body alone is their occasional cause. It is only according as they are related to the faculties of the body or to those of the soul that we distinguish them into two kinds.

How Ideas are Preserved and Renewed in Memory

But when the statue is a long time without thinking of a mode of being, what becomes during that time, of the idea it has acquired of it? Where does it come from when afterwards it is recalled in the memory? Is it preserved in the soul or in the body? In neither.

It is not in the soul, since it is sufficient to have a derangement of the brain to take away the power to recall. It is not in the body. Only the physical cause is preserved in the body and for the idea to be preserved there we should have to suppose that the brain had remained absolutely in the state in which it had been left by the sensation which the statue recalls. How can such a supposition agree with the continual movement of the animal spirits? How can we make it agree, especially when we consider the multitude of ideas with which the memory is enriched? The phenomenon can be explained in a much simpler way.

I have a sensation when a movement in one of my sense organs is transmitted to the brain. If the movement begins in the brain and is extended to the sense organ, I believe that I have a sensation which in fact I have not: it is an illusion. But if the movement begins and ends in the brain, then I recall the sensation which I have had.

When an idea is recalled by the statue, it is not, then, because it is preserved either in the body or in the soul: it is because the movement which is the physical and occasional cause of the idea is reproduced in the brain. But this is not the place to hazard conjectures on the mechanism of memory. We preserve the remembrance of our sensations. We recall them to ourselves, after having been for a long time without thinking of them. It is sufficient for this that they should have made a vivid impression on us, or that we should have experienced them on many occasions. These facts authorize me to suppose that our statue, being organized like ourselves, is like us, capable of memory.

The Self or Personality of a Man Limited to the Sense of Smell

(1) *Of the Personality of the Statue*

Our statue being capable of memory, there is no smell which does not recall to it that it was once another smell. Herein lies its personality. If it is able to say 'I' it can say it in all the states of its duration; and at each time its 'I' will embrace all the moments of which it might have preserved recollection.

(2) *It cannot Say 'I' at the First Moment of its Existence*

I admit that it could not say 'I' at the first smell. What we understand by this word 'I' seems to be only possible in a being who notices that in the present moment he is no longer what he has been. So long as there is no change, he exists without any reflexion upon himself; but as soon as he changes, he judges that he is the same as he formerly was in another state, and he says 'I'.

This observation makes it clear that at the first moment of his existence the statue is not able to form desires, for before being able to say *I desire it*, it must have said 'I' or 'me'.

(3) The 'I' is at one and the same Time the Consciousness of What it is, and the Remembrance of What Has Been

Smells of which the statue has no recollection, do not enter into the idea which it has of its personality. They are then for it, as though it had never smelled them. They are as much strangers to its 'I' as the colours and sounds of which it has as yet no knowledge. Its 'I' is only the collection of the sensations which it experiences, and those which memory recalls to it.* In a word it is immediate knowledge of what it is for itself, and remembrance of what it has been.

Footnote

*'Does the man who loves a lady for her beauty,' said Pascal, 'truly love her? No: for small-pox may destroy her beauty, without killing her, and may cause him to love her no more. And if one loves me for my judgement or memory, does one love me? No: for I may lose these qualities and still be myself. In what then does the "I" consist, if it be neither in the body nor in the soul? And how can one love body and soul except for the qualities which do not make the "I", since they are perishable? Should we then love the substance of the soul of a person abstractly with such qualities as it might possess? This is impossible and would be unjustifiable. We never, then, love the person but only the qualities. When we love a person, we must mean the assemblage of the qualities which make the person.' Pascal. *Pensées* (323, *Brunschvicg's arrangement*).

But it is not the assemblage of the qualities which make the person, for then the same man, young or old, beautiful or ugly, wise or foolish, would be so many different persons. Whatever the qualities for which you love me it is always me you love, for the qualities are only me modified differently. If someone treading on my toe were to say to me, 'I have not hurt *you*, for you could lose your toe and still be *you*,' should I be convinced? Why then should I think that, because I can lose my memory and my judgement, one cannot love me, since I am loved for these qualities? But they are perishable; what of that? Is the *me* a necessity of one's nature? Does it perish in animals? And is not man's immortality a special gift of God? In Pascal's meaning God alone can say 'I'.

How a Man Limited to Touch Discovers His Body and Learns That There is Something Outside Himself

(1) *The Statue Has Movements*

I allow the statue the use of all its members: but what is the cause which induces it to move them? It cannot be the intention of serving itself, for as yet it does not know that it is composed of articulated parts, or supported by external objects. It is to nature we must look for a beginning. Nature must produce the first movements in the statue's members.

(2) *How Movements are Produced*

If nature gives it an agreeable sensation, we may imagine that the statue is able to enjoy it, and will keep the parts of its body in the same situation in which they enjoy it. A sensation, therefore, would appear to conduce to continuous repose rather than to the production of movement. But if it is natural for the statue to give itself up to a sensation which pleases it and to enjoy it in repose, it is equally natural for it to shrink from a sensation which hurts it. It is true that it does not know how to shrink from such a sensation, but at the beginning it is not necessary for it to know, it is sufficient for it to obey nature. It is a result of its organization, that its muscles contracted by pain move its limbs, and that it moves automatically without knowing that it moves.

It can even have agreeable sensations of so vivid a character that they will not let it rest in perfect repose; in any case it is certain that the alternating passage from pleasure to pain and from pain to pleasure must occasion movements in its body. Were it not organized in such a way as to be moved upon the occasion of the pleasant or unpleasant sensations which it experiences, the perfect repose to which it would be condemned would leave it no means of seeking what would be useful to it, or of avoiding what would be harmful to it.

In accord with its organization therefore, pleasure and pain, or the passage from one to the other, cause it to have movements; it cannot then but happen that among these movements some will cut off or suspend a sensation which is hurtful, and others will procure it a sensation which is pleasurable. It will therefore have an interest in studying its movements, and consequently it will learn from them all that they are able to teach it.

It moves, naturally, mechanically, by instinct and without knowing that it does it; and it only remains to explain how it discovers, by means of movement, that it has a body and that outside it there are other bodies.

If we consider the multitude and the variety of the impressions which objects make upon our statue, we shall judge that its movements ought naturally to be repeated and to be varied. Now as soon as they are repeated and varied, it occurs to it necessarily, after many trials, to put its hands on itself and on the objects which approach it.

Placing its hands on itself it will discover that it has a body, but only when it has distinguished the different parts of it and recognized in each the same sentient being. It will discover there are other bodies when it touches things in which it does not find itself.

(3) *Sensation by means of Which the Soul Discovers that it has a Body*

It can then only owe this discovery to some particular sensation of touch. Now what is this sensation?

Impenetrability is a property of all bodies. Several things cannot occupy the same place. Each excludes all others from the place it occupies.

This impenetrability is not a sensation. We do not, strictly speaking, feel that bodies are impenetrable: we judge that they are. This judgement is a consequence of the sensations that they produce in us.

We draw this inference chiefly from the sensation of solidity; because, in two solid bodies which come into contact with one another we perceive very clearly the resistance which each maintains in order mutually to exclude the other. Could they interpenetrate the two would be confused into one: but since they are impenetrable, they are necessarily distinct and always two.

The sensation of solidity is unlike the sensations of sound or colour or smell. For in those sensations the soul does not know its own body and yet naturally perceives its modifications in which it finds itself and itself only. Since the characteristic of the sensation of solidity is to represent two things together which are mutually exclusive, the soul does not perceive solidity as one of its own modifications, it perceives it as a modification in which it finds two things which exclude one another, and consequently it perceives solidity in these two things.

Here then we have a sensation by means of which the soul passes beyond itself, and we begin to understand how it will discover bodies.

In fact, since the statue is organized to make movements only when impressions are made upon it, we may suppose that its hand will naturally be carried to some part of its body, to the chest for example. Then its hand and its chest will be distinguished from one another by the sensation of solidities which they mutually give each other, and which necessarily puts them one outside the other. But in distinguishing its chest from its hand the statue will find itself in each, because it will feel itself equally in both. Whatever other part of its body it touches it will distinguish it in the same way, and will equally discover itself there. Although this discovery may be primarily due to the sensation of solidity, it will be still more easily made if other sensations are joined with it. If the hand be cold, for example, and the chest be warm, the statue will then feel them as something solid and cold touching something solid and warm. It will learn to refer the cold to the hand, the warmth to the chest, and it will easily distinguish the one from the other. Thus, then, these two sensations, which are scarce fitted in themselves to inform the statue that it has a body, will yet contribute to give it this obvious idea when they are included in the sensation of solidity.

If now the statue's hand, in being carried from one part of the body to another, has always avoided touching the intermediary parts, it will find itself in each part as in so many different bodies and it will not yet know that altogether these parts form one body. This is because the sensations which it has experienced are not shown to be contiguous and consequently they do not form one single *continuum*.

But should it happen to run its hand along its arm and over its chest and head etc. without taking its hand off, then it will feel, to put it briefly, a continuity of itself under its hand, and this same hand, which will unite in a single *continuum* parts formerly separated, will give it evident feeling of extension.

(4) *How it Recognizes Itself*

The statue learns to know its body and to recognize itself in all its component parts, because as soon as it places its hands upon one of them, the same sentient being replies in some way from one to the other: *this is myself*. As it continues to touch itself, everywhere the sensation of solidity will represent two things which exclude one another, and which at the same time are contiguous, and everywhere the same sentient being will reply from one to the other: *this is myself, this is still myself!* It will feel itself in all parts of the body. It no longer will confuse itself with its modifications, it will no longer be warm and cold. It will feel warm in one part of its body and cold in another.

(5) *How it Discovers That There Are Other Bodies*

As long as the statue only places its hands upon itself, it must regard itself as all that exists. But if it touches a foreign body the 'I' which feels itself modified in the hand, does not feel itself modified in the foreign body. The 'I' does not receive the response from the foreign body which it receives from the hand. The statue, therefore, judges these modes to be altogether outside it. As it formed its own body it now forms all other objects. The sensation of solidity gives consistency in the one case as in the other, with this difference, that the 'I' which responded in the one case ceases to respond in the other.

(6) *What This Idea of Objects Is Reduced To*

It does not, then, perceive objects in themselves, it only perceives its own sensations. When many distinct and coexistent sensations are circumscribed by touch, in limits in which the 'I' replies to itself, it acquires the knowledge of its own body; when many distinct and coexistent sensations are circumscribed by touch, in limits in which the 'I' does not reply, it has the idea of a body different from its own. In the first case its sensations continue to be qualities of itself, in the second, they become qualities of a quite different object.

(7) *Its Surprise at Not Being All It Touches*

When it comes to learn that it is something solid, it is, I imagine, much surprised not to find itself in all it touches. It cannot know whether it will find anything there: experience alone can teach it that.

(8) *Effects of This Surprise*

From this surprise arises the anxiety to know where it is, and if I may so express it, just where it is. It takes hold and lets go, and takes hold again of everything round it; it seizes hold of itself, and compares itself with the objects it touches; and as it attains to more exact ideas so its body and the objects in contact with it appear to it to be forming under its hands.

(9) *In Each Thing It Touches It Believes It Touches Everything*

But I conjecture it will be long before it will imagine there are things beyond the objects it meets. It seems to me, that when it begins to touch, it will believe that it is touching everywhere there is; and only after it has passed from one place to another and handled many objects, will it come to suspect there are objects beyond those it grasps.

(10) *How It Learned To Touch*

But how did it learn to touch? Through movements nature has forced on it. Nature having procured for it sensations sometimes pleasant sometimes unpleasant, it will want to enjoy the one and shun the other. At first indeed it will not know how to regulate its movements. It will not know how to guide its hand so as to put it on one part of its body, rather than another. It will make many attempts, will repeat them over and over again until it succeeds. It will notice wrong movements, and avoid them. It will notice those which responded to its desires, and repeat them. In a word, it will proceed tentatively and will form by degrees a habit of movements proper for its preservation. Then will there be movements in its body corresponding to the desires of its soul. Then will it be moved by its will.

REFERENCES

Condillac, Étienne Bonnot, Abbé de. *Traité des Sensations* 1754. Trans. as *Treatise on Sensations* by Geraldine Carr. London: Favil Press, 1930, pp. 3–4, 12, 21, 43–4, 84–90
    Translation based on 1798 collected edition
Cassirer, Ernst. *The Philosophy of the Enlightenment*. Princeton, New Jersey: Princeton University Press, 1951, Chap. 1
La Mettrie, J. O. *L'Homme machine*. Trans. as *Man a Machine*. Annotated by G. C. Bussey. Chicago: Open Court, 1912

JAMES BRAID

1795–1860

JAMES BRAID, who was born in Fifeshire, later qualified as a doctor at Edinburgh University. He practised medicine in Scotland and subsequently moved to Manchester where he gained a considerable reputation.

In 1841 his attention was drawn to the so-called 'animal magnetism' by Lafontaine, a Swiss mesmerist, lecturing in Manchester. Mesmerism, to the great scandal of the medical profession, had been enthusiastically adopted from France in 1837 by Elliotson, whose support and founding of the *Zoist* in 1843 led to the establishment of various mesmeric clinics. By the time that Braid entered upon the scene the subject was already a matter of heated controversy, the possible use of 'mesmerism' as a means of producing anaesthesia in surgery soon becoming one of the major bones of contention. Between 1845 and 1851 Esdaile, working in India, produced evidence of distinctly promising anaesthetic results.

Braid, whose initial approach to the matter was highly critical, remained to the end in opposition to Elliotson and Esdaile, but came to accept the phenomena observed by the mesmerists while refuting the 'magnetic' interpretation originally put forward by Reichenbach. Braid in fact fought long and hard to establish a psychological explanation and his battling has considerable historical interest. In the 1850s his sympathetic and psychological attack on the question came to be known in France, particularly by Azam and Broca, who repeated his experiments. Their findings and favourable reports re-awakened serious interest in the phenomena reported. This lapsed but later it gave indirect impetus to the outstanding psychotherapeutic work subsequently associated with the names of Liébeault, Bernheim, Charcot, and others in the second half of the French nineteenth century. Braid's work also became known in Germany, where by 1882 most of his writings were available in translation. Readers will find a critical and often vivid account of the early days (and dangers) of mesmerism in Binet and Féré's *Animal Magnetism*.

The following extracts from a pamphlet published in 1846 show something of Braid's systematic method of investigation.

It has the sub-title: 'An experimental inquiry into the nature and cause of the phenomena attributed by Baron Reichenbach and others to a New Imponderable'. It is well to realize that Braid was not only against imponderables being multiplied without necessity but also, as a responsible doctor, he was fully aware of the dangers of experimenting in hypnotic suggestion and of the need to safeguard against misuse. His explanation, while an enormous advance, would now be regarded as only partial.

From THE POWER OF THE MIND OVER THE BODY

In Braid's time it was being argued, e.g. by Reichenbach, that 'a new imponderable' was the explanation of phenomena observed by the mesmerists, the existence of this imponderable being demonstrable only in the case of a few highly sensitive and nervous subjects. The following illustrates the kind of phenomena and the explanation put forward by Reichenbach:

Magnets of 10 lb. supporting power, when drawn along the body, without contact, produce certain sensations in a certain proportion of human beings. Occasionally, out of twenty, three or four sensitive individuals are found; and in one case, out of twenty-two females examined by the author eighteen were found sensitive.

The sensation is rather unpleasant than agreeable, and is like an aura: in some cases warm, in others cool; or it may be a pricking, or the sensation of the creeping of insects on the skin; sometimes headache comes on rapidly. These effects occur when the patient does not see the magnet, nor know what is doing; they occur both in males and females, though more frequently in females; they are sometimes seen in strong, healthy people, but oftener in those whose health, though good, is not so vigorous, and in what are called nervous persons. Children are frequently found to be sensitive. Persons affected with spasmodic diseases, those who suffer from epilepsy, catalepsy, chorea, paralysis, and hysteria, are particularly sensitive. Lunatics and somnambulists are uniformly sensitive. The magnet is consequently an agent capable of affecting the human body. . . .

Healthy, sensitive subjects observe nothing farther than the sensations above noticed, and experience no inconvenience from the approach of magnets; but the diseased sensitive subjects experience different sensations, often disagreeable, and occasionally giving rise to fainting, to attacks of catalepsy, and to spasms so violent that they might possibly endanger life. In such cases, which generally include somnambulists, there occurs an extraordinary acuteness of the senses; smell and taste, for example, become astonishingly delicate and acute; many kinds of food become intolerable, and the perfumes most agreeable at other times become offensive. The patients hear and understand what is spoken three or four rooms off, and their vision is often so irritable, that, on the one hand, they cannot endure the sun's light, or that of a fire; while, on the other, they are able, in very dark rooms, to distinguish, not only the outlines, but also the colours of objects, where healthy people cannot distinguish anything at all.

Braid maintained that with

many individuals, and especially of the highly nervous, and imaginative, and abstractive classes, a strong direction of inward consciousness to any part of the body, especially if attended with the expectation or belief of something being about to happen, is quite sufficient to change the physical action of the part, and to produce such impressions from this cause alone, as Baron Reichenbach attributes to his new force. Thus every variety of feeling may be excited from an internal or mental cause – such as heat or cold, pricking, creeping, tingling, spasmodic twitching of muscles, catalepsy, a feeling of attraction or repulsion, sights of every form or hue, odours, tastes, and sounds, in endless variety, and so on, according as accident or intention may have suggested. Moreover, the oftener such impressions have been excited, the more readily may they be reproduced, under similar circumstances, through the laws of association and habit. Such being the fact, it must consequently be obvious to every intelligent and unprejudiced person, that no implicit reliance can be placed on the human nerve, as a test of this new power in producing effects from external impressions or influences, when precisely the same phenomena may arise from an internal or mental influence, when no external agency whatever is in operation.

Believing that in Reichenbach's experiments the possible effect of 'the mental part of the process' had been overlooked, Braid decided to repeat the experiments trying to keep this factor under control. The method and results are indicated below:

In order to guard against this source of fallacy, [overlooking mental influence] therefore, I considered it would be the best mode to throw patients into the nervous sleep, and then operate on such of them as I knew had no use of their eyes during the sleep (for some patients have), and to take accurate notice of the results when a magnet capable of lifting fourteen pounds was drawn over the hand and other parts of the body without contact, after the manner described as performed by Baron Reichenbach in his experiments.

I experimented accordingly, and the results were, that in no instance was there the slightest effect manifested, unless when the magnet was brought so near as to enable the patient to feel the abstraction of heat (producing a sensation of cold), when a feeling of discomfort was manifested, with a disposition to move the hand, or head, or face, as the case might be, from the offending cause. This indication was precisely the same when the armature was attached, as when the magnet was open; and in both cases, if I suffered the magnet to touch the patient, instantly the part was hurriedly withdrawn, as I have always seen manifested during the primary stage of hypnotism, when the patients were touched with any cold object. Now, inasmuch as patients in this condition, generally, if not always, manifest their perceptions of external impressions by the most natural movements, unless the natural law has been subverted by some preconceived notion or suggested idea to the contrary, and as I have operated with similar results upon a considerable number of patients, we have thus satisfactory proof that there was no real attractive power of a magnetic or other nature, tending to draw the patient, or any of his members, so as to cause an adhesion between his body and the magnet, as between the latter and iron, as Baron Reichenbach had alleged. I conclude, therefore, that the phenomena of apparent attraction manifested in his cases were due entirely to a mental influence; and I shall presently prove that this is quite adequate to the production of such effects.

Having shown that without expectation, suggestion, and the like, the mere juxtaposition of magnets produced no unusual results, Braid proceeded to experiment with patients who were wide awake (*a*) when they could and (*b*) when they could not see what was being done. Here is the beginning of an account which he reinforces with more examples:

I shall now proceed to detail the results of experiments with patients when wide awake, and when they had an opportunity of seeing what was being done, and expected something to happen; and also when the same patients saw nothing of what was doing, but supposed I was operating, and consequently expected something to occur.

With nearly all the patients I have tried, many of whom had never been hypnotized or mesmerized, when drawing the magnet or other object slowly from the wrist to the points of the fingers, various effects were realized, such as a change of temperature, tingling, creeping, pricking, spasmodic twitching, catalepsy of the fingers, or arm, or both; and reversing the motion was generally followed by a change of symptoms, from the altered current of ideas thereby suggested. Moreover, if any idea of what might be expected existed in the mind previously, or was suggested orally, during the process, it was generally very speedily realized. The above patients being now requested to look aside, or a screen having been interposed, so as to prevent their seeing what was being done, and they were requested to describe their sensations during the repetition of the processes, similar phenomena were stated to be realized, even when there was nothing whatever done, beyond watching them, and noting their responses. They believed the processes were being repeated, and had their minds directed to the part, and thus the physical action was excited, so as actually to lead them to believe and describe their feelings as arising from external impressions.

The above fact was most remarkably evinced in a young gentleman, twenty-one years of age. I first operated in this manner on his right hand, by drawing a powerful horse-shoe magnet over the hand, without contact, whilst the armature was attached. He immediately observed a sensation of cold follow the course of the magnet. I reversed the passes, and he felt it less cold, but he felt no attraction between his hand and the magnet. I then removed the cross-bar, and tried the effect with both poles alternatively, but still there was no change in the effect, and decidedly no proof of attraction between his hand and the magnet. In the afternoon of the same day I desired him to look aside and hold his hat between his eyes and his hand, and observe the effects when I operated on him, whilst he could not see my proceedings. He very soon described a recurrence of the same sort of sensations as those he felt in the morning, but they speedily became more intense and extended up the arm, producing rigidity of the member. In the course of two minutes this feeling attacked the other arm, and to some extent the whole body, and he was, moreover, seized with a fit of involuntary laughter, like that of hysteria, which continued for several minutes – in fact, until I put an end to the experiment. His first remark was, 'Now this experiment clearly proves that there must be some intimate connexion between mineral magnetism and Mesmerism, for I was most strangely affected, and could not possibly resist laughing during the extraordinary sensations with which my whole body was seized, as you drew the magnet over my hand and arm.' I replied that I drew a very different conclusion from the experiments, as I had never used the magnet at all, nor held it, nor anything else, near to him; and that the whole proved the truth of my position as to the extraordinary power of mind over body, and how mental impressions could change physical action.

Finally Braid takes into account behaviour resulting from suggestion used at a certain stage of hypnosis.

I had long been familiar with the fact, that during a certain stage of hypnotism, patients may be made to give various manifestations, or declarations of their feelings and emotions, according to previously-existing ideas, or suggestions imparted to them during the sleep; and, moreover, that such associations once formed, were liable to recur ever after, under a similar combination of circumstances. As occurs in ordinary dreaming, they seem generally at once to adopt the idea as a reality, without taking the trouble of reasoning on the subject as to the probability of such ideas being only imaginary; and their extreme mobility in the hypnotic state at a certain stage renders them prompt with their corresponding physical response. In proof of this, and how readily those inattentive to these facts may misapprehend what they see realized in such cases, I beg to submit the following interesting illustration. When in London lately, I had the pleasure of calling upon an eminent and excellent physician, who is in the habit of using mesmerism in his practice, in suitable cases, just as he uses any other remedy. He spoke of the extraordinary effects which he had experienced from the use of magnets applied during the mesmeric state, and kindly offered to illustrate the fact on a patient who had been asleep all the time I was in the room, and in that stage, during which I felt assured she could overhear every word of our conversation. He told me, that when he put the magnet into her hands, it would produce catalepsy of the hands and arms, and such was the result. He wafted the hands and the catalepsy ceased. He said that a mere touch of the magnet on a limb would stiffen it, and such he proved to be the fact.

I now told him, that I had got a little instrument in my pocket, which, although far less than his, I felt assured would prove quite as powerful, and I offered to prove this by operating on the same patient, whom I had never seen before, and who was in the mesmeric state when I entered the room. My instrument was about three inches long, the thickness of a quill, with a ring attached to the end of it. I told him that when put into her hands, he would find it catalepsize both hands and arms as his had done, and such was the result. Having reduced this by wafting, I took my instrument from her, and again returned it, in another position, and told him it would now have the reverse effect – that she would not be able to hold it, and that although I closed her hands on it, they would open, and that it would drop out of them, and such was the case, – to the great surprise of my worthy friend, who now desired to be informed what I had done to the instrument to invest it with this new and opposite power. This I declined doing for the present; but I promised to do so, when he had seen some further proofs of its remarkable powers. I now told him that a touch with it, on either extremity would cause the extremity to rise and become cataleptic, and such was the result; that a second touch on the same point would reduce the rigidity, and cause it to fall, and such again was proved to be the fact. After a variety of other experiments, every one of which proved precisely as I had predicted, she was aroused. I now applied the ring of my instrument on the third finger of the right hand, from which it was suspended, and told the doctor, that when it was so suspended, it would send her to sleep. To this he replied, 'it never will,' but I again told him that I felt confident that it would send her to sleep. We then were silent, and very speedily she was once more asleep. Having aroused her, I put the instrument on the second finger of her left hand, and told the doctor that it would be found she could *Not* go to sleep, when it was placed there. He said he thought she would, and he sat steadily gazing at her, but I said firmly and confidently that she would not. After a considerable time the doctor asked her if she did not feel sleepy, to which she replied 'not at all;' could you rise and walk? when she told him she could. I then requested her to look at the point of the forefinger of her right hand, which I told the doctor would send her to sleep, and such was the result; and, after being aroused, I desired her to keep a steady gaze at the nail of the thumb of the left hand which could send her to sleep in like manner, and such proved to be the fact.

Having repaired to another room, I explained to the doctor the real nature and powers of my little and apparently magical instrument – that it was nothing more than my portmanteau-key and ring, and that what had imparted to it such apparently varied powers was merely the predictions which the patient had overheard me make to him, acting upon her in the peculiar state of the nervous sleep, as irresistible impulses to be affected, according to the results she had heard me predict.

Braid ends his whole discussion as follows:

In conclusion, I beg particularly to remark, that, whilst my experiments and observations are opposed to the theoretical notions of Baron Reichenbach and the mesmerists, in all the more important points, they directly confirm the reality of the facts, as to the power which we possess of artificially producing certain phenomena by certain processes; as also of intensifying aspects which arise in a minor degree, spontaneously, or by the patient's own unaided efforts. They allege that the exciting cause is the impulsion into the body of the patient from without of a portion of this new force; whilst I attribute it to a subjective or personal influence, namely, that of the mind and body of the patient acting and re-acting on each other in a particular manner, from an intense concentration of inward consciousness of one idea, or train of ideas, which may, to a certain extent, be controlled and directed by others. The latter power, however, merely arises from the mental and physical impressions producing still greater concentration of the patient's attention in a particular direction; that is to say, by concentrating their attention to the point over which they see anything drawn, or upon which a mechanical, calorific, frigorific, or electric impression is made, whereby a greater supply of nervous influence, blood, and vital action, is drawn to the part from the physical and mental resources of the patient himself, and not from the person or substance exciting those physical impressions. They enable the patient more effectually to concentrate his own vital powers, and thus to energize function; on the same principle as a patient afflicted with anaesthesia, or loss of feeling, is able to hold an object in his hand whilst he looks at it, but will allow it to drop when his eyes are averted.

It is worthy of particular remark, that my researches prove the power of concentration of attention, as not only capable of changing physical action, so as to make some patients, in the wide-waking state, imagine that they see and feel from an external influence what is due entirely to an internal or mental cause; but I have extended the researches, so as to prove that the same law obtains in respect to all the other organs of special sense, and different functions of the body. My theoretical views, therefore, instead of diminishing, rather enhance the value of this power as a means of cure. They strikingly prove how much may be achieved by proper attention to, and direction of, this power of the human mind over the physical frame, and vice versa, in ameliorating the ills which flesh is heir to. I beg further to remark, in support of my views, that in the experiments of Baron Reichenbach, and the mesmerists generally, all which I have endeavoured to prove as unnecessary for the production of the phenomena referred to is their alleged mesmeric fluid, or new force; of the latter, there is under such circumstances, as yet no direct and satisfactory proof; and it is unphilosophical to attribute to a new and extraneous force what can be reasonably accounted for from the independent physical and psychiatric powers of the patient, which must necessarily be in active operation.

The results of my experiments satisfactorily prove the efficacy of the mind and the remarkable power of the soul over the body.

REFERENCES

Binet, Alfred, and Féré, Charles. *Animal Magnetism*. London: Kegan Paul, 1887

Boring, E. G. *History of Experimental Psychology*. New York and London: Century, 1950, Chap. 7 and references

Braid, James. 'The Power of the Mind over the Body.' London: John Churchill, 1846. Quoted more fully in Dennis, Wayne. *Readings in the History of Psychology*. New York: Appleton-Century-Crofts, 1948

JOHN STUART MILL

1806–1873

JOHN STUART MILL was born in London and was the precocious son of James Mill, whose methods of education are reflected in John Stuart's *Autobiography*. Technically J. S. Mill was neither a professional philosopher nor a psychologist. He was associated with the East India Company for 35 years, in contact with current administrative and diplomatic issues. In the intervals, and after the dissolution of the Company in 1858, Mill wrote on a wide range of topics within philosophy and political and social economy.

The following extract from Mill's *A System of Logic* illustrates his treatment of body-mind problems. His grip on the philosophical issues involved can be fully realized only if the chapter is taken as a whole. The reader will note, among other points, the clear challenge Mill presents to the old assumption that cause and effect must resemble each other in some sense. His discussion could lead us into the difficult problem of the nature of explanation in psychology to which we have referred (p. 178) but whose full consideration lies outside the scope of this book.

From A SYSTEM OF LOGIC

... A part of our notion of a body consists of the notion of a number of sensations of our own, or of other sentient beings, habitually occurring simultaneously. My conception of the table at which I am writing is compounded of its visible form and size, which are complex sensations of sight; its tangible form and size, which are complex sensations of our organs of touch and of our muscles; its weight, which is also a sensation of touch and of the muscles; its colour, which is a sensation of sight; its hardness, which is a sensation of the muscles; its composition, which is another word for all the varieties of sensation which we receive under various circumstances from the wood of which it is made, and so forth. All or most of these various sensations frequently are, and, as we learn by experience, always might be, experienced simultaneously, or in many different orders of succession at our own choice: and hence the thought of any one of them makes us think of the others, and the whole becomes mentally amalgamated into one mixed state of consciousness. . . .

There is not the slightest reason for believing that what we call the sensible qualities of the object are a type of anything inherent in itself, or bear any affinity to its own nature. A cause does not, as such, resemble its effects; an east wind is not like the feeling of cold, nor heat like the steam of boiling water. Why then should matter resemble our sensations? Why should the inmost nature of fire and water resemble the impressions made by those objects upon our senses? Or on what principle are we authorized to deduce from the effects, anything concerning the cause, except that it is a cause adequate to produce those effects? It may, therefore, safely be laid down as a truth both obvious in itself, and admitted by all whom it is at present necessary to take into consideration, that, of the outward world, we know and can know absolutely nothing, except the sensations which we experience from it.

Body having now been defined as the external cause, and (according to the more reasonable opinion) the unknown external cause, to which we refer our sensations; it remains to frame a definition of Mind. Nor, after the preceding observations, will this be difficult. For, as our conception of a body is that of an unknown exciting cause of sensations, so our conception of a mind is that of an unknown recipient, or percipient, of them; and not of them alone, but of all our other feelings. As body is understood to be the mysterious something which excites the mind to feel, so mind is the mysterious something which feels and thinks. It is unnecessary to give in the case of mind, as we gave in the case of matter, a particular statement of the sceptical system by which its existence as a Thing in itself, distinct from the series of what are denominated its states, is called in question. But it is necessary to remark, that on the inmost nature (whatever be meant by inmost nature) of the thinking principle, as well as on the inmost nature of matter, we are, and with our faculties must always remain, entirely in the dark. All which we are aware of, even in our own minds, is (in the words of James Mill) a certain 'thread of consciousness'; a series of feelings, that is, of sensations, thoughts, emotions, and volitions, more or less numerous and complicated. There is something I call Myself, or, by another form of expression, my mind, which I consider as distinct from these sensations, thoughts, &c.; a something which I conceive to be not the thoughts, but the being that has the thoughts, and which I can conceive as existing for ever in a state of quiescence, without any thoughts at all. But what this being is, though it is myself, I have no knowledge, other than the series of its states of consciousness. As bodies manifest themselves to me only through the sensations of which I regard them as the causes, so the thinking principle, or mind, in my own nature, makes itself known to me only by the feelings of which it is conscious. I know nothing about myself, save my capacities of feeling or being conscious (including, of course, thinking and willing): and were I to learn anything new concerning my own nature, I cannot with my present faculties conceive this new information to be anything else, than that I have some additional capacities, as yet unknown to me, of feeling, thinking, or willing.

Thus, then, as body is the unsentient cause to which we are naturally prompted to refer a certain portion of our feelings, so mind may be described as the sentient *subject* (in the scholastic sense of the term) of all feelings; that which has or feels them. But of the nature of either body or mind, further than the feelings which the former excites, and which the latter experiences, we do not, according to the best existing doctrine, know anything; and if anything, logic has nothing to do with it, or with the manner in which the knowledge is acquired.

REFERENCE

Mill, John Stuart. *A System of Logic Ratiocinative and Inductive.* London: Longmans, 8th Edn. Reprinted 1904, pp. 36–7, 39–40

EWALD HERING

1834–1918

HERING was born in Saxony. He practised medicine in Leipzig and lectured in physiology at the University. From 1865 to 1870 he was Professor of Physiology in Vienna, and the address, part of which is quoted below, was given at the Anniversary Meeting of the Imperial Academy of Sciences in Vienna on 30 May, 1870. Hering moved to Prague, also as Professor of Physiology, in 1870 and he stayed until 1893, thereafter returning to Leipzig. He is best known to psychologists for his work on colour vision. In relation to modern treatments of perception, however, there is considerable historical interest in the arguments, between Helmholtz and Wundt on the one hand and Hering on the other, about the relative contributions of genetic development and native endowment to our modes of sensory perception (Boring).

Über das Gedächtnis was translated by Samuel Butler who appreciated Hering as much as he was infuriated by Von Hartmann's more ponderous and metaphysical speculations on the same subject. Some of these, nevertheless, Butler also brought himself to translate, and the extracts are also available in the reference cited below.

From ON MEMORY

I hope to show how far psychological investigations also afford not only permissible, but indispensable, aid to physiological inquiries.

Consciousness is an accompaniment of that animal and human organization and of that material mechanism which it is the province of physiology to explore; and as long as the atoms of the brain follow their due course according to certain definite laws, there arises an inner life which springs from sensation and idea, from feeling and will.

We feel this in our own cases; it strikes us in our converse with other people; we can see it plainly in the more highly organized animals; even the lowest forms of life bear traces of it;

and who can draw a line in the kingdom of organic life, and say that it is here the soul ceases?

With what eyes, then, is physiology to regard this two-fold life of the organized world? Shall she close them entirely to one whole side of it, that she may fix them more intently on the other?

So long as the physiologist is content to be a physicist, and nothing more – using the word 'physicist' in its widest signification – his position in regard to the organic world is one of extreme but legitimate one-sidedness. As the crystal to the mineralogist or the vibrating string to the acoustician, so from this point of view both man and the lower animals are to the physiologist neither more nor less than the matter of which they consist. That animals feel desire and repugnance, that the material mechanism of the human frame is in close connexion with emotions of pleasure or pain, and with the active idea-life of consciousness – this cannot, in the eyes of the physicist, make the animal or human body into anything more than what it actually is. To him it is a combination of matter, subjected to the same inflexible laws as stones and plants – a material combination, the outward and inward movements of which interact as cause and effect, and are in as close connexion with each other and with their surroundings as the working of a machine with the revolutions of the wheels that compose it.

Neither sensation, nor idea, nor yet conscious will, can form a link in this chain of material occurrences which make up the physical life of an organism. If I am asked a question and reply to it, the material process which the nerve fibre conveys from the organ of hearing to the brain must travel through my brain as an actual and material process before it can reach the nerves which will act upon my organs of speech. It cannot, on reaching a given place in the brain, change then and there into an immaterial something, and turn up again some time afterwards in another part of the brain as a material process. The traveller in the desert might as well hope, before he again goes forth into the wilderness of reality, to take rest and refreshment in the oasis with which the *Fata Morgana* illudes him; or as well might a prisoner hope to escape from his prison through a door reflected in a mirror.

So much for the physiologist in his capacity of pure physicist. As long as he remains behind the scenes in painful exploration of the details of the machinery – as long as he only observes the action of the players from behind the stage – so long will he miss the spirit of the performance, which is, nevertheless, caught easily by one who sees it from the front. May he not, then, for once in a way, be allowed to change his standpoint? True, he came not to see the representation of an imaginary world; he is in search of the actual; but surely it must help him to a comprehension of the dramatic apparatus itself, and of the manner in which it is worked, if he were to view its action from in front as well as from behind, or at least allow himself to hear what sober-minded spectators can tell him upon the subject.

There can be no question as to the answer; and hence it comes that psychology is such an indispensable help to physiology, whose fault it only in small part is that she has hitherto made such little use of this assistance; for psychology has been late in beginning to till her fertile field with the plough of the inductive method, and it is only from ground so tilled that fruits can spring which can be of service to physiology.

If, then, the student of nervous physiology takes his stand between the physicist and the psychologist, and if the first of these rightly makes the unbroken causative continuity of all material processes an axiom of his system of investigation, the prudent psychologist, on the other hand, will investigate the laws of conscious life according to the inductive method, and will hence, as much as the physicist, make the existence of fixed laws his initial assumption. If, again, the most superficial introspection teaches the physiologist that his conscious life is dependent upon the mechanical adjustments of his body, and that inversely his body is subjected with certain limitations to his will, then it only remains for him to make one assumption more, namely, *that this mutual interdependence between the spiritual and the material is itself also dependent on law*, and he has discovered the bond by which the science of matter and the science of consciousness are united into a single whole.

Thus regarded, the phenomena of consciousness become functions of the material changes of organized substance, and inversely – though this is involved in the use of the word 'function' – the material processes of brain substance become functions of the phenomena of consciousness. For when two variables are so dependent upon one another in the changes they undergo in accordance with fixed laws that a change in either involves simultaneous and corresponding change in the other, the one is called a function of the other.

This, then, by no means implies that the two variables above-named – matter and consciousness – stand in the relation of cause and effect, antecedent and consequence, to one another. For on this subject we know nothing. The materialist regards consciousness as a product or result of matter, while the idealist holds matter to be a result of consciousness, and a third maintains that matter and spirit are identical; with all this the physiologist, as such, has nothing whatever to do; his sole concern is with the fact that matter and consciousness are functions one of the other.

By the help of this hypothesis of the functional inter-dependence of matter and spirit, modern physiology is enabled to bring the phenomena of consciousness within the domain of her investigations without leaving the *terra firma* of scientific methods. The physiologist, as physicist, can follow the ray of light and the wave of sound or heat till they reach the organ of sense. He can watch them entering upon the ends of the nerves, and finding their way to the cells of the brain by means of the series of undulations or vibrations which they establish in the nerve filaments. Here, however, he loses all trace of them. On the other hand, still looking with the eyes of a pure physicist, he sees sound-waves of speech issue from the mouth of a speaker; he observes the motion of his own limbs, and finds how this is conditional upon muscular contractions occasioned by the motor nerves, and how these nerves are in their turn excited by the cells of the central organ. But here again his knowledge comes to an end. True, he sees indications of the bridge which is to carry him from excitation of the sensory to that of the motor nerves in the labyrinth of intricately inter-woven nerve cells, but he knows nothing of the inconceivably complex process which is introduced at this stage. Here the physiologist will change his standpoint; what matter will not reveal to his inquiry, he will find in the mirror, as it were, of consciousness; by way of a reflection, indeed, only, but a reflection, nevertheless, which stands in intimate relation to the object of his inquiry. When at this point he observes how one idea gives rise to another, how closely idea is connected with sensation and sensation with will, and how thought, again, and feeling are inseparable from one another, he will be compelled to suppose corresponding successions of material processes, which generate and are closely connected with one another, and which attend the whole machinery of conscious life, according to the law of the functional interdependence of matter and consciousness.

After this explanation I shall venture to regard under a single aspect a great series of phenomena which apparently have nothing to do with one another, and which belong partly to the conscious and partly to the unconscious life of organized beings. I shall regard them as the outcome of one and the same primary force of organized matter – namely, its memory or power of reproduction.

The word 'memory' is often understood as though it meant nothing more than our faculty of intentionally reproducing ideas or series of ideas. But when the figures and events of bygone days rise up again unbidden in our minds, is not this also an act of recollection or memory? We have a perfect right to extend our conception of memory so as to make it embrace involuntary reproductions of sensations, ideas, perceptions, and efforts; but we find on having done so, that we have so far enlarged her boundaries that she proves to be an ultimate and original power, the source, and at the same time the unifying bond, of our whole conscious life.

We know that when an impression, or a series of impressions, has been made upon our senses for a long time, and always in the same way, it may come to impress itself in such a manner upon the so-called sense-memory that hours afterwards, and though a hundred other things have occupied our attention meanwhile, it will yet return suddenly to our consciousness with all the force and freshness of the original sensation. A whole group of sensations is sometimes reproduced in its due sequence as regards time and space, with so much reality that it illudes us, as though things were actually present which have long ceased to be so. We have here a striking proof of the fact that after both conscious sensation and perception have been extinguished, their material vestiges yet remain in our nervous system by way of a change in its molecular or atomic disposition, that enables the nerve substance to reproduce all the physical processes of the original sensation, and with these the corresponding psychical processes of sensation and perception.

Every hour the phenomena of sense-memory are present with each one of us, but in a less degree than this. We are all at times aware of a host of more or less faded recollections of earlier impressions, which we either summon intentionally or which come upon us involuntarily. Visions of absent people come and go before us as faint and fleeting shadows, and the notes of long-forgotten melodies float around us, not actually heard, but yet perceptible.

Some things and occurrences, especially if they have happened to us only once and hurriedly, will be reproducible by the memory in respect only of a few conspicuous qualities; in other cases those details alone will recur to us which we have met with elsewhere, and for the reception of which the brain is, so to speak, attuned. These last recollections find themselves in fuller accord with our consciousness, and enter upon it more easily and energetically; hence also their aptitude for reproduction is enhanced; so that what is common to many things, and is therefore felt and perceived with exceptional frequency, becomes reproduced so easily that eventually the actual presence of the corresponding external *stimuli* is no longer necessary, and it will recur on the vibrations set up by faint *stimuli* from within. Sensations arising in this way from within, as, for example, an idea of whiteness, are not, indeed, perceived with the full freshness of those raised by the actual presence of white light without us, but they are of the same kind; they are feeble repetitions of one and the same material brain process – of one and the same conscious sensation. Thus the idea of whiteness arises in our mind as a faint, almost extinct, sensation.

In this way those qualities which are common to many things become separated, as it were, in our memory from the objects with which they were originally associated, and attain an independent existence in our consciousness as *ideas* and *conceptions*, and thus the whole rich superstructure of our ideas and conceptions is built up from materials supplied by memory.

On examining more closely, we see plainly that memory is a faculty not only of our conscious states, but also, and much more so, of our unconscious ones. I was conscious of this or that yesterday, and am again conscious of it to-day. Where has it been meanwhile? It does not remain continuously within my consciousness, nevertheless it returns after having quitted it. Our ideas tread but for a moment upon the stage of consciousness, and then go back again behind the scenes, to make way for others in their place. As the player is only a king when he is on the stage, so they too exist as ideas so long only as they are recognized. How do they live when they are off the stage? For we know that they are living somewhere; give them their cue and they reappear immediately. They do not exist continuously as ideas; what is continuous is the special disposition of nerve substance in virtue of which this substance gives out to-day the same sound which it gave yesterday if it is rightly struck. Countless reproductions of organic processes of our brain connect themselves orderly together, so that one acts as a stimulus to the next, but a phenomenon of consciousness is not necessarily attached to every link in the chain. From this it arises that a series of ideas may appear to disregard the order that would be observed in purely material processes of brain substance unaccompanied by consciousness; but on the other hand it becomes possible for a long chain of recollections to have its due development without each link in the chain being necessarily perceived by ourselves. One may emerge from the bosom of our unconscious thoughts without fully entering upon the stage of conscious perception; another dies away in unconsciousness, leaving no successor to take its place. Between the 'me' of to-day and the 'me' of yesterday lie night and sleep, abysses of unconsciousness; nor is there any bridge but memory with which to span them. Who can hope after this to disentangle the infinite intricacy of our inner life? For we can only follow its threads so far as they have strayed over within the bounds of consciousness. We might as well hope to familiarize ourselves with the world of forms that teem within the bosom of the sea by observing the few that now and again come to the surface and soon return into the deep.

The bond of union, therefore, which connects the individual phenomena of our consciousness lies in our unconscious world; and as we know nothing of this but what investigation into the laws of matter teach us – as, in fact, for purely experimental purposes, 'matter' and the 'unconscious' must be one and the same thing – so the physiologist has a full right to denote memory as, in the wider sense of the word, a function of brain substance, whose results, it is true, fall, as regards one part of them, into the domain of consciousness, while another and not less essential part escapes unperceived as purely material processes.

*

An organized being, therefore, stands before us a product of the unconscious memory of organized matter, which, ever increasing and ever dividing itself, ever assimilating new matter and returning it in changed shape to the inorganic world, ever receiving some new thing into its memory, and transmitting its acquisitions by the way of reproduction, grows continually richer and richer the longer it lives.

*

The brain processes and phenomena of consciousness which ennoble man in the eyes of his fellows, have had a less ancient history than those connected with his physical needs. Hunger and the reproductive instinct affected the oldest and simplest forms of the organic world. It is in respect of these instincts, therefore, and of the means to gratify them, that the memory of organized substance is strongest – the impulses and instincts that arise hence having still paramount power over the minds of men. The spiritual life has been superadded slowly; its most splendid outcome belongs to the latest epoch in the history of organized matter, nor has any very great length of time elapsed since the nervous system was first crowned with the glory of a large and well-developed brain.

Oral tradition and written history have been called the memory of man, and this is not without its truth. But there is another and a living memory in the innate reproductive power of brain substance, and without this both writings and oral tradition would be without significance to posterity. The most sublime ideas, though never so immortalized in speech or letters, are yet nothing for heads that are out of harmony with them; they must be not only heard, but reproduced; and both speech and writing would be in vain were there not an inheritance of inward and outward brain development, growing in correspondence with the inheritance of ideas that are handed down from age to age, and did not an enhanced capacity for their reproduction on the part of each succeeding generation accompany the thoughts that have been preserved in writing. Man's conscious memory comes to an end at death, but the unconscious memory of Nature is true and ineradicable: whoever succeeds in stamping upon her the impress of his work, she will remember him to the end of time.

REFERENCE

Hering, Ewald. 'On Memory as a Universal Function of Organized Matter'. Trans. by Samuel Butler in *Unconscious Memory*. London: Fifield, 1920, pp. 64–8, 68–72, 80–1, 85–6

WILHELM WUNDT

1832–1920

WUNDT was born in Baden and studied at Tübingen and Heidelberg, starting as a physiologist and qualifying also in medicine. He became assistant in a Heidelberg medical clinic but in 1856 turned once more to physiology, working initially under Johannes Müller in Berlin. In 1857 he returned, as Dozent in physiology, to Heidelberg where Helmholtz was appointed professor in 1858. Until 1871, when Helmholtz went to Berlin, they worked in the same department, Wundt slowly changing from an experimental physiologist, with wide interests in philosophy and anthropology, to an experimental psychologist. Wundt stayed at Heidelberg till 1874 with Helmholtz's successor Kühne, and then moved to Zurich. By this time he had published the *Beiträge zur Theorie der Sinnes Wahrnehmung* (1858–62), which foreshadowed his later development of experimental psychology, and also the *Grundzüge der physiologischen Psychologie* (1873–4). In arguing for psychology to be placed on a scientific basis Wundt, like Fechner, seems to have been influenced by Herbart, even though he was in a different tradition.

In 1875 Wundt went to Leipzig as Professor of Philosophy. There in 1879 he founded the first psychological laboratory to be dignified by the German administrative status of 'Institut'. His first (self-appointed) assistant was James McKeen Cattell who, as Boring recounts, insisted on studying individual differences and was regarded by Wundt as 'ganz americanisch'. For a further account of Wundt's long tenure of office at Leipzig and of his many publications the reader should consult, initially, Boring, Flügel, and Humphrey.

The following extract from *Grundriss der Psychologie*, first published in 1896, shows Wundt dealing with body and mind in the course of attempting to identify the distinctive approach of psychology. It is interesting to compare his comments with those of John Stuart Mill and with the British psychologist Ward's influential article in the *Encyclopaedia Britannica* for 1886. In Ward's hands psychology came to be described as 'the scientific study of individual experience'.

The reader can also see, below, something of the use Wundt makes of 'processes'. According to Allport in 1940, American thinking moved away from this concept, at any rate for a while. In British psychology, while most of Wundt's somewhat intellectualist and narrowly experimental attitude was modified, thinking in terms of 'processes' entrenched itself steadily at the expense of 'entities'. It has been suggested by Professor Mace that 'a person' is the only noun needed in modern British psychology.

From OUTLINES OF PSYCHOLOGY

The expressions outer experience and inner experience do not indicate different objects, but *different points of view* from which we take up the consideration and scientific treatment of a unitary experience. We are naturally led to these points of view, because every concrete experience immediately divides into *two factors*: into a *content* presented to us, and our *apprehension* of this content. We call the first of these factors *objects of experience*, the second, *experiencing subject*. This division indicates two directions for the treatment of experience. One is that of the *natural sciences*, which concern themselves with the *objects* of experience, thought of as independent of the subject. The other is that of *psychology*, which investigates the whole content of experience in its relations to the subject and also in regard to the attributes which this content derives directly from the subject. The point of view of natural science may, accordingly, be designated as that of *mediate experience*, since it is possible only after abstracting from the subjective factor present in all actual experience; the point of view of psychology, on the other hand, may be designated as that of *immediate experience*, since it purposely does away with this abstraction and all its consequences.

*

When the concept of actuality is adopted, one of the questions on which metaphysical systems of psychology have long been divided is immediately disposed of. This is the question of the *relation of body and mind*. So long as body and mind are both regarded as substances, this relation must remain an enigma in whatever way the two concepts of substance are defined. If they are like substances, then the different contents of experience as dealt with in the natural sciences and in psychology can no longer be understood, and there is no alternative but to deny the independence of one of these forms of knowledge. If they are unlike substances, their connexion is a continual miracle. If we start with the theory of the actuality of mind, we recognize the immediate reality of the phenomena in psychological experience. Our physiological concept of the bodily organism, on the other hand, is nothing but a part of this experience, which we gain, just as we do all the other empirical contents of the natural sciences, by assuming the existence of an object independent of the knowing subject. Certain components of mediate experience may correspond to certain components of immediate experience, without there being any necessity of reducing the one component to the other or of deriving one from the other. In fact, such a derivation is absolutely impossible because of the totally different points of view adopted in the two cases. Since we have here, not different objects of experience, but different points of view in looking at a unitary experience, there must be at every point a thorough-going relation between the two modes of treatment adopted in the natural sciences and in psychology. It is, furthermore, obvious that the natural sciences never exhaust the total contents of reality, there are always a number of important facts which can be approached only directly, or in psychological experience; these are all the contents of our subjective consciousness which do not have the character of ideational objects, that is, are not directly referred to external objects. This includes our whole world of feeling so long as this world is considered entirely from the point of view of its subjective significance.

The principle that all those contents of experience which belong at the same time to the mediate or natural scientific sphere of treatment and to the immediate or psychological sphere, are related to each other in such a way that every elementary process on the psychical side has a corresponding elementary process on the physical side, is known as the *principle of psycho-physical parallelism*. It has an empirico-psychological significance and is thus totally different from certain metaphysical principles which have sometimes been designated by the same name, but which have in reality an entirely different meaning. These metaphysical principles are all based on the hypothesis of a psychical substance. They all seek to solve the problem of the interrelation of body and mind, either by assuming *two* real substances with attributes which are different, but parallel in their changes, or by assuming *one* substance with two distinct attributes which correspond in their modifications. In both these cases the metaphysical principle of parallelism is based on the assumption that every physical process has a corresponding psychical process and vice versa, or on the assumption that the mental world is a mirroring of the bodily world, or that the bodily world is an objective realization of the mental. This assumption is, however, entirely indemonstrable and leads in its psychological application to an intellectualism which is contradictory to all experience. The psychological principle of parallelism, on the other hand, as above formulated, starts with the assumption that there is only *one* experience, which, however, as soon as it becomes the subject of scientific analysis, is, in some of its components, open to *two* different kinds of scientific treatment, to a mediate form of treatment, which investigates ideated objects in their objective relations to one another, and to an *immediate* form, which investigates the same objects in their directly known character, and in their relations to all the other contents of the experience of the knowing subject.

REFERENCES

Allport, G. W. 'The Psychologist's Frame of Reference', *Psychological Bulletin*. Vol. 37, 1940, pp. 1–28

Boring, E. G. *A History of Experimental Psychology*. New York and London: Century, 1929. Chap. 15

Flügel, J. C. *A Hundred Years of Psychology*. London: Duckworth, Revised Edn. 1948

Humphrey, George. *Thinking*. An Introduction to Experimental Psychology. London: Methuen, 1952

Wundt, Wilhelm. *Grundriss der Psychologie*. Translated as *Outlines of Psychology* by C. H. Judd. Leipzig: Wilhelm Engelmann. London: Williams and Norgate, 3rd Revised English Edn. from the 7th Revised German Edn. 1907, pp. 2, 363–5

WILLIAM JAMES

1842–1910

WILLIAM JAMES was born in New York and died at Chocorna, New Hampshire, after 78 years of responsive living, varied interests, and of being almost universally beloved. He achieved education by family stimulus and in Paris, Boulogne, Rhode Island, Geneva, and Bonn. He thought of becoming a painter, studied chemistry and the biological sciences at Harvard, and there after various interruptions he qualified in medicine in 1869. After illness and further travels in Europe, James returned to the United States and in 1872 was appointed Instructor in Physiology at Harvard. By 1876 he was lecturing on physiological psychology. In 1880 he became Assistant Professor in Physiology and in 1885 Professor of Philosophy. With occasional intervals he lectured at Harvard till 1907, the year of his retirement from university work. He travelled again in Europe, returning home to America just before he died.

James started the *Principles of Psychology* in 1878; it was published in 1890. While this was James' major text-book, it is only one of many publications which it is still a pleasure to read. James wrote, says Professor Mace, 'as though he supposed that human nature was a matter of interest to human beings, not merely as a "proper" but as an irresistible study for mankind.'

The first extract below introduces James thinking in terms of processes and persons. It is followed by part of his discussion of the 'self'. This should give pause to anyone tempted to identify too hurriedly with an oversimplified 'body' or 'mind'.

From PRINCIPLES OF PSYCHOLOGY

We now begin our study of the mind from within. Most books start with sensations, as the simplest mental facts, and proceed synthetically, constructing each higher stage from those below it. But this is abandoning the empirical method of investigation. No one ever had a simple sensation by itself. Consciousness, from our natal day, is of a teeming multiplicity of objects and relations, and what we call simple sensations are results of discriminative attention, pushed often to a very high degree. It is astonishing what havoc is wrought in psychology by admitting at the outset apparently innocent suppositions, that nevertheless contain a flaw. The bad consequences develop themselves later on, and are irremediable, being woven through the whole texture of the work. The notion that sensations, being the simplest things, are the first things to take up in psychology is one of these suppositions. The only thing which psychology has a right to postulate at the outset is the fact of thinking itself, and that must first be taken up and analysed. If sensations then prove to be amongst the elements of the thinking, we shall be no worse off as respects them than if we had taken them for granted at the start.

The first fact for us, then, as psychologists, is that thinking of some sort goes on. I use the word thinking . . . for every form of consciousness indiscriminately. If we could say in English 'it thinks', as we say 'it rains' or 'it blows', we should be stating the fact most simply and with the minimum of assumption. As we cannot, we must simply say that *thought goes on.*

Five Characters in Thought

How does it go on? We notice immediately five important characters in the process, of which it shall be the duty of the present chapter to treat in a general way:

(1) Every thought tends to be part of a personal consciousness.

(2) Within each personal consciousness thought is always changing.

(3) Within each personal consciousness thought is sensibly continuous.

(4) It always appears to deal with objects independent of itself.

(5) It is interested in some parts of these objects to the exclusion of others, and welcomes or rejects – *chooses* from among them, in a word – all the while.

In considering these five points successively, we shall have to plunge *in medias res* as regards our vocabulary, and use psychological terms which can only be adequately defined in later chapters of the book. But every one knows what the terms mean in a rough way; and it is only in a rough way that we are now to take them. This chapter is like a painter's first charcoal sketch upon his canvas, in which no niceties appear.

Thought tends to Personal Form

When I say *every thought is part of a personal consciousness*, 'personal consciousness' is one of the terms in question. Its meaning we know so long as no one asks us to define it, but to give an accurate account of it is the most difficult of philosophical tasks. This task we must confront in the next chapter; here a preliminary word will suffice.

In this room – this lecture-room, say – there are a multitude of thoughts, yours and mine, some of which cohere mutually, and some not. They are as little each-for-itself and reciprocally independent as they are all-belonging-together. They are neither: no one of them is separate, but each belongs with certain others and with none beside. My thought belongs with my other thoughts, and your thought with your other thoughts. Whether anywhere in the room there be a mere thought, which is nobody's thought, we have no means of ascertaining, for we have no experience of its like. The only states of consciousness that we naturally deal with are found in personal consciousnesses, minds, selves, concrete particular I's and you's.

Each of these minds keeps its own thoughts to itself. There is no giving or bartering between them. No thought even comes into direct *sight* of a thought in another personal consciousness than its own. Absolute insulation, irreducible pluralism, is the law. It seems as if the elementary psychic fact were not *thought* or *this thought* or *that thought*, but *my thought*, every thought being *owned*. Neither contemporaneity, nor proximity in space, nor similarity of quality and content are able to fuse thoughts together which are sundered by this barrier of belonging to different personal minds. The breaches between such thoughts are the most absolute breaches in nature. Everyone will recognize this to be true, so long as the existence of *something* corresponding to the term 'personal mind' is all that is insisted on, without any particular view of its nature being implied. On these terms the personal self rather than the thought might be treated as the immediate datum in psychology. The universal conscious fact is not 'feelings and thoughts exist', but 'I think' and 'I feel'. No psychology, at any rate, can question the *existence* of personal selves. The worst a psychology can do is so to interpret the nature of these selves as to rob them of their worth. A French writer, speaking of our ideas, says somewhere in a fit of anti-spiritualistic excitement that, misled by certain peculiarities which they display, we 'end by personifying' the procession which they make, – such personification being regarded by him as a great philosophic blunder on our part. It could only be a blunder if the notion of personality meant something essentially different from anything to be found in the mental procession. But if that procession be itself the very 'original' of the notion of personality, to personify it cannot possibly be wrong. It is already personified. There are no marks of personality to be gathered *aliunde*, and then found lacking in the train of thought. It has them all already; so that to whatever farther analysis we may subject that form of personal selfhood under which thoughts appear, it is, and must remain, true that the thoughts which psychology studies do continually tend to appear as parts of personal selves.

I say 'tend to appear' rather than 'appear', on account of those facts of sub-conscious personality, automatic writing, etc., of which we studied a few in the last chapter. The buried feelings and thoughts proved now to exist in hysterical anaesthetics, in recipients of post-hypnotic suggestion, etc., themselves are parts of *secondary personal selves*. These selves are for the most part very stupid and contracted, and are cut off at ordinary times from communication with the regular and normal self of the individual; but still they form conscious unities, have continuous memories, speak, write, invent distinct names for themselves, or adopt names that are suggested; and, in short, are entirely worthy of that title of secondary personalities which is now commonly given them. According to M. Janet these secondary personalities are always abnormal, and result from the splitting of what ought to be a single complete self into two parts, of which one lurks in the background whilst the other appears on the surface as the only self the man or woman has. For our present purpose it is unimportant whether this account of the origin of secondary selves is applicable to all possible cases of them or not, for it is certainly true of a large number of them. Now although the *size* of a secondary self thus formed will depend on the number of thoughts that are thus split-off from the main consciousness, the *form* of it tends to personality, and the later thoughts pertaining to it remember the earlier ones and adopt them as their own. M. Janet caught the actual moment of inspissation (so to speak) of one of these secondary personalities in his anaesthetic somnambulist Lucie. He found that when this young woman's attention was absorbed in conversation with a third party, her anaesthetic hand would write simple answers to questions whispered to her by himself. 'Do your hear?' he asked. '*No*', was the unconsciously written reply. 'But to answer you must hear.' ' *Yes, quite so.*' 'Then how do you manage?' '*I don't know.*' 'There must be some one who hears me.' '*Yes.*' 'Who?' '*Someone other than Lucie.*' 'Ah! another person. Shall we give her a name?' '*No.*' 'Yes, it will be more convenient.' '*Well, Adrienne, then.*'

The Consciousness of Self

In Chapter x of the *Principles of Psychology* James is led on to discuss first (i) the self as known or 'empirical me' and then (ii) the self as 'a unifying principle'. Those 'selves' listed under (*a*), (*b*), and (*c*) in the following passage belonging to the first and (*d*) belonging to the second.

The constituents of the Self may be divided into two classes, those which make up respectively –
   (*a*) The material Self;
   (*b*) The social Self;
   (*c*) The spiritual Self; and
   (*d*) The pure Ego.

(*a*) The body is the innermost part of *the material self* in each of us; and certain parts of the body seem more intimately ours than the rest. The clothes come next. The old saying that the human person is composed of three parts – soul, body, and clothes – is more than a joke. We so appropriate our clothes and identify ourselves with them that there are few of us who, if asked to choose between having a beautiful body clad in raiment perpetually shabby and unclean, and having an ugly and blemished form always spotlessly attired, would not hesitate a moment before making a decisive reply. Next, our immediate family is a part of ourselves. Our father and mother, our wife and babes, are bone of our bone and flesh of our flesh. When they die, a part of our very selves is gone. If they do anything wrong, it is our shame. If they are insulted, our anger flashes forth as readily as if we stood in their place. Our home comes next. Its scenes are part of our life; its aspects awaken the tenderest feelings of affection; and we do not easily forgive the stranger who, in visiting it, finds fault with its arrangements or treats it with contempt. . . .

(*b*) *A man's social Self* is the recognition which he gets from his mates. We are not only gregarious animals, liking to be in sight of our fellows, but we have an innate propensity to get ourselves noticed, and noticed favourably, by our kind. No more fiendish punishment could be devised, were such a thing physically possible, than that one should be turned loose in society and remain absolutely unnoticed by all the members thereof. If no one turned round when we entered, answered when we spoke, or minded what we did, but if every person we met 'cut us dead', and acted as if we were non-existing things, a kind of rage and impotent despair would ere long well up in us, from which the cruellest bodily tortures would be a relief; for these would make us feel that, however bad might be our plight, we had not sunk to such a depth as to be unworthy of attention at all.

Properly speaking, *a man has as many social selves as there are individuals who recognize him* and carry an image of him in their mind. To wound any one of these his images is to wound him. But as the individuals who carry the images fall naturally into

classes, we may practically say that he has as many different
social selves as there are distinct *groups* of persons about whose
opinion he cares. He generally shows a different side of himself
to each of these different groups. Many a youth who is demure
enough before his parents and teachers, swears and swaggers
like a pirate among his 'tough' young friends. We do not show
ourselves to our children as to our club-companions, to our
customers as to the labourers we employ, to our own masters
and employers as to our intimate friends. From this there results
what practically is a division of the man into several selves and
this may be a discordant splitting, as where one is afraid to let
one set of his acquaintances know him as he is elsewhere; or it
may be a perfectly harmonious division of labour, as where one
tender to his children is stern to the soldiers or prisoners under
his command. . . .

(c) By the Spiritual Self, so far as it belongs to the Empirical Me, I mean a man's inner or subjective being, his psychic
faculties or dispositions, taken concretely; not the bare principle of personal Unity, or 'pure' Ego, which remains still to be
discussed. These psychic dispositions are the most enduring
and intimate part of the self, that which we most verily seem to
be. We take a purer self-satisfaction when we think of our
ability to argue and discriminate, of our moral sensibility and
conscience, of our indomitable will, than when we survey any
of our other possessions. Only when these are altered is a man
said to be *alienatus a se*. . . .

. . . Now, *what is this self of all the other selves?*
Probably all men would describe it in much the same way up to
a certain point. They would call it the *active* element in all
consciousness; saying that whatever qualities a man's feelings
may possess, or whatever content his thought may include,
there is a spiritual something in him which seems to *go out* to
meet these qualities and contents, whilst they seem to *come in*
to be received by it. It is what welcomes or rejects. It presides
over the perception of sensations, and by giving or withholding
its assent it influences the movements they tend to arouse. It is
the home of interest, – not the pleasant or the painful, not even
pleasure or pain, as such, but that within us to which pleasure

and pain, the pleasant and the painful speak. It is the source of effort and attention, and the place from which appear to emanate the fiats of the will. A physiologist who should reflect upon it in his own person could hardly help, I should think, connecting it more or less vaguely with the process by which ideas or incoming sensations are 'reflected' or pass over into outward acts. Not necessarily that it should *be* this process or the mere feeling of this process, but that it should be in some close way *related* to this process; for it plays a part analogous to it in the psychic life, being a sort of junction at which sensory ideas terminate and from which motor ideas proceed, and forming a kind of link between the two. Being more incessantly there than any other single element of the mental life, the other elements end by seeming to accrete round it and to belong to it. It becomes opposed to them as the permanent is opposed to the changing and inconstant. . . .

James in discussing his own experience of this 'self' finds subtle feelings of bodily activity to play an important part in such experience. The Material, Social and Spiritual Me's can clearly conflict, and James' account of this is not to be missed.

Rivalry and Conflict of the Different Selves

With most objects of desire, physical nature restricts our choice to but one of many represented goods, and even so it is here. I am often confronted by the necessity of standing by one of my empirical selves and relinquishing the rest. Not that I would not, if I could, be both handsome and fat and well dressed, and a great athlete, and make a million a year, be a wit, a *bon-vivant*, and a lady-killer, as well as a philosopher; a philanthropist, statesman, warrior, and African explorer, as well as a 'tone-poet' and saint. But the thing is simply impossible. The millionaire's work would run counter to the saint's; the *bon-vivant* and the philanthropist would trip each other up; the philosopher and the lady-killer could not well keep house in the same tenement of clay. Such different characters may conceivably at the outset of life be alike *possible* to a man. But to make any one of them actual, the rest must more or less be suppressed. So the seeker of his truest, strongest, deepest self must review the list carefully, and pick out the one on which to stake his salvation. All other selves thereupon become unreal, but the fortunes of this self are real. Its failures are real failures, its triumphs real triumphs, carrying shame and gladness with them. This is as strong an example as there is of that selective industry of the mind on which I insisted some pages back. Our thought, incessantly deciding, among many things of a kind, which ones for it shall be realities, here chooses one of many possible selves or characters, and forthwith reckons it no shame to fail in any of those not adopted expressly as its own.

I, who for the time have staked my all on being a psychologist, am mortified if others know much more psychology than I. But I am contented to wallow in the grossest ignorance of Greek. My deficiencies there give me no sense of personal humiliation at all. Had I 'pretensions' to be a linguist, it would have been just the reverse. So we have the paradox of a man shamed to death because he is only the second pugilist or the second oarsman in the world. That he is able to beat the whole population of the globe minus one is nothing; he has 'pitted' himself to beat that one; and as long as he doesn't do that nothing else counts. He is to his own regard as if he were not, indeed he *is* not.

Yonder puny fellow, however, whom every one can beat, suffers no chagrin about it, for he has long ago abandoned the attempt to 'carry that line', as the merchants say, of self at all. With no attempt there can be no failure; with no failure no humiliation. So our self-feeling in this world depends entirely on what we *back* ourselves to be and do. It is determined by the ratio of our actualities to our supposed potentialities; a fraction of which our pretensions are the denominator and the numerator our success: Thus,

$$\text{Self-esteem} = \frac{\text{Success}}{\text{Pretensions}}$$

Such a fraction may be increased as well by diminishing the denominator as by increasing the numerator. To give up pretensions is as blessed a relief as to get them gratified; and where disappointment is incessant and the struggle unending this is what men will always do. The history of evangelical theology, with its conviction of sin, its self-despair, and its abandonment of salvation by works, is the deepest of possible examples, but we meet others in every walk of life. There is the strangest lightness about the heart when one's nothingness in a particular line is once accepted in good faith. *All* is not bitterness in the lot of the lover sent away by the final inexorable 'No'. Many Bostonians, *crede experto* (and inhabitants of other cities, too, I fear), would be happier men and women to-day, if they could once for all abandon the notion of keeping up a Musical Self, and without shame let people hear them call a symphony a nuisance. How pleasant is the day when we give up striving to be young, – or slender! Thank God! we say, *those* illusions are gone. Everything added to the Self is a burden as well as a pride. A certain man who lost every penny during our civil war went and actually rolled in the dust, saying he had not felt so free and happy since he was born. . . .

When James turns to the pure ego, or self as principle of personal identity, he discusses the hypothesis of an immortal soul, the associationist solution and its difficulties, then the transcendentalist answer exemplified by Kant. Of the latter he comments, with what justice the reader must decide: 'The only service that transcendental egoism has done to psychology has been by its protest against Hume's "bundle" theory of mind. But this service has been ill performed; for the Egoists themselves, let them say what they will, believe in the bundle, and in their own system merely *tie it up* with their special transcendental string invented for that use alone.'

James' own solution, to which it is essential for the reader to refer, is to deny the discrete character of psychological experience from the start. He maintains that the current passing thought, bringing with it the antecedents in the stream of thought of which it is at least partly the product, is itself the thinker.

It is important to realize that James throughout his discussion of the self is trying to identify *that which can be studied*, or can assist in explanation, and therefore what is immediately relevant to the field of psychology. He was far too good a philosopher to make dogmatic assertions outside this field.

REFERENCES

James, William. *Principles of Psychology*. New York: Holt. London: Macmillan, 2 vols, 1890. Vol. I, pp. 224–8, 292, 293, 296, 297–8, 309–10

Knight, Margaret. *William James*. Harmondsworth: Penguin Books, 1954

Mace, C. A. See Knight, *supra*, Editorial Foreword

INDEX

Abelard, 59–60
Adrian, 152
Aesclepiades, 47
Alexander the Great, 43, 214
Allport, G. W., 385–6
Anselm, St, 58
Aquinas, St Thomas, 38, 39, 53, 63, *250–3*
Aristotle, 21, 30, 37–43, 108, 173, *214–28*
Artists and Sculptors, 13, 14, 52, 60, 61–2, 63–4, 66–8, 70–3, 77, 97, 101, 111, 132, 149, 172, *and plates*
aspect theories, 19, 152, 305–29, 385–8
associationism, 140, 152, 153, 346 ff.
Augustine, St, 48–9, 53, *245–9*
Averroes, 55, 63

Bacon, Francis, 97, 128, *273–81*
Bacon, Roger, 68
Bain, Alexander, 41, 155–6
Bartolomeus Anglicanus, 105
Bell, Sir Charles, 151
Berkeley, 18, 131, 133–4
Bernard, Claude, 156, 175
Bernheim, 162
Boring, E. G., 149 ff., 153, 162, 376
Bradley, 165
Braid, James, 162, *363–72*
Brentano, Franz, 162
Brett, G. S., 44, 142
Breuer, 162
Breughel, 14
Broca, 152
Brown, Robert, 151
Browne, Sir Thomas, 125–6
Butler, Joseph, 131, 136–8

Cabanis, 131, 142
Caelius Aurelianus, 47
Caraffa, Pope Paul IV, 90, 172
Cassirer, Ernst, 127
Cattell, J. McKeen, 162
Caxton, 78
Celsus, 47
Charcot, 162
Chartres, School of, 59–60
Cicero, 47–8
Clark, Sir George, 76–7
Clark, Sir Kenneth, 14, 66
Coghill, G. E., 156 *n.*
Columbus, Christopher, 76
Columbus, Renaldo, 103–4
Condillac, 140–1, *352–62*
Copernicus, 105
Cuvier, 150

Dante, 61
Darwin, Charles, 40, 150
Darwin, Erasmus, 150
Democritus, 32, 34, 46
Descartes, 17, 18, 97, 104, 112–13, 177, *282–304*, 318–20
Donne, John, 128
Du Bois-Reymond, 151
Dürer, 92–3

Epicurus, 30, 34, 43, 45–6, 171
epiphenomenalism, 18, 152, 178
Erasmus, 87, 95

Fechner, 161
Fisher, H. A. L., 80–1, 100
Flourens, 152
Francis of Assisi, St, 61
Freud, 41, 120, 137, 147, 159, 162

Galen, 47, 96, 104, 148, *241–4*
Galileo, 97, 106 ff.

401

Galton, Sir Francis, 157–9
Galvani, 149
Ganshof, F. L., 53 ff., 67, 75
Gerson, 62
Gestalt psychologists, 162
Geulincx, 141
Giotto, 62, 66
Goethe, 120, 142, 150
Greenwood, M., 44, 47

Haller, 142
Harding, D. W., 128, 176
Hartley, David, 131, 140, *346–51*
Hartmann, von, 161, 376
Harvey, William, 97, 102, 111
Hazard, Paul, 102, 138
Heisenberg, 46
Helmholtz, 151
Helvétius, 141–2
Herbart, 160–1
Hering, 135, 152–3, *376–84*
Hippocrates, 17, 26, 32–4, 43, 47,
    96, 148, *183–7*
Hobbes, 19, 97, 114–17, 173
Homer, 25 ff.
Huizinga, 51–2, 62, 71, 95, 132
Hume, 132, 134–6, 160, 173, 177,
    339–45
Huxley, Julian, 152
Huxley, T. H., 18, 150, 152

Idealism, 18, 19, 178

James, William, 163, 172, *389–99*
Janet, Pierre, 392–3
Jowett, 37
Jung, 173

Kant, 131, 136
Kepler, 97, 105–6, 110–11

Lamarck, 150, 157
La Mettrie, 142, 352
Lashley, K. S., 152
Leibniz, 19, 123, 135, 160, *330–8*
Leipzig laboratory, 161

Liébeault, 162
Lister, J. J., 150
Locke, 99, 102, 123–4, 138–9
    160, 347, 352
logic, relational, 165–6, 177–8
logical positivism, 20
Lorenzetti, 66
Lorenzo de' Medici, 88
Lucretius, 18, 34, 45, 46, *229–40*
Lyell, 150

Mace, C. A., 389
Maine de Biran, 159–60
Majendie, 151
Malebranche, 141, 350
Malleus Maleficarum, 14, 82–4,
    263–7
Marco Polo, 74, 76
Marcus Aurelius, 48
Marsiglio, 66
materialism, 18, 19, 115–17, 152,
    178, 229–40
McDougall, William, 176
mental chemistry, 154
Mesmer, 145, 363
Mill, James, 153, 160
Mill, John Stuart, 153–5, *373–5*
Montaigne, 87, 95, 97
Montesquieu, 132, 141
Moore, G. E., 165, 177
Müller, Johannes, 151

Neutral monism, 20, 178
Newton, Eric, 13
Newton, Sir Isaac, 123, 348, 350
Nordenskiöld, E., 102 ff.
occasionalism, 350, 352

Onians, R. B., 25 ff.

Parallelism, 19, 152, 178, 330 ff.,
    387–8
Pascal, 125–6, 356
Petrarch, 67–8, 173, *254–62*
Pevsner, N., 61
physiology, 102 ff., 149 ff., 150 ff.

Piaget, 40
Pinel, 131
Plato, 26, 30, 34–7, 108, *188–213*
Plotinus, 48
Plutarch, 47
Poets, 25 ff., 32, 46, 62, 67, 70,
    71, 74, 78, 79, 86, 97, 99, 108,
    109, 120, 131, 142
Pomponazzi, 87
Prince, Morton, 18, 163

Ranke, 15, 88, 91
remembering, 49, 245–9, 354–5
Rolando, 152
Rome laboratory, 161 *n.*, 376 ff.
Rousseau, 159, 173
Rush, Benjamin, 151
Russell, Bertrand, 19, 20, 38,
    42–3, 59, 109, 134–5, 165, 172,
    177
Ryle, Gilbert, 20–1, 166

Salisbury, John of, 59, 60
Schopenhauer, 148, 161
Schwann, T., 151
Scot, Reginald, *263 ff.*
Seneca, 48
Sergi, 161 *n.*
Servet, 103–4
Sherrington, 152, 163, 164–5
Simone Martini, 66
Smith, F. V., 135
Smith, May, 44, 47

Spencer, Herbert, 156
Spinoza, 99, 102, 117–22, 127,
    148, 172, 173, *305–29*
statistics, 146, 148
Stebbing, L. S., 135
Stoics, 43, 171
Stout, G. F., 162
suggestion and hypnosis, 363, 392

Titchener, E. B., 162
Trevelyan, G. M., 78–9, 137–8
Tuke, William, 151

Unconscious functioning, 158–9,
    162, 382 ff., 393

Vives, 95–6
Voltaire, 138–9, 160, 214

Ward, James, 162, 385
Weyer, 86, 93, *263–72*
Whitehead, A. North, 15, 54,
    165, 172, 177
William of Ockham, 65, 166
Willis, T., 134, 149
witches and witch hunts, 81–4,
    91, 263 ff.
Wittgenstein, 166
Wren, Sir Christopher, 149
Wundt, 155, 159, 161, *385–8*

Zeno, 43
Zilboorg, G., 43, 44, 91, 93 ff., 162,
    264 ff.

*Some other Pelican books
are described on the
following pages*

The Wandering Scholars

HELEN WADDELL

A318

The Wandering Scholars or 'Vagantes' flourished in the later Middle Ages. They left behind them a splendid harvest of lyric poetry written in low Latin, a selection of which has been translated by Miss Waddell in her collection of *Mediaeval Latin Lyrics* (now published in Penguin Classics). Here the story of this great lyrical outpouring, shrouded in the legend, contention, and confusion of the time is revealed with great insight into its remote and fascinating spirit. The result is to open the door to one of the most delightful and hitherto inaccessible periods in the civilization of Europe.

Miss Waddell traces the origins of the movement to the pagan tradition of classical learning and then shows how in the tenth century men of a new age appeared whose comprehensive learning was a legend even among their contemporaries. Such was Gerbert, the most famous of these Wandering Scholars. But it was later in the twelfth century that in France a new general revival of humanism occurred. Miss Waddell gives a vivid picture of its centres: the monasteries at Chartres and Orleans, and the University of Paris, and of the great men – such as Peter Abelard – who dominated this intricate ecclesiastical society.

The Waning of the Middle Ages

J. HUIZINGA

A307

Since it was first published in English in 1924 this book has established itself as a leading work on the close of the Middle Ages. The author came to write it as a result, as he says, of 'endeavouring to arrive at a genuine understanding of the art of the brothers Van Eyck and their contemporaries'. In other words he was led to consider this fascinating period, between the end of one civilization and the beginning of another, through its art. For this reason it is distinguished not only by a wide range of historical knowledge and scholarship, but also by an unusual feeling and understanding for the art of the period and the way in which the culture was integrated with the entire life of the times.

'The book remains in one's mind as a *tour de force*, a work of learning which can be read easily and which impresses itself on the memory.' – History

A History of Western Literature

J. M. COHEN

A371

The History of Western Literature tells the whole story of Continental writing in the vernacular tongues from the days of the great epics and the romances of chivalry to the middle of the present century, a span of almost nine hundred years. Beginning in a narrow territory, strictly Western, the book's subject extends, with the passage of time, to take in prose and poetry written in countries as far afield as Russia and Mexico. Its unifying theme is the development, by way of a series of impulses often from without, declines, and fresh starts, of a single literary tradition which has come to influence the writing of many countries which were once independent of it.

The aim of this book, however, is not simply to present a factual account of an historical growth. Its pattern reflects its author's own judgements and valuations, arrived at in the course of almost forty years reading in the chief European languages, and develops certain ideas concerning the recurrence of literary attitudes and techniques first put forward by the German critic, Ernst Robert Curtius in his great volume *European Literature and the Latin Middle Ages*. It is therefore put forward as a work of original criticism.

Medieval Thought
from St Augustine to Ockham

GORDON LEFF

A424

In the history of ideas, there is a tendency for the old attitude to persist that between the Roman Empire and the Renaissance there was nothing of importance. It is now generally accepted that the Middle Ages, far from being a stopgap, had its own distinctive civilization, and even its doctrines were more than the mere embellishment of Catholic dogma. This book, in tracing their development over the thousand years from St Augustine to Ockham, shows that the picture was far from static or uniform. The author treats the subject historically. He begins with a discussion of the special nature of the medieval outlook and the different sources from which its thinkers drew. The book is divided into three parts, corresponding to the main phases in medieval life as well as thought, each preceded by a short historical introduction for those unacquainted with the period. Close connexion is observed between the thinkers and their cultural milieu, and educational developments, such as the rise of the universities, are considered throughout. The author is concerned neither to argue for a particular outlook nor to point the relevance of medieval belief for today. As a historian of ideas, his sole intention has been to present medieval thought as intelligibly as space will allow.

Language in History

HAROLD GOAD

A416

No one who takes the trouble to read this book can fail to be exhilarated, if not provoked. In many ways it is a remarkable book, for it was written by a remarkable man who was both deeply learned and keenly observant and who had exceptional opportunities throughout a very long life of studying languages in action in the western world. Trained as an historian at Harrow and Oxford, he gained wide experience in Mediterranean lands as liaison officer in the First World War and he chose to spend the greater part of his later life in the land of St Francis and Dante. Harold Elsdale Goad was moved to write these pages under the strong conviction that language and culture are indissolubly linked and that their survival or decline must ultimately depend upon the degree of loyalty shown by a community of people to one common purpose. His colourful description of the parts played in history by the great languages of western civilization has an obvious and immediate bearing on present problems and future hopes, and he has succeeded in presenting his theme so simply and straightforwardly that the reader can follow its main argument with complete understanding.

Landscape into Art

A369

Sir Kenneth Clark has shown the belief that art is a part of our general consciousness and gives a special value to all our experiences. In this book, which is based on his first course of lectures as Slade Professor at Oxford, he is concerned with man's relation to nature as reflected in the history of landscape painting. In the first part he considers the acceptance of descriptive symbols, the curiosity about facts, the creation of fantasy to relieve his fears, and a belief in a Golden Age of order. The great landscape painters of the nineteenth century, Constable and Corot, Turner and Van Gogh, Cézanne and Seurat, are treated in detail. Finally he considers the future of landscape painting at a time when the more vital artists have turned away from nature. The book contains 96 pages of plates.

'The importance of this book to art criticism and to the history of art can scarcely be exaggerated. Ruskin and others have written notable pages on the art of landscape painting, but no such complete work on it as a separate branch of art has appeared in English.' – *Cambridge Review*

Chinese Art

W. Y. WILLETTS

A358–9

This book, which covers more than four thousand years, describes some of China's noblest art-forms – including jade, bronze, lacquer, silk, sculpture, pottery, calligraphy, painting, and architecture. The material is strictly selected: no attempt is made to give a complete history of each art-form. Instead, each is examined at a given stage of Chinese history, and during a particular phase of its development. The phase is in some cases one of formative evolution, in others one of maturity. So jade-carving, basically a neolithic craft, is surveyed in the setting of New Stone Age life in China. Architecture, which is highly traditional in its styles and techniques, is described on the basis of architectural layouts and buildings of the last six hundred years, which alone are still standing. The chapters are arranged in chronological order; in this way *Chinese Art* may be read as a continuous record of four thousand years of Chinese art-history. Alternatively, each chapter may be regarded as a self-contained essay on the art-form with which it deals.

There are 64 pages of plates, and many line drawings in the text.

An Outline of European Architecture

NIKOLAUS PEVSNER

A109

This is a history of Western architecture as an expression of Western civilization described historically in its growth from the ninth to the twentieth century. It does not deal with the architecture of classical antiquity, or, generally, with that of the first thousand years A.D. With these exceptions, it tells the story of Western and Central European architecture during the last thousand years through the medium of its outstanding expressions in actual building. Not every architect or every work of importance is mentioned; but the styles discussed and the points raised are illustrated by descriptions of individual buildings which exemplify them. The method adopted is to discuss a few buildings of each period and country in some detail and to avoid dull cataloguing. The aim of the book is to make readers appreciate architectural values. It is written for reading, not merely for reference, and it makes interesting reading indeed in its concentration and its combination of warmth and scholarship. A revised and enlarged edition is now available with over 100 plates and many diagrams.

'It is quite the best short history of European architecture that has ever been published in this country.' – Herbert Read in the *Architects' Journal*

French Architecture

PIERRE LAVEDAN

A329

This book, of which the French version has run into many editions, is a history of French architecture from its origins until the present day. This Pelican edition is the first time it has appeared in English. Unlike many writers on architecture, Professor Lavedan does not subjugate the problems of technique and materials to aesthetic considerations. He sees that almost every major architectural innovation has resulted equally from technical and artistic demands. For this reason the first chapter of the book provides a general account of the materials and technique of building, which is not readily available in such a compact form elsewhere. The first part of the book also discusses the important question of 'style'. The rest is in the main divided into two sections dealing respectively with the history of Religious and Civil architecture from medieval times until the present. In addition there are chapters on town-planning and the planning of gardens, biographies of the chief architects discussed, and the book is illustrated with line drawings in the text and sixty-four pages of plates.

Daily Life in Ancient Rome

J. CARCOPINO

This book brings the capital of the ancient world and its people to life again, as they were in the second century A.D., when Rome ruled an Empire which 'comprehended the fairest part of the earth and the most civilized portion of mankind.' The author has drawn on sources that run all the way from ancient literature to the latest discoveries among the ruins of Roman life. Business and social activities, incomes, living conditions, marriage and the family, the religious and educational trends of the period, housing, and even plumbing are reconstructed out of the fragments that two thousand years have deposited. We see the Roman making the round of his daily business appointments, calls, and dinner engagements in the midst of the tumult of the capital. Maps and illustrations, lacking in the original French edition of the book, have been added by Professor Rowell, who has also rewritten and greatly augmented the original notes and added a new bibliography.

'Here, in extraordinarily vivid detail you have a picture of the generation born in the middle of the first century – a brilliant study.' – *Punch*

'To the common reader like myself it is of the greatest interest.' – Raymond Mortimer in the *New Statesman*